The Festive Fifty

Mark Whitby

Revised Edition - Fully Updated

MARK WHITBY

© Mark Whitby 2015. All rights reserved. No part of this publication may be reproduced, in any form or in any means, without permission from the author, except by a reviewer, who may quote brief passages for the purpose of a review.

First published in 2005

This edition published in 2015 by Unwashed Territories

This book is dedicated to all of those John Peel fans – at Dandelion Radio and on the Peel Yahoo Group and elsewhere - whose tireless efforts to keep his musical legacy alive are a constant inspiration.

CONTENTS

1. Introduction — 1
2. The John Peel Festive Fifties — 5
3. The Post-Peel Festive Fifties — 95
4. A-Z List of Featured Bands/Artists — 113
5. Top Artists in Festive Fifty History — 183
6. Top Albums in Festive Fifty History — 209
7. John Peel Sessions & The Festive Fifty — 229
8. Records & Statistics — 237
9. The 'Other' Festive Fifty Entries — 255

About the author

Mark Whitby was born in 1965 and lives in the north-west of England with his wife and two children. He first began listening to the John Peel show in 1978 and by 1983 had realised that his infatuation with the festive fifty was at a dangerously obsessive level. Following involvement with music in a variety of ways – as a promoter of a venue, occasional DJ on community radio and some half-arsed attempts to be in a band – he joined the team running Dandelion Radio in 2007 and now runs a blog devoted to new music and a small digital record label, both called Unwashed Territories. All of the above was fired by a fascination for the John Peel show and the music he was introduced to as a consequence, so it would leave a pretty big hole in his life if it had never been there, which might go some way towards explaining why he puts himself through, and even enjoys, the process of updating and revising the information in this book every so often.

markw@dandelionradio.com
Twitter - @markwdandelion
www.facebook.com/mark.whitby.923

Acknowledgements:

In updating this book, I'm extremely grateful to members of the Peel Yahoo Group both for supplying a constantly fascinating and helpful archive of Peel-related information and past shows. Ken Garner's work in rescuing the 1977 chart from historical oblivion has been invaluable, as has his book *The Peel Sessions* and the mine of information therein. Massive thanks go to Dandelion Radio and particularly those who put in so much work in to launch the station and who continue to strive to continue the true legacy of John Peel; also, of course, for continuing the great tradition of the festive fifty

INTRODUCTION

A lot of people I know seem slightly bewildered that I'm prepared to put myself through the inevitably lengthy process that leads to putting these books out. Perhaps it's odd that I don't find the ideal of listening to and reading about a lot of music that I love a particularly difficult ordeal, in fact if I had my way I'd probably devote pretty much all my time to those pursuits, pausing only to watch the occasional game of football. Having this mentality, it was I suppose inevitable that the gap between the first edition of this book, which hit an either interested or indifferent public with not much in between in 2005, and now, would start to make me fidgety. It gnawed at me that so much from the original book had become out of date and that there were also some nagging omissions and errors that had left me with so many troubled nights sleep that I really couldn't go on without doing something about them. I suspect there'll be similar obstacles to my sleep patterns after this book sees the light of day, though hopefully not as many, but in any case no doubt the process will have to begin before too long.

It seems to me, anyway, that the most important reason for putting together a book about the festive fifty is simply that there are so many fine bands that appeared in it that got, and continue to get, an unreasonably small amount of recognition. While I can't promise to remedy that injustice fully, I can at least hopefully bring as many of these bands as possible to the attention of more people. As the festive fifties broadcast from 2006 on Dandelion Radio have featured many more such bands or artists, the impulse to update the work became increasingly irresistible. Of course, the churlish (and perhaps even the not so churlish) may point out that there are loads of great bands that didn't make the festive fifty, which is of course true and I'd like to have the time to write a book about a lot of them too. We can, however, at least cover the music that, at a particular time, meant enough to enough people with the good taste to listen to an innovative and challenging radio show for them to go to the trouble to vote for it at the end of the year. Which for me seems a worthwhile thing to do.

The first edition of *The Festive Fifty* was published in 2005 and had a much greater impact on my life than I'd anticipated. Not because it made money or brought any other material benefits - it sold moderately, to an audience of committed John Peel fans – or affected the trajectory of what might be loosely termed any career ambitions I might once have had. The impact it had on my life was a much more important one in that it brought me into contact with a wide range of people for whom the John Peel show in general and the Festive Fifty in particular had been a central part of life.

At the time, a greater concern for me was not, anyway, the fate of my book but iabout what form the Festive Fifty might continue, and what form the John Peel legacy might take, if any at all. At the time the signs weren't good, although, following John Peel's untimely passing in October 2005, Radio One initially filled the slot with its *One Music* DJs, Huw Stephens, Rob Da Bank and Ras Kwarme, with a briefing to seek out and air new music in a style akin to that of the late, great Peel.

I was relieved when the three took up the mantle of the Festive Fifty at the end of 2006, but again their approach to that seemed somehow alien to the spirit of Peel and bereft of any genuine attempt to acquaint themselves with the legacy they were continuing. While Peel had often sounded, however unconvincingly, reluctant in his references to the voting period, restricting himself to announcements between the more important business of playing good music, there seemed something almost contrived about the approach that year and the somewhat giddy presentation of the results. The Radio One website at the time included a page with the DJs' personal favourites on, as if it was considered necessary to provide listeners with prompts of the kind of things they ought to be voting for. Perhaps someone at the BBC thought such a policy necessary, but clearly it's an approach that Peel would have baulked at, and quite rightly.

The countdown was broadcast with enthusiasm and evident respect for its origins by Stephens and Da Bank, but I strongly suspected that this was the last we would hear of it. Although the BBC accepted and used the amendments I suggested to what was then a horrendously accurate section on the festive fifty on their Keeping It Peel pages, they wished to have no connection with my book, sayings its content was not 'directly' related to its programme content. Which suggested there was no clear attachment on behalf of the corporation to the idea of the festive fifty or, you suspectd, the legacy of Peel. Whatever the undoubted enthusiasm of Da Bank and Stephens for the task of picking up the Peel mantel, One Music in itself had always seemed a fairly half-hearted idea on the part of the BBC, a self-conscious and tokenistic nod in the direction of 'new music' and I assumed its days were numbered.

I assumed correctly. Early the following year the BBC announced that the initiative was being abandoned and that Colin Murray (yes, Colin Murray) would be filling the hallowed 10-12 Radio One slot that had been Peel's for much of his time at the BBC and for the later period of his life   That seemed to put the lid on any hope of genuine, John Peel-inspired music shows continuing on the airwaves, and certainly it seemed to be the end of the road as far as the Festive Fifty was concerned.

That it wasn't was down to the efforts of a small group of people who will always enjoy my undying respect.

It was Sarah Nelson, whose *Listen With Sarah* project had so delighted Peel in his last years, who first hinted to me that the end of the line might not quite have been reached after all. My book was in circulation by then and Sarah had already purchased a copy. She-mailed me to inform me that her husband Peter was involved in a soon to be launched internet station called Dandelion Radio, which of course took its name from Peel's old record label and whose founders aimed to produce programmes in the spirit of the late DJ.

When Dandelion's first programmes first saw the light of day in June 2006, the results were far better than I dared hope and I became an avid listener from day one. The spirit of John Peel, although it can never be perfectly replicated by anyone, had at least been respectfully preserved by a bunch of genuine Peel listeners who financed the station themselves, thus having to make no concessions to commercial pressures, and clearly were the right custodians for this vital legacy. If we were to lose the Festive Fifty, at least we didn't have to lose completely the fresh and challenging radio that Peel had championed.

What I didn't know at the time was that Peel's former producers had approached Dandelion to ask if they'd be interested in becoming the home of the chart, as the BBC had no interest in continuing it. Had I known that it would have saved me a lot of restless searching and canvassing of opinion across the internet with the aim of finding enough like-minded souls to pull some sort of unofficial Festive Fifty together, in an effort to preserve the chart in however imperfect a manner. I'd largely given up hope of this and, in one desperate attempt at least to salvage some sort of commemorative chart to mark what would have been its thirtieth anniversary, I came up with the idea of a one-off Truly Festive Festive Fifty, made up purely of votes for people's favourite Xmas-themed records, the results of which I include here as an unofficial (and therefore not represented the book's statistical section) chart fashioned in the image of the Festive Fifty.

Even as the votes were being compiled, Dandelion's Paul Webster messaged me on myspace (at that time still the forerunner among social network sites) to tell me that Dandelion were intending, after all, to continue the festive fifty. I went ahead and published the results of The Truly Festive Festive Fifty on the web anyway, but happily left the chart's future in the more than safe hands of Dandelion Radio. The chart continues to be fascinating listening, containing the occasional surprise entry of a kind that wouldn't feature in any other chart anywhere in the world, as well as, it must be said, perhaps an over-preponderance of indie guitar bands, much as has been the case for most of its long history.

It's largely due to Dandelion Radio that you have in your hands a revised edition of this book, which includes all of the Festive Fifties since the internet station took over official responsibility for the chart. I joined the station as a DJ five months after the first one and have lived out a small dream by becoming part of the broadcast team for the chart ever since. Although this means I can no longer, as I did for decades, listen to the countdown with the rapt attention of an eager listener who doesn't quite know what's coming next, this is a small price to pay for being allowed to play a minor part in ensuring that it continues to occupy its place in the Xmas listening schedule. Although the first year's chart was aired on New Year's Day, subsequent festive fifties are now broadcast from 12 midnight at the very earliest hours of Christmas Day, and, despite that, it appears large numbers of listeners are willing to stay awake often until 5am (UK time) to listen in, while a similarly large listening audience tunes in for the first repeat airing at a more civilised time, normally late on Christmas Day afternoon.

Also included in the book are a full rundown of the 1977 chart, thankfully rescued from historical oblivion by the brilliant Ken Garner, and a few other bits that may be of interest to the avid Peel listener. I hope you enjoy it and I'm equally sure you'll let me know, in the nicest possible way, of any mistakes. Thank you for those of you who pointed these out in the first edition: you will now find them duly corrected, although inevitably, with the mass of information contained within these pages, I can't promise there won't be a few things that avid Peel historians will wish to point out or contest.

Some sections have also been revised and presented in a slightly altered format: I've chosen, for example, to give extended details of particular tracks only for charts that didn't appear in the first book. For those that did, I'd opted for a more detailed overall commentary on the chart, as this appears to be a feature that people have generally found to be most useful in the original book.

I've also chosen to cut out some of the sillier elements of the first edition, including some of the dafter statistical records (of interest, surely, only to those who are more anally retentive than me, which can't be many people) and that ludicrously stupid section at the back. No one actually contacted me to propose that these sections be removed, but I'm sure that was only due to politeness. Enjoy the book.

THE JOHN PEEL FESTIVE FIFTIES
1976-2004

In the first edition I gave commentaries on selected individual tracks. I've largely ditched that format here, only using it for the Peel-selected chart of 1977, as it's obviously a one-off and I felt it was worth commenting on several of his choices. Other festive fifties are reproduced only in list form with an overall commentary. More extended comment on individual entries can, of course, can be found in the first edition of the book and, should anyone still want a copy of that, please contact me (I've included my Dandelion Radio e-mail address in the *About the Author* section). Here, I've concentrated more on providing more detailed overall commentaries on the charts than appeared in the first edition which, on the basis of the feedback I received, seemed to be what people valued more.

Where possible, I've tried to identify the actual version of each track played in the countdown. In most of the earlier, 'all time' charts I've not repeated this information unless Peel played the track from a different source subsequently. The majority of the information has been taken from the immensely valuable Peel wiki pages, so massive thanks to those who've taken the trouble to piece that together..

1975
John Peel's Top Fifteen Singles –A Festive Fifty Precursor?

In his show of 19 December 1975, John Peel revealed his top fifteen singles of the year. Although there was no mention of the intention to instigate a yearly chart at the time, many consider this to be the first stirring of the germ of an idea that was to become the festive fifty.

The list is interesting in several respects. Later Peel listeners are often surprised by its content, and understandably so for the fifteen singles chosen contain eight that had appeared in the top thirty of the UK singles chart that year, including two number ones, from 10cc and Rod Stewart, on the verge of transforming himself from top bloke and Peel favourite to vapid MOR hit monster, something that perhaps had its starting point on the day of this broadcast when, as Peel announced with regret during the countdown, his much-anticipated split with The Faces was formally announced. At first glance there is scant evidence here of the John Peel that would become, and had indeed been, the champion of new bands. It's superficially tempting to view the chart as evidence of the generally dismal state of British music in the mid-seventies limiting his choice, were it not for the fact that during the broadcast Peel comments on what a good year it had been and alludes to the difficult selection process he'd had to go through to produce it. He even states that all of the singles in his top five would feature in his personal all-time top fifty.

Only two singles in this chart would appear in the first festive fifty of 1976. While there would be records from 1975 in that list, of those featured here only Bob Marley and Roy Harper would muscle their way on board. Indeed, the 1976 Festive Fifty would contain a large proportion of album tracks, not surprising considering the Peel audience demographic in the mid-seventies, which makes it perhaps even more curious that Peel should produce a list drawn only from singles here. Doubtless it made the shortlisting of his favourites a marginally easier process, but prior to the punk boom that revived the 7" form, Peel had been in the vanguard, along with the Old Grey Whistle Test, of a musical culture that regarded the LP as a format of interest to 'serious' music aficionados.

But then Peel was nothing if not a challenger of his audience's expectations and perhaps we should view his top fifteen singles in this light. Despite its commercial moments, it's an eclectic enough selection, with manic folk from Jack the Lad and a rare solo curiosity from Bob Seargent, who would soon become a highly sought after producer, nestling up against Marley's reggae and a number one from a band who remain one of the key links between the largely polarised sensibilities of the early and late seventies. While many might see the Laurel & Hardy track as a curious choice, airplay from Peel was crucial in getting it into the high position it eventually occupied in the singles charts and it represents a taste for the the odd and curious that would have a place in the DJ's shows until the end. It was a song originally written in 1913 that took its artistic inspiration from John Fox Jr's novel of the same name and this version was recorded by the comedy duo for their film Way Out West in 1937. Laurel & Hardy's finest musical moment would take its place alongside the likes of Laurie Anderson's 'O Superman' and The Cuban Boys' 'Intelligentsia v Cognoscenti', firm Peel favourites yet largely got play on daytime radio due to a presumed novelty appeal. There are actually four vocalists on the recording, with professional singers taking on Laurel's falsetto and baritone moments and the song was only prevented from reaching number one in the UK by Queen's 'Bohemian Rhapsody'.

Mike Oldfield's 'In Dulce Jubilo' originated from a Bach composition reinterpreted by R.L. Pearsall. Peel had been a major supporter of Oldfield, giving vital early impetus to what would become the massively successful *Tubular Bells* and in the process helping the fledgling Virgin label to establish itself as the major concern it would eventually become. Thus did Peel play a small and unwitting part in the establishment of Richard Branson's business empire. Another artist on the way to the big time was Joan Armatrading – the only lead artist with two tracks here (although guitarist Peter Carr contributed to both the Rod Stewart and Millie Jackson singles). Peel's support for Armatrading in the years since 1972, where she had effectively been in recording exile due to a label dispute, had been crucial in sustaining her profile. During that time, the Peel sessions she recorded accounted for pretty much her sole recorded output, sustaining her until she returned in 1975 with her Back to the Night album, a collection much championed by Peel, which included the two singles listed here. She appeared in session eight times on the Peel show between 1972 and 1976, after which her self-titled album and single 'Love and Affection' would propel her into the big time.

Peter Frampton was another on the verge of a major commercial triumph. His 'Show Me the Way' would appear on his ground-breaking live album *Frampton Comes Alive!,* which sold over six million copies in the United States alone, remarkably becoming the best-selling LP in America in both 1976 and 1977. John Lennon, on the other hand, was about to enter a period of self-imposed hibernation. Many will be surprised to see his 'Imagine' featured here: it's a song which, following his death five years later, took on an almost schmalzy, over-sentimentalised veneer. Indeed Chumbawamba would smash it to pieces in the *Revolution* EP that yielded their 1985 entry and it would also be reworked by Wax Audio as 'Imagine This', with vocals cut and pasted from George W. Bush speeches, the results appearing in the OneMusic festive fifty in 2005. When originally released in 1971, however, the 'communism with a sugar coating' label attached to it by its creator still very much held, perhaps due to it sharing space on an album with other uncompromising statements like 'I Don't Wanna Be a Soldier' and 'Gimme Some Truth'. Reissued as a single in this year, Peel still clearly reserved a lot of affection for the tune, as indeed he did for Lennon himself. Since then, the tune has shared the fate of Blake's 'And Did Those Feet', coopted into an establishment that either doesn't look too closely at its radical lyrical content or seeks to neutralise it. Thus, Errol Brown could sing it about imagining no possessions to a Tory rally at the height of Thatcherism to unanimous applause. Incidentally, Peel mentions in the broadcast that his wife, had she had a say, would have placed the tune even higher.

Perhaps the most pleasing entry is Jack the Lad's energetic rendition of 'Gentlemen Soldier', an old English folk song that had been recorded by Martin Carthy and Dave Swarbrick in 1967 and would later be covered by, among others, The Pogues and Steeleye Span. The song's origins date back at least to the nineteenth century. Though the first known recorded mention occurred in 1907, when the collector Miss A. G. Gilchrist was given the lyrics by Thomas Coomber, Rudyard Kipling had quoted a fragment of the lyrics in his Soldiers Three collection of poems, first published in 1888 and alternative versions of the song have separate and lengthy histories in Irish and Scottish folk balladry. Jack the Lad's spirited version brings out the ballad's bawdy character arguably more successfully even than the fine treatment it received at the hands of The Pogues on the *Rum, Sodomy & The Lash* album.

Interestingly, when Peel came to making a selection from this year for his 1999 Peelenium, only Millie Jackson's 'Loving Arms' reappeared from this list. His other choices were David Bowie's 'Fame', Burning Spear's 'Slavery Days' and Little Feat's 'Long Distance Love', the last of which the Peel audience would deem fit for inclusion in the following year's inaugural festive fifty. Jackson's appearance at number two reflects Peel's oft-stated admiration for an artist whose style always set her apart from the rest of the soul and R&B pack and probably denied her the kind of success enjoyed by so many of her contemporaries. Often explicit and raunchy, especially during live performances, and later counting among her album covers a close-up of her cleavage and a photograph of her sitting on the toilet, she didn't make too many concessions to conservative America. 'Loving Arms', however, is simply one of the most powerful soul ballads ever, sung by one of the great soul voices.

It's beaten to the number one slot by Be Bop Deluxe and a single from their *Futurama* album. Peel's 'wait till you hear the new album' teaser at the end of the broadcast refers to the soon to be released *Sunburst Finish* LP which would take this highly influential seventies band into the top twenty of the albums chart. Led by Bill Nelson, the band merged elements of glam and progressive rock but Nelson's constant determination not to be pigeonholed appeared to supply them with a formidable enough sound to survive the artistic upheavals wrought by punk and the new wave. Frequent line-up changes led to an always volatile existence, however, and the band would disband completely in 1978, leaving Nelson to pursue an idiosyncratic solo career that never got close to the flirtations with success of his former band, of which he appeared to care little.

Another item of interest here is how, before announcing the number three, Peel voices his disappointment that none of his personal top four was a hit and says he was particularly surprised about this in the case of Lack the Lad. Just over two years, later, in his 28 December 1977 show, in reference to the Boomtown Rats, he mentions the song making the charts before declaring that this is not a fact he has any interest in whatsoever. One of many comments that perhaps illustrate his changing expectations of the music he played either side of the punk revolution.

John Peel's Top Fifteen Singles of 1975
Broadcast date: 19 December

15. Hold On To Love – Peter Skellern (Decca 7")*(Peter Skellern – piano/vocals)*

14. The Trail of the Lonesome Pine – Laurel & Hardy (United Artists 7")*(Stan Laurel – vocals; Oliver Hardy – vocals; Chill Wills – vocals; Rosina Lawrence – vocals; Marvin Hatley – score)*

13. In Dulci Jubilo – Mike Oldfield (Virgin 7")*(Mike Oldfield – guitar/piano/synthesizers; Leslie Penning – recorder/kortholt; William Murray – snare drum)*

12. Back to the Night – Joan Armatrading (A&M 7")*(Joan Armatrading – vocals; Pete Gage – giutar; Colin Pincott – guitar; Phil Chen – bass; Jean Roussel – piano; Tony Newman – drums; Gasper Lawall – percussion)*

11. I'm Not In Love – 10cc (Mercury 7")
(Eric Stewart – keyboards/vocals; Lol Creme – guitar; Graham Gouldman – bass; Kevin Godley – drums)

10. First Starring Role – Bob Sargeant (RCA 7")
(Bob Sargeant – guitar/keyboards/vocals; Clive Chaman – bass; Mike Garson – keyboards; Mike Bailey – trumpet; Paul Nieman – trombone; Ritchie Dharma – drums; Dennis McKay – percussion)

9. Show Me The Way – Peter Frampton (A&M 7")
(Peter Frampton – guitar/keyboards/vocals; Andy Bown – bass; John Siomos – drums)

8. No Woman No Cry – Bob Marley & The Wailers (Island 7")

7. Dry Land – Joan Armatrading (A&M 7")
(Joan Armatrading – piano/vocals; Pete Gage – synthesizer)

6. Imagine – John Lennon (Apple 7")
(John Lennon – piano/vocals)

5. Sailing – Rod Stewart (Warner Bros 7")
(Rod Stewart – vocals; Pete Carr – guitar; Bob Glaub – bass; Barry Beckett – keyboards; David Lindley – violin; Al Jackson – drums)

4. When An Old Cricketer Leaves The Crease – Roy Harper (Harvest 7")

3. Gentleman Soldier - Jack the Lad (Charisma 7")
(Phil Murray – bass/vocals; Billy Mitchell – guitar; Simon Cowe – keyboards; Walter, aka Ian Fairbairn – banjo/violin; John Kirkpatrick – accordion; Ray Laidlaw – drums)

2. Loving Arms – Millie Jackson (Polydor 7")
(Millie Jackson – vocals; Jimmy Johnson – guitar; Pete Carr – guitar; David Hood – bass; Barry Beckett – keyboards; Roger Hawkins – drums)

1. Maid in Heaven – Be Bop Deluxe (Harvest 7")
(Bill Nelson – guitar/voals; Charlie Tumahai – bass; Andrew Clark – keyboards; Simon Fox – drums/percussion)

1976

Even as the votes were being collected for the first Festive Fifty, Led Zeppelin were releasing the costly and indulgent *The Song Remains The Same* concert film, Rick Wakeman was returning to Yes and Pink Floyd allowed an inflatable pig to escape from just over Battersea Power Station, threatening aeroplane flight paths. The excellent *The Last Waltz* would eventually commemorate The Band's final concert, which also took place that month. The film's name and the concert's timing couldn't have been more appropriate, as the likes of Dylan, Van Morrison, Neil Young and Eric Clapton joined the band on stage where, although they didn't know it, they were assembling an old order that would enjoy relatively unchallenged adulation for the last time.

The Peel show as they knew it was already sliding pretty rapidly out of existence. While a glance at the Peel sessions played during November and December might suggest nothing out of the ordinary was brewing – featured artists included Blue, Van Der Graaf Generator and Bridget St John – the barricades had gone up, amidst great publicity and interest from a music press that was already having its head turned in new directions, with Peel's punk special broadcast on 10 December and a session from The Damned, following one from The Vibrators in the previous month, were the more significant signposts to the future. The following autumn would show the extent to which this laid the ground for what was to come: among the session guests in the period between September and November 1977 were Buzzcocks, XTC, The Slits, The Lurkers, Skrewdriver, the Tom Robinson Band, Siouxsie & The Banshees, Suburban Studs and Sham 69. Apart from the Sex Pistols, Eddie & The Hot Rods and session guests The Damned, the 1976 special had been a non-British, and mainly US, affair, necessarily so because in those days Peel was restricted, session material aside, to playing official releases only. The momentum that had been stirring in UK music was already apparent in the live music scene, however, and the 1976 festive fifty would become, as well as the first of its kind, the one that would find itself consigned to history with greatest haste by what would become, within the next twelve months, a new Peel listening audience.

But, as the chart below reveals, change was slow to come about, at least for much of the audience he still had. Peel had been playing the first Ramones album, but was receiving angry letters from listeners appalled that such obvious lack of technical expertise should be rewarded with airplay from the programme that for so long had been known as a champion for musical innovation. And musical innovation had, to them, tended to mean never using three chords when you could at least attempt to use them all. The Ramones didn't figure in the festive fifty; many of those who joined The Band onstage did.

They feature in a festive fifty of extraordinary length. While most top tens of the future would fit easily on one side of a ninety minute cassette, this one comprises ten tracks that collectively last well over seventy minutes. There are three tracks that, individually, last far longer than a full side of many punk albums and three, by Pink Floyd, Genesis and Yes that are little less than rock 'symphonies' in several movements. Little wonder that the voters responsible for it reacted so strongly to the two minute, three chord stabs of anger and adolescent trauma that soon began to fill airtime in their favourite radio show.

The debate represented conceptual extremes, but the celebrated musical legacy of the late sixties – if it isn't difficult or 'serious' it should be ignored – had swelled to the point that, like an over-inflated balloon, its eventual bursting would be pretty much instantaneous. The unintended forefathers of this unplanned, and soon to be largely forgotten, child were the much-lauded figures in this list who helped lift rock and roll from the primordial soup: The Beatles, Dylan, The Doors and the Rolling Stones.

The unplanned child itself, the beast of progressive rock, stands astride this list like a colossus, though one that was being slain even as the votes were being collected. The Damned and the Pistols had released the first British punk singles, with 'Anarchy in the UK' blasting the mildewed ear of the British charts even as its record company was withdrawing it from sale following the Grundy appearance. The balloon had duly been pricked.

Although it was becoming anachronistic even while in the process of being collated and played, this all-time chart remains of considerable interest and no little quality. If punk did us the favour of getting us to see that a pseudo-classical approach to rock and roll had led us down an especially dull and unproductive alley, in time it would also stand guilty of encouraging us to neglect, for a time, some genuine creative peaks from the pre-punk period and there are several of those on this list. Take the crazed and deranged proto-psychobilly of the Legendary Stardust Cowboy, for instance, with a track that could take on any punk track in the ring of caustic brilliance and come out on top. Or the ever-majestic Captain Beefheart, a creature whose significance would duly be assessed and eventually recognised as at least as crucial as as Iggy Pop or the New York Dolls in engineering the insane creative peak that mu would reach in the late seventies. Interestingly in the light of Peel's comments during later festive fifty countdowns, here he anticipates such an objection coming from listeners before hitting them with the Legendary Stardust Cowboy track, indeed commenting that during the early voting 'Paralysed' had spent some time in the number one position.

Many of the performers here would be similarly significant. Who can put a value on Marley's popularisation of reggae, travelling at this point in a separate geneological chain that would eventually meet punk at an unexpected crossroads and with it forge a source of much inspiration for the period to come? Jimi Hendrix, appearing three times here, would find himself temporarily written off as a relic from the rock star past, while in truth his revision of the vocabulary of the blues was at least as important as that of Beefheart in asking questions that needed to be asked of the music of the time even if many of his imitators would miss the point. The same could be said of Led Zeppelin and Jimmy Page, of course and, if it was never likely that the new generation would have much truck with 'Whole Lotta Love' or, at number one, 'Stairway to Heaven', the strains of 'Kashmir' would ring through the guitars of thousands of aspring garage experimenters to highly productive effect well into the future. The Beatles, joining the two previous artists with three entries, would be similarly written off by the punk crowd before being quickly reassimilated by the Liverpudlian indie scene that came out of the late seventies and whose three leading acts – Wah!, The Bunnymen and The Teardrop Explodes – would all dig into their heritage to find much to inspire; ditto the Mancunian scene of the late eightes. Jackson Browne would find resonance in the work of Elvis Costello right through Aztec Camera and beyond, in artists who would recognise his extraordinary observational skill as a lyricist, even if just now he was being poo pooed in a classic singer-songwriter pigeonhole that was temporarily thrown out along with the rest of the early seventies bathwater. Jonathan Richman also finds a place here with 'Roadrunner', a genuine precursor of the new wave to come and the clearest signpost in this chart towards future festive fifties.

The highest place track released in 1976 would come from Welsh band Racing Cars, a band with little connection with the punk dynamic and yet one that would retain a magic for Peel for some time to come. Dylan is the only artist to place four tracks in the chart, a man for whom the punk idea of ripping up the rule book and upsetting the old audience was something he could justly claim to have been doing while many of them were still in their prams, resonating here with 'Like a Rolling Stone' all the way up to the more recent rage against injustice that was the incredible 'Hurricane'.

There are also, it's fair to say, also several musical moments here that thoroughly deserved to be erased from history, while another striking feature of the chart is the presence of a mere two women: Grace Slick of Jefferson Airplane and Linda Thompson. Perhaps more surprisingly, the largely male dominated environs of the festive fifty would persist for quite a few years beyond this one.

1976 Festive Fifty

Broadcast dates: 24, 27, 28, 29 & 30 December; 3 January

50. And You & I – Yes (Atlantic LP *Close to the Edge*)
49. Willin' – Little Feat (Warner Bros LP *Sailin' Shoes*)
48. Go to Rhino Records – Wild Man Fischer (Rhino 7")
47. When an Old Cricketer Leaves The Crease – Roy Harper (Harvest 7")
46. O Caroline – Matching Mole (CBS LP *Matching Mole*)
45. Light My Fire – The Doors (Elektra LP *The Doors*)

44. Hurricane – Bob Dylan (CBS LP *Desire*)
43. Fountain of Sorrow – Jackson Browne (Asylum LP *Late For The Sky*)
42. The Weaver's Answer – Family (Reprise LP *Family Entertainment*)
41. I Want To See The Bright Lights Tonight – Richard & Linda Thompson (Island LP *I Want To See The Bright Lights Tonight*)
40. Dark Star – Grateful Dead (Warner Bros LP *Live/Dead*)
39. Jumping Jack Flash – Rolling Stones (Decca 7")
38. Jessica – Allman Brothers Band (Capricorn LP

Brothers & Sisters)
37. Hey Joe – Jimi Hendrix Experience (Track 7")
36. Kashmir – Led Zeppelin (Swan Song LP *Physical Graffiti*)
35. Late For The Sky – Jackson Browne (Asylum LP *Late For The Sky*)
34. Maggie May – Rod Stewart (Mercury 7")
33. Roadrunner – Jonathan Richman & The Modern Lovers (Beserkley 7")
32. No Woman, No Cry – Bob Marley & The Wailers (Island 7")
31. Supper's Ready – Genesis (Charisma LP *Foxtrot*)
30. I Can Take You to the Sun – The Misunderstood (Fontana 7")
29. Won't Get Fooled Again – The Who (Track LP *Who's Next*)
28. Rocky Mountain Way – Joe Walsh (ABC 7")
27. Pickin' the Blues – Grinderswitch (Capricorn LP *Macon Tracks*)
26. Long Distance Love – Little Feat (Warner Bros LP *The Last Record Album*)
25. Child In Time – Deep Purple (Harvest LP *Deep Purple In Rock*)
24. White Rabbit – Jefferson Airplane (RCA 7")
23. Visions of Johanna – Bob Dylan (CBS LP *Blonde On Blonde*)
22. Riders on the Storm – The Doors (Elektra LP *LA Woman*)
21. Madame George – Van Morrison (Warner Bros LP *Astral Weeks*)
20. Freebird – Lynyrd Skynyrd (MCA 7")
19. Whole Lotta Love – Led Zeppelin (Atlantic LP *Led Zeppelin II*)
18. Big Eyed Beans From Venus – Captain Beefheart & The Magic Band (Reprise LP *Clear Spot*)
17. Strawberry Fields Forever – The Beatles (Parlophone 7")
16. Voodoo Chile – Jimi Hendrix Experience (Reprise LP *Electric Ladyland*)
15. Paralyzed – Legendary Stardust Cowboy (Mercury 7")
14. Hey Jude – The Beatles (Apple 7")
13. Brown Sugar – Rolling Stones (Rolling Stones 7")
12. Cortez the Killer – Neil Young & Crazy Horse (Reprise LP *Zuma*)
11. Rose of Cimarron – Poco (ABC LP *Rose of Cimarron*)
10. Like a Rolling Stone – Bob Dylan (Columbia 7")
9. A Day in the Life – The Beatles (Parlophone LP *Sgt Pepper's Lonely Hearts Club Band*)
8. Shine on You Crazy Diamond – Pink Floyd (Harvest LP *Wish You Were Here*)
7. They Shoot Horses, Don't They? – Racing Cars (Chrysalis 7")
6. Alright Now – Free (Island 7")
5. All Along the Watchtower – Jimi Hendrix Experience (Track 7")
4. Echoes – Pink Floyd (Harvest LP *Meddle*)
3. Desolation Row – Bob Dylan (Columbia LP *Highway 61 Revisited*)
2. Layla – Derek & the Dominoes (Polydor 7")
1. Stairway To Heaven – Led Zeppelin (Atlantic LP *Led Zeppelin IV*

1977

Most of us had long given up hope of the 1977 chart ever re-surfacing in full. At the time of publishing the first edition of this book, all that was in circulation was its top thirteen, to which I gave a brief mention. It is therefore with considerable excitement that Peel fans recieved the news that Ken Garner, in his book *The Peel Sessions* had, through meticulous research of listener diaries and tapes, managed to piece together the full list. Not a festive fifty at all, it emerged, but a whopping 61 tracks of Peel's personal favourites during a crucial year for his show and for music in general.

As has been well-documented, we didn't get a listeners' chart that year. As a result of a number of factors, family issues and the rapidly changing music scene among them, Peel decided not to run a chart in the manner of that of the previous year, but instead to broadcast his own choices. What resulted is a fascinating run-down of favourite Peel tunes in a watershed year, in which, as Peel himself has acknowledged, the bulk of his audience changed overnight. While it would have been interesting to find out what that changing audience made of its favourite music in arguably the most important year in the history of music (and certainly British music), Peel's own views on the matter were certainly of no less interest and in retrospect it's good that we got this one-off glimpse into how a festive fifty might have looked had he got his own way.

Had there been a listeners' chart that year, who knows what it might have looked like? There must have been a serious possibility that the aggrieved old school elements in his audience would have bandied together to place 'Stairway To Heaven' at number one again, or even that a top ten might, despite Peel's embracing of a punk scene that was revitalizing and challenging tastes like nothing before or since, once again be dominated by the likes of Led Zeppelin, Pink Floyd and Dylan. And of course the situation wasn't one in which those on either side of the barricades would have cheerfully accepted a mixed chart: a 50-50 result would have antagonised the year zero crowd of punk as much as it would the alleged dinosaurs they sought to consign to pre-history. One of the reasons why Peel and Walters had devised the chart in the first place was to improve audience numbers that had been falling off in a fallow period for new music: the potentially damaging effect of a series of a bunch of unpalatable selections getting into the chart might well have killed the idea in its infancy. The fact that a number of what might be termed pre-1976 bands still managed to gatecrash the following year's festive fifty renders a concern that a fair number of them would have turned up here entirely credible.

I'm not suggesting anything cynical on the part of Peel or Walters in refusing to gather votes for a listeners' chart, simply that both music and the Peel show had changed so radically within a single year there was therefore a good chance that an end of year chart might well not have been reflective of the show and its new direction, and that it's therefore probably a good thing that a vote didn't take place that year. Peel had done what he'd always done on most spectacularly, following his instinct, lurching left-field to leave floundering like spent fish those who weren't inclined to join him on his fantastic journey: given the concerns he would raise later about overly conservative festive fifties, would he have viewed a chart skewed by the votes of those spent fish as reason to ditch the idea before his new audience could get used to having it around?.

Peel was, however, a lover of variety and of challenging musical preconceptions more than anything else. Although he'd already emerged as the foremost champion of the positive influence of punk, he wasn't about to subscribe to the 'year zero' narrowness that was already afflicting many among his new audience. The mixture we have here - featuring the likes of Ry Cooder, Jeck Beck and Status Quo among others - is pretty representative of the Peel shows at the time. History has sometimes painted a misleading picture of the mid to late seventies period Peel shows. Just as some of those who rarely or never listened to his show in the eighties assumed all he was playing were indie guitar bands, so many imagine the shows from this period consisted of wall-to-wall punk records. Indeed, as a young punk-influenced kid discovering the Peel show for myself in 1978, what struck me, as I suspect is the case with those who first listened in in any period, was its unexpected variety, of a kind reflected in this chart. A typical show of the period, if such a thing exists, would contain a welcome number of punk-influenced tunes, but with much else besides, much like this list. Anyone from his new audience tuning in to this chart wouldn't find anything especially unusual or amiss about finding a number of non-punk interlopers being in there: that was already an accepted part of the Peel experience.

The same couldn't be said, of course, of the majority of his pre-1977 audience, who would be repulsed by much of what's here, if they were listening to it at all, of course. They'd been abandoned to history by their former DJ idol. At least Bob Harris on Whistle Test was making clear his disquiet about the likes of New York Dolls and The Ramones forcing themselves between Focus and Barclay James Harvest and disrupting the long-accepted dynamic of his show. Peel, they were apalled to find, was positively embracing the upstarts who were muscling in on territory they'd always regarded as rightfully theirs.

Had he not done so, and we can sometimes now ignore what a courageous and iconoclastic action he took, the Peel show might well have ceased very quickly to lay claim to the important place it had occupied and would continue to occupy in music. This chart gives a fascinating insight into what was going on in his mind at the time, its combination of great new punk tunes – some already taking their place within a new musical canon, some peripheral and marginal but no less invigorating – and what continued to be of interest from elsewhere. It's also, sadly but inevitably, the only chart in the history of the Festive Fifty to allow reggae releases a proportion of the place more in line with their importance to the Peel musical legacy.

When you collect it all together, you're left with one of the most impressive festive fifty charts in existence. Perhaps we can go further and regard what is below as something of a never-to-be-lived-up-to model for future fifties and the reason for Peel's frequently expressed disappointment that the outcome was seldom – if ever – close to its mix of the cutting edge, the diverse, the rare and what was best of the popular. It's as if Peel bestowed on us some platonic template that we would inevitably struggle collectively to live up to.

The 1977 Forgotten Fifty (or Sixty-One)
Broadcast dates: 22, 23, 26 & 27 December 1977

61. God Save The Queen – Sex Pistols (Virgin 7")

It's widely thought that Peel started his show with this 'extra' track as a provocative gesture in the face of the BBC 'ban' on the single. Peel had played it prior to the furore surrounding its release in the queen's silver jubilee year and also appeared to claim, during the countdown of the 1999 all-time chart, that he had never been restricted from playing the single by his employers Whatever the truth, commencing his end of the year show with the tune was a typically defiant piece of broadcasting by this most playlist-resistant of all DJs as well as the best possible way to begin a chart of the year's most interesting releases.

60. Rocket In My Pocket – Little Feat (Warner Bros. LP *Time Loves A Hero*)
59. Whatever Happened To – Buzzcocks (United Artists 7")
58. Jocko Homo – Devo (Stiff 7")
57. Beginning of the End – Eddie & The Hot Rods (Island LP *Life On The Line*)
56. Bring in the Morning Light – The Motors (Virgin LP, *1*)
55. Watching The Detectives – Elvis Costello & The Attractions (Stiff 7")
54. Capital Radio – The Clash (CBS 7" EP *Capital Radio*)
53. Stepping Razor – Peter Tosh (CBS LP, *Equal Rights*)

In which Peel rights the considerable wrong of Tosh's omission from the remainder of festive fifty history. This is a Joe Higgs composition that appeared on Tosh's second album *Equal Rights*. Higgs was a teacher of singing and harmony in Tosh's native Jamaica and was instrumental in the development of his early work in the sixties with Bob Marley and Bunny Wailer in the first incarnation of The Wailers.

52. John Willie's Ferret – Oldham Tinkers (Topic LP, *For Old Time's Sake*)

One of several notable Lancastrian folk bands who emerged during the sixties, this trio adopted their name in support of travellers in their local town who had come into conflict with the local council. The eponymous ferret is one of several of John Willie's possessions celebrated in their music, along with his horse, his ragtime band and his performing newt. Their radical east Lancastrian heritage was also celebrated in renditions of songs like 'The Stockport Strike', 'Old King Coal' and 'Peterloo'.

51. Pretty Vacant – Sex Pistols (Virgin 7")
50. I.R.T. – Snatch (Bomp Then Lightning 7")

A single that was a massive favourite of *Sniffin' Glue*, that flagship of the nascent fanzine movement. Snatch were Patti Palladin and Judy Nylon, American emigrants living in London, and this was from a raw double A-side single that featured two tracks (the other was 'Stanley') recorded in the duo's London flat. Although Palladin would go on to achieve greater notoriety in the early eighties Snatch remains her finest musical achievement and the duo's significance in the emerging New York/London cultural exchange that went on in the punk years has been largely underplayed: the duo frequently hobnobbed and performed with fixtures of the NY punk scene like Johnny Thunders, Jerry Nolan and Wayne County.

49. Wild Dub – Generation X (Chrysalis 7" *Wild Youth* B-side)
48. Green Onions – Roy Buchanan (Atlantic LP *Loading Zone*)

In its original Booker T & the MGs form, this tune would thrill a new generation of followers as a result of its appearance in the *Quadrophenia* film a couple of years later. Guitarist Roy Buchanan turns it into a meandering, eight minute monster, eschewing the clipped style of Steve Cropper (you can't out-Cropper Cropper so it's best not to try) in favour of a wailing, growling blues howl duelling with the familiar signature organ riff.

47. Whole Wide World – Wreckless Eric (Stiff 7")

A track that seemed to represent the unique ethos of Stiff Records in the late seventies more than any other, a lament to having nobody to love delivered with a dollop of innocent desperation aligned with a smidgeon of malice from the perpetual cigarette-adorned mouth of pub rock's finest troubadour.

46. Away From the Numbers – The Jam (Polydor LP *In The City*)
45. I Knew the Bride – Dave Edmunds (Swan Song 7")

One of many tracks down the years able to transform itself from Peel favourite to Radio Two playlist fodder and back again with seamless ease. Edmunds' ability to deliver a cheeky pop number with enough raw flavour to satisfy the pub rock crowd and whistling milkmen alike would see his appeal span the seventies, surviving the punk year zero blitz with ease and finding willing acolytes like Elvis Costello and Nick Lowe, who wrote this.

44. Feel Like Making Love – Elizabeth Archer & The Equators (Lightning Records 7")

Good to see a place in this chart for some cool lovers' rock, especially this, which is one of a perhaps unexpectedly large number of cover versions to feature here, this a version of the Roberta Flack classic. There are certain reggae tracks that you feel could go on forever and you'd happily live the rest of your life within their grooves, and this is one of them. And the dub version on the b-side is perhaps even better. The Equators were initially signed by Stiff Records and then Two-Tone, meaning they had a crack at two of the freshest and most infuential labels of the late seventies yet were perhaps too stylistically diverse ever to make the kind of breakthrough of many of their record company peers.

43. Questions – Suburban Studs (Pogo 7")

Birmingham punk band who provided early support slots for both the Pistols and The Clash but, despite a distribution deal with WEA through which they put out an album, and a notoriously frenetic gigging schedule, they largely disappeared from sight when original lead singer Eddy Zipps left the band. This was from their first single. Their second 'I Hate School', previewed in their only Peel session of December 1977, would be their final release in 1978.

42. The Dark End of the Street – Ry Cooder (Warner Bros. LP *Show Time*)

If the post-77 crowd could still find a place in its raw heart for Dave Edmunds, the same could barely be said of Ry Cooder, whose precocious talent had thrilled on the first Beefheart album but whose work since had been associated with the kind of technically perfect, muso stylings that no self-respecting punk kid would even waste a carefully propelled gollop phlegm over. This track, a cover of a Penn/Moman soul classic, showcased Cooder's impeccable musical vocabulary well enough and retains enough of its original soul smoothless to render it appealing. Whether it's up there with other classic renditions by Percy Sledge, June Tabor and James Carr, among others, is another question.

41. Neat Neat Neat – The Damned (Stiff 7")
40. No Man's Land – June Tabor (Topic LP *Ashes & Diamonds*)

Version of the Eric Bogle classic that would later resurface in a Festive Fifty with The Men They Couldn't Hang, re-named as 'The Green Fields of France'. Tabor remains one of the great voices of folk music and has the ability to infuse traditional and well-known tunes with an element of newness and spontaneity, something that's certainly in evidence here.

39. Lookin' After No 1 – Boomtown Rats (Mercury 7")
38. Oh Bondage Up Yours! – X Ray Spex (Virgin 7")

Another band who've had their scandalous omission from festive fifty history rectified thanks to Ken Garner's research, with a track that arguably reflects the spirit of the age as good as anything that came out of this vibrant period. The frantic disharmony of Poly Styrene's voice battling Laura Logic's saxophone was a hell of a two fingers to those former Peel listeners still stuck in their pre-1977 ways.

37. Sick of You – The Users (Raw 7")

Classic punk vinyl: rudimentary production, wobbly sound levels and crassly enunciated New York-esque drawl., bass and drums submerged between an overriding and disarmingly basic guitar riff. The Users were from Cambridge and this almost archetypal punk gem founds its way into Peel's little red box of favourite records that he kept down the years, as well as being a declared influence on the emerging Dead Kennedys.

36. 'Heroes' – David Bowie (RCA 7")
35. (I'm) Stranded – The Saints (EMI LP *(I'm) Stranded*)

Premier Aussie punk band with a record that'd easily muscle its way into many people's top fifty punk singles, including mine. It was actually released as a single back in September 1976, before any UK punk singles had seen the light of day, and qualifies here by virtue of its appearance on the album of the same name. The single had originally been released on the band's own Fatal label but they'd quickly become part of the major label feeding frenzy that saw pound signs in the blood left on the ground after the punks' violent dismemberment of their industry. Famously, Sounds reviewer Jonh Ingham declared it 'Single of this and every week' and he had a point.

34. The Cruel Brother – Five Hand Reel (RCA LP *For A' That*)

Sounds great when played closely after those X Ray Spex, Users and Saints singles – try it. Dick Gaughan solo single that followed him into the repertoire of his later band The Boys of the Lough, a Celtic folk band of joint Scottish and Irish ancestry. Gaughan has hailed the contribution of drummer Dave Tulloch to this version of the tune as so integral that he's since refused to perform it as a solo artist. This is from the album 'For A' That', its title taken from the Robert Burns poem, a rendition of which also appears here.

33. Paradise – Dr Feelgood (United Artists LP *Sneakin' Suspicion*)
32. Waiting In Vain – Bob Marley & The Wailers (Island LP *Exodus*)
31. Love Story – The Lurkers (Beggars Banquet 7" single *Shadow* B-side)
30. Nobody Go Run Me – King Short Shirt (Weed Beat 7")

King Short Shirt is the alias of Emmanuel McLean, the Antiguan calypso legend whose uncompromising stance and absorption of the politics of the black power movement into his lyrics brought him into repeated conflict with the authorities. His legacy as one of the most important calypso artists of all time remains unchallenged.

29. Your Generation – Generation X (Chrysalis 7")
28. Success – Iggy Pop (RCA LP *Lust For Life*)
27. White Riot – The Clash (CBS 7")
26. Blue Wind – Jeff Beck with the Jan Hammer Group (Epic LP *Live*)

Difficult to think of a track in this list that proclaims Peel's independence of the punk Year Zero ethos more than this one, the closing track from a live album put out by a proclaimed guitar hero and former acolyte of Eric Clapton and Jimmy Page and the keyboardist who first found fame with the Mahavishnu Orchestra. In Beck's case, Peel would go on featuring some of his more experimental solo recordings for years to come.

25. Can't Give You More – Status Quo (Vertigo LP *Rockin' All Over The World*)

It's always surprised me when I hear younger Peel fans comment that Peel must have included 'Down Down' in his singles box as a joke, and that there was a similar tongue-in-cheek reason for including it in his DJ sets. Older listeners would undoubtedly be aware that 'the Quo' remained for many years one of his favourite bands. They survived the punk revolution perhaps without even really being aware it had happened.

24. Freedom Connection – Jah Woosh (Jamaica Sound 12")

Pretty obscure reggae tune, even moreso at the time because it didn't receive an official release until 1978 when it became the first single issued by the London-based Jamaica Sound, a label whose mission was informed by a desire to ensure that such gems did not find themselves completely bypassed by history, that I would contend never put out a bad record.

23. Pinhead – The Ramones (Sire LP *Leave Home*)

The only appearance by The Ramones in any Festive Fifty is this track from their second album, which quickly became a favoured anthem among their fans. The song was inspired by the brilliant 1932 film *Freaks*.

22. I Don't Wanna – Sham 69 (Step Forward 7")

If the pre-1976 crowd were balking at the likes of The Users and X Ray Spex, they were probably chucking their radios out of the window the first time John Peel played Sham, if they were still around to hear it. I can think of few bands I've had more heated debates over down the years. Even to many who thrilled at the punk explosion, they were viewed as inarticulate meatheads, flirting dangerously with crass slogans and working class tribalism that was inevitably going to appeal to some of the more unpleasant elements on the fringes of the punk contingent. Despite this, I was one of those who found a lot in them, my adolescent self loving such crude and confrontational diatribes as this one, their first single for the independent Step Forward label, which was produced by none other than John Cale. It wouldn't be long before Polydor snapped them up and this unlikely bunch of street urchins became UK chart regulars, proclaimed, probably accurately, as the most working class chart band in history.

21. London Lady – The Stranglers (United Artists 7" single *(Get A) Grip (On Yourself)* B-side)
20. Box Number – The Boys (NEMS LP *The Boys*)

19. The Worm Song – The Yobs (NEMS 7" single *Run Rudolph Run* B-side)

As Ken Garner notes, the two entries above placed together probably represented some anagrammatic schedule tinkering of the kind Peel loved. The two were, however, the same band. The Boys were a very early punk band, formed in late 1975. Like Sham 69 they enjoyed the patronage of John Cale and supported him on tour in 1977. 'Box Number' was a track from their eponymous album – which only record company delays prevented from being the first UK punk album release – and also made an appearance in the much loved Peel session of that year. The Yobs were their novelty persona for Xmas releases only, The Worm Song' being the B-side to their cover of Chuck Berry's 'Run Rudolph Run'.

18. Emergency – The Motors *(*Virgin *LP, 1)*
17. See Them a Come – Culture (Joe Gibbs Music LP *Two Sevens Clash*)

Peel would in later years go onto say that, has he been able to make the necessary arrangements, Culture would have recorded as many sessions as The Fall. This is from their classic debut album, rightly acknowledged as one of the standards against which all great roots reggae should be measured.

16. New Religion – Some Chicken (Raw 7")

I've regularly put in a claim for this as the ultimate punk tune and I'm sticking to that claim. The sound isn't just basic, it's dementedly simplistic to a barely inimitable degree, its music so rudimentary that the brief three chord (if that) guitar line that breaks out after the second verse sounds almost sophisticated in comparison. Despite this, the sheer earnestness of the vocal delivery and a guitarist who's clearly working at the top of his range – there's no sense of a Mick Jones performing within himself, but of a guy giving it absolutely everything he has – make this an absolute two minutes of joy that's never lost a bit of its appeal. It's the kind of thing we should be packing into time capsules and projecting into space because any being that found it would either be exactly the kind of alien it would be good to make contact with or else leave us well alone.

15. Incendiary Device – Johnny Moped (Chiswick 7")
14. Pigs – Pink Floyd (Harvest LP *Animals*)
13. Truly – The Jays & Ranking Trevor (Revival 7")

Plenty of uncertainty about this release, whose label credits the artist as 'J.Ayes & Ranking Trevor' but this is widely held to be a misprint. Whatever the case, it's sublime enough to include a repeated 'Here Comes The Bride' riff and get away with it.

12. Shadow – The Lurkers (Beggars Banquet 7")

Uxbridge punks who released this, the first single ever to appear on the highly durable Beggars Banquet label, in summer 1977. Its B-side 'Love Story' also appeared in this chart, making it the first ever single to register both its A-side and B-side in a festive fifty.

11. Holidays In The Sun – Sex Pistols (Virgin 7")
10. Be Good To Yourself – Frankie Miller (Chrysalis 7")

Massive Peel favourite for whom this was a breakthrough release, getting into the top thirty of the UK singles chart. Produced by Chris Thomas, a producer whose remarkable range of credits include Pink Floyd's *Dark Side of the Moon*, Pulp's *Different Class*, and the Sex Pistols, who he produced while at the same time working with Paul McCartney

9. Complete Control – The Clash (CBS 7")
8. Like A Hurricane – Neil Young & Crazy Horse (Reprise 7")
7. Right Track – Marlene Webber (Jama 7" split w/ David Issaacs' 'Place in the Sun')

Version of a Phyllis Dillon tune that appeared as the B-side of David Isaacs' 'Place in the Sun' single. Absolute class from an unfairly obscure singer whose other releases include scintillating versions of 'Stand By Your Man' and 'The First Cut is the Deepest'. Before that Marlene performed in The Webber Sisters with her sibling Joyce.

6. Smokescreen – Desperate Bicycles (Refill 7")

Among the most fervent and dedicated advocates of punk's DIY spirit, the band allegedly formed purely to release this, their first single on their own label, then decided to carry on, resolutely independent to the end, which didn't come until 1981.

5. Suspended Sentence – John Cooper Clarke (Rabid 7" EP *Innocents*)

Salford's bard can delight even with an ad-libbed aside so an entire poem set to music, especially when supported by the producer-genius Martin Hannett (then as Martin Zero), here with the first of many Festive Fifty entries, scarcely ever even came close to missing the mark. This was a track from his debut EP on Hannett's own Rabid indie label. Soon Clarke would be in demand as a support act and releasing singles on CBS. This is a brilliant put-down of the tabloid hang-'em-flog-'em brigade as Clarke relates deadpan, with Swiftian bathos, a dystopian society wherein capital punishment is not merely legal but compulsory.

4. I Can't Stand My Baby – Rezillos (Sensible 7")
3. You Beat The Hell Out of Me – The Motors (Virgin 7")
2. Uptown Top Ranking – Althea & Donna (Lightning Records 7")

If ever asked to compile a top twenty of the ultimate Peel recordings, it would be hard not to include this which, early in 1978, would shock pretty much everybody – including the duo themselves – by making number 1 in the UK charts. It wasn't that it was unusual for reggae tunes to enjoy mass popularity, but this song, with its undiluted doggerel, sheer sense of enjoyment and abandon and complete lack of concessions to the commercial market, broke down a highly significant barrier and, in an age when the National Front was in the midst of an all-too effective recruitment campaign, this refreshing, unabashed slice of Afro-Caribbean culture seemed, in its own apolitical way, to point the way forward towards a positive future in deeply negative times. One of the greatest of all Peel-instigated success stories.

1. Dancing The Night Away – The Motors (Virgin 7")

With this The Motors, essentially a pub rock band who grew out of the ashes of the influential Ducks Deluxe, trumped both the Pistols and The Clash with regard to the number of entries in this chart as well as finding themselves at the top of the pile of Peel's favourite releases of the year. The tune would peak just outside the top forty, but The Motors would soon follow Althea & Donna to the top reaches of the charts with 'Airport', a number five hit in early 1978.

1978

If there had been an artistic upheaval like the one between the first festive fifty and this one every few years, perhaps the all-time format would have endured. Only seven tracks remained from 1976 following a two year period during which Peel's show went through the transformation that changed his listening audience to an extent that was never again matched throughout his broadcasting life.

Regarding Peel himself, and the alleged 'betrayal' of musical sensibilities advanced by those in his previous audience who considered the embracing of punk as something akin to the Pope discovering a hitherto latent affection for Aleister Crowley, the signs that he would warm to such a thing had actually been there all along. Even before he joined Radio One, in a Perfumed Garden of 12 July 1967, he's heard referring to listener's complaints about him playing Jimmy Reed who, those listeners protest, is far too 'basic'. There's nothing wrong with 'basic', is his response, defending himself and Reed while simultaneously rejecting the artistic ethos some members of his audience chose to associate him with. If they ignored such signs, that was their problem: all punk did was bring to the surface a love for the basic and rudimentary, not to mention the anti-establishment, which had always been there.

Far better qualified writers than me have probed the sociological and political context of punk, but I'll take a philosophical view and say that punk's real legacy was a kind of Cartesian revolution applied to music. Just as in philosophy Descartes sought to question and, if necessary, demolish his previous beliefs and thought systems in the search for indubitable truth, so punk questioned accepted musical ideals and paradigms in search of something less narrow and truer a spirit of rock and roll that had somehow got badly distorted and compromised. If such questioning occasionally kicked over undeserving statues, then that was an inevitable part of the process: they might be returned to their prior positions should the severe critical examination they were undergoing deem them worthy, or they might not. What came out as a result of this was simply a re-examination of what was valued in music, and the Peel show would be the place where the best, most varied and most uninhibited of the examinations would be aired. As such, the relatively short-lived punk movement's lasting role was chiefly as a midwife to a far more interesting musical future, and the 1978 Festive Fifty was the Peel audience's first opportunity to record the fruits of its initial phase. If, as his critics stated, Descartes was only really seeking a stronger foundation for beliefs he already held, punk had no such motive: part of the excitement of the period was in not knowing what the midwife might pull kicking and screaming into the world, or what the hell it would resemble, if anything.

If the 1978 festive fifty gives a reasonably accurate image of the new canon that replaced the old, it perhaps fails to capture the true breadth of the excitement of the period. Peel's own 1977 chart had allowed us perhaps a broader glimpse of what was afoot, allowing us to behold the wonder of such unlikely luminaries as Johnny Moped, Some Chicken and Suburban Studs as they were going about their uncouth business. In some ways 1978 gives a picture of what had happened now that the dust had settled to some extent on the upheaval wrought a year earlier.

So, instead of some of the great one-off singles that made such a massive contribution to the energy of the period, we see here the acknowledged masters of the scene, new heroes to replace the old, most of whom by this point have signed to major labels meaning that, unlike the chart of the previous year, there's no place for such names as Pogo, Raw, Bomp Then Lightning or even Chiswick while reggae, as would be largely the case throughout festive fifty, is entirely absent save for its appropriation by The Clash.

What comes across here is how efficiently the majors had already hoovered up most of the leading players. The only genuine indie to secure an entry for more than one artist is Stiff, foreshadowing the longevity of this impudent and brilliant upstart of the period. Rough Trade, which would later establish itself as the greatest festive fifty label of all time, only scores through the reliable offices of Stiff Little Fingers, while the other 'indie' entries come from the short-lived Mancunian label New Hormones and Sensible, via the Rezillos, with one of only seven tunes to survive from the previous year's top fifty. It was a period in which indies were more vibrant than at any time in British music history, and there's no question that they're under-represented here.

One of the many spurious notion to be debunked during the period was the one that decreed that the great songwriters must be, of necessity, also intellectuals or even something akin to the Nietzshean ubermensch. Thus the point came to be missed completely when it concerned the likes of Jim Morrison or John Lennon: great artists both but never intellectuals or philosophers. Morrison's half-digested and idealised consumption of Nietzsche and Lennon's heart-felt but trite politics ought never to have been taken as seriously as they were and it led to a deification of brilliant creative figures (both 'Riders on the Storm' and 'Strawberry Fields Forever' from the 1976 chart were the products of a stunning artistic imagination) which was as unnecessary as it was wide of the mark.

While punk clearly had much to say, it seemed unlikely that any of the great songwriters emerging in the late seventies would be hailed as proto-philosophers, or anything that placed them an inch above the concerns of their own listeners. Many of the best of them feature in this chart: Elvis Costello, for instance, who for the next six years would be driven by that creative energy that derives from the conviction that you were only as good as your last song, and John Lydon who, both with the Pistols and his new band Public Image Ltd, would respond with a characteristic sneer to any attempt to intellectualise what he did, with a result that the profundity of many of his lyrics and musical experimentation would be underplayed, even to this day. Howard Devoto's restless artistic spirit would bring about his early departure from Buzzcocks and the formation of Magazine, perhaps the first band to show the way forward after punk by inverting its own premises almost as they were still being formed. Even Springsteen, much derided by Peel and rightly so despite his appearance here, would understand that the future lay in the fierce adoption of blue collar no-bullshit values as opposed to any imitation of the rock heroes who preceded him, even if many of the postures struck had an off-putting air of familiarity about them.

What we were witnessing was not a constantly recurrent revolution in British music – and, with the exception of Springsteen, all the new music that entered the chart since 1976 came from Britain or Ireland – but literally a new, and far more open belief system. Much of what would become accepted into the punk canon is already evident here: it didn't emerge, at least for the Peel audience, with the benefit of hindsight or the application of nostalgia. The festive fifties of this late seventies period celebrated with intuitive precision the great majority of those punk records that would come to be regarded as true classics of the era. We heard 'Suspect Device' and instantly knew it would keep us company for the rest of our lives; and we were right, just as we were about 'White Man in Hammersmith Palais', 'Boredom', 'Teenage Kicks' and so many others.

Also evident here is the original template for what might be termed Banshees Syndrome, whereby a popular Peel group releases a numger of spectacularly good tracks and its fan base are divided on which is the best, resulting in a split vote. The Banshees created a record (though admittedly a short-lived one) of seven entries in a single festive fifty but, because of the split, the highest is only at number 22.

The opposite is true in the case of the Sex Pistols, with their first three singles already hailed as classics and all featuring in the top six, with the fourth at number 18. A number of tracks in this chart would continue to be residents of the festive fifty until all-time format was abandoned four years later, and a fair number would still be there when it briefly reappeared in 1999. It's worthy of note, also, that there was a massive increase in voters compared with the only previous festive fifty of two years earlier: four or five times more, according to Peel's own estimation. Clearly there was powerful evidence that his and Walters' idea of generating more interest for the show via the introduction of the chart had been successful, though it's very doubtful either of them had anticipated the enormous culture change that had presumably played a major part.

There were five tracks that managed to survive the great artistic cull that occurred between the 1976 chart and this one. The previous number one, 'Stairway to Heaven' stuck out like a sore thumb that had then been run over repeatedly by a steamroller at number 14. Van Morrison's 'Madame George' actually managed to hold its position at number 21 and, most remarkably, Lynyrd Skynyrd's 'Freebird' even went up from its position two years earlier. The song represents pre-punk sentiments perhaps more than any other and, if any band could stand as a paradigm for rock and roll excess in the period, it was Skynyrd, so its elevated position might be best explained by two things: one, it was a track that many of those who remained of the Peel audience's 'old guard' gravitated towards to reassert old fashioned values and, two, the death of three of their members in a 1977 plane crash offered further reason to commemorate them, especially as a new line-up wouldn't re-emerge until 1979, meaning the band at the time voting took place for this chart were officially defunct, the song itself taking on further poignance en route to its cigarette-lighters-in-the-air deification by the resurgent rock crowd who would use it to restate territorial rights once the sackers of punk had moved on.

The other thing that probably needs to be commented on is that, apart from Siouxsie's multiple appearances, women have only slightly more representation in this chart than they had in the male-dominated 1976 festive fifty. One of the barriers punk had been so celebrated for breaking down was the gender divide in rock and yet only Fay Fife of the Rezillos and Flying Lizard Deborah Evans join Siouxie here. X-Ray Spex, the Slits, Penetration, The Adverts, Lene Lovich, just to name a small number of bands with female members, all of whom recorded a Peel session during the year, were absent; they would never get a sniff of the action in future festive fifties either. Nor would the situation alter much in the following year.

Despite that, this is a list of absolute stormers. Peel, during the broadcast, declared himself 'knocked out' by the quality of the chart and commented that the top six would probably feature in any all-time top twenty of his own.

1978 Festive Fifty

Broadcast dates: 26, 27 & 28 December; 1 January

50. Metal Postcard (Mittageisen) – Siouxsie & The Banshees (Polydor LP *The Scream*)
49. Emerald – Thin Lizzy (Warner Bros LP *Live & Dangerous*)
48. Like a Hurricane – Neil Young & Crazy Horse (Reprise LP *American Stars & Bars*)
47. Summertime Blues – Flying Lizards (Virgin 7")
46. Desolation Row – Bob Dylan
45. EMI – Sex Pistols (Virgin LP *Never Mind The Bollocks*)
44. In The City – The Jam (Polydor 7")
43. Jigsaw Feeling – Siouxsie & The Banshees (Polydor LP *The Scream*)
42. Mirage – Siouxsie & The Banshees (Polydor LP *The Scream*)
41. Switch – Siouxsie & The Banshees (Polydor LP *The Scream*)
40. London Lady – The Stranglers (United Artists LP *Rattus Norvegicus*)
39. My Generation – The Who (Brunswick 7")
38. Overground – Siouxie & The Banshees (Polydor LP *The Scream*)
37. Alison – Elvis Costello (Stiff 7")
36. Like A Rolling Stone – Bob Dylan (Columbia LP *Highway 61 Revisited*)
35. Dancing The Night Away – The Motors (Virgin LP *1*)
34. Helter Skelter – Siouxsie & The Banshees (Radio promo, Polydor LP *The Scream*)
33. No More Heroes – The Stranglers (United Artists LP *No More Heroes*)
32. Hanging Around – The Stranglers (United Artists LP *Rattus Norvegicus*)
31. Layla – Derek & The Dominoes (Polydor LP *Layla & Other Assorted Love Songs*)
30. Moving Away From The Pulsbeat – Buzzcocks

(United Artists LP *Another Music In A Different Kitchen*)
29. Shine On You Crazy Diamond – Pink Floyd
28. Sultans Of Swing – Dire Straits (Vertigo LP *Dire Straits*)
27. Sex & Drugs & Rock & Roll – Ian Dury & The Blockheads (Stiff 7")
26. Born To Run – Bruce Springsteen (Columbia LP *Born To Run*)
25. Watching The Detectives – Elvis Costello & The Attractions (Stiff 7")
24. Down In The Tube Station At Midnight – The Jam (Polydor 7")
23. Police & Thieves – The Clash (CBS LP *The Clash*)
22. Hong Kong Garden – Siouxsie & The Banshees (Polydor 7")
21. Madame George – Van Morrison
20. Can't Stand My Baby – The Rezillos (Sensible 7")
19. Freebird – Lynyrd Skynyrd (MCA LP *Pronounced*)
18. Holiday in the Sun – Sex Pistols (Virgin LP *Never Mind The Bollocks*)
17. Another Girl, Another Planet – The Only Ones (Columbia LP *The Only Ones*)
16. "Heroes" – David Bowie (RCA LP *"Heroes"*)
15. White Riot – The Clash (CBS LP *The Clash*)
14. Stairway To Heaven – Led Zeppelin
13. New Rose – The Damned (Stiff 7")
12. Boredom – Buzzcocks (New Hormones 7" EP *Spiral Scratch*)
11. Alternative Ulster – Stiff Little Fingers (Rough Trade LP *Inflammable Material*)
10. Teenage Kicks – The Undertones (Sire 7")
9. Public Image – Public Image Ltd (Virgin LP *Public Image*)
8. What Do I Get? – Buzzcocks (United Artists 7")
7. (White Man) In Hammersmith Palais – The Clash (CBS 7")
6. Pretty Vacant – Sex Pistols (Virgin LP *Never Mind The Bollocks*)
5. Shot By Both Sides – Magazine (Virgin 7")
4. Suspect Device – Stiff Little Fingers (Rough Trade 7")
3. God Save The Queen – Sex Pistols (Virgin LP *Never Mind The Bollocks*)
2. Complete Control – The Clash (CBS 7")
1. Anarchy In The UK – Sex Pistols (Virgin LP *Never Mind The Bollocks*)

Top Fifteen of 1978?

What would the 1978 chart look like if the format adopted in later years were in use then? In other words, if only tracks released in 1978 could be voted for. Of course, it's impossible to know, but from the list above we can compile a top fifteen tracks released in that year and speculate, based on the order in which they appeared, that this is how the top end might have looked:

1. Suspect Device – Stiff Little Fingers
2. Shot By Both Sides – Magazine
3. White Man in Hammersmith Palais – The Clash
4. Public Image – Public Image Ltd
5. Teenage Kicks – The Undertones
6. Alternative Ulster – Stiff Little Fingers
7. Another Girl, Another Planet – The Only Ones
8. Can't Stand My Baby – The Rezillos (*Released as a single in 1977, but eligible because of its appearance on the Can't Stand The Rezillos album*)
9. Hong Kong Garden – Siouxsie & The Banshees
10. Down in the Tube Station at Midnight – The Jam
11. Sex & Drugs & Rock & Roll – Ian Dury & The Blockheads
12. Sultans Of Swing – Dire Straits
13. Moving Away From the Pulsebeat – Buzzcocks
14. Helter Skelter – Siouxsie & The Banshees
15. Overground – Siouxsie & The Banshees

1979

The remarkable changes recently wrought in the British musical landscape were even more evident in this year's chart. Only five tracks in it could be said to be untouched by the influence of punk and its immediate aftermath – even fewer than the previous year – and that only three were pre-1977 releases shows the era-defining 'year zero' approach fervently at work. Much of the chart's top end was little more than the 1978 Festive Fifty re-shuffled: nine of the top ten were in last year's fifty, which you might expect to be leading Peel already to harbour doubts about whether an all-time chart had a future as an annual event. Not a bit of it, it seemed: after all, despite a certain stylistic consistency prevailing, there were 19 tracks from 1979 and the number of new entries (23) made up almost half of the chart, something Peel drew attention to as he commenced his broadcast of the first instalment.

All of those new entries, it's fair to note, bore the very distinctive stamp of punk's influence. Some were new releases from established bands of the period: the Jam scored with two singles – 'Strange Town' and 'Eton Rifles' – that joined 'Down in the Tube Station of Midnight' in that fine run of releases that few bands in the future would ever come close to matching. There were more entries for the Undertones too, still carrying the banner of Peel's favourite band, with 'Jimmy Jimmy' also revealed by the DJ as a great favourite of his children. Peel was less complimentary about Stiff Little Fingers' cover of 'Johnny Was', another track that represented the reggae-punk crossover, this time via a song that relocated an incident that had its genesis downtown Jamaica to the troubled streets of Northern Ireland. The song had been showcased in the band's debut Peel session in 1978 and, despite Peel's reservations, became a great favourite with his listeners, one of many songs in the chart that reflected a broadening the punk template beyond the brief, energetic statements that had characterised its initial flowering.

Very much emerging as the man leading the charge away from those origins was one of its architects . As what remained of the Pistols became focused by Malcolm McLaren on an attempt to rewrite their history as a deliberate scam, John Lydon, nee Rotten was offering what ultimately became a more convincing version, specifically as what remained of the rest of the Pistols appeared more inclined to a life of simply playing bad heavy metal and getting wasted. Lydon was showing he'd been the vital element of the band that had raised it above the level of crassness to which it had hitherto sunk and, with Public Image Ltd, he was exploring ways of taking music beyond the narrow confines punk had imposed. While their ground-breaking *Metal Box* wouldn't get a taste of the action until the following year, their 'Death Disco' could make a good case for being the most important release of the year, a tune that combined a twisted reimagining of Tchaikovsky with uncomfortably personal subject matter that, when it appeared on Top of the Pops, seemed literally to stop the show, so clearly were its presenters and audience, all of whom continued to look completely unaffected by the upheavals of punk, stunned by the experience.

Lydon appeared six times in the top thirty, courtesy of the combined works of his two groundbreaking bands, and there were places for many others who were illuminating interesting roads into the future. Gang of Four, a group of Leeds University students who would become one of the most influential of all late seventies bands, made an appearance, though only with a single track from their debut album *Entertainment*, a masterpiece that stood out even in this innovative period, utilising Brechtian alienation effects and unapologetically literary wordplay to toss more and more possibilities into the post-punk cauldron.

Also from Leeds, The Mekons scored their only festive fifty entry with a piece of sharply observed punk that would barely hint at the potential of this band to outlast pretty much every other group from the period. Elsewhere, the excellent Ruts, a band who I still recall hearing with a mixture of shock and awe when they came out of the transistor radio I held next to my ear under the bedclothes appeared twice, while a single American entry came from Dead Kennedys, a band who pretty much ditched the US art-punk template and went straight for the jugular in the manner of their British counterparts. They possessed, in East Bay Ray, one of the period's finest guitarists, a man who could rudely seize his Californian heritage and twist a surf riff into a twisted punk masterpiece in a manner that would be copied by so many of the skatepunk bands who'd crop up in his neck of the woods more than a decade later, but never fully emulated.

Perhaps the two new bands who most vividly portrayed the vast mass of disparate possibilities open to music in this era, and the remarkable commercial potential they enjoyed during this period, were Gary Numan's 'Tubeway Army' and, coming out of nowhere (well, Coventry) with a breath of fresh air arguably, in a period of breaths of fresh air, more eagerly drawn in than any other, The Specials and the Two-Tone label.

Numan would soon abandon Tubeway Army and continue under his own name, but not before he hit number one with a track that was the result of his band ditching their origins as a pretty ordinary 'punk'-inspired band in favour of embracing electronic music. It was a moment that synergised the Bowie Boys, who'd persisted in the clubs throughout the period and stayed aloof from the punk crowd (Peel commented that there were fewer votes for Bowie himself this year), and the till then largely unexplored influences of Kraftwerk and which kickstarted the whole 'cult with no name' that would soon be appropriated by a media keen to drag music away from those dirty punks.

Fundamentalists in the punk crowd, who associated the synthesizer with those prog rock bands they'd spent so much energy and spit trying to get rid of, balked at the direction taken by Numan. Along with his musical direction, he was a Tory and outspoken nationalist who, when questioned about his voting intentions by Sounds in 1983, came out unequivocally for Thatcher, informing another magazine that his favourite piece of music was 'Land of Hope & Glory'. Peel, however, despite clearly having no truck with his politics, remained a supporter long after the music press had written him off as a tiresome reactionary and he would be welcomed back for session appearances as late as 2000 and 2001.

The Specials couldn't have been further apart from Numan either political or stylistically. They kick-started the Two-Tone movement with a manifesto of racial tolerance and a voice for the downtrodden you could dance to. Merging ska and punk into an infectious hybrid, Two-Tone was arguably the last genuinely live musical movement and one that attained a level of commercial success of which most punks bands could only have dreamed. The Specials had the chart's highest new entry, the brilliant 'Gangsters', which took the relationship between the band and former Clash supremo Bernie Rhodes and turned it into a microcosm for internal industry tensions, Terry Hall's laconic vocals underpinned by an upbeat ska swagger in a brilliantly conceived musical contrast that would move the self-financed single from the Peel show and, almost without pausing for breath, onto daytime radio. 'Gangsters' would be the first of eight Specials singles to go top ten in the UK singles charts while, down the list, 'Too Much Too Young' – in its original, slowed-down version – gave notice of its potential to excite: the track would be released in its speeded up live version the following year and become a UK number one.

It may seem from these observations that there were a hell of a lot of commercially successful tunes in this chart, and that would be correct. More than half of what's in here had made the UK top forty during an all-too brief period in which artistic excellence and commercial potential could enjoy a reasonably harmonious relationship. Despite that, the entry that resonated down the years most of all was that of The Fall at number forty, with a small but significant step on their journey to becoming the most prolific festive fifty band of all time. Since then, there have been only three festive fifties in which the band has not appeared. The Cure, while clearly not able to make such a claim, also made the first appearance of what would become a sustained five-year period of chart activity.

Punk had also, for the first time in British music (notwhstanding the efforts of The Kinks and Small Faces, and discounting, as we surely should, the contribution of Gerry & The Pacemakers), brought locality and national identity to the fore in a sustained way: four of the top six tracks here refer directly to an area of the UK, whether the nation as a whole, a part of it or the microcosm of a tube station. In a similar spirit, there is again only one track in here by a band from outside Britain and Northern Island.

Peel drew attention to the fact that practically every track The Jam had ever recorded received at least some votes, making note of what we termed 'Banshees Syndrome' a year earlier by commenting on that long-standing festive fifty quirk that would deem that such bands would inevitably suffer from a split vote whereas those with fewer releases – in this case the likes of The Specials, The Ruts, Magazine and others – would find it easier to pool together whatever votes came in from their audience and thus achieve a placing higher up the chart. Arguably, the Pistols would benefit from this more than anyone, their vast influence restricted to one magnificent LP that this year saw them occupy four of the top sixteen places. They remained at number one, 'Anarchy in the UK' this year beating off the challenge from The Undertones comfortably, with around twice as many votes.

Festive Fifty 1979

Broadcast dates: 20, 24, 26 & 27 December; 1 January

50. What Do I Get? – Buzzcocks
49. Police & Thieves – The Clash
48. Hong Kong Garden – Siouxsie & The Banshees
47. Babylon's Burning – The Ruts (Virgin LP *The Crack*)
46. Helter Skelter – Siouxsie & The Banshees
45. No More Heroes – The Stranglers
44. Playground Twist – Siouxsie & The Banshees (Polydor LP *Join Hands*)
43. 10:15 Saturday Night – The Cure (Fiction LP *Three Imaginary Boys*)
42. Jigsaw Feeling – Siouxsie & The Banshees
41. Where Were You? – The Mekons (Fast Product 7")

40. Rowche Rumble – The Fall (Step-Forward 7")
39. Are 'Friends' Electric? – Tubeway Army (Beggars Banquet LP *Replicas*)
38. Switch – Siouxsie & The Banshees
37. Into The Valley – The Skids (Virgin LP *Scared To Dance*)
36. Too Much Too Young – The Specials (Two Tone LP *Specials*)
35. Icon – Siouxsie & The Banshees (Polydor LP *Join Hands*)
34. "Heroes" – David Bowie
33. California Uber Alles – Dead Kennedys (Optional 7")
32. My Generation – The Who
31. Jimmy Jimmy – The Undertones (Sire LP *The Undertones*)
30. Shine On You Crazy Diamond – Pink Floyd
29. You've Got My Number (Why Don't You Use It?) – The Undertones (Sire 7")
28. Death Disco – Public Image Ltd (Virgin 7")
27. Strange Town – The Jam (Polydor 7")
26. White Riot – The Clash
25. Boredom – Buzzcocks
24. Stairway To Heaven – Led Zeppelin
23. Damaged Goods – Gang of Four (EMI LP *Entertainment!*)
22. Love Song – The Damned (Chiswick 7")
21. Love in a Void – Siouxsie & The Banshees (Polydor 7")
20. Another Girl, Another Planet – The Only Ones
19. The Eton Rifles – The Jam (Polydor 7")
18. Wasted Life – Stiff Little Fingers (Rough Trade 7" single *Suspect Device* B-side)
17. Shot By Both Sides – Magazine
16. Pretty Vacant – Sex Pistols
15. Johnny Was – Stiff Little Fingers (Rough Trade LP *Inflammable Material*)
14. Holidays in the Sun – Sex Pistols
13. God Save The Queen – Sex Pistols
12. Get Over You – The Undertones (Sire 7")
11. In A Rut – The Ruts (People Unite 7")
10. New Rose – The Damned
9. Public Image – Public Image Ltd
8. Suspect Device – Stiff Little Fingers
7. Gangsters – Special AKA (Two Tone 7")
6. Alternative Ulster – Stiff Little Fingers (Rough Trade LP *Inflammable Material*)
5. Complete Control – The Clash
4. Down in the Tube Station at Midnight – The Jam
3. White Man in Hammersmith Palais – The Clash
2. Teenage Kicks – The Undertones
1. Anarchy in the UK – Sex Pistols

Top Twenty of 1979?

Due to the appearance of Stiff Little Fingers' *Inflammable Material* album, the band would have been eligible to secure the number one position again, had an annual chart existed, although their putative e FF-topper of the previous year would have dropped to number three. It perhaps stresses the huge popularity of the band at this time that this would have resulted in their securing four of the top seven places in the chart.

1. Alternative Ulster – Stiff Little Fingers
2. Gangsters – Special AKA
3. Suspect Device – Stiff Little Fingers
4. In A Rut – The Ruts
5. Get Over You – The Undertones
6. Johnny Was – Stiff Little Fingers
7. Wasted Life – Stiff Little Fingers
8. The Eton Rifles – The Jam
9. Love in a Void – Siouxsie & The Banshees
10. Love Song – The Damned
11. Strange Town – The Jam
12. Death Disco – Public Image Ltd
13. You've Got My Number (Why Don't You Use It?) – The Undertones
14. Jimmy Jimmy – The Undertones
15. California Uber Alles – Dead Kenneys
16. Icon – Siouxsie & The Banshees
17. Too Much Too Young – The Specials
18. Into The Valley – The Skids
19. Are 'Friends' Electric? – Tubeway Army
20. Rowche Rumble – The Fall

THE FESTIVE FIFTY

1980

Given the format of the early festive fifties, tactical voting was to some extent inevitable. Why waste your vote on a much-loved obscure track that stood no chance of charting when you could renew the unfinished business of last year of trying to push 'Complete Control' towards the number one slot? Of course, attempts at mild rigging of the vote would remain a feature of the chart long after this early format had been abandoned, but there was no question that repeating an 'all-time' chart on an annual basis gave would-be tactical voters an awful lot of information to go in terms of determining their priorities and it was perhaps inevitably that the chart of the last two years clearly had an influence on how a large proportion of this chart would look.

Despite this, the all-time format was perhaps given a stay of execution due to the emergence of Joy Division who, with seven entries, not only took over the mantle of most featured band from Siouxsie & The Banshees, but also managed to do what the Banshees had never done and take some those entries into the higher reaches of the chart. A sharing of the vote among Joy Division fans didn't prevent the band from placing two tracks in the top three and another further down the top ten. And there was even more of a sign that the winds of change were originating firmly from a direction out towards Salford when a band called The Fall indicated their sole appearance of the previous year represented something more than a mere brief flirtation with the festive fifty when they matched the four tracks registered by the Banshees.

As was the case in the previous year, Peel did his best to generate drama with the material he had by continuing a narrative around what clues might be discerned from movements within the chart. He even ponders aloud whether the drop of 'Rowche Rumble' to number 49 signals a decline in the FF fortunes of The Fall. In the first announcement of its kind during a festive fifty countdown – though certainly not the last – Peel proclaimed their 'How I Wrote Elastic Man' his favourite single of the year.

Joy Division aside, there was a general paucity of bands entering the chart for the first time. It was good to see an appearance for Adam & The Ants before they submitted to unrelenting crapness. Such was the quck transition of Adam, who moved from photogenic pirate, to highwayman, to fairytale prince with unrelenting ease, the excitement generated by a genuine ex-first generation punk making unmistakeable moves on the top of the singles charts was already quickly wearing off when this chart was broadcast. However, it's a pleasing, if minor, feature of this festive fifty that we were allowed to record that there was a time, between the old Ants and the appalling artistic decline that set in with 'Prince Charming' and reached a pitiful low with 'Antrap', when they were a genuinely welcome addition to the commercial mainstream.

The Teardrop Explodes never did become crap, of course, but they also make an appearance in a period prior (yes, there was such a period) to Julian Cope discovering hallucinogenics, with the Mick Finkler line-up that some hard-line scouse fans of the group will insist they were never the same after, and who dismiss my arguments in favour of the much-maligned *Wilder* album with a derisory snort. If this added a much needed freshness to the early chart, then so did Spizz's legendary 'Where's Captain Kirk?', the two singles also building on the bursting open of the doors on behalf of independent labels by Two-Tone the previous year by ensuring representation for Liverpool's Zoo label and Rough Trade respectively. Zoo would prove only occasional visitors to the chart, while the latter, alongside its importance in the centre of the UK's indie distribution network, was now beginning its climb to the status of the most decorated label in festive fifty history.

In fact, bolstered by the Fall and Joy Division entries, this was the best year so far for independent labels, Rough Trade tying with Factory for the accolade of label with most entries and leaving the majority of majors trailing some way behind, though Polydor offered some sort of challenge, with four entries from Siouxsie & The Banshees (a significant decline, with the highest only at number 37) and a couple from The Jam representing what turned out to be a final attempt to arrest the march into the indie eighties. It would not be until 1992 that a major would again enjoy a position at the top of the pile, and there have been very few such challenges since.

Killing Joke gave notice of their arrival with a couple of entries and it was good to see appearances from a couple of Clash songs: the widely loved 'Armagideon Time' and the much derided 'Bankrobber'. The release of the latter had, in the music press, seen the band endure the must sustained backlash yet, though much of it concentrated not on the music but on the outlaw chic pose adopted by Joe Strummer despite it now being common knowledge that he was the son of a high ranking civil service official. Whatever you felt about Strummer, it all seemed to have very little to do with the song's actual quality it made the single's appearance here, however low down, particularly gratifying. Peel, a vocal supporter of the single, commented on this also. While there are certainly allegations you could make against The Clash – signing for a major label and Strummer sending his son to a boarding school after distancing himself from his own past so fervently are often more convincingly cited – surely what parents you have is one of the few things in life you can havean control over whatsoever.

But there can be no question that it was the music of Joy Division that did most to enliven, and perhaps rescue, an annual all-time chart in danger of growing stale. Some assumed then it was merely the death of Ian Curtis during the year that brought about their seven entries, but time would record that their arrival represented far more than an epitaph for the singer. No band since the arrival of punk has exerted more of an influence over music and the same might also be said of the Factory label.

The highest place Joy Division song, 'Atmosphere', wasn't a Factory release, at least not in its original form. It appeared via the Sordide Sentimental label in France, limited to 1578 copies. Coupled with 'Dead Souls', it came out under the title 'Licht und Blindheit' and became immediately collectable in its original version. As its popularity among Joy Division fans became evident, it was given a single release by Factory in September with a new version of 'She's Lost Control' on the B-side.

Had it not been for Joy Division and a few other things, of course, there wouldn't have been an awful lot to set this chart apart from the one the previous year and few would give the all-time format much chance of surviving as a permanent fixture of the Christmas period. Disillusionment hadn't yet in for the DJ, however, and the days of mildly laconic cynicism with regard to the festive fifty were clearly some way off as he announced at the end of the first broadcast how he did 'really enjoy this – I must admit'.

1980 Festive Fifty
Broadcast dates: 22, 23, 24, 29 & 30 December

50. Damaged Goods – Gang Of Four
49. Rowche Rumble – The Fall
48. White Riot – The Clash
47. Hong Kong Garden – Siouxsie & The Banshees
46. Bankrobber – The Clash (CBS 7")
45. Icon – Siouxsie & The Banshees
44. Switch – Siouxsie & The Banshees
43. Treason – The Teardrop Explodes (Mercury LP *Kilimanjaro*)
42. Smash It Up – The Damned (Chiswick LP *Machine Gun Etiquette*)
41. Twenty Four Hours – Joy Division (Factory LP *Closer*)
40. Where's Captain Kirk? – Spizzenergi (Rough Trade 7")
39. Armagideon Time – The Clash (CBS 7")
38. Fiery Jack – The Fall (Step-Forward 7")
37. Jigsaw Feeling – Siouxsie & The Banshees
36. Psyche – Killing Joke (Malicious Damage 7")
35. Requiem – Killing Joke (EG 12")
34. Careering – Public Image Ltd (Virgin LP *Metal Box*)
33. Poptones – Public Image Ltd (Virgin LP *Metal Box*)
32. Gangsters – Special AKA
31. California Uber Alles – Dead Kennedys
30. Kings of the Wild Frontier – Adam & The Ants (Epic LP *Kings of the Wild Frontier*)
29. Love Song – The Damned (Chiswick LP *Machine Gun Etiquette*)
28. Another Girl, Another Planet – The Only Ones
27. Wasted Life – Stiff Little Fingers
26. How I Wrote 'Elastic Man' – The Fall (Rough Trade 7")
25. God Save The Queen – Sex Pistols
24. Suspect Device – Stiff Little Fingers
23. Pretty Vacant – Sex Pistols
22. She's Lost Control – Joy Division (Factory 12")
21. Totally Wired – The Fall (Rough Trade 7")
20. New Dawn Fades – Joy Division (Factory LP *Unknown Pleasures*)
19. In a Rut – The Ruts

18. A Forest – The Cure (Fiction LP *Seventeen Seconds*)
17. Get Over You – The Undertones
16. Johnny Was – Stiff Little Fingers
15. Complete Control – The Clash
14. Decades – Joy Division (Factory LP *Closer*)
13. Going Underground – The Jam (Polydor 7")
12. Holidays In The Sun – Sex Pistols
11. Public Image – Public Image Ltd
10. Transmission – Joy Division (Factory 7")
9. Alternative Ulster – Stiff Little Fingers
8. New Rose – The Damned
7. Teenage Kicks – The Undertones
6. Holiday in Cambodia – Dead Kennedys (Cherry Red 7")
5. (White Man) In Hammersmith Palais – The Clash
4. Down In The Tube Station At Midnight – The Jam
3. Love Will Tear Us Apart – Joy Division (Factory 7")
2. Atmosphere – Joy Division (Factory 12")
1. Anarchy in the UK – Sex Pistols

Top Twenty of 1980?

As details of what lay just outside the 1980 Fifty were made available in 1980, it's possible gain to give a hypothetical top twenty again featuring tracks released only during that year. It marks clearly the dynamic shift of the balance of power from Stiff Little Fingers – who had so many 1979 entries and yet whose highest placing this year would have been a speculative number 18 – to Joy Division, who occupy the top two positions and six slots in the top twenty. The potential for The Fall to figure prominently when annual charts came into being a couple of years hence was also demonstrated by the appearance of two of their tunes in the top ten.

1. Atmosphere – Joy Division
2. Love Will Tear Us Apart – Joy Division
3. Going Underground – The Jam
4, Decades – Joy Division
5. A Forest – The Cure
6. Totally Wired – The Fall
7. She's Lost Control – Joy Division (eligible due to inclusion on Factory release of *Atmosphere* single)
8. How I Wrote 'Elastic Man' – The Fall
9. Kings of the Wild Frontier – Adam & The Ants
10. Requiem – Killing Joke
11. Pssyche – Killing Joke
12. Twenty Four Hours – Joy Division
13. Treason – The Teardrop Explodes
14. Bankrobber – The Clash
15. Wardance – Killing Joke
16. Dog Eat Dog – Adam & The Ants
17. West One (Shine On Me) – The Ruts
18. White Mice – The Mo-dettes
19. Tin Soldiers – Stiff Little Fingers
20. Dead Souls – Joy Division

1981

Joy Division served convincing notice that, if the all-time format was here to stay, they intended to dominate it for some years to come by increasing their representation in the chart: their feat of placing four tracks in the top seven would be repeated, by themselves, the following year, but it's something that's only been emulated once since. This year they placed eight tracks in the Festive Fifty overall with another, 'She's Lost Control', only just failing to make it in. New Order added two tracks, to make it a round ten for the three surviving members.

Indeed, there were almost as many Joy Division/New Order tracks in the chart as there were new tracks in total, with only ten new acts featuring. Because of this, it didn't come as much of a surprise that this would be the last year the festive fifty would be heard solely in this format. To provide a further clue that changes might be afoot, the 1981 broadcast featured Peel's first real statement of outright dissatisfaction with the results. Prior to the countdown, he stated for the first time that he didn't enjoy the broadcasts, a significant change from the almost giddy excitement that accompanied his revelation of the 1978 countdown and a complete reversal of the sentiments expressed only the previous year.

Among the new appearances were two tracks from Altered Images, a band greatly loved by Peel but who, in broader terms, were almost perpetually lampooned and trivialised. Their debut single 'Dead Pop Stars' made it to number 15 in this list, but had perhaps had the misfortune to appear in the aftermath of several high profile rock and roll deaths - most notably those of Ian Curtis and John Lennon - with the result that many people cynically attributed to the band an attempt to be clever or profound that was clearly never intended. When 'Happy Birthday' appeared, the band encountered allegations from the opposite end of the seriousness spectrum, with many failing to see beyond its frothy, playful exterior. In some ways, the band suffered from being ahead of their time: like their fellow Scots on the Postcard label, they anticipated mid-eighties indie in an age in which dark cynicism largely held sway and where a band's failure either to be archly political or dourly existential somewhere in their make-up was treated as a deficiency by many 'serious' commentators. In less cynical times, The Wedding Present would have no problems at all carrying off a fine cover of 'Happy Birthday' in their very 1988 Peel session.

If this sounds like an allegation that we'd gone full circle and returned back at 1976, then it isn't. The very fact that a band like Altered Images could ride a wave like this and still retain a healthy regard among sections of fans and critics, against any prevailing sniffiness, is characteristic of an age that seemed constantly engaged in a highly productive form of Hegelian dialectic. If in the future the world would quickly tire of a British music press that constantly sought to rubbish what they'd proclaimed as essential six months earlier, then its origins lay back in that volatile ground for music that was the period roughly between 1979 and 1983, where musical sensibilities in a music press that, with the internet not enough a glint in an American general's eye, continued to act as the most important source for new information, were picked up and discarded on an almost monthly basis.

In this period, Peel performed arguably his most important role. It's no coincidence that this was the year in which Sounds launched a number of off-shoot periodicals, such as the new pop inclined Noise and Punk's Not Dead, and also the metal magazine Kerrang!, which would go on to outlive its father publication easily. If the late seventies had provided a vibrant melting pot of styles, what had emerged from the melting pot were a number of stylistic dictats that appeared not to want to challeng pre-existing rules but set and establish new ones intertwined with subcultural norms: neu punk, the new wave of British heavy metal, new romanticism and new pop being among the more prominent It's no coincidence that the word 'new' features in all these labels, appropriated by the followers and cheerleaders of the respective tribes to proclaim themselves guardians of the future of music. As always, Peel stood aloof from such tribalism and, almost alone in this period, kept the flag flying for a cross-generic appreciation of music that, more than ever, was becoming an increasingly alien perspective and would only become more so in years to come as the unrelenting march of brand identity and distinct consumer groups made its serious play for dominance both within music and outside it.

The other new bands in this chart provide helpful illustrations of the constantly shifting dynamic at play. In heavy contrast to the charm of Altered Images, for instance, were the outwardly surly and dangerous Birthday Party, who came from down under brandishing a strangely compelling torrent of apocalyptic fervour emanating from the mouth of a demented preacher atop guitars that were by turns swarthy and brutal. Noisy and raw though it was, stylistically it was a million miles from what the neu punks were up to and, though the band were marshalled into an image-camp alongside the goths by those who had to have their music that way, in truth what they produced came out of somewhere else entirely, and I don't mean Australia, though they were, it's only right to note, the very first band from the southern hemisphere to be voted into a festive fifty (Saints having made it in via selection by John Peel in 1977). The Birthday Party and Altered Images co-existed in a chart that also had a place, among other things, for the jazz-fuelled frenzy of Pigbag and the sparse experimentalism of Laurie Anderson, both of which, and particularly the latter, became unlikely 'crossover' hits.

Meanwhile, Theatre of Hate embarked on their brief flirtation with the festive fifty, Killing Joke extended a residence that would peter out more quickly than many expected and Scritti Politti, in that glorious middle period in transition from bedsit ideologues to new pop stars, added to the Rough Trade roster with the much-loved, by Peel and others, 'The Sweetest Girl': their re-appropriation of various pop forms forced to take a back seat during punk would find an influence across the commercial landscape, most notably in the music of the soon to be huge Culture Club, and added a melodic punch to the chart that was embellished also by the aforementioned Altered Images and the excellent B-Movie, whose gentle yet irresistable 'Remembrance Day' was an unexpected and refreshing new entrant.

Perhaps unsurprising in what was a highly divisive political period for the UK, direct political comment would become a prevalent feature in festive fifties over the next few years and, even aside the more familiar clarion calls from The Jam and The Clash. the mood was beginning to stir here, with a place for Heaven 17, formed from the ashes of the old Human League, and their timely denunciation of Thatcherism and Reaganomics and, with probably the most important release of the year, The Specials' 'Ghost Town', whose uncannily timed appearance at the top of the UK singles charts coincided with the inner city riots to provide one of the most pertinent musical soundtracks heard in any political period. Here, the number one changed for the first time since 1978, with 'Anarchy in the UK' being temporarily deposed by Joy Division's 'Atmosphere', effectively dispelling any lingering beliefs that its high appearance last year was due only to the mourning of Ian Curtis. Dispelling it even further was the appearance of five Joy Division tracks in the top eleven, including the original B-side of 'Atmosphere', making it the most successful double-sided record in festive fifty history, an accolade it holds to this day.

1981 Festive Fifty
Broadcast dates: 23, 24, 28, 29 & 30 December

50. Happy Birthday – Altered Images (Epic LP *Happy Birthday*)
49. Switch – Siouxsie & The Banshees
48. Procession – New Order (Factory 7")
47. Lie Dream of a Casino Soul – The Fall (Kamera 7")
46. Over The Wall – Echo & The Bunnymen (Korova LP *Heaven Up Here*)
45. Pssyche – Killing Joke (EG 7")
44. Isolation – Joy Division (Factory LP *Closer*)
43. Twenty Four Hours – Joy Division
42. California Uber Alles – Dead Kennedys
41. Another Girl, Another Planet – The Only Ones
40. Icon – Siouxsie & The Banshees
39. Papa's Got A Brand New Pigbag – Pigbag (Y Records 7")
38. God Save The Queen – Sex Pistols
37. Israel – Siouxsie & The Banshees
36. Remembrance Day – B Movie (Deram 12")
35. Jigsaw Feeling – Siouxsie & The Banshees
34. O Superman – Laurie Anderson (One Ten 7")
33. How I Wrote 'Elastic Man' – The Fall
32. Suspect Device – Stiff Little Fingers
31. In A Rut – The Ruts
30. Fiery Jack – The Fall
29. (We Don't Need This) Fascist Groove Thang – Heaven 17 (Virgin 7")
28. Follow The Leaders – Killing Joke (EG 7")
27. Requiem – Killing Joke
26. Public Image – Public Image Ltd
25. Legion – Theatre of Hate (Burning Rome LP *He Who Dares Wins*)
24. Johnny Was – Stiff Little Fingers
23. Going Underground – The Jam
22. The Sweetest Girl – Scritti Politti (Rough Trade 7")
21. Ghost Town – The Specials (Two-Tone 12")
20. Get Over You – Undertones
19. Release The Bats – Birthday Party (4AD 7")
18. Complete Control – The Clash
17. Holidays in the Sun – Sex Pistols
16. Alternative Ulster – Stiff Little Fingers
15. Dead Pop Stars – Altered Images (Epic 7")
14. Transmission – Joy Division
13. Down in the Tube Station at Midnight – The Jam
12. New Rose – The Damned
11. Dead Souls – Joy Division (Factory LP *Still*)
10. (White Man) In Hammersmith Palais – The Clash
9. Holiday in Cambodia – Dead Kennedys
8. A Forest – The Cure (Fiction 12")
7. Decades – Joy Division
6. Teenage Kicks – Undertones
5. New Dawn Fades – Joy Division
4. Ceremony – New Order (Factory 7")
3. Love Will Tear Us Apart – Joy Division
2. Anarchy in the UK – Sex Pistols
1. Atmosphere – Joy Division

Top fifteen of 1981?

1. Ceremony – New Order
2. Dead Pop Stars – Altered Images
3. Release the Bats – The Birthday Party
4. Ghost Town – The Specials
5. The Sweetest Girl – Scritti Politti
6. Legion – Theatre of Hate
7. Follow the Leaders – Killing Joke

8. (We Don't Need This) Fascist Groove Thing – Heaven 17
9. O Superman – Laurie Anderson
10. Remembrance Day – B Movie
11. Israel – Siouxsie & the Banshees
12. Papa's Got a Brand New Pigbag – Pigbag
13. Over the Wall – Echo & the Bunnymen
14. Lie Dream of a Casino Soul – The Fall
15. Procession – New Orde

1982

There would still be an all-time festive fifty in 1982 but Peel decided also to broadcast a chart purely made up of tracks released in that calendar year only and this would henceforth become the established format of future charts, not entirely unexpectedly. Peel positively purred with satisfaction over the top five of the yearly countdown, claiming he would have found it difficult to predict that four of the tracks (presumably the exception was the number one) would have been so high.   It was clear to all, including the DJ, that the new format would avoid the obvious drawbacks and inherent predictability of the old one, though in truth future top fives would rarely be as difficult to forecast as Peel found this one to be.

What the new format allowed was for highly popular and important bands of the day (for the Peel listening audience anyway) to have their current output sifted and graded in order of importance to listeners of the time. This would quickly lead, in the mid-eighties, to dominance of the chart by certain bands, chiefly The Smiths, The Fall and The Wedding Present, but for now it allowed The Clash, for example, to register four tracks from their *Combat Rock* album. Whatever the merits of that collection, it's doubtful that Peel listeners as a body would collectively regard it as their best, but the new format allowed its popularity to be reflected in sharp contrast to, say, *London Calling* which, though regarded by many as the band's most important album, failed to register a single FF entry in the more competitive arena of the all-time chart. Had the currrent format existed back in the late seventies, it's hard to imagine that Clash tracks like '1977' or 'Guns of Brixton' wouldn't have found a place in it. As it stood, those tracks, along with many others of the late seventies, have been denied a place in festive fifty history.

Despite Peel's obvious appreciation of the 1982 yearly chart, the most striking feature to the modern observer is probably its generally commercial nature. More than thirty of the tracks were hit singles in the UK charts, a total that's never been matched since and which it's hard to see ever being achieved again. While itt's possible there was some uncertainty among voters regarding how to approach the new format (in the interests of getting a much-loved track in, was it necessary to vote for tracks that had achieved some significant level of appreciation?), we should be cautious in making such a judgment. Although a large number of tracks herein achieved commercial success, only one of them – 'Come On Eileen' – was not played by Peel during the year (for the record, one other track on the chart shared this distinction, Weekend's excellent 'A View From Her Room', not a single to trouble the compilers of the top forty, but presumably in due to airplay from David Jensen's show, which in those days preceded Peel's on the air and which clearly shared a significant proportion of its listening audience).

While Peel listeners in the future might look at the many hit singles included here and consider it difficult to believe that Peel would have played them, this wasn't the case at all. Peel was a great champion of the early work of, for example, Tears For Fears, Yazoo and Musical Youth, and the singles contained here that went on to achieve such success were great favourites of his in 1982. Simple Minds were already clearly heading in the direction of stadium rock sterility, but their *New Gold Dream* album – which yielded three entries, all of them UK hit singles – was also much loved by Peel, as had been the band's previous releases. And of course The Clash and The Jam were established heavyweights among Peel listeners, who'd managed to secure success without shedding their artistic credibility, whatever some of the more cynical among late seventies musical connoiseurs might have been claiming at the time.

 Since 1978, 'good' records had been finding it less difficult to get into the UK singles charts and secure airplay on daytime radio than might now be supposed. While it's easy to dismiss this as nostalgia for a bygone age from someone who, like myself, was then enduring his teenage years, consider that 1981 had seen The Jam (twice), Blondie (three times), The Police, The Pretenders and The Specials all spending periods at number one. These were all bands that had grown, in different ways, out of the punk era and, though not all of them had Peel credentials, they illustrate how the commercial airwaves and hence the national singles chart were hospitable to a lot of the music that had emerged in the post-punk aftermath. Consider the success of the small Coventry Two-Tone label and especially The Specials, who'd had an unbroken run of eight top ten singles, all in their way uncompromising in a musical or political context or both. An agenda had, for five or six years, been successfully forced on the music industry and the door it opened to more innovative bands is reflected here. In short, it's not that Peel was playing more commercial stuff, but that the stuff he was playing was, at the time, finding it easier to make the leap from the Peel show to daytime airplay and Top of the Pops.

This was, sad to say, a period that was already on the wane as the dubious gods of new pop began to absorb that territory and the 1982 chart would be left to appear a conspicuous and, it would seem, never to be repeated historical event. Whatever honeymoon period punk was still apparently enjoying, The Jam would announce their split during the year (Peel commends Weller for the bravery of his decision during the countdown) and The Clash would never be the same musical force again. The Specials had already splintered and, while both they and Two-Tone would remain in some form, their days as a force for taking radical music consistently into the top ten were pretty much over. Their absence would leave a vacuum which, for a time, would throb with uncertainty about what shape music would take in the future: a period of crisis, perhaps, but also one of excitement and creative suspense. Because of this the 1983 chart would be one of the most anticipated of all time, and it wouldn't disappoint, but the number of tunes in it that crossed over to achieve any significant level of commercial appreciation would be greater reduced and, with a brief lapse in the mid-nineties, this trend would continue in future festive fifties.

Some of the figures who would make that 1983 listing are represented here: the Cocteau Twins make their first appearance in a festive fifty and would look ahead to a richest 24 months of recorded output in the history of music; the appearance of Manchester bands such as The Passage and Chameleons, not to mention New Order, gave evidence of the persistent creativity stirring in that part of the world, soon to explode once again with the rapid rise of The Smiths; Redskins are here too, a band with a powerful and uncompromising left-wing message as well as a potent musical force who helped drive an entirely welcome wedge between bands with skinheads and the politics of the National Front.

Alongside Redskins, old Peel favourite Robert Wyatt, one of the few members of the old musical guard to have found himself warmly embraced by the post-punk community, finds himself at number two with 'Shipbuilding', a single that still sounds utterly startling even today, balancing a melancholy given shape by Wyatt's unique voice with a forceful anti-war statement that rendered it simultaneously understated yet powerful, reflecting an emerging political comment in this chart that would again find fuller voice in 1983. With the ever-increasing threat of nuclear weapons, the Falklands conflict and the forthcoming miner's striker, the years of 1982-85 were a period in which no one with a properly functioning mind could refuse to stand up and be counted and this was another factor that would give shape to a fascinating, though short-lived, period for the festive fifty.

This is also a year in which the future rules of the yearly chart haven't yet been fixed, either by Peel or by potential voters. It wouldn't be until 1984 that Peel would rule that a track could enter in successive years if it appeared on another release in that year and so, for instance, 'The Sweetest Girl' by Scritti Politti appears in the all-time chart but not the 1982 listings, despite presumably being eligible due to featuring on the *Songs to Remember* album: the fact that two other tracks from that release do appear suggest either that voters didn't feel they were allowed to vote for a track in the new chart that had appeared in an early festive fifty or else they did but Peel at this stage was applying different rules. The only track to appear in both charts was New Order's 'Temptation' (number one in the yearly festive fifty), which suggests an unwillingness among voters to select a track for both charts, despite the fact that the festive fifties between 1978 and 1981 had always contained a number of new entries from that calendar year.

A real historical curiosity is the absence of The Fall from either chart. While 'Look Know' landed just outside the yearly chart, it's odd that, in a year in which they released two studio albums – *Room to Live* and the classic *Hex Enduction Hour* – neither should produce an entry. Their absence from the all-time chart is just as intriguing: they'd placed four tracks in the 1980 chart and three in 1981. Indeed, in every year between 1980 and 1988, the band would never dip below three entries, apart from here. There is the possibility that, having such a large number of options, the Fall vote had splintered to such an extent that no one track could secure sufficent votes and it's also reasonable to remember that The Fall weren't yet the band who would become regulars of the top ten, their absence from the festive fifty unthinkable. That would come soon (they would feature in every top ten between 1983 and 1987) but at this point they had even failed to crack the top twenty. Part of the explanation might also be that 1982 was only one of two years in which the band didn't record a Peel session while, through the rest of the eighties, session material provided an especially rich source of festive fifty appearances (see section six of this book for more on this).

Nonetheless, it remains strange that there was no place for this already eminent Peel band among the hundred places here, although 'The Classical' from *Hex Enduction Hour* would turn up in the next all-time chart some seventeen years later. It wouldn't be until 2006, a year with no Fall releases save a limited edition cover of The Monks, that they would miss out on the festive fifty action again.

1982 All-Time Festive Fifty

Broadcast dates: 15, 16, 20, 21, 22, 23, 27, 28, 29 & 30 December. The two charts' run-downs were broadcast concurrently, with alterating tracks played from each. This format became somewhat confusing and Peel would abandon it, favouring two separate broadcasts, when the next all-time chart was broadcast seventeen years later.

=49. Love Song – The Damned
=49. O Superman – Laurie Anderson
48. The Eternal – Joy Divison (Factory LP *Closer*)
47. Shot By Both Sides – Magazine
46. Hong Kong Garden – Siouxsie & The Banshees
45. Icon – Siouxsie & The Banshees
44. Pretty Vacant – Sex Pistols
43. Ghost Town – The Specials
42. Switch – Siouxsie & The Banshees
41. She's Lost Control – Joy Division
40. Armagideon Time – The Clash
39. Jigsaw Feeling – Siouxsie & The Banshees
38. Isolation – Joy Division
37. Holidays in the Sun – Sex Pistols
36. Get Over You – Undertones
35. In A Rut – The Ruts
34. Pssyche – Killing Joke
33. Legion – Theatre of Hate (SS 7" *Original Sin* B-side)
32. Requiem – Killing Joke
31. Suspect Device – Stiff Little Fingers
30. Procession – New Order
29. Johnny Was – Stiff Little Fingers
28. Release The Bats – Birthday Party
27. The Sweetest Girl – Scritti Politti
26. Transmission – Joy Division
25. God Save The Queen – Sex Pistols
24. Another Girl, Another Planet – The Only Ones
23. Twenty-Four Hours – Joy Division
22. Over the Wall – Echo & The Bunnymn
21. Dead Pop Stars – Altered Images
20. Public Image – Public Image Ltd
19. Complete Control – The Clash
18. Temptation – New Order (Factory 7")
17. Going Underground – The Jam
16. Alternative Ulster – Stiff Little Fingers
15. Israel – Siouxsie & The Banshees (Polydor LP *Once Upon A Time/The Singles*)
14. Holiday In Cambodia – Dead Kennedys
13. New Rose – The Damned (Big Beat LP *Another Great Record From The Damned: The Best of The Damned*)
12. Joy Division – Dead Souls (Sordide Sentimentale 7")
11. Down in the Tube Station at Midnight – The Jam
10. (White Man) In Hammersmith Palais – The Clash
9. Bela Lugosi's Dead – Bauhaus (Small Wonder 7")
8. Teenage Kicks – Undertones
7. Decades – Joy Division
6. Ceremony – New Order
5. A Forest – The Cure
4. New Dawn Fades – Joy Division
3. Love Will Tear Us Apart – Joy Division
2. Atmosphere – Joy Division
1. Anarchy in the UK – Sex Pistols

1982 Festive Fifty

50. I Think I Need Help – Farmer's Boys (Waap 7")
49. Melt – Siouxsie & The Banshees (Polydor 12")
48. Suicide Bag – Action Pact (Fallout 7" EP *Suicide Bag*)
47. Conspiracy – The Higsons (Waap 7")
46. Third Uncle – Bauhaus (Beggars Banquet LP *The Sky's Gone Out*)
45. Glittering Prize – Simple Minds (Virgin LP *New Gold Dream*)
44. Remember – Shambeko Say Wah! (Eterna 7")
43. A View From Her Room – Weekend (Rough Trade 7")
42. In Shreds – Chameleons (Epic 7")
41. XOYO – The Passage (Cherry Red LP *Degenerates*)
40. Rock The Casbah – The Clash (CBS LP *Combat Rock*)
39. The Bitterest Pill (I Ever Had To Swallow) – The Jam (Polydor 7")
38. Love on the Terraces – Serious Drinking (Upright 7")
37. Wax & Wane – Cocteau Twins (4AD LP *Garlands*)
36. Pass The Dutchie – Musical Youth (MCA 7")
35. Feel Me – Blancmange (London LP *Happy Families*)
34. Living on the Ceiling - Blancmange (London LP *Happy Families*)
33. A Strange Day – The Cure (Fiction LP *Pornography*)
32. Someone, Somewhere in Summertime – Simple Minds (Virgin LP *New Gold Dream*)
31. Peasant Army – Redskins (CNT 7" *Lev Bronstein* B-side)
30. Promised You A Miracle – Simple Minds (Virgin 12")
29. Love My Way – Psychedelic Furs (CBS 7")
28. The Figurehead – The Cure (Fiction LP *Pornography*)
27. Know Your Rights – The Clash (CBS LP *Combat Rock*)
26. Should I Stay Or Should I Go – The Clash (CBS LP *Combat Rock*)
25. The Hanging Garden – The Cure (Fiction LP *Pornography*)
24. Pillar To Post – Aztec Camera (Rough Trade 7")
23. Slowdive – Siouxsie & The Banshees (Polydor 12")
22. African & White – China Crisis (Inevitable 7")
21. Whatever Is He Like? – Farmers Boys (Backs 7")
20. Empire Song – Killing Joke (EG 7")
19. Come On Eileen - Dexy's Midnight Runners (Mercy LP *Too-Rye-Ay*)
18. Asylums In Jerusalem – Scritti Politti (Rough Trade LP *Songs To Remember*)
17. Hurt – New Order (Factory 7" *Temptation* B-side)
16. Fireworks – Siouxsie & The Banshees (Polydor 7")
=14. Ziggy Stardust – Bauhaus (Beggars Banquet 7")
=14. Party Fears Two – Associates (Associates 7")
13. Faithless – Scritti Politti (Rough Trade LP *Songs To Remember*)
12. Only You – Yazoo (Mute LP *Upstairs At Eric's*)
11. A Town Called Malice – The Jam (Polydor 7")
10. Revolutionary Spirit – Wild Swans (Zoo 7")
9. Into The Garden – Artery (Red Flame LP *Oceans*)
8. Do You Believe in the Westworld? – Theatre of Hate (Burning Rome LP *Westworld*)
7. The Story of the Blues – Wah! (Eternal 7")
6. Straight To Hell – The Clash (CBS LP *Combat Rock*)
5. Mad World – Tears For Fears (Mercury 7")
4. The Back of Love – Echo & The Bunnymen (Korova 7")
3. The Message – Grandmaster Flash & The Furious Five (Sugar Hill 12")
2. Shipbuilding – Robert Wyatt (Rough Trade 7")
1. Temptation – New Order (Factory 7")

MARK WHITBY

1983

A golden year for the festive fifty. Few tears were shed for the all-time chart as listeners voted in a memorable listing in a year in which there was much of quality to choose from. As punk and its immediate legacy now faded decently into happy and inspirational memory, its influence thankfully didn't wane and mid-eighties 'indie' was being born with innumerable creative pathways opening up.

Indicative of this are the first stirrings of The Smiths and Billy Bragg, plus the continuing emergence of the Cocteau Twins as a powerful force, in addition to their label, Ivo Watts-Russell's 4AD, which would still be turning out festive fifty entries almost three decades later. Not only did Watts-Russell discover and release the music of the Cocteau Twins, but also the powerful and influential Birthday Party and a whole range of new bands with whome he managed somehow to combine a distinct label ethos with a fascinating and eclectic roster. His This Mortal Coil project, also represented here, broadened the listening experience of many in the post-punk audience who'd been invigorated by the 'year zero' excitement of punk, but now had their ears opened to some of the artistic luminaries from the years before who had gone into a kind of enforced artistic suspended animation between 1977 and 1982. This Mortal Coil matched 4AD artists with songs by the likes of Roy Harper, Gene Clark, Syd Barrett and, perhaps most notably, Tim Buckley and did much to broaden the record collections of listeners of a certain age, including myself, who might otherwise have taken years to catch up with their musical legacies, if they ever did.

While Factory had achieved unprecedented domination over the 1982 all-time chart, their entries had all been Joy Division and New Order recordings; 4AD became the first indie to achieve a level of dominance of a festive fifty with entries (ten here) spread across four different bands. One of them, Xmal Deutschland, also became the first band from a non-English speaking nation ever to feature in the festive fifty. Their 'Incubus Succubus' would remain the highest-placed track recorded by a non-British/Irish European act until the Sugarcubes in 1987, while Xmal's achievement as the only continental European act with two entries in the same chart would stand until Solex emulated it in 1998.

Despite that, the festive fifty remained overwhelmingly British/Irish, the only other exceptions the entries from the Birthday Party and SPK, both hailing from Australia, and a single US band, Peel favourites of the time 10,000 Maniacs, still in that interesting period before they became darlings of US college radio and British sixth-formers. A significant legacy of punk remained in the stranglehold held by the cities of what was once the industrial north: the Manchester/Salford area remained particularly strong, mainly because of New Order, The Smiths and the Fall, who between them shared six of the top nine places, but there was space in the chart also for The Chameleons and Tools You Can Trust, while bands from Liverpool, Sheffield, York, Leeds and Hull all contributed to this artistic reversal of the economic north-south divide and gained representation here. Scottish bands continued to be well-served by festive fifty voters, with East Kilbridge's Aztec Camera appearing again alongside the Cocteau Twins and the engaging duo Strawberry Switchblade, from Glasgow, with 'Trees & Flowers', a plaintive and engaging tune inspired by agorophobia.

They contributed to another small rise in representation of women in the chart. The 1982 yearly chart had featured five bands with female members, the best yet but only a small increase on what had gone on before. Here, seven of the 30 acts featured had female vocalists, a small increase again, accounting for thirteen of the entries between them, dwarfing the numbers of previous years, though it would take another decade before the gender imbalance would be fully addressed.

Peel professed himself surprised at another appearance for Redskins, whose 'Lean On Me' is too often overlooked as one of the great political battle cries of the early eighties: awarded greater status are the two Elvis Costello songs here, his version of 'Shipbuilding' and the acerbic 'Pills & Soap'. Less direct, filled with oblique commentary on the politics of the day are the Bunnymen's 'The Cutter' and 'Never Stop'. Hull's Red Guitars beat them all, though, in terms of a festive fifty position and arguably in creating the most stunning politically inspired song of the year: the dystopian 'Good Technology', a brilliant debut single and the first of a great triumvirate from the band that went on to include 'Fact' and 'Steel Town', which landed just outside the top ten. The band would be short lived in their original and most dynamic form, effectively ceasing to exist within the following year, the departure of Jeremy Kidd leading to a change of direction that would remove much of the intoxicating spikiness from their sound.

The battle for the number one spot, such as it was, gave notice of the broad form festive fifty top tens would begin to take over the next four years, where a small number of bands would often provide a large proportion of the entries between them. Here, effectively three bands shared the top six places (if we consider that This Mortal Coil's entry featured only the two members that then made up Cocteau Twins), with at the top one of the most predictable number ones in the chart's history. Indeed, Peel revealed he'd received pleas from some listeners to fix the chart in order to stop it getting there. New Order's gaining of two of the top three places emulated the achievement of their previous band and their five entries overall made them unquestionably the first winners of what would become in the mid-eighties an annual battle of the festive fifty heavyweights. The Smiths gave a stirring performance on the back of only singles and session appearances and their position on the threshold of a glorious festive fifty career must have been evident to just about everybody. Four entries, three of which were in the top nine, remains the best chart performance of any band without an album release behind them and it's unlikely it will ever be matched.

Perhaps of interest to festive fifty obsessives only is the curiosity surrounding the track just outside the top fifty. In the countdown, Peel mentioned that an unspecified Cocteau Twins track was at number 51. However, during a show in 1984, he made a different suggestion, claiming that Howard Devoto's 'Rainy Season' occupied that position (thanks to the guy who messaged the Dandelion Radio Facebook page to point this out). It probably shouldn't be enough to keep anyone awake at night but, on belatedly discovering the contrary information, I have to admit to losing a few hours.

1983 Festive Fifty

Broadcast dates: 21, 22, 27, 28 & 29 December

50. War Baby – Tom Robinson (Panic 7")
49. The Walk – The Cure (Fiction 7")
48. Shipbuilding – Elvis Costello (F-Beat LP *Punch The Clock*)
47. Trees & Flowers – Strawberry Switchblade (92 Happy Customers 7")
46. Sonny's Burning – Birthday Party (4AD 12" EP *The Bad Seed*)
45. The Village – New Order (Factory LP *Power, Corruption & Lies*)
44. Fascination – Cabaret Voltaire (Virgin 7")
43. Deep in the Woods – Birthday Party (4AD 12" EP *The Bad Seed*)
42. Somewhere – Danse Society (Society 7")
41. New Year's Day - U2 (Island 7")
40. Wings – The Fall (Rough Trade 7" *Kicker Conspiracy* B-side)
39. Metal Dance – SPK (Desire 12")
38. Hitherto – Cocteau Twins (4AD 12" EP *Sunburst & Snowblind*)
37. Television/Satellite – Sophie & Peter Johnston (Peel Session 22.2.83)
36. Doppelganger – Luddites (Xcentric Noise 7" EP *Strength Of Your Cry*)
35. Kicker Conspiracy – The Fall (Rough Trade 7")
34. Working & Shopping – Tools You Can Trust (Red Energy Dynamo 7")
33. Handsome Devil – The Smiths (Rough Trade 7" *Hand In Glove* B-side)
32. Qual – Xmal Deutschland (4AD 7")
31. Second Skin – Chameleons (Statik LP *Script of the Bridge*)
30. Lean On Me – Redskins (CNT 7")
29. Oblivious – Aztec Camera (Rough Trade LP *High Land Hard Rain*)
28. Peppermint Pig – Cocteau Twins (4AD 7")
27. Alice – Sisters of Mercy (Merciful Release 7")
26. My Mother The War – 10,000 Maniacs (Reflex 12")
25. Leave Me Alone – New Order (LP *Power, Corruption & Lies*)
24. Pills & Soap – The Imposter (Elvis Costello) (F-Beat LP *Punch The Clock*)
23. Never Never – The Assembly (Mute 7")
22. The Cutter – Echo & The Bunnymen (Korova 7")
21. The Man Whose Head Expanded – The Fall (Rough Trade 7")
20. Dear Prudence – Siouxsie & The Banshees (Wonderland 7")
19. Temple of Love – Sisters of Mercy (Merciful Release 7")
18. Your Silent Face – New Order (Factory LP *Power, Corruption & Lies*)
17. Never Stop – Echo & The Bunnymen (Korova 7")

16. From The Flagstones – Cocteau Twins (4AD 12" EP *Sunburst & Snowblind*)
15. The Love Cats – The Cure (Fiction 7")
14. Sugar Hiccup – Cocteau Twins (4AD 12" EP *Sunburst & Snowblind*)
13. Incubus Succubus – Xmal Deutschland (4AD 7")
12. This is Not a Love Song – Public Image Ltd (Virgin 7")
11. Good Technology – Red Guitars (Self Drive 7")
10. Picture On The Wall – Naturalites & The Realistics (CSA LP *Picture On The Wall*)
9. Hand In Glove – The Smiths (Rough Trade 7")
8. Eat Y'self Fitter – The Fall (Peel Session 23.3.83)
7. A New England – Billy Bragg (Utility/Go! Discs 12" EP *Life's a Riot with Spy Vs Spy*)
6. Reel Around The Fountain – The Smiths (Peel Session 31.5.83)
5. Musette & Drums – Cocteau Twins (4AD LP *Head Over Heels*)
4. Song to the Siren – This Mortal Coil (4AD 7")
3. Age of Consent – New Order (Factory LP *Power, Corruption & Lies*)
2. This Charming Man (New York Vocal) – The Smiths (Rough Trade 12")
1. Blue Monday – New Order (Factory 12")

1984

If the 1978-82 festive fifty years can be viewed as reflective of the punk honeymoon period, 1983's signalling of the emergence of a mid-eighties era of indie creativity was to become a double edged sword as, far from extending the trend of varied quality that had been a feature of recent charts, festive fifties of the mid-eighties would come to be categorised by declining numbers of voters and an increasing conservatism.

While 1984 offered another strong chart, it also contained those seeds of threatened dominance by a small number of prominent bands that very quickly came to fruition. We see here the growing strength of The Smiths, the continued presence of New Order and, more short-lived, another fine showing for the Cocteau Twins. While The Fall only feature three times, they manage to pierce the top ten for the second year running, clear evidence that, despite that curious no-show in 1982, the band's festive fifty star was now seriously rising.

Peel revealed that he'd actually considered not doing a festive fifty this year, voicing his concern that the chart was becoming a Christmas tradition along the same lines as the queen's speech, but said he'd been swayed by voters' pleas to retain it as a cherished fixture of the period. While such incidents would become fairly regular in coming years, it also appeared that, on the face of it, it generally took very little prompting to get him to change his mind.

If Peel was concerned about the chart's potential absorbtion into conservatism, this may have been tempered by a satisfaction that mid-eighties political voices remained healthily in evidence and that both his programme and the festive fifty were, within their varied remits, offering them a forum in what was an increasingly difficult period for those of us on the political left. Three tracks in the top ten offered some kind of critique of the times,, though The Men They Couldn't Hang's reworking of an Eric Bogle folk song about the first world war seemed somehow the most poignant, even moreso in retrospect, with the forthcoming scandal caused by the BBC's screening of *The Monocled Mutineer* and a clear resistance from the right-wing press and the Thatcher government towards any critique of the British military so soon after the Falklands war. In a Britain that had witnessed the temporary banning of Lennon's 'Give Peace a Chance' by the BBC, as well as what passed at the time for a relatively serious debate about whether Julie Covington's 'Don't Cry For Me Argentina' pissed off Argentinians enough for it to escape a similar ban, the refreshing opportunity to hear songs like this was a reminder that not everyone had completely taken leave of their senses, as much as it was a welcome voice against the prevalent spirit of jingoism that was infecting the nation.

These were indeed confusing times. Redskins, in their professed aim to talk like the Clash and walk like the Supremes, gained a top ten entry through a release on a major label,, while the largely unpoliticised Frankie Goes To Hollywood produced the most commercially successful comment ever on the subject of nuclear war when 'Two Tribes' (a song that had originally appeared in the band's Peel session of 1982) spent nine weeks at number one but retained enough significance among discerning Peel listeners to grab a place at number 25 here. Billy Bragg's 'Between The Wars' was a poignant and affecting commentary on the time, though his Red Wedge initiaitive was roundly condemned by the Redskins and at times deliberately sabotaged by a Militant Tendency openly celebrated by the Mighty Wah! in 'Come Back'. All of which says much about the lack of consensus among leftist political voices of the period, which was clearly part of the problem.

Though their earlier work had shown little passion for direct political comment, The Smiths' session recording 'Nowhere Fast' proclaimed an intention to drop their trousers in front of the queen ahead of their *Meat Is Murder* manifesto the following year and was duly rewarded with a festive fifty appearance. The band also provided the first instance of a track being voted into two successive festive fifties in the new yearly format. 'Reel Around the Fountain' had appeared as a session track in 1983 and now gained enough votes to feature again following its appearance in a different form on the band's debut LP and also in its original session version on the *Hatful of Hollow* compilation (the version played during the broadcast). Peel admitted that he thought about excluding it but ultimately allowed it in, partly because he couldn't think of a good enough reason not to do so and partly because he wanted to hear it again himself. His reasoning on this point set a precedent for future festive fifties; had he gone another way, while subsequent charts would have suffered mainly minor changes as a result, in both 1995 and 1998 we would have had a different number one.

In some ways the most significant releases of any sort of political hue occurred in the bottom ten of the chart. While New Model's 'Vengeance' gave the band their only festive fifty appearance, tracks from the Special AKA, Bronski Beat and Working Week were indicative of the British left's increasingly more productive movement during the rest of the decade, where the power of calls for social justice gained ground as economic battles were being lost. Both 'Nelson Mandela' and 'Venceramos' gave support to political prisoners persecuted by regimes that Thatcher had refused to condemn and even openly supported, the apartheid government in South African (husband Dennis was busily profiting from shares in a gold mine that employed child labour for slave wages) and Pinochet's right-wing regime in Chile. While left-wing councils around Britain found a way of articulating a different view of the future by offering support to the oppressed opposition in these countries, Special AKA's taking up of Mandela's case was a significant stage in the generation of a political momentum that would lead to the end of apartheid by the end of the decade, and Peel commented during the countdown that he felt it ought to have been placed a lot higher. The plaintive, deeply personal tale resonance of 'Smalltown Boy' was imbued with a courage it's often difficult to appreciate today, its tale of a young gay man's ostracism by his own family and community against the backdrop of a parliament calling for the banning of any such 'promotion' of homosexuality. Ultimately this was ground on which the left could fight and eventually win against the draconian Clause 28, rights for homosexuals eventually becoming a course that even many on the political right would drop their opposition to.

A rather less politicised voice in the chart was that of gothic rock, which was reaching its peak with the Sisters of Mercy's best festive fifty year and the appearance of The Cult and Flesh For Lulu, while the faux cabaret of Japan's Frank Chickens saw the first ever entry for an Asian band and Unknown Cases offered the first of what would prove to be only occasional stirrings of African music in festive fifties, albeit via a duo of German origin with a track that had actually been released in Britain in 1983.

Prior to announcing the chart, Peel assured listeners that it was as 'straight as we can get it', acknowledging that occasional postal votes arrived that were a bit suspicious, the first outright allusion to potential vote-rigging in festive fifties. While there have been subsequent vague confessions of targetted voting for certain punk tracks in the late seventies, the motive for this appears to have been no more than an effort to assure 'Stairway to Heaven' didn't make it to number one again alongside the possible piling up of tactical votes for songs that already had a chart pedigree, such was the nature of the all-time listing back then. Peel now hinted that he felt there was evidence that certain bands might be making efforts to push their own tunes up the chart and, while he was convinced this was having little impact, it would be a subject that would be returned to with increasing levels of concern over the years. Prior to announcing the number six, he did reveal that a suspicious number of votes had come in during the same week and all from the same county, making 'Spike Milligan's Tape Recorder' by The Membranes the first festive fifty entry to be officially suspected of vote rigging. Peel said he'd left the votes as they were but would be forced to review this approach in future years. The issue would remain dormant for a considerable period but, certainly from 1998 onwards, the suspicion of vote-rigging and vote canvassing would become a major topic of concern.

Peel had confessed to having to pull his car over to the kerb when he heard Cocteau Twins' 'Pearly Dewdrops'

Drops' on the radio for the first time, so taken aback was he by what he heard, yet he appeared almost dismissive of its appearance at number two, saying he was more of a 'Spangle Maker' man, showing a perfectly understandable affection for the track at number four. He also said he was pleased to see The Men They Couldn't Hang at number three and had already proclaimed the number five track as his favourite of the year, saying he thought it should have been higher. So, despite his earlier voicing of doubts about continuing the chart, it would appear that the top five contained one track good enough to reduce him to tears and at least another three that he liked even more.

1984 Festive Fifty

Broadcast dates: 18, 19, 25 & 26 December & 1 January

50. Venceremos (We Will Win) – Working Week (Virgin 7")
49. Pepper Tree – Cocteau Twins (4AD 12" *Pearly Dewdrops'* Drops B-side)
48. Smalltown Boy – Bronski Beat (Forbidden Fruit 7")
47. Thorn of Crowns – Echo & The Bunnymen (Korova LP *Ocean Rain*)
46. Dirty (Extended Version) – Hard Corps (Survival 12")
45. Dark Streets of London – The Pogues (Stiff LP *Red Roses For Me*)
44. No Bulbs – The Fall (Beggars Banquet LP *The Wonderful & Frightening World of The Fall*)
43. Vengeance – New Model Army (Abstract LP *Vengeance*)
42. Blue Canary – Frank Chickens (Peel Session 3.4.84)
41. Nelson Mandela – Special AKA (Two-Tone 7")
=39. Beatrix – Cocteau Twins (4AD LP *Treasure*)
=39. Subterraneans – Flesh For Lulu (Polydor 7")
38. Pandora – Cocteau Twins (4AD LP *Treasure*)
37. Upside Down – Jesus & Mary Chain (Creation 7")
36. Reel Around The Fountain – The Smiths (Rough Trade LP *Hatful of Hollow*)
35. Biko – Robert Wyatt (Rough Trade 12" *Work in Progress*)
34. My Suitor – Berntholer (Blue Feather 7")
33. Another Day – This Mortal Coil (4AD LP *It'll End in Tears*)
32. Bias Binding – Yeah Yeah Noh (In Tape 7" *EP Cottage Industry*)
31. Dr Mabuse – Propaganda (ZTT 12")
30. Spiritwalker – The Cult (Beggars Banquet LP *Dreamtime*)

29. The Saturday Boy – Billy Bragg (Go! Discs LP *Brewing Up With Billy Bragg*)
28. Please Please Please Let Me Get What I Want – The Smiths (Rough Trade LP *Hatful of Hollow*)
27. The Bushes Scream While My Daddy Prunes – Very Things (Reflex LP *The Bushes Scream While My Daddy Prunes*)
26. Masima Bele – Unknown Cases (Rough Trade 12" Released 1983: eligible release was Roadrunner Dutch import 12")
25. Two Tribes (Carnage Mix) – Frankie Goes To Hollywood (ZTT 12")
24. Heaven Knows I'm Miserable Now – The Smiths (Rough Trade LP *Hatful of Hollow*)
23. William, It Was Really Nothing – The Smiths (Rough Trade LP *Hatful of Hollow*)
22. Domino – Cocteau Twins (4AD LP *Treasure*)
21. Kangaroo – This Mortal Coil (4AD LP *It'll End in Tears*)
20. Murder – New Order (Factory Benelux 12")
19. The Killing Moon – Echo & The Bunnymen (Korova LP *Ocean Rain*)
18. C.R.E.E.P. – The Fall (Beggars Banquet 7")
17. What Difference Does It Make? – The Smiths (Rough Trade 7")
16. Ivo – Cocteau Twins (4AD LP *Treasure*)
15. Emma – Sisters of Mercy (Peel Session 19.6.84)
14. Nowhere Fast – The Smiths (Peel Session 9.8.84)
13. Between The Wars – Billy Bragg (Peel Session 20.9.84)
12. Lonesome Tonight – New Order (Factory 12" *Thieves Like Us* B-side)
11. Saint Huck – Nick Cave & The Bad Seeds (Mute LP *From Her to Eternity*)
10. Keep On Keeping On – Redskins (Decca 7")

9. Lay of the Land – The Fall (Beggars Banquet LP *The Wonderful & Frightening World of The Fall*)
8. Walk Away – Sisters of Mercy (Merciful Release 7")
7. Thieves Like Us – New Order (Factory 12")
6. Spike Milligan's Tape Recorder – The Membranes (Criminal Damage 7")
5. Come Back – The Mighty Wah! (Beggars Banquet 7")
4. The Spangle Maker – Cocteau Twins (4AD 12" *Pearly Dewdrops' Drops* A-side)
3. The Green Fields of France (No Man's Land) – The Men They Couldn't Hang (Imp 7")
2. Pearly Dewdrops' Drops – Cocteau Twins (4AD 12")
1. How Soon Is Now? – The Smiths (Rough Trade LP *Hatful of Hollow*)

1985

Although there were, as Peel announced himself, only two tracks on the chart that he didn't play during 1985, you sensed a simmering discontent that, in contrast to the brief statements regarding continuation the chart in both 1981 and 1984, were not on this occasion balanced by much enthusiasm elsewhere. As would become the case often in the ensuing years, the cause of such mild chagrin was not so much the lack of quality in the chart as its somewhat unadventurous nature. You sense that, in the period 1981-84, eclecticism had clung tenaciously to some parts of the charts however predictable were several of the other entries. Here, this precarious attachment appeared to give way significantly.

It would remain thus for several years to come. The 1985 chart was arguably, in its way, as much a signal of a new direction for the festive fifty as was that of 1982, when the baton was handed over from the all-time chart to annual listings. It's not so much that many of Peel's favourites of the year didn't make it in, because that had always been the case to an extent. It would be unfair, for instance, to lay the blame at 1985's feet for refusing to recognise bands or artists such as 3 Mustaphas 3, Boothill Foot Tappers or Ivor Cutler, all of whom had recorded memorable sessions for the show that year, because such blame might easily be levelled at festive fifties of the past and well into the future. But add to that no recognition for the likes of Bogshed. Terry & Gerry or Microdisney plus the rude termination of Yeah Yeah Noh's tenure after a single entry the previous year, and you begin to get the impression of a chart beginning to become attached to its originator more than ever before; perhaps most surprisingly, there was nothing from Half Man Half Biscuit's debut album, a release rapturously received by Peel and many others alike. You sense there was something here akin to a proclamation on the voting audience's behalf that what they liked was a rather narrower selection of music than Peel was offering. The increase in voting numbers that took place that year perhaps suggested a motivation on their part to make these voices fervently heard.

Although it's been presumed elsewhere that the two (unnamed) tracks in the chart were Sisters of Mercy entries, Peel often voiced his dislike for the number four entry here, 'She Sells Sanctuary' by The Cult, a single that enjoyed a remarkably long residency in the UK chart and became a staple of that growing feature of the mid-eighties, the indie club night. Perhaps this was the chart's most significant symptom of the rallying call of the constituency of voters referred to above. 'Indie' had changed, moving from its punk association in the late seventies, through the innovative spirit of post-punk, moving into a variety of sub-genres in the early eighties eventually to be reclaimed in a distinctive form now, where The Smiths were the new gods and where guitarists took their lead from anti-rockism and the Rickenbacker jangle of Johnny Marr, providing a new generation of non-mainstream teens with their signature motif. Meanwhile opposing voices at the back of the indie club clung to a lineage that went back to the Banshees and The Cure and, in the transition from Southern Death Cult to The Cult, found heroes with the potential to retain their cherished sensibilities while even offering a path into the singles charts.

There were exceptions. It was extremely gratifying to see The Vibes making an appearance (Peel commented that he might well have voted for that himself), finally some recognition for Husker Du, plus three tracks for The Pogues (a band I got to see live that year, a live experience that has still never been beaten) and an unexpectedly high entry for Chumbawamba, their only appearance in a festive fifty until they made a triumphant, if brief, return in 1993, with a typically uncompromising anthem of the period. Peel announced the entry as 'Revolution', perhaps indicating that votes had come in for the thematically-linked EP of that name as a single release, but the 'Liberation' track from the EP was the one played. Such surprises were few, and Peel often grumbled laconically through the countdown, even pausing to note that the number 42 entry was a rare example of a Fall track he didn't like much and declaring his lack of appreciation for the number 7 entry, which had been acclaimed by many for its imposing of a Cocteau Twins aesthetic on the music of Felt (Felt hadn't liked the results much either) before reaching the aforementioned Cult offering, though there will have been some satisfaction in finding more cherished tracks occupying the three highest positions.

It's not a criticism of thpse acts who made their debut here to say that many of them had some link with the past or carried some stamp of approval from elsewhere. James and The Woodentops, while both very fine bands, gained much in credibility among festive fifty voters, you suspect, from the patronage of Morrissey. It was great to see the Three Johns in there, with their only ever appearance, but of course they linked back to the past via John Langford to The Mekons. Even The Cure, now fully reinvented as a commercially successful pop band, managed an unlikely appearance, while the high placing for Felt, with the aforementioned 'Primitive Painters', was probably due to the involvement of Robin Guthrie as producer and Liz Fraser's vocal contributions more than anything else: it gave Cocteau Twins fans somewhere to go, lacking this year the multiple options to choose from during the band's prolific years of 83 and 84.

Despite the proliferation of Smiths and Fall tracks, it was the Jesus & Mary Chain who took most of the plaudits, becoming the first band ever to seize the top two slots in a festive fifty. Their exquisite indie pop shrouded in buzzsaw sub-Velvets feedback undoubtedly gave the year some of its finest moments and their eminence had been anticipated by Peel when, on playing their debut 'Upside Down' in the 1984 chart, he confidently voiced his expectation that there would be several tracks from the band in this year's chart. In fact, their representation was limited to their three singles, which carried large numbers of votes between them to leave other tracks from their stunning debut album *Psychocandy* outside the chart. The album managed to offer both a manifesto for indie pop and a radical reappropriation of *White Light White Heat* noise manipulation, taking the cherished aesthetic that underpinned much of this chart and both distorting and radicalising it. The Mary Chain's musical approach, controversial name and violent early gigs marked them out as perhaps the first genuine folk devils the eighties had produced: unlike many of those the music press had attempted to saddle with a 'new Pistols' label, they had some of the hallmarks of punk but what really struck home was how, when you stripped away the surface veneer of that early notoriety, what was left behind was even better..

1985 Festive Fifty
Broadcast dates: 16, 17, 18, 23 & 25 December

50. All Day Long – Shop Assistants (Subway Org 7" EP *Shopping Parade*)
49. Like One Thousand Violins – One Thousand Violins (Dreamworld 12" *Halcyon Days* B-side)
48. Well Well Well – The Woodentops (Rough Trade 7")
47. The Wind of Change – Robert Wyatt & The SWAPO Singers (Rough Trade 7")
46. Makes No Sense At All – Husker Du (SST LP *Flip Your Wig*)
45. Face Up – New Order (Factory LP *Low-Life*)
44. It Happens – Primal Scream (Creation 7" *All Fall Down* B-side)
43. Some Kind of Stranger – Sisters of Mercy (Merciful Release LP *First & Last & Always*)
42. L.A. – The Fall (Beggars Banquet LP *This Nation's Saving Grace*)

41. Well I Wonder – The Smiths (Rough Trade LP *Meat Is Murder*)
40. Between The Wars – Billy Bragg (Go! Discs 7" EP *Between The Wars*)
39. Couldn't Get Ahead – The Fall (Beggars Banquet 7")
38. Faron Young – Prefab Sprout (Kitchenware LP *Steve McQueen*)
37. I'm in Pittsburgh (And It's Rainin') – The Vibes (Chainsaw 12" EP *The Inner Wardrobes of Your Mind*)
36. Marian – Sisters of Mercy (Merciful Release LP *First & Last & Always*)
35. Tupelo – Nick Cave & The Bad Seeds (Mute LP *The First Born Is Dead*)
34. A Hundred Words – The Beloved (Peel Session 15.1.85)

33. Gut of the Quantifier - The Fall (Beggars Banquet LP *This Nation's Saving Grace*)
32. Meat Is Murder – The Smiths (Rough Trade LP *Meat Is Murder*)
31. That Joke Isn't Funny Anymore – The Smiths (Rough Trade LP *Meat Is Murder*)
30. Motor City – Age of Chance (Riot Bible 7")
29. The Headmaster Ritual – The Smiths (Rough Trade LP *Meat Is Murder*)
28. Hymn From a Village – James (Factory 7" *James II*)
27. In Between Days – The Cure (Fiction LP *The Head on the Door*)
26. L.A. Rain – Rose of Avalanche (Leeds Independent 7")
25. I'm A Man You Don't Meet Every Day – The Pogues (Stiff LP *Rum, Sodomy & The Lash*)
24. Sunrise – New Order (Factory LP Low-Life)
23. Spoilt Victorian Child – The Fall (Beggars Banquet LP *This Nation's Saving Grace*)
22. V2 – That Petrol Emotion (Noiseanoise 7")
21. Bring on the Dancing Horses – Echo & The Bunnymen (Korova 7")
20. A Pair of Brown Eyes – The Pogues (Stiff LP *Rum, Sodomy & The Lash*)
19. Move Me – The Woodentops (Rough Trade 7")
18. Sub-culture – New Order (Factory LP *Low-Life*)
17. All That Every Mattered – Shop Assistants (Peel Session)
16. Love Vigilantes – New Order (Factory LP *Low-Life*)
15. Go Out & Get 'Em Boy – The Wedding Present (Reception 7")
14. Death of the European – Three Johns (Abstract 7")
13. Sally MacLennane – The Pogues (Stiff LP *Rum, Sodomy & The Lash*)
12. You Trip Me Up – Jesus & Mary Chain (Blanco y Negro LP *Psychocandy*)
11. Ironmasters – The Men They Couldn't Hang (Imp LP *The Night of a Thousand Candles*)
10. Flag Day – The Housemartins (Go! Discs 7")
9. Perfect Kiss – New Order (Factory LP *Low-Life*)
8. The Boy With the Thorn in His Side – The Smiths (Rough Trade 7")
7. Primitive Painters – Felt (Cherry Red LP *Ignite The Seven Cannons*)
6. Revolution (Liberation) – Chumbawamba (Agit Prop 7" EP)
5. Aikea-Guinea – Cocteau Twins (4AD 12" EP *Aikea-Guinea*)
4. She Sells Sanctuary – The Cult (Beggars Banquet LP *Love*)
3. Cruiser's Creek – The Fall (Peel Session 3.6.85)
2. Just Like Honey – Jesus & Mary Chain (Blanco y Negro LP – *Psychocandy*)
1. Never Understand - Jesus & Mary Chain (Blanco y Negro LP – *Psychocandy*)

1986

My comments here in the first edition appear to have been not so much misinterpreted as interpreted all too accurately, my own failings having rendered them rather more negative than I'd intended them to be. I'll attempt some qualification here and emphasise my remark that there was a lot of good stuff here but, in place of 'not of vintage quality' perhaps emphasise that really it's the lack of variety rather than quality that makes this a less than vintage festive fifty. If this sounds much the same as the reservations voiced over 1985 then consider that to be so, with knobs on.

In his regular column in The Observer, Peel made it clear he felt the festive fifty was becoming a slightly stale affair, lamenting the lack of music by black artists in particular. He certainly had a point. While no end of year chart had ever fully reflected Peel's tastes (aside from 1977 of course) and none could be expected to, the content of the mid-eighties festive fifties offered a particularly poor reflection of the content of the Peel shows of the period. The mid-eighties Peel shows, among other things, offered a vibrant showcase for, among other things, much of the excellent African music appearing during the period as well as a healthy amount of good hip-hop. Both are entirely absent here and would only make sporadic appearances thereafter.

There are, it's fair to say, some varied elements in the list. A first and only appearance in a festive fifty for Freiwillige Selbstkontrolle was perhaps most pleasing for Peel, although he also voiced his satisfaction that Nick Cave eased into the chart with his version of Jimmy Webb's 'By the Time I Get to Phoenix'. There are three tracks here that he hadn't previously played on the radio and he does mildly chide himself for not having shared with us the Elvis Costello and The The singles before now.

And there is much quality here, even though it often comes from predictable sources. Although there is a sniffiness among some hardline Fall fans around the Brix Smith period and the generally less caustic edge to their music during that time, *Bend Sinister* remains a very fine album, as of course does The Smiths' *The Queen is Dead*: both albums are duly rewarded with five entries here, alongside respective classic singles 'Living Too Late' and 'Panic' (for The Smiths, 'Ask' also makes an appearance). In the case of The Smiths, Peel would amuse himself by commenting on the lack of entries as he counted down the chart, knowing they had placed an unprecedented six in the top twelve, including four in the top seven, the latter emulating the feat of Joy Division in 1981 and the former trumping it. In 'There is a Light That Never Goes Out', The Smiths provided the first album-only track to be voted as number one since 'Stairway to Heaven'. Filling the slots immediately beneath it were the two highest placed cover versions in festive fifty history, with Age of Chance's release apparently putting in a spirited late run in an ultimately unsuccessful attempt to deny The Smiths their second number one in three years and Manchester its fifth in six years.

There's little doubt however that, aside from the punk years, there's never been a festive fifty whose content might be so easily labelled, whether you preferred 'indie pop', the popular term at the time of 'shambling' or simply C86, the name of an NME cassette that featured many of the period's best new bands and which came to be used as a shorthand term for bands with a predilection for jangly guitars, short tunes and, often, anoraks, despite the fact that the content of the cassette had been far more varied, including less easily pigeon-holed bands like Stump and Bogshed. The music press had, in its way, got all misty-eyed and romantic in commemorating the tenth anniversary of the punk explosion, declaring with no real evidence whatsoever that music operated in ten year cycles and proclaiming the aforementioned bands as some kind of new 'movement'.

In a decade of spurious arguments, this one was right up there among the least convincing. Did rock and roll really begin in 1956? And wasn't 1966 more of an intake of breath between the British beat boom and psychedelia? In 1987, some of those understandably underwhelmed by the championing of C86 denied it had represented anything significant whatsoever, manipulating history again in order to make the same claims for acid house.

C86 and those associated with it, in making up much of this festive fifty, is largely responsible for the generally unremarkable nature of this chart. While there are a number of undeniably very good indie guitar bands herein, and some creditable blasts of inspiration, as the chart wore on there was a nagging feeling that what was being played had already appeared further down the chart. When Peel actually did this at one point, not subsequently realising his error (and therefore rendering The Wedding Present's 'This Boy Can Wait' the first entry in the chart not to be broadcast, though not the last), the error seemed loaded with unintended irony.

One thing that can be said about the 1986 chart, however, concerns the pleasing variety of independent labels herein, many of them new to the chart. This is a positive feature of C86 that is all too commonly overlooked but, if the explosion of small labels could hardly be said to match the one that happened after the dawning of punk, the debut here of labels like Girlie, Glass, Lazy and Raw TV, plus further outings for 53rd % 3rd, Liverpool's always excellent, and still active Probe Plus, 53rd & 3rd and the then vibrant Creation label, provide evidence that the mid-eighties scene contained an enormous swell of passionate grass roots activity that is sometimes overlooked, and the 1986 chart does reflect this far better than did the more celebrated festive fifty of 1978.

More trivially, at this stage the Peel programme was still a CD-free zone, although this would change, albeit slightly, in the following year At the end of the programme, Peel mentions that at the time he only owned three of these maligned objectc, one each by Joy Division and New Order, the other the soundtrack to *Amadeus*.

1986 Festive Fifty

Broadcast dates: 22, 23, 24, 29 & 30 December

50. The Body of an American – The Pogues (Stiff 7" EP *Poguetry in Motion*)
49. Serpent's Kiss – The Mission (Chapter 22 12")
48. Dktr Faustus – The Fall (Beggars Banquet LP *Bend Sinister*)
47. Take the Skinheads Bowling – Camper Van Beethoven (Rough Trade 12")
46. The Official Colourbox World Cup Theme – Colourbox (4AD 7")
45. By the Time I Get to Phoenix – Nick Cave & The Bad Seeds (Mute LP *Kicking Against The Pricks*)
44. Is There Anyone Out There? – Mighty Mighty (Girlie 7")
43. I Don't Want To Be Friends With You – Shop Assistants (Blue Guitar 7")
42. I Could Be In Heaven – The Flatmates (Subway Org. 7")
41. Greetings To The New Brunette – Billy Bragg (Go! Discs LP *Talking to the Taxman About Poetry*)
40. I Want You – Elvis Costello (Demon LP *Blood & Chocolate*)
39. Dickie Davies Eyes – Half Man Half Biscuit (Probe Plus 7")
38. Those Eyes, That Mouth – Cocteau Twins (4AD 12" *Love's Easy Tears* B-side)
-7. Lucifer Over Lancashire (Alternative Version) – The Fall (Melody Maker 7" V/A EP *Vinyl Conflict 2*)
36. Felicity – The Wedding Present (Peel Session 26.2.86)
35. Cemetry Gates – The Smiths (Rough Trade LP *The Queen is Dead*)
34. Like An Angel – Mighty Lemon Drops (Dreamworld 7")
33. I Wish I Could Sprechen Sie Deutsch – Freiwillige Selbstkontrolle (Peel Session 13.8.86)
32. Heartland – The The (Epic 7")
31. Rules & Regulations – We've Got A Fuzzbox & We're Gonna Use it (Vindaloo 7" EP *Rules & Regulations*)
30. This is Motortown – Very Things (DCL 7")
29. It's a Good Thing – That Petrol Emotion (Demon 7")
28. You Should Always Keep In Touch With Your Friends – The Wedding Present (Reception 7" *This Boy Can Wait* B-side)
27. Bible of the Beats – Age of Chance (Riot Bible 7")
26. Realm of Dusk – The Fall (Peel Session 9.7.86)
25. Whole Wide World – Soup Dragons (Subway Org. 7")
24. Levi Stubbs' Tears – Billy Bragg (Go! Discs 12")
23. Truck Train Tractor – The Pastels (Glass 7")
22. Really Stupid – The Primitives (Lazy 7")
-21. Love's Easy Tears – Cocteau Twins (4AD 12")
-20. Bournemouth Runner – The Fall (Beggars Banquet LP *Bend Sinister*)
19. Therese – The Bodines (Creation 7")
18. This Boy Can Wait – The Wedding Present (Reception 7")
17. Hang Ten! – Soup Dragons (Raw TV 7")
16. Once More – The Wedding Present (Reception 7")
15. Living Too Late – The Fall (Beggars Banquet 7")
14. Trumpton Riots – Half Man Half Biscuit (Probe Plus 7")
13. Almost Prayed – Weather Prophets (Creation 7")
12. Bigmouth Strikes Again – The Smiths (Rough Trade LP *The Queen is Dead*)
11. Ask – The Smiths (Rough Trade 7")
10. US 80s-90s – The Fall (Beggars Banquet LP *Bend Sinister*)
9. Some Candy Talking – Jesus & Mary Chain (NME V/A 7" EP *NME's Big Four*)
8. Safety Net – Shop Assistants (53rd & 3rd 7")
7. The Queen is Dead – The Smiths (Rough Trade LP *The Queen is Dead*)
6. I Know It's Over – The Smiths (Rough Trade LP *The Queen is Dead*)
5. Panic – The Smiths (Rough Trade 7")
4. Velocity Girl – Primal Scream (Creation 7" single *Crystal Crescent*)
3. Mr Pharmacist – The Fall (Beggars Banquet 7")
2. Kiss – Age of Chance (Riot Bible 7")
1. There is a Light That Never Goes Out – The Smiths (Rough Trade LP *The Queen is Dead*)

1987

The Smiths' split of 1987 remains one of the landmark events of modern music and it was inevitable that the festive fifty would mark it in a fairly extreme way. It didn't let the band's fans down in that respect, with a mammoth eleven tracks entering the chart, consigning another Joy Division record to the history books. To a superficial observer, it all began tamely enough, with the band's last two non-album singles already accounted for by the time we'd reached number 34. Such was the obsessive pull of the band, however, seasoned observers would know that this was nothing to go by. B sides from those releases would turn up further up the chart and, by the time we'd finished, eight of the eleven tracks on their swansong *Strangeways Here We Come* album had made an appearance. Peel's protests were inevitable, preceded by the words 'I mean I like The Smiths too, you know I do, but...'

'Faintly ridiculous,' he would call it, yet the band had their farewell party gatecrashed by impudent rising festive fifty stars from the east. The Wedding present had surfaced at number 31 with their thrilling cover of Girls At Our Best's 'Getting Nowhere Fast' after which a strange silence had prevailed, the reason becoming clear when we got to the top ten and found the Leeds band in there four times, something that only Joy Division and The Smiths had ever achieved before and something that has never been matched since.

Although his comment at the start of the broadcast that he'd been tempted to fiddle the chart was clearly tongue in cheek, once again, Peel would use his Observer column to express his disappointment at much of the content, though his tone was slightly less aggrieved than in the previous year. Clearly his displeasure was softened slightly due to a few hip-hop records being voted in and admittedly brief intrusions from house and African music.

The most notable feature of the 1987 festive fifty, though, lies in a heightened recognition in general for what was coming out of the United States, certainly in comparison with previous festive fifties. It always struck me as curious that, pre-1987, the chart had been so dominated by UK acts. Here, alongside hip-hop, were the first stirrings of Sonic Youth along with a smattering of other notables including Big Black and Butthole Surfers, neither of whom were ever to trouble the festive fifty scorers again. Peel was clearly especially delighted by Colorblind James Experience sneaking into the lower reaches and, although Sonic Youth's appearance at number 13 would signal the high point for American tunes in this chart,, the total of eleven records of US origin was easily the highest since that first chart of 1976. Stateside labels like Def Jam, Blast First, Touch & Go and Fourth & Broadway all got their first taste of festive fifty action. While there would be UK-dominated festive fifties in the future, these would be infrequent events and the days of perpetual US-free zones were over for good.

All of which, on the surface, would suggest reason for more than muted celebration on behalf of Peel, especially when you throw in the figure of twenty new acts appearing, the highest since 1982, perhaps suggesting that the relative sterility that had taken hold of the chart during the previous two years was coming to an end. That he refused to partake in any orgies of optimism was, you suspect, due largely to the Smiths' dominance. While the demise of the band was certainly something to be regretted, for Peel as much as anyone else, at least there was a hope it would put a stop to their stranglehold on this chart.

There was, in any case, a Banshees-like spread of the vote over a large number of Smiths tunes which led to only one of them making the top ten and only two others reaching the top twenty. The aforementioned domination of the top ten by the Wedding Present's *George Best* album allowed them to grab a big chunk of the top end action, with a couple of entries for fellow heavyweights The Fall, something from New Order and one from That Petrol Emotion, now the vehicle for Peel's much-loved former Undertones the O'Neill brothers. Just outside the top ten, I, Ludicrous achieved the highest placing at that point for a non-official release, in the form of a flexidisc for the *Blah Blah Blah* magazine. Among the achievements of The Smiths and The Wedding Present it should not go unnoticed that The Sugarcubes, from Iceland, became the first non-British act to take the number one spot.

1987 Festive Fifty

Broadcast dates: 22, 23, 28, 29 & 30 December

50. Talulah Gosh – Talulah Gosh (53rd & 3rd 7")
49. Rok Da House – Beatmasters/Cookie Crew – (Rhythm King 12")
48. Breaking Hands – Gun Club (Red Rhino LP *Mother Juno*)
47. Considering a Move to Memphis – Colorblind James Experience (Earring LP *Colorblind James Experience*)
46. Pump Up The Volume – M/A/R/R/S (4AD 12")
45. Shoplifters of the World Unite – The Smiths (Rough Trade 7")
44. 22 Going On 23 – Butthole Surfers (Blast First LP *Locust Abortion Technician*)
43. 1963 – New Order (Factory 12" *True Faith* B-side)
42. L Dopa – Big Black (Touch & Go LP *Songs About Fucking*)
41. Nine Million Rainy Days – Jesus & Mary Chain (Blanco y Negro LP *Darklands*)
40. I Started Something I Couldn't Finish – The Smiths (Rough Trade LP *Strangeways Here We Come*)
39. Kill Surf City – Jesus & Mary Chain (Blanco y Negro 7" *April Skies* B-side)
38. You're Gonna Get Yours (Dub/Terminator X Getaway Version) – Public Enemy (Def Jam 12")
37. (I Got A) Catholic Block – Sonic Youth (Blast First LP *Sister*)
36. I Know You Got Soul – Eric B. & Rakim (Cooltempo 7")
35. Frans Hals – McCarthy (The Pink Label 7")
34. Sheila Take A Bow – The Smiths (Rough Trade 7")
33. Blow Up – James Taylor Quartet (Re-Elect The President 7")
32. Sign O' The Times – Prince (Paisley Park 7")
31. Getting Nowhere Fast – The Wedding Present (Reception 12" *Anyone Can Make A Mistake* B-side)
30. My Foolish Heart – Bhundu Boys (WEA LP *True Jit*)
29. I Won't Share You – The Smiths (Rough Trade LP *Strangeways Here We Come*)
28. Brighter – Railway Children (Factory LP *Reunion Wilderness*)
27. Paid In Full (Seven Minutes of Madness: The Coldcut Remix) – Eric B. & Rakim (Fourth & Broadway 12")
26. Athlete Cured – The Fall (Peel Session 11.5.87)
25. Death of a Disco Dancer – The Smiths (Rough Trade LP *Strangeways Here We Come*)
24. Half A Person – The Smiths (Rough Trade 7" *Shoplifters of the World Unite* B-side)
23. Sweet & Tender Hooligan – The Smiths (Rough Trade 7" *Sheila Take A Bow* B-side: originally broadcast in Peel Session 17.12.86)
22. Big Rock Candy Mountain – The Motorcycle Boy (Rough Trade 7")
21. Paint a Vulgar Picture - The Smiths (Rough Trade LP *Strangeways Here We Come*)
20. You Sexy Thing – Cud (Peel Session 30.6.87. Also released that year on Strange Fruit 12" EP *The Peel Sessions*)
19. Stop Killing Me – Primitives (Lazy 7")
18. Colombian Necktie – Big Black (Touch & Go LP *Songs About Fucking*)
17. Sharp as a Needle – Barmy Army (On-U Sound 7")
16. April Skies – Jesus & Mary Chain (Blanco y Negro LP *Darklands*)
15. Girlfriend in a Coma – The Smiths (Rough Trade LP *Strangeways Here We Come*)
14. Rebel Without A Pause – Public Enemy (Def Jam 7")
13. Schizophrenia – Sonic Youth (Blast First LP *Sister*)
12. Stop Me If You Think You've Heard This One Before - The Smiths (Rough Trade LP *Strangeways Here We Come*)
11. Preposterous Tales – I, Ludicrous (Blah Blah Blah magazine flexidisc)
10. Anyone Can Make A Mistake – The Wedding Present (Reception LP *George Best*)
9. Hit The North (Part 1) – The Fall (Beggars Banquet 7")
8. A Million Miles – The Wedding Present (Reception LP *George Best*)
7. True Faith (Shep Pettibone Remix) – New Order

(Factory 12")
6. My Favourite Dress – The Wedding Present (Reception LP *George Best*)
5. Last Night I Dreamt That Somebody Loved Me – The Smiths (Rough Trade LP *Strangeways Here We Come*)

4. Big Decision – That Petrol Emotion (Polydor 7")
3. Everyone Thinks He Looks Daft - The Wedding Present (Reception LP *George Best*)
2. Australians in Europe – The Fall (Peel Session 11.5.87)
1. Birthday – Sugarcubes (One Little Indian 7")

1988

In his show of 19 December, Peel responded to a listener who enquired about the possible return of an all-time chart by saying that his reluctance to do so was partly fuelled by a concern that 'Stairway To Heaven' would return to the number one spot. It was probably pushing it a bit for anyone to make such an enquiry anyway, given that the future of the current chart still remained insecure. Peel used the phrase 'young boys strumming guitars' to denounce its conservatism in the last of the five broadcasts. It was a phrase he would repeat or offer mild variations on over the years. Once again, he voiced his regret at the lack of black music in particular.

While he certainly had a point, it would be fair to say the 1988 festive fifty was an improvement on the low point of 1986 in terms of variety. While the preponderance of guitar music in the chart was an understandable bone of contention, this was true of festive fifties long before the mid-eighties, including the 1978 chart that Peel had lavished so much praise on. And black music had been largely absent from the festive fifty since its inception, with only his own selection in 1977 containing more tracks featuring black musicians than the 1987 chart had. Admittedly the chart this year showed a reduction and perhaps that was a source of particular disappointment.

Despite the lukewarm reception Peel gave the chart in his Observer column, he did welcome the appearance of a couple of his favourite US records (from Mudhoney and Spit, the latter with a track he would have considered voting for himself, he revealed in the broadcast) and there were a number of appreciative comments as he went along. McCarthy, although they qualified for the tag of young boys strumming guitars if anyone did, were warmly received at number 38; a first chart appearance for Inspiral Carpets was welcomed and there was a smattering of praise for Morrissey's 'Disappointed', or at least seven or eight seconds of it. He also noted with appreciation the variety of countries he'd received votes from, including Nepal, Brunei and a single vote from New Zealand, which doesn't sound much to write home about but perhaps says something about the state of play before then, as well as hinting at the reason why so many festive fifties had been dominated by UK bands.

Peel played the wrong record during the countdown for the second time in a festive fifty, this time broadcasting 'River Euphrates' by the Pixies rather than 'Bone Machine'. Although he recognized the error and claimed it had never happened before, he had done so just two years earlier but never acknowledged it at the time. Is it that he simply never realised his mistake? Hard to believe, as you'd think some FF observers would surely have been willing to point this out. This time it caused scheduling problems, meaning he was a record behind after the first show, and further problems occurred the second night when the Lockerbie bombing led to an extended new bulletin. Peel apologised for following the news of the crash with what he labelled 'trivial nonsense'.

It's perhaps a source of surprise to later Peel listeners that the only track in this chart not played in the Peel show that year was from Cocteau Twins, making their final appearance in any festive fifty. After their debut EP 'Lullabies' in 1982 every official release from the band had made some contibution to the chart until the *Tiny Dynamine/Echoes in a Shallow Bay* EPs ended the run towards the end of 1985, something that was probably attributable to their release very late in the year. In 1983, Peel had even declared the Cocteau Twins (not The Fall) to be his favourite band. However, 1986's *Victorialand* album had failed to yield a single entry and a year of little activity in 1987 pretty much signalled the end of their festive fifty legacy, with 'Carolyn's Fingers' providing a belated, if high quality, swansong. With its release as a single in the US, the track kick-started the second wave of the Twins' career, with their *Heaven Or Las Vegas* album in 1990 well received in very different critical circles.

Although the chart offered significantly more variety and interest than had 1986, the top end remained territory largely inhabited by the indie club night brigade. New darlings House of Love gained the number one spot (Peel commented that it had the best ending of any record on the chart that year), beating off a couple of Wedding Present favourites, once of which – 'Take Me I'm Yours' - set a new festive fifty record for a track only available in its session version. Its number four placing remains unassailed by any session recording since. Jesus & Mary Chain also predictably made a strong showing, while the indie clubbers' fave 'Freak Scene' by Dinosaur Jr sailed in at number five. At least, on the Peel show, it was possible to listen to the song without a bunch of kids with floppy hair shouting 'fuck off' at an opportune moment over the radio edit. It's a stereotype, but a pretty accurate one as such things go. Or maybe I was just getting too old for those clubs at this point.

Dinosaur Jr's compatriots Pixies sprang into festive fifty life with four tracks from their debut *Surfer Rosa* album, which also generated the first chart action as a producer for Steve Albini, who'd debuted as a performer with Big Black in the previous year's chart. Although there were slightly fewer entries for records by US bands than had been the case a year earlier, Pixies became the first from that side of the Atlantic to place this many entries in a festive fifty and over the next four charts they'd go on to become the highest achieving American band in chart history.

1988 Festive Fifty
Broadcast dates: 20, 21, 26, 27 & 28 December

50. Night of the Living Baseheads – Public Enemy (Def Jam LP *It Takes A Nation of Millions to Hold Us Back*)
49. Don't Laugh – The Wedding Present (Reception 12" *Nobody's Twisting Your Arm* B-side)
48. Wrote For Luck – Happy Mondays (Factory 7")
47. Shame On You – Darling Buds (Native 7")
46. Crash – Primitives (RAC 7")
45. Bone Machine – Pixies (4AD LP *Surfer Rosa*)
44. Fine Time – New Order (Factory 7")
43. Miles Apart – Mega City Four (Primitive 7")
42. Shimmer – The Flatmates (Subway Org. 7")
41. Collision – Loop (Chapter 22 12")
40. Guest Informant – The Fall (Beggars Banquet 12" *Victoria* A-side, additional track)
39. River Euphrates – Pixies (4AD LP *Surfer Rosa*)
38. Should The Bible Be Banned? – McCarthy (September 12")
37. Samora Machel – Shalawambe (Peel Session 12.9.88)
36. Jerusalem – The Fall (Beggars Banquet LP *I Am Kurious Oranj*)
35. Charlton Heston – Stump (Ensign LP *A Fierce Pancake*)
34. On Tape – Pooh Sticks (Fierce LP *Alan McGee*)
33. What For – James (Sire LP *Strip-mine*)
32. Road Pizza – Spit (Nailed For Sound 12")
31. Sweet Young Thing Ain't Sweet No More – Mudhoney (Sub Pop 7")
30. Where Is My Mind? – Pixies (4AD LP *Surfer Rosa*)
29. Silver Rocket – Sonic Youth (Blast First LP *Daydream Nation*)
28. 14 Days in May – Overlord X (Hardcore 12")
27. I Am Kurious Oranj – The Fall (Beggars Banquet LP *I Am Kurious Oranj*)
26. Carolyn's Fingers – Cocteau Twins (4AD LP *Blue Bell Knoll*)
25. Waiting For The Great Leap Forwards – Billy Bragg (Go! Discs LP *Workers' Playtime*)
24. New Big Prinz – The Fall (Beggars Banquet LP *I Am Kurious Oranj*)
23. Disappointed – Morrissey (HMV 7" *Every Day is Like Sunday* B-side)
22. Late Night Maudlin Street – Morrissey (HMV LP *Viva Hate*)
21. Something Nice – Robert Lloyd & The New Four Seasons (In-Tape 7")
20. Deus – The Sugarcubes (One Little Indian LP *Life's Too Good*)
19. Teenage Riot – Sonic Youth (Blast First LP *Daydream Nation*)
18. Love in a Car – House of Love (Creation LP *The House of Love*)
17. Feed Me With Your Kiss – My Bloody Valentine (Creation LP *Isn't Anything*)
16. Bremen Nacht – The Fall (Beggars Banquet LP *The Frenz Experiment*)

15. I'm Not Always So Stupid – The Wedding Present (Reception 12" *Nobody's Twisting Your Arm* B-side)
14. Cab It Up! – The Fall (Beggars Banquet LP *I Am Kurious Oranj*)
13. Suedehead – Morrissey (HMV LP *Viva Hate*)
12. Every Day Is Like Sunday - Morrissey (HMV LP *Viva Hate*)
11. Keep the Circle Around – Inspiral Carpets (Playtime 7")
10. The Mercy Seat – Nick Cave & The Bad Seeds (Mute LP *The Mercy Seat*)
9. Christine – House of Love (Creation LP *The House of Love*)
8. Why Are You Being so Reasonable Now? – The Wedding Present (Reception 7")
7. Gigantic – Pixies (4AD LP *Surfer Rosa*)
6. You Made Me Realise – My Bloody Valentine (Creation 7" EP *You Made Me Realise*)
5. Freak Scene – Dinosaur Jr (Blast First 7")
4. Take Me I'm Yours – The Wedding Present (Peel Session 30.5.88)
3. Sidewalking – Jesus & Mary Chain (Blanco y Negro 7")
2. Nobody's Twisting Your Arm – The Wedding Present (Reception 7")
1. Destroy the Heart – House of Love (Creation 7")

1989

On a personal level, looking through this list reminds me of the astonishing number of gigs I must have gone to around that time. Represented within it are the best band I saw in that period (Pixies) and the worst (Jesus Jones), who incidentally provide the only non-Stone Roses track (more of which a little further on) in this chart not to have been played by Peel during the year.   Inspiral Carpets, Galaxie 500, Pale Saints, House of Love and the amazing Cud were among the other live delights I witnessed (as well as, more obviously The Fall and, on multiple occasions, The Wedding Present), and all of whom made the 1989 festive fifty cut.

I also managed to see the Stone Roses, who joined Tom Waits and Patti Smith among my list of musical obsessions that Peel didn't share. Although he was at pains to stress during the countdown that he didn't hate the band, he did admit he found their appeal difficult to understand.   He gave faint praise when stating that 'Made of Stone' had 'agreeable singalong potential' and caustically citing a typo when announcing 'She Bangs the Drums'. Although it's certainly the case that other bands have appeared in festive fifties despite not finding favour with Peel, Stone Roses' achievement of placing five entries in the chart, including four from their debut album, makes them unique in securing such a strong showing despite quite clearly never being a 'Peel band'.   Incidentally, I still find people who are willing to argue very strongly that Peel played tracks from their album in this show during the year. If this is correct, I'm still yet to find evidence of it (aside from in the festive fifty countdown, of course). He certainly played their debut single 'So Young' back in 1985 but, as is heard in this countdown, was pretty dismissive of whatever the band did after that.

Of the great Madchester triumvirate, he was always far more of a Happy Mondays or Inspiral Carpets man and the latter here are rewarded with five entries while the former, with a remix of the previous year's entry 'Wrote For Luck', make it into the top five. While the number of tracks of Mancunian/Salfordian origin in the top ten (five) actually fell one short of the city's high water mark in 1983, a whopping nineteen entries (more than a third of the chart) had their origins in the area.   Despite this, the Factory label saw less of the action than they had during that early eighties Mancunian FF uprising, with only that Mondays entry and a solitary New Order track to show for being the ones to have set the ball rolling. However, the two featured tracks did allow the label to secure a tenth consecutive year of residence in the chart. Peel came to the defence of that other Mancunian institution Morrissey, whose material that year, especially the 'Ouija Board, Ouija Board' single, had received the kind of critical panning you suspected sections of the music media had been itching to give him for some time. Peel dissented, as did enough Morrissey fans to place his two of the three singles he released that year in the top twenty, while the other made an appearance lower down. This meant his first five singles had made the festive fifty, something that had only hitherto been achieved by The Wedding Present, Jesus and Mary Chain and his former band.

The Fall also contributed little to the total, managing only a single entry, with 'Dead Beat Descendant' allowing them to continue a post-1982 run of consecutive appearances that still had more than a decade's worth of fuel in the tank. The band's album output that year had been limited to the release of *Seminal – Live*, a contractual obligation release which did contain new material but very little of it. Like their blank year of 1982, 1989 contained no new session material from the band (a new session was recorded for broadcast on New Year's Day 1990), unless you count a live set broadcast from London's Subterrania in August.

Peel will have been disappointed that the bulk of festive fifty voters appear to have been bypassed by the acid house phenomenon, as indeed they appeared to be by forms of dance music, despite its growing cultural significance. Madchester did open the door for 808 State to register their only festive fifty entry but, given the nature of the changes music was undergoing at this point, this was fairly small beer and there was, in truth, far more for the countdown's host to find fault with this year than there had been in either of the previous two years. While it may be tempting to see the Roses as a curious festive fifty aberration, perhaps they were simply the latest and most pronounced example of a growing tendency in recent years to ignore, or at best only tacitly acknowledge, the musical diet Peel was serving up.

At the top end, we had the closest battle for the number one ever, a three song scrap eventually won by The Sundays, but with the voting so close that, had 'Debaser' received one more vote in first place, The Pixies would have seized the top spot. Thus the opportunity of becoming the first American band to achieve a festive fifty number one was denied them; similarly denied were The Wedding Present, who got even closer, although they would eventually put this right 24 years in the future. The Sundays, incidentally, were one of only two bands in the fifty solely fronted by a female lead singer. The predominantly male make-up of bands in the chart is something that we've commented on earlier in the book; there had been a small upsurge in the mid-eighties and there were bands here (such as Pixies and Galaxie 500) whose line-ups included female personnel, but the curious gender imbalance in the festive fifty that had survived the equality drives of both punk and C86 was still a few years away from being addressed.

1989 Festive Fifty
Broadcast dates: 20, 21, 26, 27 & 28 December

50. She Comes in the Fall – Inspiral Carpets (Peel Session 5.4.89)
49. Directing Traffic – Inspiral Carpets (Peel Session 9.10.89)
48. Tom Verlaine – Family Cat (Bad Girl 7")
47. Interesting Drug – Morrissey (HMV 7")
46. Landslide – Popguns (Medium Cool 7")
45. What Have I Said Now? – The Wedding Present (RCA LP *Bizarro*)
44. Not Listening – Snuff (Workers' Playtime LP *Snuffsaidgorblimeyguv –stonemeifhedidntthrowa wobblerchachachachachachachachahcahcahca- youregoinghomeinacosmicambience*)
43. Dead – Pixies (4AD LP *Doolittle*)
42. Too Much Kissing –Senseless Things (Way Cool LP *Postcard CV*)
41. Don't Let Our Youth Go to Waste – Galaxie 500 (Aurora LP *Today*)
40. Paradise – Birdland (Lazy 7")
39. Swerve – Dub Sex (Cut Deep 12")
38. Dead Beat Descendant – The Fall (Beggars Banquet 7" *Cab It Up* B-side)
37. Here Comes Your Man – Pixies (4AD LP *Doolittle*)
36. Wave of Mutilation - Pixies (4AD LP *Doolittle*)
35. So This Is How It Feels – Inspiral Carpets (Peel Session 9.10.89)
34. Eye Know – De La Soul (Big Life LP *3 Feel High & Rising*)
33. Hypnotized – Spacemen 3 (Fire 7")
32. Info Freako – Jesus Jones (Food 7")
31. Convenience – Bob (House of Teeth 7" EP *Convenience*)
30. The Perfect Needle – Telescopes (What Goes on 12")
29. I Wanna Be Adored – Stone Roses (Silvertone LP *The Stone Roses*)
28. Hollow Heart – Birdland (Lazy 7")
27. Vanishing Point – New Order (Factory LP *Technique*)
26. Sensitive – Field Mice (Sarah 7")
25. She Rides the Waves – Pale Saints (4AD 12" EP *Barging into the Presence of God*)
24. Bewitched – The Wedding Present (RCA LP

Bizarro)
23. Fools Gold – Stone Roses (Silvertone 12")
22. Pacific State – 808 State (ZTT 12" *Quadrastate*)
21. Find Out Why – Inspiral Carpets (Cow 7")
20. Ouija Board, Ouija Board – Morrissey (HMV 7")
19. Brassneck – The Wedding Present (RCA LP *Bizarro*)
18. Last of the Famous International Playboys – Morrissey (HMV 7")
17. Made of Stone – Stone Roses (Silvertone LP *The Stone Roses*)
16. You Got It (Keep It Outta My Face) – Mudhoney (Sub Pop LP *Mudhoney*)
15. Only a Prawn in Whitby – Cud (Imaginary LP *When In Rome...Kill Me*)
14. Take Me! – The Wedding Present (RCA LP *Bizarro*)
13. Blues From a Gun – Jesus & Mary Chain (Blanco y Negro LP *Automatic*)
12. Just Like Heaven – Dinosaur Jr (Blast First 7")
11. Sight of You – Pale Saints (4AD 12" EP *Barging Into the Presence of God*)
10. I Don't Know Why I Love You – House of Love (Fontana 7")
9. Joe – Inspiral Carpets (Cow 12")
8. Sit Down – James (Rough Trade 7")
7. She Bangs the Drums – Stone Roses (Silvertone LP *The Stone Roses*)
6. I Am the Resurrection – Stone Roses (Silvertone LP *The Stone Roses*)
5. Monkey Gone To Heaven – Pixies (4AD LP *Doolittle*)
4. W.F.L. (Vince Clarke Mix) – Happy Mondays (Factory 7")
3. Debaser – Pixies (4AD LP *Doolittle*)
2. Kennedy – The Wedding Present (RCA LP *Bizarro*)
1. Can't Be Sure – The Sundays (Rough Trade 7")

1990

The format that had served the festive fifty well since the late seventies – that of neatly counting down 10 tunes a night over five nights – was abandoned for good as changing time slots for the Peel show necessitated a spread over four nights and never again would there be a settled, permanent pattern to something that had become as much a part of Christmas as cheap crackers and your uncle's stale farts. Much gnashing of teeth in particular was heard among those for whom recording the countdown had become a familiar and necessary ritual: the old days, when more often than not a nightly portion of the FF would fit on on side of a C90 cassette were now gone, forever as it turned out.

It would be going too far to say that things would never be the same again, but the changing broadcast format would coincide, with an eight year period of volatility for the festive fifty, during which we would witness some spectacular ups and downs: Peel's complete refusal, one year, to broadcast the chart at all, another in which a truncated version of the FF would be broadcast only after pleas for listeners, and yet there would also be one chart that Peel would declare an unmitigated triumph, the first time such a thing had happened since the halcyon year of 1978.

But that was the near future. For now, the first chart since Thatcher was forced out of office and the Berlin Wall came down certainly left traces of a world very different from that of only a few years earlier. Not that there was much comment on events of historical magnitude in the tunes themselves: only Fatima Mansions, fronted by Cathal Coughlan. formerly of Peel favourites Microdisney, who amazingly was making his first appearance in the festive fifty, came close with their savage ode to the deposed Romanian dictator Ceaucescu.

But the changes in music, and indeed the wider world of youth culture, that had been wrought since 1986 were certainly in evidence. If 1989 had been the high point for Manchester music in the fifty (this year eleven tunes with Mancunian/Salfordian origins made the chart, and that's if we allow the dubious claims made on behalf The Charlatans), then there was no question that the wider cultural influence of its scene the area generated is acutely in evidence. Who'd have imagined, back in the late seventies, that two of the first ten entries in a festive fifty countdown would contain the word 'groove' or derivatives thereof and another would carry the title 'Little Fluffy Clouds'? Or that the top twenty would contain a cover of a Mike Nesmith tune, a reworking of a John Kongas hit, a song about Karen Carpenter's death and a twenty minute sound collage?

After many years as Peel favourites, scousers The Farm donned flares and got on the Manchester gravy, sorry groovy, train, did a baggy cover of 'Stepping Stone' and found themselves in a festive fifty for the first time while enjoying long-elusive commercial success. The Shamen were undergoing a comparable period of transition from indie wannabes to chart-toppers during which they made their most interesting music; they appear here, together with Deee-lite, with a tune that it would have been impossible to imagine gaining favour in the circles it now did only a couple of years previously. The indie kids, whether fuelled by narcotics or not, had discovered it was safe to come out of their bedrooms and OK to dance, even if they retained a certain narrowness about what they were prepared to take the floor to: Happy Mondays had outlived the short blossoming of the Stone Roses, had beaten Inspiral Carpets 2-1 in this important annual fixture and had, when the dust settled, pretty much established the preferred template that accompanied the flinging open of those bedroom doors, falling pictures of Morrissey trampled underfoot in the process. Even The Fall (with 'Telephone Thing') and My Bloody Valentine (with the ante-post favourite for the number one, 'Soon') could not with any integrity declare themselves to be untouched by the prevailing mood. Morrissey himself, who was pretty much untouched by it, duly made his last appearance in a Peel-presented festive fifty with 'November Spawned a Monster', a track that brought his uninterrupted run of festive fifty singles, solo and with The Smiths, to a remarkable seventeen. The run came to an end when 'Piccadilly Palare' failed to garner the necessary votes and Morrissey's only subsequent appearance would be in the very first Dandelion Radio chart some sixteen years hence.

Despite that, the two tunes in this chart that most productively built on the post-Mondays Mancunian template – New FADS' 'Big' and Paris Angels' 'All On You (Perfume)' found themselves beaten to the top of the pile not only by a surprise number one for The Fall (their first) but by a 2-3-4 run for Creation Records and two bands seen as the standard bearers for the so-called shoegazing scene. If MBV's number two tune at least bore some of the hallmarks of the changing creed, two entries right beneath them for Oxford's Ride gave a clear hint of another swift volte-face in British music in favour of kids who wore their fringes long and, if you accept the stereotype, kept those heads resolutely down, in deep contrast with the 'look-you-straight-in-the-eye' approach that reverberated following the impact of the Madchester. Meanwhile, at number 23, were the stirrings of a new wind blowing in from Seattle, of which more later.

In short, change kept coming and, despite the troubled period for the festive fifty we were in, the 1990 chart was a pretty good one, in many ways no less interesting to those of 1983 and 84 in the way it fired off all sorts of possible new directions. The problem for the future certainly wouldn't be MBV, Ride or Nirvana, but that rather too many would express their adoration for them in unimaginative and often derivative ways, leaving music stuck in too many evident cul-de-sacs rather than opening up brand new, expansive and inviting thoroughfares.

Peel's new favourites, Babes in Toyland, snuck in with an entry, one of ten from the US as a whole, giving America its strongest ever showing in a festive fifty to date. The Sub Pop label placed three singles in the chart, and Pixies contined their fine run with a four entries, even if this year the upper reaches of the chart kept them at arm's length. At the top there was yet another close scrap for number one and Peel declared himself both pleased and surprised at the eventual winner. After so many years of missing out on the number one spot, it was curious that The Fall should finally make it with such an understated tune as 'Bill is Dead'. It had apparently been a close call, with only one 'slightly soiled' voting paper denying My Bloody Valentine the triumph many had anticiapted.

Incidentally, I'm as devoted to pedantry in English grammar as the next man, but those who accused me in the first edition of a misused apostrophe for the number 12 entry might wish to note that the band put it there, not me.

1990 Festive Fifty
Broadcast dates: 22,23, 29 & 30 December

50. Beast Inside – Inspiral Carpets (Peel Session 5.6.90)
49. Dig For Fire – Pixies (4AD LP *Bossanova*)
48. Alison – Pixies (4AD LP *Bossanova*)
47. Groovy Train – The Farm (Produce 7")
46. Stepping Stone – The Farm (Produce 7")
45. Nothing Special – Bastro (Clawfist split 7" w/My Dad is Dead)
44. Groove is in the Heart – Deee-lite (Elektra 12")
43. God Knows It's True – Teenage Fanclub (Paperhouse 7")
42. Little Fluffy Clouds – The Orb (Big Life 12")

41. Chicago, Now! – The Fall (Cog Sinister LP *Extricate*)
40. Kool Thing – Sonic Youth (Geffen LP *Goo*)
39. Dalliance – The Wedding Present (Peel Session 28.10.90)
38. House – Babes In Toyland (Sub Pop US import 7")
37. Any Way That You Want Me – Spiritualized (Dedicated 7")
36. Here's Where the Story Ends – The Sundays (Rough Trade LP *Reading, Writing & Arithmetic*)
35. Telephone Thing – The Fall (Cog Sinister LP *Extricate*)
34. Pro>gen – The Shamen (One Little Indian 12")
33. Blues For Ceaucescu – Fatima Mansions (Kitchenware 7")
32. Kinky Afro – Happy Mondays (Factory 7")
31. Velouria – Pixies (4AD LP *Bossanova*)
30. Blood Outta Stone – The Fall (Cog Sinister 12" *White Lightning* B-side)
29. The Wagon – Dinosaur Jr (Sub Pop 7")
28. Polar Bear – The Charlatans (Situation Two LP *Some Friendly*)
27. Sweetness & Light – Lush (4AD 7")
26. Kill Your Television – Ned's Atomic Dustbin (Chapter 22 7")
25. Taste – Ride (Creation LP *Nowhere*)
24. The Happening – Pixies (4AD LP *Bossanova*)
23. Sliver – Nirvana (Sub Pop 7")
22. Crawl – The Wedding Present (RCA 12" EP *3 Songs*)
21. Kaleidoscope – Boo Radleys (Rough Trade 12" EP *Kaleidoscope*)
20. Heather – The Wedding Present (Peel Session 28.10.90)
19. The Ship Song – Nick Cave & The Bad Seeds (Mute LP *The Good Son*)
18. Don't Talk, Just Kiss – The Wedding Present (RCA 12" *Brassneck* B-side)
17. The Only One I Know – The Charlatans (Situation Two LP *Some Friendly*)
16. November Spawned a Monster – Morrissey (HMV 7")
-15. White Lightning – The Fall (Cog Sinister 12")
14. Big – New Fast Automatic Daffodils (Playtime 12")
13. Different Drum – The Lemonheads (Roughneck 7")
12. I'm Hardly Ever Wrong – Would Be's (Decoy 7")
11. Everything Flows – Teenage Fanclub (Paperhouse LP *A Catholic Education*)
10. Loving You – The Orb (Peel Session: 3.12.89)
9. Corduroy – The Wedding Present (RCA 12" EP *3 Songs*)
8. Step On – Happy Mondays (Factory 12")
7. Make Me Smile (Come Up & See Me) – The Wedding Present (RCA 12" EP *3 Songs*)
6. All On You (Perfume) – Paris Angels (Sheer Joy 7")
5. Tunic (Song For Karen) – Sonic Youth (Geffen LP *Goo*)
4. Like a Daydream – Ride (Creation 12" EP *Play*)
3. Dreams Burn Down – Ride (Creation LP *Nowhere*)
2. Soon – My Bloody Valentine (Creation 12" EP *Glider*)
1. Bill is Dead – The Fall (Cog Sinister LP *Extricate*)

1991

First, we should be clear that in December 1991 Peel didn't, as is often claimed, collect the votes, decide the chart was crap and refuse to play it. He actually binned it half way through the voting process, with the determining factor the low number of votes rather than the poor quality of what listeners were choosing. While many appear to think the 1991 chart had proved to be one conservative festive fifty too many, the facts suggest it was rather the listeners themselves, and not Peel, who were finding little interest in the vote. Just because the chart did, eventually, turn out to be a fairly predictable one shouldn't be used to justify a revisionist account of what actually happened. If the first edition contributed to that misunderstanding, I apologise: it was essentially a lazy judgement on my part (and arose partly because I really liked the phrase 'the predictable indulgence the chart had become' and wanted to use it), and something that I'm keen to correct here.

In some ways, this may have acted as a helpful 'good behaviour' warning to voters, who campaigned repeatedly for some time for this chart to be broadcast and would, perhaps, be less likely again to risk the future of a much loved institution due to their own tardiness. That the same thing never happened again perhaps suggests that it either worked, or that Peel was unwilling to put himself in the position again of standing in the way of those who loved the chart, whatever its blemishes, however long it might take them to get their act together and actually put a vote in, knowing that he'd never hear the last of it. It's almost as if the festive fifty had taken on a kind of Frankensteinian life of its own where apathy from either voters or Peel himself could never quite kill what had been created, however occasionally monstrous Peel found it.

Following continued pressure throughout 1992, Peel began to relent, saying he wouldn't compile the chart himself or broadcast it but, should a listener be willing to do so, he'd send him or her the entries to carry out the task on his behalf. There was little doubt that someone would take up the offer and eventually the chart was put together by a listener in Sheffield. The 1992 chart went ahead as planned and then, at the beginning of 1993, Peel announced that he would broadcast the 1991 results after all, not in a series of special shows, but track by track during the year. He did so and the number one was finally revealed and broadcast in July 1993, not that there was any great surprise surrounding the selection.

While it's hard to contest the prevailing view that the chart was of a generally predictable nature, perhaps this was understandable in a year that saw the breakthrough success of Nirvana's *Nevermind* as well as The Wedding Present's powerful resurfacing with *Seamonsters*. Add in a popular Fall LP and the final offering from the much-loved Pixies and you could probably have accounted for around a third of the chart before we got started. Another band to join them with multiple entries were Peel favourites Babes In Toyland, who followed a single entry in 1990 with four tracks of the seven on the mini-LP *To Mother*, plus an entry for the 'Handsome & Gretel' single – not something that would have displeased the DJ, you imagine.

Amazingly, this was also the first festive fifty in which the number of bands featuring at least one female member finally reached double figures. Make of that what you will, but it was an area in which the 1991 chart could hardly be accused of merely mimicking the pattern of most festive fifties since the mid-eighties. Other notable appearances included a first festive fifty outing for Pavement (well, unless you count the 1992 chart, which had already been broadcast before this was heard, of course), alongside what we assumed would be a last appearance for My Bloody Valentine but wasn't. There was a final appearance also for Factory Records after twelve successive years in the chart, courtesy of Electronic's 'Get the Message', although the by then dead and much lamented label would return for a triumphant cameo in the all-time chart of 1999.

Slint got a deserved entry, from their *Spiderland* LP, a release that would go on to be among the most influential of the nineties, while Peel favourites like 70 Gwen Party and Foreheads in a Fishtank enjoyed a solitary encounter apiece with the chart. The Too Pure label, which would go on to be a frequent visitor to these parts during the decade to come, appeared for the first time, with two entries including the first from PJ Harvey, who'd still be around more than twenty years hence with little sign of running out of steam.

And then there were the 'shoegazers', among the most maligned and stereotyped of all musical sub-genres. Taking their inspiration from such fine eighties bands as Cocteau Twins, Jesus and March Chain and My Bloody Valentine, they mixed the ethereal, the enigmatic and the feedback drenched while, so it was alleged, looking at their shoes. Ride had broken down the door in the previous year and through it they swept, including Moose, who many continue to regard as the band who originated the phrase, so intense was the inspection of their own shoelaces while they , and here joined by the likes of Slowdive and Chapterhouse, plus FF non-virgins the Boo Radleys, in the greatest festive fifty love-in for their often derided creed. While Peel loved many of these bands, what they represented en masse contributed greatly to the chart's conservatism: this was, when it came down to it, very much a festive fifty for those who loved their guitars so much they could barely look up from them.

The 1991 chart does feature the second narrowest spread of acts since the all-time charts ended: 28 in all, which is one higher than the Smiths-dominated year of 1987. Yet in terms of the number of new bands and artists, the number (18) is the same as the previous year and only one year (also, perhaps strangely, 1987) had featured more debutants. While a very good argument could be advanced for the tracks concerned showing less quality than in other years, such a criticism had been levelled by Peel at several of its predecessors and therefore it's hard to make a special case of pointing the finger at this one. Howver, if it's true – as appears the case – that fewer voters took part than in previous years, it would have been nice if they'd taken advantage of the presumably lower threshold needed for entry to get a bit more variety in there.

1991 Phantom Fifty
Broadcast dates: 8 January to 2 July 1993

50. Nick Cave Dolls – Bongwater (Shimmy Disc LP *The Power of Pussy* – actually released 1990)
49. Car Wash Hair – Mercury Rev (Mint Films 7")
48. Breed – Nirvana (Geffen LP *Nevermind*)
47. Bird Dream of the Olympus Mons – Pixies (4AD LP *Trompe Le Monde*)
46. Motorway to Roswell – Pixies (4AD LP *Trompe Le Monde*)
45. Missing The Moon – Field Mice (Sarah 12")
44. Gorgeous Blue Flower in My Garden – Th' Faith Healers (Too Pure 12" EP *A Picture of Health*)
43. So What About It? – The Fall (Cog Sinister LP *Shift-work*)
42. Ripe – Babes In Toyland (Twin-Tone LP *To Mother*)
41. The Mixer – The Fall (Cog Sinister LP *Shift-work*)
40. Get the Message – Electronic (Factory 7")
39. Primus – Babes In Toyland (Twin-Tone LP *To Mother*)
38. No Escape from Heaven – Curve (Anxious 12" EP *Blindfold*)
37. To Here Knows When – My Bloody Valentine (Creation LP *Loveless*)
36. Like a Virgin – Teenage Fanclub (Creation LP *The King*)
35. The War Against Intelligence – The Fall (Cog Sinister LP *Shift-work*)
34. Summer Babe – Pavement (Drag City 7")
33. Pearl – Chapterhouse (Dedicated 7")
32. Octopussy – The Wedding Present (RCA LP *Seamonsters*)
31. Laugh My Head Off – Babes In Toyland (Twin-Tone LP *To Mother*)
30. Catatonic - Babes In Toyland (Twin-Tone LP *To Mother*)
29. Sexuality – Billy Bragg (Go! Discs 7")
28. Auto Killer UK – 70 Gwen Party (Snape 7" *Helier Party* B-side)
27. Siva – Smashing Pumpkins (Caroline LP *Gish*)
26. Planet of Sound – Pixies (4AD LP *Trompe Le Monde*)
25. Lithium – Nirvana (Geffen LP *Nevermind*)
24. High Tension Line – The Fall (Cog Sinister 7" – released December 1990)
23. Good Morning, Captain – Slint (Touch & Go LP *Spiderland*)
22. Rotterdam – The Wedding Present (RCA LP *Seamonsters*)
21. Happy Shopper – Foreheads in a Fishtank (Stuf 7" *She Loves You Yeah* B-side)
20. Catch the Breeze – Slowdive (Creation 12" EP *Holding Our Breath*)
19. Finest Kiss – Boo Radleys (Rough Trade 12" EP *Every Heaven*)
18. Handsome & Gretel – Babes In Toyland (Peel Session 18/8/91)
17. Suzanne – Moose (Hut 12" EP *Cool Breeze*)
16. Drain You – Nirvana (Geffen LP *Nevermind*)
15. Black Metallic – The Catherine Wheel (Fontana 7")
14. Fleshworld – The Wedding Present (RCA 12" *Lovenest* B-side)
13. Some Fool's Mess – Gallon Drunk (Clawfist 7")
12. Dare – The Wedding Present (RCA LP *Seamonsters*)
11. Higher Than The Sun – Primal Scream (Creation LP *Screamadelica*)
10. Teenage Whore – Hole (Caroline LP *Pretty on the Inside*)
9. A Lot of Wind – The Fall (Cog Sinister LP *Shift-work*)
8. Dalliance – The Wedding Present (RCA LP *Seamonsters*)
7. Burn Black – Hole (Sub Pop US Import 7" *Dicknail* B-side)

6. The Concept – Teenage Fanclub (Creation LP *Bandwagonesque*)
5. Star Sign – Teenage Fanclub (Creation LP *Bandwagonesque*)
4. Edinburgh Man – The Fall (Cog Sinister LP *Shiftwork*)
3. Ten Little Girls – Curve (Anxious 12" EP *Blindfold*)
2. Dress – PJ Harvey (Too Pure 7")
1. Smells Like Teen Spirit – Nirvana (Geffen LP *Nevermind*)

1992

I suppose the obvious question to ask is why, after ditching the festive fifty so dramatically a year earlier, Peel chose to reinstate it or even show any apparent reluctance to do so. We've perhaps already answered it: ultimately this is a listener's chart and, following its abandonment due to voter apathy, it was returned to its rightful place in the Xmas schedule largely because listeners had been making their displeasure about the decision known throughout the year: even if Peel had wanted to see the back of it, and there's no solid evidence that he did, he may well have asked himself whether it was worth the hassle. By this stage, Peel had already agreed to allow the 1991 votes to be counted and this had been the clearest indication among those who, like me, fretted about the threat of a permanent abandonment that the festive fifty wasn't quite dead and buried yet.

Indeed, it seemed Peel's listeners were determined to enforce their right to have whatever chart they bloody well liked because this festive fifty contained the largest number of tracks never before played by Peel in any chart before or since (seven), including the three tracks from Sugar's *Copper Blue* album. Similarly, the failure to place The Fall's 'Kimble' any higher than number 34 despite John's ceaseless advocation of its merits was, on its own, the most obvious display of voter independence since the Stone Roses rebellion of 1989. Surprisingly, however, he revealed during the broadcast that his own number one would have been a different Fall track, their version of 'Legend of Xanadu' which became the highest placed track from a magazine compilation in festive fifty history.

A second question might be, having reinstated it, what made Peel refrain this year from chucking the votes into a drawer again. Presumably voters, chastened from the experience of last year, had got more involved in the process from a decently early stage this time. Despite the 'Kindle' and *Copper Blue* incidents, presumably he was also a little bit happier this year with what the votes were coming in for. While The Wedding Present, who'd released a single a month in that year, were always firm favourites to have the most entries, their overall total of seven (6 A-sides and 1 B) was only one more than refreshing new(ish) band on the festive fifty block Pavement. 'Getting a bit silly' was Peel's comment on The Wedding Present's accumulation of entries, but presumably the inclusion of tracks by Disposable Heroes of Hiphoprisy, Datblygu, Future Sound of London and Dr Devious did much to pacify those who, like Peel, yearned for a more varied chart. A certain sparkle was added that had arguably been lacking too often in recent years and, if listeners chose to be contrary and vote in Suede as well, perhaps this displayed a kind of awkwardness on their part that he could reluctantly admire.

That said, the decision to broadcast this chart and not that of the previous year certainly can't have had anything to do with an increase in the range of new or different bands. There were 18 acts new to the festive fifty here, exactly the same as in 1991, while the number of different acts featured overall – 29 – was only one more than in the previous year's abandoned listing.

The shadow of 1991 hung across the chart in other ways, with several of the entries having histories going well back into the previous year. The excellent Welsh band Datblygu's 'Popeth' had come out on a cassette the previous year. The song had also appeared in a Peel session in that year, subsequently released in 1992, hence its qualification for this chart. Both Pavement's 'Summer Babe' and Babes In Toyland's 'Handsome & Gretel' made the chart for the second successive year, by virtue of their appearances on the *Slanted & Enchanted* and *Fontanelle* albums respectively. The entry for KLF & Extreme Noise Terror's '3 am Eternal' arose from a recording of their performance of the song on Top of the Pops at Christmas 1991, while Pond's 'Young Splendor' had also had a release in late 1991.

The phenomenon affected the top of the chart too. The third placed track, Ministry's 'Jesus Built My Hotrod had been released as a single on 7 November 1991 and therefore had had an additional two months to build up its momentum among FF voters before its appearance on the *Psalm 69* album secured its eligibility here. And, as if to ensure that the ghost of that gap year of 1991 was determined to cast its aggrieved influence over this chart to a maximum degree, the number one single didn't enjoy any form of release in 1992. It was a close thing too, with Bang Bang Machine's 'Geek Love' edging out PJ Harvey only on a count of the most number one votes after the two tracks had finished level on points. 'Geek Love' is indeed a superb record and a deserved number one and Peel had stated of the self-released single that had the band never released another record, they'd still have achieved more than most people do in their lives. Yet it's questionable whether the single should have qualfied for this festive fifty at all. It appeared as the lead track on the *Geek* EP in late 1991, having been recorded in August and September prior to its release soon afterwards. The single's release date is crucial here because, if it enjoyed a release in December, festive fifty precedent would have rendered it eligible for the 1992 festive fifty. As a home-made release, though, its date of issue remains unclear, hence the questions regarding its eligibility.

Peel played the track for the first time in his show of 5 January 1992, which perhaps helped him to decide on its viability for inclusion here. In the event, he allowed it in, in the process denying PJ Harvey the number one and, we would subsequently discover, placing her at number two for the second successive year. At over nine minutes in length, 'Geek Love' also topped the long-standing record of 'Stairway To Heaven' as the longest track to make number one in a festive fifty, although the record has been beaten since. Ignore me at your peril, 1991 seemed to be saying; I will cast a shadow over you, your children and your children's children. Or over the following year, anyway.

1992 Festive Fifty

Broadcast dates: 18, 19 & 25 December; 1 January

50. The Birmingham School of Business School – The Fall (Fontana LP *Code: Selfish*)
49. All in the Mind – Verve (Hut CD single)
48. Helpless – Sugar (Creation LP *Copper Blue*)
47. Conduit For Sale – Pavement (Big Cat LP *Slanted & Enchanted*)
46. Falling – The Wedding Present (RCA 7" *Silver Shorts* B-side)
45. Taillights Fade – Buffalo Tom (Situation Two CD single)
44. 3 am Eternal – KLF & Extreme Noise Terror (KLF Communications 7")
43. On the Road Again – Big Stick (Albertine US CD *Drag Racing Underground* – released 1991)
42. Circa 1762 – Pavement (Peel Session 23/6/92)
41. Sticky – The Wedding Present (RCA 7")
40. Leave Them All Behind – Ride (Creation 12")
39. Lazarus – Boo Radleys (Creation 12")
38. Television, the Drug of the Nation – Disposable Heroes of Hiphoprisy (4th & Broadway CD *Hypocrisy is the Greatest Luxury*)
37. Summer Babe (Winter Version) – Pavement (Big Cat LP *Slanted & Enchanted*)
36. Tearing Water – Love Cup (Twelve Inch 7" *1*)
-35. In the Mouth a Desert – Pavement (Big Cat LP *Slanted & Enchanted*)
34. Kimble – The Fall (Peel Session 19/1/92)
33. Teethgrinder – Therapy? (A&M 7")
32. Favor – Arcwelder (Duophonic 7")
31. Happy Busman – Frank & Walters (Go! Discs/Setanta 7")
-30. The Language of Violence – Disposable Heroes of Hiphoprisy (4th & Broadway CD *Hypocrisy is the Greatest Luxury*)
29. Popeth – Datblygu (Ankst LP *BBC Peel Sessions*. Session was broadcast 9.2.91 but collection released in 1992)
28. Winona – Drop Nineteens (Hut 12")
27. Young Splendor – Pond (Tim/Kerr 7" – released 1991. Also on Sub Pop LP Pond, released 2.1.93)
26. Theresa's Sound World – Sonic Youth (Geffen LP *Dirty*)
25. Cyber Dream – VR ft Dr Devious & His Wisemen (Indisc CD)
24. Blue Eyes – The Wedding Present (RCA 7")
23. 100% - Sonic Youth (Geffen LP *Dirty*)
22. Handsome & Gretel – Babes In Toyland (Southern LP *Fontanelle*)

21. A Good Idea – Sugar (Creation LP *Copper Blue*)
20. Blue Room (Pt 1)– The Orb (Big Life 12" single)
19. Love Slave – The Wedding Present (RCA 7")
18. Silver Shorts – The Wedding Present (RCA 7")
17. Sugar Kane – Sonic Youth (Geffen LP *Dirty*)
16. Changes – Sugar (Creation LP *Copper Blue*)
15. The Drowners – Suede (Nude 12")
14. Flying Saucer – The Wedding Present (RCA 7")
13. Reverence – Jesus & Mary Chain (Blanco y Negro 7")
12. Ed's Babe – The Fall (Fontana CD single)
11. Papua New Guinea – Future Sound of London (Jumpin' & Pumpin' 12")
10. Here – Pavement (Big Cat LP *Slanted & Enchanted*)
9. Bruise Violet – Babes In Toyland (Southern LP *Fontanelle*)
8. Trigger Cut – Pavement (Big Cat LP *Slanted & Enchanted*)
7. Youth Against Fascism – Sonic Youth (Geffen LP *Dirty*)
6. Free Range – The Fall (Cog Sinister 7")
5. The Legend of Xanadu – The Fall (NME V/A CD Ruby Trax)
4. Come Play With Me – The Wedding Present (RCA 7")
3. Jesus Built My Hotrod – Ministry (Sire 12")
2. Sheela-Na-Gig – PJ Harvey (Too Pure LP *Dry*)
1. Geek Love – Bang Bang Machine (Jimmi Kidd Rekordz 12" – released 1991)

1993

The first ever festive fifty to be broadcast in one show, on Christmas Day evening, continued the chart's rehabilitation following its near-death experience in 1991 and, with the unpleasantness around the phantom fifty by now neatly cleared up and filed away, it seemed we could get on with the business of generating a yearly top fifty with the threat of any further repercussions, if not lifted, then at least greatly reduced. In that spirit, a number of historic barriers were broken down. The uncompromising title of the number one was hailed by Peel as a welcome message in 'this depraved year', its literal call to arms against the far right seeing Chumbawamba make a triumphant return to the festive fifty, alongside Credit To The Nation, who'd by now established themselves as the indie kids' hip hop band of choice.

Peel Session entries featured frequently in the countdown. Although some of these, such as The Fall's 'Ladybird (Green Grass)' were purely selections the DJ preferred over the LP version, PJ Harvey's 'Wang Dang Doodle' and 'Naked Cousin' were both recorded exclusively for a session, though the former had since gained an official release as the B-side to Harvey's 'Man-Size' singlw (its main track was the artist's first A-side not to feature in a festive fifty, incidentally). Peel also chose the session version of Transglobal Underground's 'Sirius B' for broadcast, over the 12" single's wonderfully titled 'Eating Mum & Dad For Breakfast' mix or the version on the *Dream of 100 Nations* album. And we also got the very first festive fifty airing for a session track from someone else's show when Peel chose to play the Mark Goodier session version of 'Glam Racket' in the countdown.

Interestingly, The Fall's achievement of ten entries was not greeted with anything like the displeasure generated by The Smiths' mass domination of 1987 or even Peel's mildly caustic reaction to The Wedding Present's seven entries in 1992. His comment that the situation was 'thoroughly bizarre' might suggest Peel was applying a different logic when it came to his favourite band, although it's not as if the two other bands were very far down his personal approval list either. Perhaps it was simply another welcome sign that, with the impact of greater variety elsewhere in the chart, his tolerance levels had been adjusted accordingly.

One of the undoubted highlights of the chart came with the appearance of New Bad Things with 'I Suck' at number 16. Although the record would gain an official release (with different, and nowhere near as good, lyrics) in the following year, the original release proved impossible to track down in the UK even on import and, as Peel mentioned in the broadcast, it became commonly accepted that he possessed the only copy in the country, which suggests that those who voted for it here had either taped it from the radio or simply had it lodged blissfully in their memories, which would be understandable, or that the votes all came from abroad. There were, after all, 610 copies of this disc somewhere in the world. Anyway, it was a gratifyingly high placing for a unique record and one of those occasions where an entry in the FF genuinely reflected what the Peel show was really about. The applause after the singer reveals he doesn't have a job, incidentally, was sampled from Cheap Trick's *Live At Budokhan* album.

When playing the entry from Cornershop at number 17, Peel noted that this was probably the best ever year for bands of Asian origin. While the threshold for this achievement was a pretty low one, it was certainly the case that Senser, Transglobal Underground, Cornershop and, yet to be announced at that point, Voodoo Queens all added more than simple ethnic variety to this festive fifty. With the exception of the last band, who were pleasing on the ear but had nothing especially new to offer, all added something genuinely dynamic and innovative to the chart, though only Cornershop went on to enjoy any kind of extended relationship with it.

The Domino label secured its first ever festive fifty entry, kind of. The label was responsible for the UK release of Sebadoh's 'Soul & Fire' but Peel opted to play the US Sub Pop release in the broadcast. This minor setback wouldn't hold the label back from becoming a force in the chart right into the Dandelion years, becoming a home to, among others, Will Oldham, who made the first of surprisingly few appearances here in his Palace Brothers guise, also on the US Drag City release as opposed to the Big Cat one available within these shores.

In the battle for the top spot, I had 'French Disko' as a nailed-on certainty, so experienced that all-too familiar feeling of top end dizziness and existential crisis when it came in at number five. Got to be 'Rid of Me' then, I thought, only for it to be announced at number four, giving PJ Harvey her third top five entry in as many years. Didn't anticipate the real number one – got to be honest - or even the rest of the top three. Peel drew attention to the fact that there were a lot of females at the top end of the chart this year: indeed, the lead vocalist on each of the top six entries was a woman. As it was only two years since bands including female members had got into double figures for the first time, this represented a significant change that had taken a peculiarly long time to come about: nineteen of the tracks in the chart were by bands that featured at least one female member.

1993 Festive Fifty
Broadcast: 25 December

50. War – The Fall (Volume Magazine V/A CD *Volume Eight*)
49. Sirius B – Transglobal Underground (Peel Session 2.4.93)
48. It's a Curse – The Fall (Permanent LP *The Infotainment Scan*)
47. Beautiful Son – Hole (City Slang 12")
46. Lip Gloss – Pulp (Island CD single)
45. Rape Me – Nirvana (Geffen LP *In Utero*)
44. Lights Go Down – Madder Rose (Seed CD *Bring It Down*)
43. Behind the Counter – The Fall (Permanent 12" EP *Behind the Counter*)
42. Get Me – Dinosaur Jr (Blanco y Negro LP *Where You Been*)
41. A Past Gone Mad – The Fall (Permanent LP *The Infotainment Scan*)
40. Scentless Apprentice – Nirvana (Geffen LP *In Utero*)
39. Jenny Ondioline – Stereolab (Duophonic 7" *French Disko* B-side)
38. Stutter – Elastica (Deceptive 7")
37. City Sickness – Tindersticks (This Way Up 7")
36. Beautiful John – Madder Rose (Seed CD *Bring It Down*)
35. Barney (...And Me) – Boo Radleys (Creation CD *Giant Steps*)
34. Good Judge of Character – J Church (Allied Recordings US Import LP *Quetzalcoatl*)
33. Atta Girl – Heavenly (Sarah 7")
32. Naked Cousin – PJ Harvey (Peel Session – 12.3.93)
31. Creep – Radiohead (Capitol CD single)
30. Marbles – Tindersticks (This Way Up LP *The First Tindersticks Album*)
29. Ladybird (Green Grass) – The Fall (Peel Session 13.3.93)
28. Timebomb – Chumbawamba (One Little Indian 7")
27. Raindrops – Tindersticks (This Way Up LP *The First Tindersticks Album*)
26. Service – The Fall (Permanent LP *The Infotainment Scan*)
25. Olympia – Hole (Peel Session 16.4.93)

24. Call it What You Want – Credit to the Nation (One Little Indian CD single)
23. Web In Front – Archers of Loaf (Alias US import 7" EP *The Loaf's Revenge*)
22. I'm Going to Spain – The Fall (Permanent LP *The Infotainment Scan*)
21. Eject – Senser (Ultimate CD single)
20. Glam Racket – The Fall (Mark Goodier Session 17.5.1993)
19. Lost in Music - The Fall (Permanent LP *The Infotainment Scan*)
18. Wang Dang Doodle – PJ Harvey (Island CD single *Man-size* B-side – originally recorded for Peel Session broadcast 12.3.93)
17. England's Dreaming – Cornershop (Wiiija CD single *Lock Stock & Double Barrel*)
16. I Suck – New Bad Things (Rainforest US 7" *Concrete* B-side)
15. 50 Ft Queenie – PJ Harvey (Island CD *Rid of Me*)
14. Razzamatazz – Pulp (Gift CD single *Razzmatazz*)
13. Regret – New Order (London LP *Republic*)
12. Hear No Bullshit (On Fire Mix) – Credit to the Nation & Chumbawamba (One Little Indian CD single)
11. Why Are People Grudgeful? – The Fall (Permanent 7")
10. Government Administrator – Eggs (Hemiola 7")
9. Ohio River Boat Song – Palace Brothers (Drag City US 7")
8. Cannonball – The Breeders (4AD CD single)
7. Soul & Fire – Sebadoh (Sub Pop US 7")
6. Supermodel Superficial - Voodoo Queens (Too Pure 7")
5. French Disko – Stereolab (Duophonic 7")
4. Rid of Me – PJ Harvey (Island CD *Rid of Me*)
3. Her Jazz – Huggy Bear (Wiiija/Catcall 7")
2. Swim – Madder Rose (Seed 7")
1. Enough is Enough – Chumbawamba & Credit to the Nation (One Little Indian CD single)

1994

Although Mark E. Smith would add to his increasing collection of festive fifty records by becoming the first, and so far only, artist to appear in the top two positions with two different bands, there was to be no continuation of The Fall's chart domination from the previous year. Indeed, we got past the number three position having heard only twice from them, both in the chart's lower reaches. Do we conclude from this that the *Middle Class Revolt* album was spectacularly less well-received than the previous year's multiply represented album? Or that Fall voters felt embarrassed at their extravagances of the previous year and determined to cast their nets more widely this time round? Or perhaps it was simply the case that, given the triumphant nature of Mr Smith's collaboration with fellow Manc legends Inspiral Carpets together with the peculiar magnificence of 'Hey! Student', all the Fall votes got funneled into a much smaller space.

Whatever was the case, both The Fall and The Wedding Present occupied a far smaller proportion of the chart than had been the case in recent times. The latter's *Watusi* fell someway short of the performance of their first three albums, though it still generated four entries, albeit one broadcast in its Peel Session form. With Nirvana saying farewell to the chart for rather different reasons, this festive fifty had about it a sense of zealous foraging for new heroes: both Pulp and Ash gave warning of their intentions for the following year, while Elastica and to a lesser extent Sleeper stamped the chart with the unquestionable buzz of excitement that followed them around on the fringes of what was known as Britpop.

For the second year running, Peel made reference in the countdown to the number of records featuring female vocalists in the chart, noting that Sleeper's number twenty entry was the ninth such entry: there would go on to be fifteen in total. He also made another reference to the number of tunes featuring 'cute kids slapping guitar' in the early stages of the second broadcast, though given that four of the six tracks he referred to were Fall and Wedding Present efforts, the word 'kids' seemed a trifle misplaced. It was also a slightly less convincing critique, certainly in comparison with the previous occasion on which he'd used a similar term, as the earlier part of the chart had allowed in the likes of Transglobal Underground and Underworld and he'd later express great pleasure at the appearance of H Foundation's

'Laika' at number eleven and LSG's 'Hearts' at five, both examples of the kind of sumptuous electronica he was introducing his audience to in those days which, you sense, wouldn't have got a sniff in the late eighties. Orbital also made their first appearance, while the most notable label debut was from Warp, whose entry via Sabres of Paradise would be the first in a lengthy and varied association with the chart that would see them do much to eat into the 'guitars only' ethos that so stifled the chart in the eighties.

Three of the four most successful American bands in festive fifty history (Pixies being the other) all figured, with Nirvana and Sonic Youth signing off with some brilliantly executed cover versions (Leadbelly and Bowie for the former, The Carpenters for the latter). Nirvana also added 'About a Girl', an old song revisited for the band's MTV acoustic session, which had got a release in the year following Cobain's death and was thus responsible for all three entries from the band. The third of the great triumvirate, Pavement, continued to make inroads, with the magnificent 'Range Life' another particular top twenty delight, though their relationship with the chart was also on the decline ahead of a period where a return to the predominantly British nature of the early charts was on the horizon. Some might put that, rather lazily, down to Britpop, but in truth it probably had more to do with the absence in the future of these great standard-bearers of US music.

As it was, 1994 still retained a distinctly transatlantic feel to it. Hole managed a couple of entries, Sebadoh made their second and final visit to the chart and there were top ten places for festive fifty one-offs from Veruca Salt and Done Lying Down. Madder Rose notched two further appearances, one of which ('Panic On') had never been played by Peel, one of only two such entries, the other coming from another American band, Mazzy Star. Beck also secured his only entry, with his iconic slacker anthem 'Loser', with Peel commenting during the countdown that he didn't believe him to be the fly-by-night flavour of the month so many assumed him to be. He was certainly right on that score, although Beck would play little part in the Peel shows of the future and absolutely no part in any other festive fifty. Steve Albini, having appeared in the past with Big Black and as the producer of a whole load of successful festive fifty acts, also got back into the festive fifty as a recording artist, with Shellac.

Nirvana'a 'About a Girl' wasn't the only track to enjoy a revival here. Pulp, now in the full flush of commercial success over ten years after their first Peel Session had been broadcast, scored an entry with 'Babies', which had initially been released as a single two years earlier. They also appeared twice more, including an entry for 'Common People', which was then only available in session form and would return to the chart, gloriously, in the form of its official release the following year.

1994 Festive Fifty

Broadcast dates: 17 & 23 December (Bit of a strange one: the first eight tracks were revealed in the first programme, with the rest of the chart in the second one. That 17 December show is a bit of a belter though, featuring as it does special Xmas sessions recorded by The Fall and Elastica)

50. Taal Zaman – Transglobal Underground (Nation LP *International Times*)
49. Angel in a Half Shirt – Tuscadero (Teenbeat US import 7")
48. Swallow – Sleeper (Indolent 7")
47. Superstar – Sonic Youth (A&M V/A CD *If I Were a Carpenter*)
46. Girl With a Crooked Eye – ROC (Little Star CD single)
45. Doll Parts – Hole (Geffen 7")
44. About a Girl – Nirvana (Geffen CD *MTV Unplugged in New York*)
43. Dirty Epic – Underworld (Junior Boys's Own CD *Dubnobasswithmyheadman*)
42. Line Up – Elastica (Deceptive CD single)
41. M5 – The Fall (Peel Session 12.1.94)
40. Where Did You Sleep Last Night? – Nirvana (Geffen CD *MTV Unplugged in New York*)
39. Spangle – The Wedding Present (Peel Session 16.4.94)
38. City Dweller – The Fall (Permanent CD *Middle Class Revolt*)
37. So Long, Baby – The Wedding Present (Island CD *Watusi*)
36. Charged Up – Salt Tank (Internal 12")
35. Panic On – Madder Rose (Atlantic LP *Panic On*)
34. Cut Your Hair – Pavement (Big Cat CD single)
33. Petrol – Ash (Infectious CD *Trailer*)

32. Loser – Beck (Geffen CD *Mellow Gold*)
31. Are We Here? (Industry Standard Edit) – Orbital (Internal CD single)
30. Click Click – The Wedding Present (Island CD *Watusi*)
29. Wilmot – Sabres of Paradise (Warp CD *Haunted Dancehall*)
28. Uncle Pat – Ash (Infectious CD *Trailer*)
27. The Man Who Sold the World – Nirvana (Geffen CD *MTV Unplugged in New York*)
26. One Summer Night – that dog (Volume Magazine V/A CD *Volume Nine*)
25. Fade Into You – Mazzy Star (Capitol CD *So Tonight That I Might See*)
24. The Dog & Pony Show – Shellac (Touch & Go CD *At Action Park*)
23. Babies – Pulp (Island 12"EP *The Sisters*)
22. Gold Soundz – Pavement (Big Cat 7")
21. Common People – Pulp (Peel Session 22.10.94)
20. Delicious – Sleeper (Indolent 7")
19. Car Song – Madder Rose (Atlantic CD *Panic On*)
18. Crow – Shellac (Touch & Go CD *At Action Park*)
17. Miss World – Hole (Geffen CD *Live Through This*)
16. Rebound – Sebadoh (Domino 7")
15. Swimming Pools, Movie Stars – The Wedding Present (Island CD *Watusi*)
14. Range Life – Pavement (Big Cat LP *Crooked Rain, Crooked Rain*)
13. Do You Remember the First Time? (Radio Edit) – Pulp (Island CD single DJ Promo)
12. Jack Names the Planets – Ash (LaLaLand 7")
11. Laika – H Foundation (Bomba 12")
10. Just a Misdemeanour – Done Lying Down (Abstract Sounds 7")
9. Ping Pong – Stereolab (Duophonic CD single)
8. Sour Times – Portishead (Go! Beat CD *Dummy*)
7. Waking Up – Elastica (Melody Maker V/A Cassette – Recording from Radio One Evening Session)
6. Hearts – LSG (Supersition German Import 12" EP *Blueprint*)
5. Caught by the Fuzz – Supergrass (Parlophone CD single)
4. Connection – Elastica (Deception CD single)
3. Seether – Veruca Salt (Hi-Rise 12")
2. Hey! Student– The Fall (Peel Session 12.1.94, entitled 'Student')
1. I Want You – Inspiral Carpets ft Mark E.Smith (Mute CD single)

1995

And then, seemingly out of nowhere, came a festive fifty that Peel lavished praise on from beginning to end. He'd already employed the phrase 'top quality stuff' four tracks in and, following the broadcast of the Van Basten track, he observed that this was becoming of the best festive fifties in quite some time. Before revealing the number one, he commented that the chart had been 'an especially good one'. In what's understood to be a unique act, he even repeated the top fifteen twice in his broadcasts for the British Forces Broadcasting Service. Although this was at the request of a listener, there's no evidence of his acceding to a similar request before or since.

Dreadzone's *Second Light* and Pulp's *Different Class* albums, two particular favourites of the DJ during the period, featured heavily. Dreadzone also threw in a couple of tracks from their *Maximum* EP, making it six entries in all, topping the five that Stone Roses had achieved in 1989 to achieve the distinction of most appearances in a festive fifty for a band making all of its appearances in a single year. The two albums came from the rather well-established stables of Island and Virgin, ensuring a significant presence in the chart for major labels. However, more significantly in the longer-term, there was a debut for the Scottish indie Chemikal Underground, which featuredwith Bis at number 47.

Bis were one of those bands whom Peel's listeners either took too or declared a distinct animosity for, and there's plenty of that kind of thing in this chart too, which may another reason why it held so much affection for him. The 'I Liked Pulp in the Eighties and they were better then, a faction that clearly didn't include Peel, were out in force, stung by their heroes' adoption by the Britpop publicity machine. Similarly The Bluetones contained rather more than a tincture of commercial Britpop sensibility and thus had little appeal for a section of Peel's audience, many of whom also regarded the presence of Ash, now reaching the peak of their FF powers, as little more than a pretty ordinary guitar band. Peel stuck by them all, while also revelling in the presence here of the likes of Van Basten and Dave Clarke, a reminder that – as with his adoption of Altered Images in the early eighties – he wasn't only about challenging his audience in terms of championing the raucous, uncompromising and vulgar: a good tune was a good tune and what really made him happy, as his reaction to this chart demonstrates, was recognition for both.

In many ways, it's the broadcast itself that makes this such an invigorating experience, variety being offered by the broadcast of some cracking session tracks rather than official versions and even live festival versions of tracks by Zion Youth and Pulp adding to the sense of enjoyment enhanced by Peel's unusually upbeat delivery. Indeed, when I got leathered one evening in a caravan in Wales, this was the festive fifty recording to put on. The listening experience, I can now confirm, is enhanced still further when you yomp around bollock naked wearing only a dog poop bag (unused) on one's nether regions.

Peel played a number of tracks recorded in session in previous years, opting for the version of Dreadzone's 'Maximum' that was broadcast in August 1994, Pulp's 'Underwear, featured in session a month later, and the version of 'Feeling Numb' by The Fall that was one of the 'secular' tracks in the Xmas session broadcast in late November of that year. In the case of Hole's 'Violet', the version played had actually been broadcast in session back in 1991 but was eligible here due to its appearance on the *Ask For It* album. The Flaming Stars track was the first festive fifty entry for a band who would record more Peel sessions during the nineties (six) than anyone other than The Fall.

With the aforementioned band already well ahead of everyone else in the top band in festive fifty history stakes, Mark E. Smith took it upon himself to acquire another record, becoming the first and so far only individual to appear with three different acts in the same chart, appearing with D.O.S.E. and Long Fin Killie alongside The Fall (curiously, their appearance at number 30 with 'Bonkers in Phoenix' was the only occasion during the countdown that Peel expressed his disapproval for an entry).

At the top of the chart, with Dreadzone looking like the overall winners, if such a thing had any meaning, as we got past the number three broadcast, anyone assuming so had figured without Pulp emulating the achievement of the Jesus & Mary Chain exactly ten years earlier and grabbing the top two spots, with the track at number one becoming the first in the history of the yearly charts to do so despite having appeared in another form (due to an appearance in the same session, in fact, from which 'Underwear' had been broadcast) the previous year's festive fifty. And of course no truly great festive fifty should be without a cock-up: Peel broadcast the wrong Stereolab track at number 33, playing 'The Extension Trip' rather than the announced 'Pop Quiz'.

1995 Festive Fifty

Broadcast dates: 29 & 30 December

50. You Can't – Safe Deposit (Urban Trance 12" *Network Analysis Vol. 1*)
49. The Joke – The Fall (Permanent LP *Cerebral Caustic*)
48. Live, Love & Unity – Dreadzone (Virgin LP *Second Light*)
47. School Disco – Bis (Chemikal Underground 7" *Disco Nation 45*)
46. Thunder (Red Three) – Dave Clarke (Deconstruction – 12" EP Red Three)
45. Vow – Garbage (Discordant 7")
44. Plug Myself In (Nero Mix) - D.O.S.E ft Mark E. Smith (Coliseum/PWL International 7")
43. Angel Interceptor (Infectious CD single)
42. Is This What You Call Change? – Harvey's Rabbit (Rotator 7")
41. Afro-Left – Leftfield (Liberation CD *Leftism*)
40. Father to a Sister of Thought – Pavement (Big Cat CD *Wowee Zowee*)
39. Not Here – Solar Race (Silvertone 7")
38. King of Death Posture (Attack Version) – Van Basten (Brute 12")
37. Northern Industrial Town – Billy Bragg (Live Peel Session 13.10.95)
36. 6 am Jullander Shere – Cornershop (Wiiija CD *Woman's Gotta Have It*)
35. Captain Dread – Dreadzone (Virgin CD *Second Light*)

34. To Bring You My Love – PJ Harvey (Island CD *To Bring You My Love*)
33. Pop Quiz – Stereolab (Duophonic CD *Music for the Amorphous Body Study Center;* however the track played was 'The Extension Trip' from the Melody Maker cassette *Reading Present*)
32. Bugs – Spare Snare (Prospective 7")
31. Underwear – Pulp (Peel Session 22.10.94. Eligible version: Island LP *Different Class*)
30. Bonkers in Phoenix – The Fall (Permanent LP *Cerebral Caustic*)
29. Kiss Tomorrow Goodbye – Flaming Stars (Peel Session 8.7.95)
28. Violet – Hole (Caroline US import LP *Ask For It*. Released 1995 but featured in Peel Session broadcast 5.1.92)
27. Disco 2000 – Pulp (Island LP *Different Class*)
26. Nitro – Dick Dale (Peel Session 8.4.95)
25. My Sister – Tindersticks (This Way Up LP *Tindersticks*)
24. Don't Call Me Darling – The Fall (Permanent LP *Cerebral Caustic*)
23. Little Britain – Dreadzone (Virgin CD *Second Light*)
22. Black Steel – Tricky (Fourth & Broadway/Island *Maxinquaye*)
21. Slight Return – The Bluetones (Superior Quality Recordings 7")
20. All-Nighter – Elastica (Deceptive CD *Elastica*)
19. If Fingers Were Xylophones – Gorky's Zygotic Mynci (Ankst 7")
18. Bleed – Catatonia (Nursery CD single)
17. Down By the Water – PJ Harvey (Island CD *To Bring You My Love*)
16. Fight the Power 95 (Dreadzone Remix) – Dreadzone (Virgin 12" EP *Maximum*)
15. Bluetonic – The Bluetones (Superior Quality Recordings 7")
14. Dance of Live (live) – Zion Train (Live Recording from Camden Festival)
13. Alright – Supergrass (Peel Session 4.2.95)
12. Mis-Shapes – Pulp (Island LP *Different Class*)
11. Send His Love To Me – PJ Harvey (Island LP *To Bring You My Love*)
10. Heads of Dead Surfers – Long Fin Killie with Mark E.Smith (Too Pure 7")
9. Maximum – Dreadzone (Peel Session 24.9.94. Elgible version: Virgin 12" EP *Maximum*)
8. I Spy – Pulp (Island LP *Different Class*)
7. Feeling Numb – The Fall (Peel Session 17.12.94, then entitled 'Numb at the Lodge')
6. Kung Fu – Ash (Infectious 7")
5. Zion Youth – Dreadzone (Virgin CD *Second Light*)
4. Girl From Mars – Ash (Infectious 7")
3. Sucker – The Wedding Present (Self-released tour 7")
2. Sorted for E's & Whizz – Pulp (Live recording from Glastonbury Festival)
1. Common People – Pulp (Island LP *Different Class*)

1996

The warm reception Peel gave to the 1995 chart suggested he was, after all, perfectly happy with a festive fifty that featured several multiple entries, despite his indications to the contrary in other years. The important thing for him, it seemed, was getting the mix right: understandably, really, because when it came down to it that was exactly what made a regular Peel show such an invigorating experience. Quality without variety wasn't enough. With that in mind, it was curious that he refrained from lavishing any such praise on the 1996 chart which not only didn't feature any band or artist more than three times, for the first time ever, but also ushered in a short three-year era in which such diversity became the norm. Not that he expressed any displeasure; indeed, the fact that he didn't comment at all on the overall quality of the chart might be regarded as some kind of tacit approval of its content: 1995 had, after all, provided a rare case of positive commentary against a recent historical background where any observations from Peel had been largely inspired by negative sentiments.

Whatever Peel's view, for a short period, it seemed that those bonds of allegiance to favourite bands that had so dictated voting patterns in the eighties no longer held sway over the chart. While the period of scattered entries that was ushered in proved a relatively show one,. even after the 1996-98 period, the phenomenon of chart domination by a band or small number of bands would be much rarer and far more understated. Just three years on from their festive fifty peak, The Fall would now find themselves in the strange position of appearing only three times yet still find themselves the most placed band, tying with Stereolab.

A fascinating eclecticism wasn't the only note struck by this chart that jarred with festive fifty history. It followed and even extended the pattern of the previous year in continuing a kind of electrification of the chart: Orbital and Underworld both made the top ten, and there were places for DJ Shadow, Forcer & Styles, Dave Clarke and Aphex Twin, among others. Super Furry Animals, Broadcast and The Delgados also made their first appearances and there was a place for the first time for eleven years for a UK number one single in the shape of Prodigy's 'Firestarter', a tune rightly celebrated for terrifying the life out of Top of the Pops-watching parents watching Top of the Pops across the nation.

Beggars Banquet made a return to the festive fifty, having had the solid good sense to put out Dick Dale's *Calling Up Spirits* album and there was even an entry for Chrysalis, who'd previously enjoyed only a minor role in the chart's history. Their release here, White Town's 'Your Woman', however, was significant as one of those records, such as Althea & Donna's 'Up Town Top Ranking' and, soon, Cornershop's 'Brimful of Asha', that followed an appearance in the festive fifty with considerable commercial success, reaching number one early the following year.

Much consternation surrounded the number 43 track. It was perhaps inevitable that at some point in a festive fifty there'd be a tune that Peel couldn't locate, but few would have guessed it would have be by Half Man Half Biscuit. At the time, when apologising for not having it to play, Peel commented that he believed there had only been one instance of his failing to play a track in a festive fifty before. Peel observers have generally regarded this as a reference to the broadcast of the wrong Stereolab track in the previous year, but in fact that had been one of three such instances. He did of course fail to play The Wedding Present's 'This Boy Can Wait' in 1986 but never appeared to realise his mistake, but did acknowledge his error after playing the wrong Pixies track a year later. This current case wasn't an error, of course, but a simple and highly unlikely case of not being able to find a track that made the chart, and it remains a singular event, not repeated even in the post-Peel years, hence my reason for considering it at some length.

Although the track in question would feature on HMHB's 'Voyage to the Bottom of the Road' album, the following year, in the process kicking off a still uninterrupted run of the the band's albums in festive fifties, at the time it had featured only in session form, and not for Peel's regular show, hence the difficulty he experienced in locating it and the reason why even the Probe Plus label couldn't help out. He had in fact broadcast the track before because the band had performed it in a session for Mark Radcliffe's show when Peel was sitting in for him. He'd eventually discover this and play the track on 28 December, just prior to re-commencing the chart at number 26. Against patterns of recent years, this was the only session track played in the countdown, in contrast to the previous year where he'd managed to play a record eight session tracks during the festive fifty. It would usher in a period in which it became much rarer for Peel to opt to play a session version over an official recording in the countdown: there would be only eleven session tracks over the remaining seven festive fifty broadcasts he oversaw, eight of these because they were only available in that form.

At the top end, having seen Bis continue their successful launch last year with a hit in both the festive fifty and the national charts, Chemikal Underground showed they really meant business by grabbing the number two and three slots. Scotland has a history of performing conspicuously well in festive fifties, but this year the nation secured a particularly impressive showing in the top five, only punctuated by two Kenickie tracks, which remain their only entries in a festive fifty. Peel said he'd assumed the band would have more entries than this in the chart: presumably their prospective domination was thwarted by Kenickie fans opting in large numbers for these two tracks. The CU label placed two Scottish bands – label owners The Delgados and the excellent Arab Strap - and both made their debut in a top four made up entirely of bands that had never featured in a previous festive fifty, the first time this had happened since 1978. Underworld, who'd only scraped into the lower reaches before that, came in at number five. It always seemed to me that the Arab Strap song was a more deserving number one, though Peel received warmly the Kenickie tune that beat them to it, which in the process became the shortest song ever to hit the top of a festive fifty.

1996 Festive Fifty

Broadcast dates: 21, 22, 28 & 29 December

50. Les Yper Yper Sound – Stereolab (Duophonic 10" *Cybele's Reverie* B-side)
49. God Show Me Magic – Super Furry Animals (Creation CD *Fuzzy Logic*)
48. The Face on the Bar Room Floor – Flaming Stars (Vinyl Japan LP *Songs from the Bar Room Floor*)
47. Out There Somewhere? (Parts I & II) – Orbital (Internal LP *Insides*)
46. Go Man Go – The Wedding Present (Cooking Vinyl CD *Mini*)
45. Kewpies Like Watermelon – Urusei Yatsura (Che Trading LP *We Are Urusei Yatsura*)
44. Sore Loser – Soul Bossa (Dishy 7")
43. A Shropshire Lad/Paintball's Coming Home – Half Man Half Biscuit (Mark Radcliffe Session 14.10.96)
42. A Design For Life – Manic Street Preachers (Sony CD *Everything Must Go*)
41. Race – Tiger (Trade 2 CD *We Are Puppets*)
40. Living Room – Broadcast (Duophonic 7")
39. Teenage Angst – Placebo (Virgin/Elevator Music CD *Placebo*)
38. Oh Yeah – Ash (Infectious CD *1977*)
37. Firestarter – The Prodigy (XL 12")
36. 2,3, Go – The Wedding Present (Cooking Vinyl CD *Saturnalia*)
35. Stem – DJ Shadow (Mo Wax CD *Introducing...*)
34. The Book Lovers – Broadcast (Duophonic CD EP *The Book Lovers*)
33. Lies, Lies & Government – Calvin Party (Probe Plus LP *Lies, Lies & Government*)
32. Babylon's Burning – Zion Train (China 12")
31. Your Woman – White Town (Chrysalis EP *Abort, Retry, Fail? (Your Woman)*)
30. Fireworks – Force & Styles (Essential Platinum 12")
29. Girl/Boy Song – Aphex Twin (Warp CD *Richard D. James LP*)
28. The State I Am In – Belle & Sebastian (Electric Honey LP *Tigermilk*)
27. Nitrus – Dick Dale (Beggars Banquet LP *Calling Up Spirits*)
26. Stunt Girl – AC Acoustics (Elemental CD single)
25. No One's Driving – Dave Clarke (Deconstruction 12")
24. Friend – Quickspace (Kitty Kitty Corporation 7")
23. Taut - John Parish & Polly Jean Harvey (Island CD *Dance Hall at Louse Point*)
22. Two Kindsa Love – John Spencer Blues Explosion (Mute CD *Now I Got Worry*)
21. Djed – Tortoise (City Slang CD *Millions Now Living Will Never Die*)
20. Fluourescences – Stereolab (Duophonic CD EP *Fluourescences*)
19. Abba on the Jukebox – Trembling Blue Stars (Shinkansen 7")
18. Ten Foot Tall – Flaming Stars (Vinyl Japan 7")
17. That Was My Veil - John Parish & Polly Jean Harvey (Island CD *Dance Hall at Louse Point*)
16. Hostile – The Fall (Jet CD *The Light User Syndrome*)
15. Goodnight – Baby Bird (Echo 7")
14. Kandy Pop – Bis (CD EP *The Secret Vampire Soundtrack*)
13. The Chiselers – The Fall (Jet CD single)
12. Brickbat – Billy Bragg (Cooking Vinyl CD *William Bloke*)
11. Cybele's Reverie – Stereolab (Duophonic CD single)
10. Girl About Town – Helen Love (Nana V/A 7" EP *Astral Angora*)
9. Why – The Sweeney (Rotator 7")
8. Patio Song – Gorky's Zygotic Mynci (Fontana CD single)
7. The Box – Orbital (Internal CD *Insides*)
6. Cheetham Hill – The Fall (Jet LP *The Light User Syndrome*)
5. Born Slippy (NUXX) – Underworld (Premier soundtrack LP *Trainspotting*)
4. Punka – Kenickie (Premier CD single)
3. Under Canvas Under Wraps – The Delgados (Chemikal Underground CD *Domestiques*)
2. The First Big Weekend – Arab Strap (Chemikal Underground CD *The Week Never Starts Around Here*)
1. Come Out 2 Nite – Kenickie (Fierce Panda 7" EP *Skillex*)

1997

Prior to the start of the countdown of what would be a truncated chart, Peel revealed, perhaps surprisingly, that he'd 'always quite enjoyed doing them'. Perhaps the much-lauded chart of 1995 and the greater spread of artists in 1996 had an influence on how he came to view the chart in that period; or perhaps his occasionally expressed reservations have led some to exaggerate his dissatisfaction with the chart. Certainly, in the years since his death, it's been common to hear and read the view that Peel hated the chart and only continued to broadcast it because of its popularity among listeners. While he did mention in 1985 that he'd considered discontinuing the festive fifty, there had been few such hints since and his that he'd deliberated in that direction and, as has been covered elsewhere in this book, the 1991 chart was abandoned largely as a result of lack of involvement from the voters rather than its inherently predictable nature. However, especially in the light of the enthusiasm he expressed, it remains a curiosity that there was only a Festive Thirty-One this year, and even that only came about late in the day and after much pleading from listeners.

Back when the first edition of this book came out, I received several requests to 'piece together' the remaining nineteen tracks, but I'm afraid I don't have the material to hand that would allow me to do so. Many have assumed that the remaining tracks played on the show on the night of broadcast, minus the Pavement session, constitute the rest of the fifty. Some have even gone so far as to suggest that it contains releases (The Verve's 'Sonnet' is the most cited example) that he would never have played were this not the case. This is completely incorrect. The other tracks are drawn from favourites of the year from John Peel's family as well as some listeners ('Sonnet' was his daughter's choice). What is baffling is that the show contains no 'new' material, making it all the more strange that it was decided there was insufficient time for a full festive fifty: he actually played 54 tracks in total during the programme.

Despite its relative brevity, it's a cracking chart, cementing any claim the mid-to-late nineties may have to the accolade of best ever festive fifty period, something which, given his comments here and elsewhere, Peel may well have agreed with himself. Stereolab came out with most entries for the second year running, including an uncanny second entry for 'Fluourescences' (not a different version – exactly the same one that was in the same position in the previous year) and the remarkable result of a collaboration with Nurse With Wound. Despite the *Levitate* album being high on the list of many fans' least favourite Fall albums, it managed a couple of entries, while the emerging Scottish powerhouses of The Delgados, Mogwai and Belle and Sebastian served notice of their longer-term intentions. Although B&S's 'Lazy Line Painter Jane' only made number five here, it would be the only track from this chart to register in the all-time festive fifty compiled two years hence.

Many of the delights of this chart, however, come not from the heavyweights but from a whole series of high quality one-off entries. 'Rapunzel' from Novak is a relentless earhole pounder of a record that lodges itself in your brain because or in spite of the random numbers in its opening and apparent Pied Piper-like tendency to drag you off somewhere and leave you entirely bewildered when you come to. Betty Davis & The Balconettes reappropriated the *Champion the Wonder Horse* theme tune to brilliant effect in celebration of kidnapped racehourse Shergar, chucking an entirely unbelievable happy ending into the mix as they did so. The Hitchers produced one of the greatest football songs of all time, seizing on the rare and subsequently unimaginable achievement of the 1992 Leeds United football team to devise and deliver the brilliant 'Strachan'.

Yet the most memorable entry was one that divided opinion in the manner of those great obscure punk records so beloved of the show twenty years earlier. A quick trawl through the internet will find records of 'critics' frothing at the mouth at the temerity of Period Pains and their attack on the depressingly popular Spice Girls. Others, including Peel, delighted in the record's awkwardly amateur stylings, enough to propel the record to the number three position. Its propensity to piss off the purists was perhaps only rivalled here by an appearance for Blur, Peel having become a great admirer of the band during that period after which they'd sat in a room with all those Pavement records to, it has to be said, highly pleasing effect. Indeed, Blur had that year become the first ever band to play a set at Peel Acres, something that would become a regular feature of the show from 1999 onwards.

Peel also paid tribute to the number of excellent small labels that both made 1997 such a memorable year and rightly gained recognition here. His comment related to the Wiiija label at number 22, but it might easily have been applied to the two entries each for Wurlitzer Jukebox and Damaged Goods, or for gratifying appearances in the top ten for Aladdin's Cave of Golf and Kitty Kitty Corporation.

Also at the top end were the highest ever placed entry for Helen Love, enjoying a brief period of omniprescence in the top ten of the chart, a telling debut from Mogwai and the first record ever to secure the distinction of number one in a festive fifty and the British singles chart. Cornershop would have to wait for the latter until 1998, courtesy of a Norman Cook remix that did much to strip away the appeal of the version that was played here, but still provided a welcome event for all that.

The chart is very much a throwback to those festive fifties that were dominated by acts from the UK and Ireland. Peel himself noted that the number 13 track was the first to originate from outside these nations and, although Daft Punk would strike a blow for France in the top ten, that would largely be the case for the remainder of the fifty. It's the only festive fifty ever not to feature a single band or artist from the United States. Unless you want to include those Pavement records devoured by Blur, of course, which would be stretching it a bit.

1997 Festive Thirty-One
Broadcast date: 23 December

31. Teenage Girl Crush – Angelica (Incredible 7")
30. Slash/Oblique – Prolapse (Radar CD *The Italian Flag*)
29. Seventeen – Hybirds (Heavenly CD EP *Take You Down*)
28. Velvet Pants – Propellerheads (Wall of Sound CD single *Spybreak!*)
27. Pull the Wires from the Wall – The Delgados (Peel Session 26.7.97)
26. Miss Modular – Stereolab (Duophonic CD single)
25. If I Die I Die – Dream City Film Club (Beggars Banquet 7")
24. Autocade – Prolapse (Radar CD single)
23. Dandelion Milk Summer – Secret Goldfish (Creeping Bent CD single)
22. Sweet Shop Avengerz – Bis (Wiiija 7")
21. Strachan – The Hitchers (Murgatroid CD *It's All Fun & Games Til Someone Loses an Eye*)
20. Fluourescences – Stereolab (Duophonic CD EP *Fluourescences*)
19. I Messiah Am Jailer – AC Acoustics (Elemental CD single)
18. Ladies & Gentlemen We Are Floating in Space – Spiritualized (Dedicated CD *Ladies & Gentlemen We Are Floating in Space BP*)
17. I'm a Mummy – The Fall (Artful CD *Levitate*)
16. Hey! Fever – Arab Strap (Chemikal Underground CD EP *The Girls of Summer*)
15. Shergar – Betty Davis & The Balconettes (Damaged Goods 7")
14. Simple Headphone Mind – Stereolab & Nurse With Wound (Duophonic 12")
13. We Crossed the Atlantic – Hydroplane (Wurlitzer Jukebox 7")
12. Dog on Wheels – Belle & Sebastian (Jeepster CD EP *Dog on Wheels*)
11. Song 2 – Blur (Food CD single)
10. The Holiday Girl (Don't Die Just Yet – Arab Strap Mix) – David Holmes (Go! Beat CD single)
9. IPC Subeditors Dictate Our Youth – Clinic (Aladdin's Cave of Golf 7")
8. Rollin' & Scratchin' – Daft Punk (Virgin CD *Homework*)
7. 4½ Inch - The Fall (Artful CD *Levitate*)
6. Rapunzel – Novak (Kitty Kitty Corporation 7")
5. Lazy Line Painter Jane – Belle & Sebastian (Jeepster CD EP *Lazy Line Painter Jane*)
4. Spice Girls (Who Do You Think You Are?) – Period Pains (Damaged Goods CD single)
3. Does Your Heart Go Boom? – Helen Love (Che Trading CD single)
2. New Paths to Helicon – Mogwai (Wurlitzer Jukebox 7")
1. Brimful of Asha (Album Version) – Cornershop (Wiiija CD single)

1998

Even set against the rollercoaster jollities of the years 1995-1997, could 1998 claim to be the most varied festive fifty ever? The trend of a wider spread of artists continued, with this time only The Delgados achieving three entries. During the countdown, Peel released the information to us that only one band would achieve this feat, meaning that anyone with at least an elementary grasp of arithmetic and anal retentive tendencies got to the number two position knowing it was now a straight fight between Gorky's Zygotic Mynci, Belle & Sebastian, Boards of Canada, Ten Benson, Clinic, Ten Benson, Solex and of course The Delgados. And those who could go beyond that and had been listening with any regularity to the Peel show during the previous months could judge pretty well where the smart money was going.

There were 41 different acts on the chart, one more than the previous record established only two years earlier, and considerable variety in style throughout, the chart only really becoming predictable at the very top end. Even so, nine different bands feature in the top ten and we did get, to date, the highest ever entry from a Japanese band, indeed the highest entry for a band from outside Europe or North America, at number five.

During the countdown, Peel mentioned a listener called Tony who'd proposed an alternative voting system for the festive fifty, giving a weighting to bands according to the number of releases they'd put out this year, presumably in an effort to give fair voice to those artists whose selections were spread across a wide range of tracks and avoid their suppressed representation, something that Peel had alluded to in the case of the Jam some two decades earlier, although he hinted that it may also be employed in reverse to engineer a situation that would avoid the dominance The Smiths and others had once enjoyed. I'm not clear how that would have come about exactly, but if that was the intention it was a slightly odd suggestion given that the established process was now doing a pretty good job of avoiding a repeat of such scenarios. Peel said he found the idea 'pretty' but rejected it due to the complicated process involved.

As with the previous year, there are pleasing successes for a whole range of small labels, with Pickled Egg emerging, somewhat curiously, as one of three labels with four entries each. The others were Warp and Chemikal Underground. More of the latter in a moment, but debate about the Pickled Egg entries would be the first recent stirrings of something that would cast a shadow over the chart for years to come, as the spectre of vote-rigging allegations began to cloud the festive fifty. Eyebrows were certainly raised as to why a small label should spring out of nowhere with so many entries, one of was a highly unexpected number five. The fact that there were two other entries on the chart for bands who'd subsequently signed with the label compounded the allegations. We can't prove there were any distasteful shenanagins afoot of course, but looking back it would appear to be part of a steady build-up to the highly dubious chart of 2002, of which more later. Certainly the increasing numbers of e-mailed votes during this period would make vote rigging far easier to pull off than it had been in the rapidly diminishing days of postal voting.

However plausible the achievements of Pickled Egg, it was another label, Chemikal Underground, that made festive fifty history by becoming the first to seize the top two slots with tracks from two different artists. The Delgados' 'Pull the Wires from the Wall' emulated Pulp's 'Common People' in being voted number one after appearing as a session track in the previous year's chart, and it did so after securing twice as many votes as the number two record. Mogwai were runners up for the second year running, with the first song to make the festive fifty with a festive title, while a number three for Belle and Sebastian secured a 1-2-3 for Scotland.

1998 Festive Fifty
Broadcast dates: 22, 23 & 29 December

50. Is This Desire? – PJ Harvey (Island CD *Is This Desire?*)
49. Shake-Off – The Fall (Peel Session 14.11.98)
48. fold4, wrap5 – Autechre (Warp CD *LP5*)
47. Evil Heat – Ten Benson (Deceptive CD *Ten Fingers of Benson*)
46. The Kids Are Solid Gold – Sportique (Roxy 7")
45. Turnstyle – Sodastream (Aquadmudvuv Australian CD *Enjoy*)
44. Went to Town – Rooney (Common Culture CD EP *Got Up Late*)
43. Pull Yourself Together – Hefner (Too Pure CD

single)
42. Radar Intruder – Derrero (Big Noise CD single)
41. Roygbiv – Boards of Canada (Warp CD *Music Has the Right to Children*)
40. Alison's Room – 60 Ft Dolls (Indolent CD single)
39. If I Were a Carpenter – Quickspace (Peel Session 10.10.98)
38. The Actress – The Delgados (Chemikal Underground CD *Peloton*)
37. Stimulus For Revolting Virus – Melt Banana (A-Zap CD *Charlie*)
36. Hush the Warmth – Gorky's Zygotic Mynci (Mercury CD *Gorky 5*)
35. Sweet Johnny (Radio Edit) - Gorky's Zygotic Mynci (Mercury CD single)
34. Powder Blue – Elbow (Self-Released EP Noisebox)
33. Goddess on a Hiway – Mercury Rev (V2 CD *Deserter's Songs*)
32. My Own Private Patrick Swayze – Male Nurse (Guided Missile 7")
31. Widdershins – Freed Unit (Pickled Egg 7")
30. Way Over Yonder in the Minor Key – Billy Bragg (Elektra CD *Mermaid Avenue*)
29. Ice Hockey Hair – Super Furry Animals (Creation CD single)
28. Rockafeller Skank (Skint CD You've Come a Long Way Baby)
27. Monkey on Your Back – Clinic (Aladdin's Cave of Golf CD single)
26. Sleep the Clock Around – Belle & Sebastian (Jeepster CD *The Boy with the Arab Strap*)
25. Turn a Blind Eye – Half Man Half Biscuit (Probe Plus CD *Four Lads Who Shook the Wirral*)
24. Lemming – Melys (Arctic CD single)
23. One Louder Solex – Solex (Peel Session 9.6.98)
22. Oh Happy Day – (Live recording from Meltdown 98, Royal Festival Hall)
21. Teardrop – MassiveAttack (Virgin CD *Mezanine*)
20. Rebel Without a Pause (Whipped Cream Mix) – Evolution Control Committee (Eerie Materials 7". Selection announced by Peel as 'Copyright Violation for the Nation')
19. Solex All Lickety Split – Solex (Matador 7")
18. Aquarius – Boards of Canada (Warp CD *Music Has the Right to Children*)
17. Soleil – L'augmentation (Pickled Egg 7")
16. Plock – Plone (Warp 12")
15. Kerry Kerry – Cinerama (Cooking Vinyl CD single)
14. I Need a Sign – Badly Drawn Boy (Twisted Nerve 7" EP *EP3*)
13. Cement Mixer – Clinic (Aladdin's Cave of Golf 7")
12. Dream Scream – Daniel Johnston (Pickled Egg 7")
11. Cracking Up – Jesus & Mary Chain (Creation CD single)
10. Long Live the UK Music Scene – Helen Love (Che Trading CD single)
9. Everything Goes Around the Water – The Delgados (Chemikal Underground CD single)
8. This is Hardcore – Pulp (Island CD single)
7. Eurodisco – Bis (Wiiija CD single)
6. Oh My God! They Killed Kenny! – Cuban Boys (Rough Trade Shops 7")
5. Unworldly – Pop Off Tuesday (Pickled Egg 7")
4. The Claw – Ten Benson (Sweet 7")
3. The Boy with the Arab Strap – Belle & Sebastian (Jeepster CD *The Boy with the Arap Strap*)
2. Xmas Steps – Mogwai (Chemikal Underground Promo CD *No Education = No Future (Fuck the Curfew)*)
1. Pull the Wires from the Wall – The Delgados (Chemikal Underground CD *Peloton*)

1999

For the first time, Peel allowed himself the indulgence of preceding the countdown with what he called 'an honorary number 51': 'Injured Birds' by Monkey Steals the Drum, one of his favourites of the year and a track that, he revealed, finished just outside the chart.

The broadcast is characterised by an unusual number of false starts, even for Peel. We hear the start of Monkey Steals the Drum again when Peel first attempts to reveal the number 50 record; we almost get Broadcast again rather than Smog at number 35 and the beginning of 'I See A Darkness' plays rather than the intended 'I Stole a Bride' at number 22. Finally, we are initially led to conclude that Half Man Half Biscuit have their first festive fifty number one, albeit rather bafflingly with a tune that's already been in the chart, but it turns out to be another broadcasting mishap and the correct number one is then revealed. Perhaps a combination of still not having entirely come to terms with CD decks (all the problems occur when he's trying to line up a CD) and the added complication of getting the Pig to announce the tunes resulted in a case of too many plates to balance.

Despite these interruptions, which always added to the appeal of any Peel show anyway, this is a very fine chart. Peel teases us about the potential omission of the Fall from the festive fifty before revealing that two have cropped up at numbers 4 and 7, with 'the master' also cramming an appearance with Elastica between them, in the process equalling Amelia Fletcher's achievement of appearing in the festive fifty with five different acts, secured only six days earlier when she appeared with Marine Research.

This was the year in which the influential Warp and Domino labels really began flex their festive fifty muscles. Having snaffled up Clinic and Pavement, both with recent chart pedigree, a good showing for Domino was always on the cards. They also supplied Will Oldham's second appearance in a festive fifty (this time under what was to become hs regular pseudonym of Bonnie 'Prince' Billy) and oversaw a chart debut for the excellent Smog. Warp, having secured the services of Broadcast, played a little of that game too and also gained second entries for the fantastically underrated Plone and the rather more celebrated Aphex Twin.

Warp unquestionably played a major part in ensuring the festive fifty could no longer be considered a largely electronica-free zone, but they weren't alone: entries for Kraken, Orbital and Sonic Subjunkies did their bit too, while it could be argued that the Mute label finally recaptured their early vision represented by the likes of The Normal by scoring with singles from Appliance and Add N to (X). There was a mild German flavor to some of the chart, moreso than in other years anyway: Sonic Subjunkies therewere joined by impudent noisemakers Atari Teenage Riot while Six By Seven got in with a German language version of Bowie's 'Heroes'.

Despite the absence of Helen Love after a three year residence, Welsh bands secured two places in the top ten via a best ever placing for Gorky's Zygotic Mynci and a surprisingly high appearance for Murry the Hump, who Peel rightly names as the first band from Aberyswyth ever to make a festive fifty. Super Furry Animals also had their best year, charting with three tracks from their critically lauded *Guerilla* album.

But ultimately, if the chart belonged to anyone, it was to Hefner and the Cuban Boys. The former became the first band since 1993 to place as many as five entries in a single festive fifty. Two of their three 'hymns' probably took votes off each other in the fight for the number one spot, leaving them at numbers 2 and 3. In any case It was unlikely either would have succeeded, with the Cuban Boys apparently winning by some distance: 'ran away with it' in Peel's words. This was, after all, the year of the hamster dance, with 'Cognoscenti Vs Intelligentsia' roundly embraced by a wider audience that knew what it liked and what it liked was an unmitigated novelty record. Not having the interest in music or general curiosity to check out who the Cuban Boys actually were, they placed the record next to 'Agadoo' and 'Barbie Girl' in their collections and smiled, watching the release make its familiar way towards the top of the charts, unfazed when they saw it stall before reaching number one, because they'd probably also bought the number one anyway.

EMI duly snapped the band up on the strength of the release and it duly gave the record company their first festive fifty number one since 'Anarchy in the UK'*. Such an achievement, had anyone from the record company been interested, might well have acted as a warning sign that another fractious relationship was about to take place with a band whose artistic interests might be rather different from those of the label, particularly given their fondness for the uncredited and well-used sample. It was, inevitably, a short-lived relationship with Cuban Boys precitably displaying just about the right level of contempt for EMI and any potential road to commercial respectability and, to the delight of the rest of us, carrying on exactly as they were.

To be honest, recognising the millennium in any serious way is something I didn't really expect Peel to do, yet he did so, not only with the fascinating Peelenium – where he selected four records a show from every year of the twentieth century over the closing months of 1999 and the early part of 2000, but also with an unexpected one-off return of the all-time festive fifty.

Although Peel sounded understandably disappointed by much of the predictable content of the first all-time chart for seventeen years, it did offer an interesting insight into what had changed and what had stayed the same in terms of listener preferences during that period. Joy Division and New Order figured heavily, securing an impressive nine entries between them, and in their case it was almost as if the intervening time period had barely even happened.

For other former heavyweights, it was a different picture. There wasn't a single entry for the Banshees and whatever head of steam The Cure had built up in the period between 1979 and 1982 had completely dissipated. Perhaps both suffered from a subsequent association with the by now much-maligned gothic rock creed, however unfairly. Stiff Little Fingers also failed to record a single entry and, though punk was pretty well represented, what was there perhaps indicated a narrowing of the canon between then and now. The Damned's 'New Rose' retained its post-1978 ever-present status, as did two tracks from the Pistols and two from The Clash and the inevitably high placed 'Teenage Kicks'. Perhaps the most surprising omission was 'God Save the Queen', a single that, you would anticipate, is one from the period that has lost none of its potential to shock and delight, yet there was no place at all for it in the fifty alongside the other Pistols entries. 'Anarchy in the UK' recorded its lowest ever position in a chart, but still came in at number four while 'Pretty Vacant' also made it in lower down.

In every other all-time chart 'Down in the Tube Station at Midnight' had been The Jam's best-placed entry, yet here, not only did it take second place to 'Going Underground', it was removed from the fifty all together. The Fall got three entries, including 'The Classical', a track that had never appeared in a festive fifty before, curiously making its belated debut despite the fact that Fall fans had dozens of previously recognised track to choose from. Perhaps it was some collective (in a Jungian sense, rather than a vote-rigging one) attempt to put right one of the great wrongs of festive fifty history: that the great *Hex Enduction Hour*, for many still the greatest Fall album of all time, had never had a track featured, until now. A slightly similar oddity, though not quite so extreme, was the case of 'Brassneck' appearing as one of two Wedding Present entries. The band had achieved twelve top ten entires in their illustrious history, and yet this single had settled only at number 18 back in 1999, and was only three places below that here. It hadn't even been the highest placed track on the *Bizarro* album, beaten easily by both 'Kennedy' and 'Take Me', neither of which got a sniff of the action here ten years later. Those other great festive fifty heavyweights The Smiths were rather more predictably represented, with both of their number ones and their one number two track featuring,, but there was no place at all for other big-hitters of the eighties such as Cocteau Twins or the Jesus & Mary Chain, nor did those perennial Peel favourites Half Man Half Biscuit manage to gain entry.

New entries included a couple of surprises from the Beach Boys, an artistic entity that tends to go in and out of fashion and which it would have been hard to visualise the post-punk audience ever going for, but whose best output certainly deserves recognition and it's this that is recognised here, through entries for 'Good Vibrations' and the best-known track from the *Pet Sounds* album. The Beatles returned to the chart, but with a different track from the three that made it in 1976 – the obtuse depth of 'I Am the Walrus' having attained a timeless and mesmerising quality over the years despite originally being stuck away on the B-side of 'Hello Goodbye', and thoroughly deserving its belated recognition.

A place each for the Velvet Underground and Nick Drake was less surprising, both having had their neglected legends thoroughly reassessed and given a decisive thumbs up during the eighties, while it was also good to see a first appearance for Tim Buckley.. Like me, I expect Peel listeners of a certain age got turned on to Buckley after This Mortal Coil's version of 'Song to the Siren', which would explain why it's this track that appears for Buckley, as well as in its cover version form, making it the first song in festive fifty history to appear in a single festive fifty in recordings of two different artists. It's rare enough for a song to appear in two versions in two different fifties, but two that have achieved that unusual feat – 'Shipbuilding' and 'There is a Light…' (albeit in the latter case via a radical subsequent re-imagining from Schneider TM that wouldn't appear until next year) - also appeared here.

Another remaining act to make a belated return were Culture, whose only previous entry had been in the Peel-selected chart of 1977 and whose appearance provoked enormous on-air excitement from Peel who then made a mistake setting up the next track due to, he confessed, 'shrieking along' to 'Lion Rock'. That such glee should greet the appearance of one of the greatest of all Peel bands in the lowly position of number 48 illustrates again just how badly neglected reggae has been in festive fifties down the years.

Only a few entries returned from the very first festive fifty: Captain Beefheart, Bob Dylan and Jimi Hendrix all made welcome appearances, now released from their post-punk classification as old farts and having in the elapsed period between 1982 and 1999 had their legacies more fairly reassessed. It would be good to think that Beefheart in particular had never been so dismissed, particularly as punk luminaries like Joe Strummer always cited him as a major influence, but the fact he'd never featured in the charts between 1978 and 1982 tells a rather different story.

*Although he played the Virgin *Never Mind the Bollocks* version in those earlier countdowns.

1999 Festive Fifty

Broadcast dates: 23, 28 & 29 December

50. Don't I Hold You – Wheat (City Slang CD *Hope & Adams*)
49. Hymn for the Things We Didn't Do – Hefner (Ovni 7" EP *The Hefner Heart*)
48. Living City Plan – Miss Mend (Piao! 7")
47. Parallel Horizontal – Marine Research (K LP *Sounds from the Gulf Stream*)
46. The Free Design – Stereolab (Duophonic LP *Cobra & Phases Group Play Voltage into the Milky Night*)
45. Carrot Rope – Pavement (Domino 7")
44. Food Music – Appliance (Mute CD single)
43. Helden – Six By Seven (Mantra CD single *Ten Places to Die*)
42. Windowlicker – Aphex Twin (Warp CD single)
41. Once Around the Block – Badly Drawn Boy (Twisted Nerve CD single)
40. Tender – Blur (Food CD *13*)
39. Revolution Action – Atari Teenage Riot (Digital Hardcore CD *60 Second Wipeout*)
38. Plot in a Pot – Melt Banana (Skin Graft LP *Scratch or Stitch*)
37. Metal Fingers in My Body – Add N to (X) (Mute CD single)
36. Echo's Answer – Broadcast (Warp CD single)
35. Cold Blooded Old Times – Smog (Domino CD single)
34. Be Rude to Your School – Plone (Warp LP *For Beginner Piano*)
33. As Good As It Gets – Gene (Polydor CD single)
32. I Took Her Love For Granted – Hefner (Too Pure CD *The Fidelity Wars*)
31. Major Leagues – Pavement (Domino CD *Terror Twilight*)
30. Twenty-Four Hour Garage People – Half Man Half Biscuit (Peel Session 3.9.99)
29. Science Fiction Freak – Dawn of the Replicants (Eastwest CD *Wrong Town Wrong Planet Three Hours Late*)
28. Flossie's Alarming Clock (Peel show exclusive recording)
27. The Turning Tide – Super Furry Animals (Creation CD *Guerilla*)
26. Side Effects – Kraken (Underfire V/A LP *Blazin'*)
25. Stanley Kubrick – Mogwai (Chemikal Underground CD EP *EP*)
24. Northern Lites – Super Furry Animals (Creation CD *Guerilla*)
23. I See a Darkness – Bonnie 'Prince' Billy (Domino CD *I See a Darkness*)
22. I Stole a Bride – Hefner (Too Pure CD *The Fidelity Wars*)
21. Hung Over as the Oven at Maida Vale – Godspeed You Black Emperor! (Peel Session 19.1.99)
20. The Second Line – Clinic (Domino CD single)
19. Look Left – Salako (Jeepster CD *Musicality*)
18. Kings Cross – Cinerama (Elefant 7" *Pacific* B-side)
17. Fire in My Heart – Super Furry Animals (Creation CD single)
16. Do You Even Know who You Are? – Sonic Subjunkies (Iris Light CD *Molotov Lounge*)
15. Style – Orbital (FRRR 12")

14. Cody – Mogwai (Chemikal Underground CD *Come On Die Young*)
13. Pacific – Cinerama (Elefant 7")
12. Waiting For a Superman – Flaming Lips (Warner Bros CD *The Soft Bulletin*)
11. Look Dad No Tunes – Half Man Half Biscuit (Probe Plus CD single)
10. Immune – Low (Tugboat 7")
9. Thrown Like a Stone – Murry the Hump (Shifty Disco 7")
8. Race For the Prize – Flaming Lips (Warner Bros CD *The Soft Bulletin*)
7. F-Oldin' Money – The Fall (Artful CD single)
6. How He Wrote Elastica Man – Elastica with Mark E. Smith (Deceptive CD *The Menace*)
5. Spanish Dance Troupe – Gorky's Zygotic Mynci (Mantra CD *Spanish Dance Troupe*)
4. Touch Sensitive – The Fall (Artful CD *The Marshall Suite*)
3. The Hymn for the Alcohol – Hefner (Too Pure CD – *The Fidelity Wars*)
2. The Hymn for the Cigarettes - Hefner (Too Pure CD – *The Fidelity Wars*)
1. Cognoscenti Vs Intelligentsia (Original Mix) – Cuban Boys (EMI promo CD)

1999 All-Time Festive Fifty

Broadcast dates: 4, 5, 6, 12, 13, 18, 19, 20, 25 & 26 January. Peel declared he was revealing the chart in ten parts because it was, he stated before broadcast, somewhat predictable and he therefore didn't want to devote a large portion of a single show to it.

50. Here – Pavement (Big Cat CD *Slanted & Enchanted*)
49. Sheela-Na-Gig – PJ Harvey (Too Pure 7")
48. Lion Rock – Culture (Strange Fruit 12" EP *The Peel Sessions*. Originally broadcast 11.1.83)
47. Can't Be Sure – The Sundays (Rough Trade LP *Reading, Writing & Arithmetic*)
46. Good Vibrations – Beach Boys (Capitol LP *Best of the Beach Boys Vol. 2*)
45. I Am the Walrus – The Beatles (Parlophone LP *Magical Mystery Tour*)
44. Visions of Johanna - Bob Dylan (CBS LP *Blonde On Blonde*)
43. Northern Sky – Nick Drake (Island LP *Bryter Layter*)
42. Heroin – The Velvet Underground (MGM LP *The Velvet Underground & Nico*)
41. God Only Knows – Beach Boys (Capitol LP *Pet Sounds*)
40. Song to the Siren – Tim Buckley (Straight LP *Starsailor*)
39. New Rose – The Damned (Stiff 7")
38. The Classical – The Fall (Kamera LP *Hex Enduction Hour*)
37. All Along the Watchtower – Jimi Hendrix Experience (Polydor LP *Electric Ladyland*)
36. French Disko – Stereolab (Duophonic CD single)
35. Going Underground – The Jam (Polydor 7")
34. Totally Wired – The Fall (Rough Trade 7")
33. Complete Control – The Clash (CBS 7")
32. True Faith – New Order (Factory LP *Substance*)
31. Lazy Line Painter Jane – Belle & Sebastian (Jeepster CD *EP Lazy Line Painter Jane*)
30. Debaser – Pixies (4AD LP *Doolittle*)
29. Pretty Vacant – Sex Pistols (Virgin 7")
28. Transmission – Joy Division (Factory LP *Substance*)
27. You Made Me Realise – My Bloody Valentine (Creation 7")
26. Pull the Wires from the Wall – The Delgados (Chemikal Underground CD single)
25. My Favourite Dress – The Wedding Present (Reception LP *George Best*)
24. How I Wrote Elastic Man – The Fall (Rough Trade 7")
23. Birthday – Sugarcubes (One Little Indian 7")
22. This Charming Man – The Smiths (Rough Trade 7")
21. Brassneck – The Wedding Present (RCA CD single)
20. She's Lost Control – Joy Division (Factory LP *Unknown Pleasures*)
19. Temptation – New Order (Factory 12")
18. Another Girl Another Planet – The Only Ones

(CBS 7")
17. Ceremony – New Order (Factory 7")
16. Soon – My Bloody Valentine (Creation 7")
15. New Dawn Fades – Joy Division (Factory LP *Unknown Pleasures*)
14. Holiday in Cambodia – Dead Kennedys (Cherry Red 7")
13. Big Eyed Beans from Venus – Captain Beefheart & The Magic Band (Reprise LP *Clear Spot*)
12. Common People – Pulp (Island CD single)
11. Shipbuilding – Robert Wyatt (Rough Trade 12")
10. Song to the Siren – This Mortal Coil (4AD LP *It'll End in Tears*)
9. There is a Light That Never Goes Out – The Smiths (Rough Trade LP *The Queen is Dead*)

8. Smells Like Teen Spirit – Nirvana (Geffen LP *Nevermind*)
7. How Soon is Now? – The Smiths (Rough Trade 12" *William, It Was Really Nothing* B-side)
6. Blue Monday – New Order (Factory LP *Substance*)
5. (White Man) in Hammersmith Palais – The Clash (CBS 7")
4. Anarchy in the UK – Sex Pistols (EMI 7")
3. Love Will Tear Us Apart – Joy Division (Factory LP *Substance*)
2. Teenage Kicks – Undertones (Good Vibrations 7" EP *Teenage Kicks*)
1. Atmosphere – Joy Division (Factory CD EP *Joy Division 1979*)

2000

'What a fantastic year 2000 has been for music,' declared Peel at the end of the broadcast, repeating a comment he'd mae following the number 44 entry, finishing the year on a highly optimistic note and hinting, however indirectly, that he'd felt the chart had adequately reflected his passion.

As was the case in 1995, Peel didn't appear to allow the fact that several bands enjoyed multiple entries to affect his enjoyment: indeed, at the time of writing, the festive fifty of 2000 is the last that could be said to have been largely dominated by a small group of albums, all released by firm Peel favourites. There were four tracks each from PJ Harvey's *Stories of the City, Stories of the Sea*, Hefner's *We Love the City* and *The Great Eastern* by The Delgados, while The Fall appeared three times with *The Unutterable*, an album that, following the massive upheavals and conflict that had occurred within the band over the previous three years, managed to stun us with a magnificence that perhaps illustrated more than any other Fall release to the tenacity and durability of Mark E. Smith. Peel hailed it, rightly, as a release that was as good as anything they'd ever put out previously and as one his three favourite albums of the year. If the days when we could expect such a collection to yield even more entries were gone, it did manage to emulate or exceed the achievements of their three immediately previous albums in festive fifty terms. Also in there with three entries was Laura Cantrell's *Not the Tremblin' Kind*, an album that, Peel declared, he loved 'to the point of madness'. Between them, these five albums managed to be responsible for close to two-fifths of the chart.

Not that this detracted one iota from the eclectic nature of the 2000 festive fifty overall. Peel was greatly pleased by the appearance of Mighty Math in the lower echelons, and an entry for Lab 4 a little further up wasn't, you suspect, any less welcome. Peel favourites Herman Dune enjoyed their only flirtation with a festive fifty, as did Calexico, with the standout track from their *Hot Rail* album.

They played a small role in making the 2000 chart one of those that gave due recognition to high quality American acts, the most prominent element of whom was Neko Case at number one, something that both pleased and amazed Peel. She thus emulated the feat of Bang Bang Machine by making her only appearance in a festive fifty in the number one slot.

Not everyone among Peel's audience shared his enthusiasm for Case and her fellow country chanteuse Cantrell. With elements of country influence clearly discernible also in the Calexico entry and Cat Power's extraordinary version of 'Wonderwall', which beats the pants off the original, there was more than enough here to make a strong case for Half

Man Half Biscuit's 'Irk The Purists' entry being almost an unofficial theme tune for the chart. The DJ had always loved a bit of country, of course, but in the later years of his life he admitted a tendency to be moved by the genre more than ever, to the point that he'd often find himself weeping uncontrollably. While Case possessed perhaps enough rock and roll raunchiness to pacify those who didn't share his emotional proclivities, music forums across the internet abounded with disparaging comments by those who found his love for Cantrell at best mystifying and at worst a betrayal. Not for the first time, the response of the anti-punk brigade and the Altered Images haters of the early eighties was recalled and we were reminded, as we perhaps needed to be every now and again, that perhaps the most enduring element of the Peel show down the years was his tendency to throw us a musical googly every now and then, something that arose not, you suspect, froma tendency to be awkward or difficult, but purely due to the open sincerity of his musical convictions.

Purists might also have raised an eyebrow at Cowcube, from just down the road from Peel, and his appearance with 'The Popping Song', a ditty that was inclined to delight and grate on listeners in roughly equal proportions. He fought the corner also for Radiohead's *Kid A* album: the globally successful band had troubled the festive fifty scorers seven years earlier when their signature tune 'Creep' had entered despite being ignored by the DJ. *Kid A* was a fascinating album, and one that raised a glorious middle finger to those of a puritanical bent within the band's own considerable fan base: duly, it was the release that really turned Peel on the band's charms and found a home here. We might be more inclined to consider a sampling of the theme from *Countdown* and a tune consisting of little beyond stereotypically upper class expressions in the same light, were they not products of the audaciously likeable Cuban Boys, whose short-lived mainstream success had predictably come to a jarring close but whose position as Peel legends was secured for ever.

There were several relatively obscure firsts around in the first festive fifty of the new millennium and, as this is a book that has an irrational fondness for such things, I feel bound to bring them to your attention. For the first time ever, two tracks from the same film soundtrack made it into the festive fifty, Orbital and New Order both scoring with tunes from *The Beach*. We also had, for the first time, a children's refrain featuring on two relatively high placed entries – Hefner's 'Day That Thatcher Dies', which featured a couple of kids, one of whom was Jack Hayter's son – and the single version of The Delgados' 'No Danger', which added a children's choir to a track that had happily existed without one on the album, yet managed to make it work brilliantly, more than justifying that version's inclusion here.

2000 Festive Fifty
Broadcast dates: 26, 27 & 28 December

50. The Crystal Lake – Grandaddy (V2 CD *The Sophtware Slump*)
49. I Fought in a War – Belle & Sebastian (Jeepster LP *Fold Your Hands Child, You Walk Like a Peasant*)
48. Ideoteque – Radiohead (Parlophone LP *Kid A*)
47. Svefn-g-englar – Sigur Ros (Fat Cat CD *Agaetis Byrjun*)
46. Little Boy Blue – Bonnie 'Prince' Billy (Western Vinyl 7")
45. Beached – Orbital & Angelo Badalamenti (FFRR/London 12")
44. Painting & Kissing – Hefner (Too Pure CD *We Love the City*)
43. W.B. – The Fall (Eagle CD *The Unutterable*)
42. Queen of the Coast – Laura Cantrell (Spit & Polish CD *Not the Tremblin' Kind*)
41. Manhattan – Cinerama (Cooking Vinyl CD *This is Cinerama*)
40. Dress Sexy at My Funeral – Smog (Domino CD *Dongs of Sevotion*)
39. Soul Boy – Mighty Math (Different Drummer CD *Up Life Gone Star*)
38. Witness – The Delgados (Chemikal Underground CD *The Great Eastern*)
37. Irk the Purists – Half Man Half Biscuit (Probe Plus CD *Trouble Over Bridgewater*)
36. Fresher Than the Sweetness in Water – Gorky's Zygotic Mynci (Mantra CD *The Blue Trees*)
35. Candyman – Lab 4 (One Inch 12")
34. Theme From Prim & Proper – Cuban Boys (Prim & Proper 7" *Old Skool For Scoundrels*)
33. Wonderwall – Cat Power (Peel Session 20.7.00)
32. Twenty Four Hour Garage People – Half Man Half Biscuit (Probe Plus CD *Trouble Over Bridgewater*)
31. Drug Dealer in the Park – Herman Dune (Prohibited CD *Turn Off the Light*)
30. Popping Song – Cowcube (CD white label)

29. Vinyl Countdown – Cuban Boys (CD EP white label *Cuban Boys On TV*)
28. The Second Line – Clinic (Domino LP *Internal Wrangler*)
27. Two Seconds – Laura Cantrell (Spit & Polish CD *Not the Tremblin' Kind*)
26. Brutal – New Order (London V/A Soundtrack CD *The Beach*)
25. Kid A – Radiohead (Parlophone CD *Kid A*)
24. The Whores Hustle and the Hustlers Whore – PJ Harvey (Island CD *Stories from the City, Stories from the Sea*)
23. Two Librans – The Fall (Eagle CD *The Unutterable*)
22. Ballad of Cable Hogue – Calexico (City Slang CD *Hot Rail*)
21. Somewhere, Some Night – Laura Cantrell (Spit & Polish CD *Not the Tremblin' Kind*)
20. In a Beautiful Place Out in the Country – Boards of Canada (Warp CD single)
19. Prayer to God – Shellac (Touch & Go CD *1000 Hurts*)
18. The Mess We're In – PJ Harvey (Island CD *Stories from the City, Stories from the Sea*)
17. Wow (Extended Version) – Cinerama (Scopitones CD *Disco Volante*)
16. Your Charms – Cinerama (Scopitones CD *Disco Volante*)
15. Good Fruit – Hefner (Too Pure CD *We Love the City*)
14. Accused of Stealing – The Delgados (Chemikal Underground CD *The Great Eastern*)
13. I Hate Scotland – Ballboy (Peel Session 21.3.00)
12. The Day That Thatcher Dies – Hefner (Too Pure CD *We Love the City*)
11. Dinosaur Act – Low (Tugboat CD single)
10. American Trilogy – The Delgados (Chemikal Underground CD *The Great Eastern*)
9. No Danger (Kids' Choir) – The Delgados (Chemikal Underground 7")
8. The Light 3000 – Schneider TM KPT michi.gan (City Slang CD *Binokular*)
7. The Greedy Ugly People – Hefner (Too Pure CD *We Love the City*)
6. Big Exit – PJ Harvey (Island CD *Stories From the City, Stories From the Sea*)
5. Come On Let's Go – Broadcast (Warp CD single)
4. Mistakes & Regrets - ...And You Will Know Us By the Trail of Dead (Domino CD single)
3. Dr Buck's Letter – The Fall (Eagle CD *The Unutterable*)
2. Good Fortune – PJ Harvey (Island CD *Stories From the City, Stories From the Sea*)
1. Twist the Knife – Neko Case & Her Boyfriends (Mint CD *Furnace Room Lullaby*)

2001

The first festive fifty since 1982 to contain no session tracks in the broadcast nonetheless provided a rare example in recent times of Peel's listeners' choices overlapping, however coincidentally, with rather less reliable organs of taste in the mainstream music press. Which is not, incidentally, a roundabout way of saying the chart was crap. Although it would be difficult for anyone who'd not spent the last year in Antarctica or on Mars to argue that the chart contained a lot of surprises, it was a pretty solid effort overall, open to criticism perhaps only for a general domination at the hands of guitars that had been levelled at so many festive fifties.

The Strokes' *Is This It* became not only the latest example of a band firing on all its festive fifty cylinders in one year and using them up (following the example of Dreadzone and Stone Roses), but also the last time to date that an album has placed as many as five tracks in a single chart, in the process also becoming the most successful debut album in festive fifty terms since Pavement's *Slanted & Enchanted*. The New York band also had versions of three of the four tracks they recorded for their one and only Peel session in the chart, again the last time a single session would generate this many entries..

They were one of a number of bands who fired the imagination of Peel voters in a festive fifty that did much to reclaim this ground for those who brandished their guitars as potential weapons of destruction rather than mere instruments of convention, providing a reminder that – despite guitar-based charts having been so often frowned upon down the years – a hell of a lot could still be achieved with a standard guitar-bass-drums set up and a dollop of inspiration and/or fire in your belly.

A band who possessed quite a bit of the latter were Sweden's The Hives, fired by their nation's often unfairly overlooked role as a driving force in the history of garage rock but with more than enough of their own creative juice to add greater power to a well-used but much loved old engine. Miss Black America who, like The Strokes, would generate five festive fifty entries from a single album but do so over this and the following year, and Antihero, who also did much to make 2001 arguably the loudest and most impertinent festive fifty since the late seventies. The latter two bands recorded the unique achievement of gaining an entry for both sides of a split 7" single. Indeed, it was perhaps the best year for the split release in festive fifty history, with further entries for tracks from Saloon and Melys that orginated on one side of similar releases.

Others who fell very much into the category of bands who blazed a fearsome trail only to burnt out rather than suffering the ignominy of fading away were single entrants like Ikara Colt, whose session that year Peel had purred and exclaimed his way through and, with one of his favourite singles of the year, Detroit Cobras. Of course, Detroit's influence on the chart didn't stop there. The White Stripes had emerged during the year following Peel's discovery of their early albums in a Dutch record shop. He bought them, he claimed, purely because the red and white sleeves reminded him of Liverpool FC. Within months the duo had risen to something approaching international stardom, ultimately becoming the last band broken by Peel to reach such stellar heights and, in doing so, opening the floodgates to a vibrant Detroit scene that contained such rock and roll monsters as the Cobras and Von Bondies, who would appear in the chart next year, not to mention high quality non-FF entrants like The Dirtbombs and Soledad Brothers. The four entries from the two Detroit bands also gave Sympathy For the Record Industry, one of Peel's favourite labels of the time, its first taste of festive fifty action..

On the subject of record labels, their success with The Strokes meant Rough Trade gained the accolade of most entries for the first time since the Smiths-dominated year of 1987, the label's revival in the modern era allowing it to pass Factory's record of most festive fifty entries, though this year a returning New Order at least struck an honorary blow on behalf of their old label.

While the aforementioned Strokes and White Stripes carved up four of the top seven places between them, those with less abrasive musical sensibilities were still well in evidence towards the top of the chart. Saloon's surprisingly high position of number 12 foreshadowed their victorious appearance in the controversial festive fifty of 2002, while a number one for Melys, with what Peel reckoned to be one of those singles that would stand out in any year, was less surprising. Similarly pleasing for the DJ was the appearance of Bearsuit at number four: the chart's most significant debutants had come into being after following that beloved Peel model of a bunch of people who couldn't play deciding to form a band. The approach has always defied logic and demonstrated that logic, after all, had no role whatsoever in producing great music. It gave them an idiosyncratic freshness that would make them frequent visitors to the chart in the ensuing years. Another first festive fifty appearance was chalked up by Camera Obsura, another band in the great Scottish indie tradition and another of whom we would not by hearing the last. The single was produced by Belle & Sebastian's Stuart Murdoch, whose band also featured twice.

The most requested track of the year on his show, according to Peel, was Greenskeepers' 'Low & Sweet', a track capable of provoking strong degrees of attachment and specular levels of irritation in roughly equal proportions. Whatever its merits, you could sense a collective sigh of relief among listeners when it settled in only at number 24.

While having its fair share of long tracks (the two from Mogwai coming top in that respect), the 2001 festive fifty is notable for containing more sub-two minute tracks than any other, topped off by the achievement of Half Man Half Biscuit's 'Vatican Broadside' not just in beating one of the longest-standing of all chart records, that of the shortest track in a festive fifty, until now held by Wild Man Fischer from way back in 1976. My thanks to A Reader (sorry, I lost all my e-mail records at some point so don't have a record of the relevant person's name) for pointing out my error in omitting Wild Man Fischer's achievement fro the first edition. No track since has ever come close to matching the brevity of the Half Man Half Biscuit track but it would be a rash act to predict that none ever will.

Regarding other festive fifty heavyweights, Mogwai, with two entries of over ten minutes here, became the first band to feature two tracks of such length in a single chart and brought their total of nine-minute plus entries to three, also a record at the time. Meanwhile, Cinerama got David Gedge back into the familiar environs of the top three, we saw the brief return of Pulp to a festive fifty and said goodbye to both Stereolab and Hefner, both of whom would grace a festive fifty for the last time.   One of the most stirring entries of the chart came from Meanwhile Back in Communist Russia, whose brief existence packed one hell of a wallop, three great Peel sessions, consisting of two great albums. and one great festive fifty entry, before the band split asunder after a bare five years of existence.

2001 Festive Fifty
Broadcast dates: 25-27 December

50. Chard – Poco (Demo CD)
49. Free Fall – Saloon (Track & Field 7")
48. Giant Robo – Rock of Travolta (Juggernaut CD *My Band's Better Than Yours*)
47. Hate to Say I Told You So – The Hives (Poptones CD *Your New Favourite Band*)
46. Someday - The Strokes (Rough Trade CD *Is This It*)
45. Captain Easychord - Stereolab (Duophonic CD EP *Captain Easychord*)
44. The Dark is Rising – Mercury Rev (V2 CD *All is Dream*)
43. New Slang – The Shins (Sub Pop CD *Oh, Inverted World*)
42. Don't Speak My Mind – Miss Black America (Dental Sounds split 7" w/Antihero)
41. I've Got Pictures of You in Your Underwear – Ballboy (SL CD EP *Girls Are Better Than Boys*)
40. Pyramid Song – Radiohead (Parlophone CD *Amnesiac*)
39. Falling From Cloud 9 – Lift to Experience (Bella Union CD *The Texas-Jerusalem Crossroads*)
38. Who's Looking Out For Number One? – Antihero (Dental Sounds split 7" w/Miss Black America)
37. Sensational Vacuum – Seedling (Transformed Dreams CD *Elevator Tourist*)
36. This is Love – PJ Harvey (Island CD single)
35. I Don't Believe in You – Melys (Sylem/Transformed Dreams split 7" w/Seedling)
34. Superman – Cinerama (Scopitones CD single)
33. One Note – Ikara Colt (Fantastic Plastic CD single)
32. I'm Waking Up to Us – Belle & Sebastian (Jeepster CD EP *I'm Waking Up to Us*)
31. Alan Bean – Hefner (Too Pure CD *Dead Media*)
30. I Wake Up in the City – The Fall (Flitwick 7" *Rude (All the Time)* B Side)
29. Trees – Pulp (Island CD *We Love Life*)
28. New York City Cops – the Strokes (Rough Trade CD *Is This It*)
27. These Are the Days - Lift to Experience (Bella Union CD *The Texas-Jerusalem Crossroads*)
26. They'll Hang Flags From Cranes Upon My Wedding Day – Ballboy (SL CD EP *Girls Are Better Than Boys*)
25. Dead Leaves and the Dirty Ground – White Stripes (Sympathy For the Record Industry LP *White Blood Cells*)
24. Low & Sweet – Greenskeepers (Classic 12" EP *What's Your Man Got to Do With Gan?*)
23. Drink Drink Drink – Cuban Boys (Sanctuary Promo CD *Drink*)
22. 2 Rights Make 1 Wrong – Mogwai (Southpaw CD *Rock Action*)
21. (Drawing) Rings Around the World – Super Furry Animals (Epic CD *Rings Around the World*)
20. My Red Hot Car – Squarepusher (Warp CD *Go Plastic*)
19. Sunrise – Pulp (Island CD *We Love Life*)
18. The Modern Age – The Strokes (Rough Trade CD *Is This It*)
17. Jonathan David – Belle & Sebastian (Jeepster CD EP *Belle and Sebastian Sing Jonathan David*)
16. Vatican Broadside – Half Man Half Biscuit (Probe Plus CD EP *Editor's Recommendation*)
15. Shout Bama Lama – Detroit Cobras (Sympathy For the Record Industry CD *Life, Love & Leaving*)
14. Human Punk – Miss Black America (R>E>P>E>A>T CD EP *Adrenaline Junkie Class-A Mentalist*)
13. Bob Wilson Anchorman – Half Man Half Biscuit (Probe Plus CD EP *Editor's Recommendation*)
12. Impact – Saloon (Glamour Puss split 7" w/Sonic Catering Band)

11. Morning After Pill – Meanwhile, Back in Communist Russia (Jitter CD *Indian Ink*)
10. My Father My King – Mogwai (Rock Action CD single *My Father My King*)
9. Crystal – New Order (London CD single)
8. Eighties Fan – Camera Obscura (Andmoresound 7")
7. Hard to Explain – The Strokes (Rough Trade CD *Is This It*)
6. Fell in Love With a Girl – White Stripes (Sympathy For the Record Industry LP *White Blood Cells*)
5. Last Nite – The Strokes (Rough Trade CD *Is This It*)
4. Hey Charlie Hey Chuck – Bearsuit (Sickroom Gramophone Collective 7")
3. Health & Efficiency – Cinerama (Manifesto CD single)
2. Hotel Yorba – White Stripes (XL CD single)
1. Chinese Whispers – Melys (Sylem CD single)

2002

For only the second time, the festive fifty was broadcast in all its glory on a single night, meaning that my normal Boxing Day habits of watching football and drinking my way through the afternoon before passing out in the evening now had to be revised in order to accommodate the need to stay up until 1am. I duly kept the footie in its rightful place and paced my alcohol consumption so that the latter stages of the chart were absorbed in a boozy haze and no shortage of disbelief.

This was not a good sort of disbelief, I hasten to add, such as the kind that brought delight to the 2000 festive fifty with the revelation that Neko Case had beaten allcomers to the top spot, but to a cheated kind informed by the sure knowledge that the chart had been contaminated like never before by mass vote-rigging. This was obvious from the start when a clearly disgruntled John Peel played the Dawn Parade at number 50 before announcing that, sadly, many votes for the band had been discounted due to block-voting on an unprecedented level. Clearly the time-honoured process of simply adding up the votes to see who wins was giving way to an era in which the end results had to be scrutinized and questioned to some extent before he could end up with a chart that was reasonably 'clean' and reflected the wishes of voters. The Dawn Parade's case illustrated how difficult it was, because the band's relative prominence that year, which had seen them break through from much-loved Suffolk 'locals' to monthly magazine championed contenders in a very short time, probably meant an uncontaminated vote would have placed them higher and might well have seen them chart more than once. In the event, however, it was difficult to see what else Peel could have done.

By the time we'd got to the end of the countdown it was difficult to know how much of what we'd heard had been untainted by something similar. Much of the chart appeared legitimate enough and there had been several highlights, the appearance of Jeffrey Lewis being on and Asa Chang & Junray with arguably the most challenging track ever to make a top twenty another, while The Datsuns gave the chart its highest ever entry from New Zealand (compatriots the D4 had appeared lower down). However, the relevation that Saloon were at number one left a seriously nasty taste in the mouth. This is not to say that Saloon weren't a fine band – they were – but their surprising appearance at number 12 in the previous year's chart was suddenly shown in a new light as surely most listeners became aware that all was not right with the vote that had thrust them into such lofty positions. Peel commented that there had never been such an unlikely number one in a festive fifty.

Despite his understandable reservations about the results, Peel did note when commencing the countdown that a large number of good records had made the chart that year. He teased listeners by playing Ballboy's 'All the Records on the Radio are Shite' as part of the non-chart broadcast before revealing that it also featured into the chart, repeating what he'd done with the White Stripes the previous year. He also made the curious decision to break off the excellent Burning Love Jumpsuit track around half way through, saying that he felt he'd played the part of the track that voters had wanted, although it seems odd that such a thing would have been specified en masse when voting.

How much necessarily manipulation of the vote went on beyond the Dawn Parade we don't know, and we also don't know how much it contributed to a return to the spread of the vote we'd become familiar with in the 1996-98 years, with only one two bands (Low and Miss Black America) placing as many as three tracks on the chart. It's also worth recording that, whatever had gone on with Saloon or others, the top ten featured a whole bunch of Peel-approved tunes, including an appearance for the heavily championed Nina Nastasia, another for Laura Cantrell and a great favourite at number nine courtesy of Marc Smith Vs Safe N Sound. Cinerama edged closer again to the top spot, and indeed some might judge they'd been wrongly deprived of the number one in highly suspicious circumstances, to give David Gedge his third appearance at number two. At number three, Miss Black America continued to serve notice of an impending world domination that, sadly, never came.

2002 Festive Fifty
Broadcast date: 26 December

50. The Hole in My Heart – Dawn Parade (Sugartown CD *Electric Fence Your Gentleness*)
49. This is a Campaign – Aphrodisiacs (White Label CD Single)
48. Green Grass of Tunnel - Mum (Fat Cat CD *Finally We Are No One*)
47. Get Loose – D4 (Infectious CD single)
46. Celebrate Your Mother – Eighties Matchbox B-Line Disaster (Island CD single)
45. Infinite Chinese Box – Miss Black America (Integrity CD single)
44. Coming in From the Cold – The Delgados (Mantra CD single)
43. So Good – Melys (Sylem CD single)
42. Obstacle 1 – Interpol (Matador CD single)
41. Cheerleader – Burning Love Jumpsuit (BSM/Grayslate LP *Please Pull Apart*)
40. To Hell With Good Intentions – McLusky (Too Pure LP *McLusky Do Dallas*)
39. Cat Girl Tights – Cinerama (Scopitones CD *Torino*)
38. Breaking News – Half Man Half Biscuit (Probe Plus CD *Cammell Laird Social Club*)
37. You Got Nothing – Antihero (Peel Session 28.5.02)
36. (That's How You Sing) Amazing Grace – Low (Rough Trade LP *Trust*)
35. Alan is a Cowboy Killer – McLusky (Too Pure LP *McLusky Do Dallas*)
34. 99.9 – Wire (Peel Session 17.9.02)
33. It Came From Japan – Von Bondies (Sympathy For the Record Industry LP *Lack of Communication*)
32. Mannequin Hand Trapdoor I Reminder – Boom Bip & Dose One (Lex LP *Seed to Sun*)
31. Seventeen – Ladytron (Invicta Hi Fi CD single)
30. Drinkink – Bearsuit (Sickroom 7")
29. Mr Blue Sky – The Delgados (Peel Session 16.10.02)
28. Your Song – Cranebuilders (Skinny Dog CD single)
27. Fall in Love with a Girl – White Stripes (XL CD single)
26. Have You Seen the Light? – Saloon (Track & Field 7")
25. Staging the Plaguing of the Raised Platform – Cornership (Wiiija LP *Handcream for a Generation*)
24. Where Do the Nights of Sleep Go When They Do Not Come To Me? – Ballboy (SL CD single)
23. The Chelsea Hotel Oral Sex Song – Jeffrey Lewis (Rough Trade CD *The Last Time I Did Acid I Went Insane*)
22. Susan Vs Youth Club – The Fall (Action CD single)
21. In Love – The Datsuns (V2 7")
20. You Don't Send Me – Belle & Sebastian (Peel Session 25.7.02)
19. Democracies – Coin Op (Fierce Panda CD single)
18. Canada – Low (Rough Trade CD single)
17. Hana – Asa-Chang & Junray (Leaf LP *Junray Song Chang*)
16. In the Drugs – Low (Rough Trade LP *Trust*)
15. Dead Leaves and the Dirty Ground – White Stripes (XL CD single)
14. The Light at the End of the Tunnel (Is the Light of an Oncoming Train) – Half Man Half Biscuit (Probe Plus CD *Cammell Laird Social Club*)
13. Careless – Cinerama (Scopitones CD *Torino*)
12. Bang – Yeah Yeah Yeahs (Shifty CD *Master/Machine*)

11. Miss Black America – Miss Black American (Integrity CD *God Bless Miss Black America*)
10. All the Records on the Radio Are Shite – Ballboy (White Label CD single)
9. Identify the Beat – Marc Smith Vs Safe N Sound (Nu Energy 12")
8. So Over You - Pindrop (White Label CD single)
7. Too Late For Tonight – Laura Cantrell (Spit & Polish CD *When the Roses Bloom Again*)
6. Hey Gravity – MASS (White Label CD single)
5. Rolling Stones T-Shirt – Antihero (Integrity CD single)
4. Ugly Face – Nina Nastasia (Touch & Go LP *The Blackened Air*)
3. Talk Hard – Miss Black America (Integrity CD single)
2. Quick Before It Melts – Cinerama (Scopitones CD single)
1. Girls are the New Boys – Saloon (Track & Field 7")

2003

How fitting that the very last festive fifty to be broadcast by John Peel should conclude with what by all accounts was a close scrap for the number one slot between the chart's most prolific performers, Mark E. Smith Vs David L. Gedge. Of course we didn't know it would be his last at the time: if we had we might have found added poignancy in the return of the Undertones to the chart in which they graced so majestically in the years 1978-82 and that other serial entrants like Ballboy, Mogwai, Belle & Sebastian, the White Stripes and Darren Hayman (with his new, short-lived band the French) should all be here too along with other Peel favourites like Melt Banana and Nina Nastasia. Or, perhaps most poignantly of all, that CLSM's 'John Peel is Not Enough' should ring out at number nine. You sensed there would be general agreement among his listeners: John Peel really was not enough but he was all we'd had, something that would be all too clear when we soon had to face up to life without him.

After the number 49 record, Peel claims it's the first time he's ever given the name of the artist before the track. I suspect even he must have known this was not the case had he given the matter some thought and that the majority of festive fifties had occasionally included tracks introduced in this manner. Introductions after the track had by this point, however, become the generally established way of doing things, and when those who acquired responsibility for the chart in subsequent years failed to follow this rule, it caused a genuine ripple of annoyance among listeners, however unreasonable that might appear to the unfamiliar.

Peel also states that he believes this to be a 'pure' festive fifty, following the shenanagins of the previous year: steps had been taken during the voting process to eliminate or at least minimise such behaviour this year. The chart certainly has a more genuine feel about it and indeed the top end was more than a tad predictable.

Given the band's profile by that time, It might have been anticipated that at least one of the two White Stripes tracks would have been higher but, as Peel hints following the playing of 'Black Math', he'd been prevented from broadcasting much of their *Elephant* album after a legal intervention from the XL record label's lawyers. Prior to the album's release, Peel had played three tracks from it and had intended to carry on in this manner over the next few shows. XL, clearly unhappy regarding the potential for illegal taping this presented, made their move and prevented him from doing so. A hugely ironic act, given that we were at a moment in history where the potential for illegal downloads would present far greater opportunities for listener skullduggery than Peel had ever made possible and that this band, almost uniquely in recent history, would never have got anywhere close to their level of stardom had it not been for this man's championing of them (to be fair to the Stripes, there was no suggestion that they supported their label's intervention). So their new record company effectively prevented a man who had done more than anyone else to make the band into the commercial proposition they now were from giving them airplay, over which Peel felt understandably aggrieved.

It was a close thing at the top, with The Fall only one vote behind Cinerama in that battle for the number one spot.

Peel commented, with misplaced certainty, that this had been the closest festive fifty of all time, of course forgetting the 1990 chart, where only a spoiled postal vote prevented My Bloody Valentine from being top, and the dead heat and decision by highest number of first choices that gave Bang Bang Machine the top spot in 1992.

2003 Festive Fifty
Broadcast dates: 24 & 25 December

50. I'm Going – The Vaults (Red Flag 10")
49. You Can See the Paint – Freddy Fresh (Howlin' CD *Have Records Will Travel*)
48. Ain't No Stoppin' This – Blizzard Boys (Blizzard Tracks 12")
47. Keep It Clean – Camera Obscura (Elefant LP *Underachievers Please Try Harder*)
46. Slow Life – Super Furry Animals (Epic CD *Phantom Power*)
45. Dr Dre Buys a Pint of Milk – Grandmaster Gareth (Awkward LP *Introduction to Minute Melodies*)
44. Tokyo Invention Registration Office – Hyper Kinako (GoJonnnyGoGoGoGo V/A 7" EP *Untitled*)
43. Stay Loose – Belle & Sebastian (Rough Trade LP *Dear Catastophe Waitress*)
42. Renaissance Kids – Golden Virgins (Hex CD single)
41. Strength of Strings – The Keys (Too Pure CD single)
40. Pendulum – Broadcast (Warp CD single)
39. Werewolf – Cat Power (Matador CD *You Are Free*)
38. Born in the USA – Ballboy (SL CD *The Sash My Father Wore & Other Stories*)
37. There There – Radiohead (Parlophone CD *Hail to the Thief*)
36. Gabriel in the Airport – The French (Too Pure LP *Local Information*)
35. Live a Little – MASS (Mandita CD single)
34. Have Love Will Travel – Black Keys (Fat Possum CD *Thickfreakness*)
33. Sex, God, Money – Neulaner (Disko B 10")
32. Open Field – Maher Shalal Hash Baz (Geographic LP *Blues Du Jour*)
31. Does This Train Stop on Merseyside?- Amsterdam (Beat Crazy CD single)
30. Suspended From Class – Camera Obscura (Elefant CD *Underachievers Please Try Harder*)
29. The Owls Go – Architecture in Helsinki (Trifekta CD *Fingers Crossed*)
28. It Makes the Room Look Bigger – Half Man Half Biscuit (Probe Plus CD EP *Saucy Haulage Ballads*)
27. Porn Shoes – The French (Too Pure LP *Local Information*)
26. Green Eyed Loco Man – The Fall (Action LP *The Real New Fall LP*)
25. First Day – Futureheads (Fantastic Plastic CD single)
24. Shotgun Funeral – Party of One (Fat Cat 7")
23. I Gave Up My Mind to a Man Who Was Blind – Ballboy (SL CD *The Sash My Father War & Other Stories*)
22. Oh Please – Undertones (Sanctuary LP *Get What You Need*)
21. I Am the Party – Million Dead (Integrity 7")
20. I Believe in a Thing Called Love – The Darkness vs SFB (White Label 12")
19. At the Back of the Chapel – Broken Family Band (Snowstorm CD single)
18. Maps – Yeah Yeah Yeahs (Dress Up LP *Fever to Tell*)
17. Black Math – White Stripes (XL LP *Elephant*)
16. Piece of You – Sluts of Trust (Chemikal Underground 7")
15. Noir Desir – Vive La Fete (Surprise 12")
14. The Sash My Father Wore – Ballboy (SL CD *The Sash My Father War & Other Stories*)
13. You Her & Me – Nina Nastasia (Touch & Go LP *Run to Ruin*)
12. Shield for Your Eyes, a Beast in the Well on Your Hand – Melt Banana (A-Zap LP *Cell Scape*)
11. Step Into My Office, Baby – Belle & Sebastian (Rough Trade LP *Dear Catastrophe Waitress*)
10. Seven Nation Army – White Stripes (XL LP *Elephant*)
9. John Peel (Not Enough) (Fergus Mayhem Remix) (G-Core 12")

8. Baby Boom – The Crimea (Boobytrap CD single)
7. Tending the Wrong Grave for 23 Years – Half Man Half Biscuit (Probe Plus CD EP *Saucy Haulage Ballads*)
6. Ratts of the Capital – Mogwai (Matador CD *Happy Songs for Happy People*)
5. Itsuko Got Married – Bearsuit (Bearslut 7")
4. Thrill Me – Undertones (Sanctuary LP *Get What You Need*)
3. Hunted By a Freak – Mogwai (Matador CD *Happy Songs for Happy People*)
2. Theme From Sparta FC – The Fall (Action LP *The Real New Fall LP*)
1. Don't Touch That Dial – Cinerama (Scopitones CD single)

2004

Of course, when 2004 began we had no idea that, sadly, we'd already heard the last chart presented by John Peel. Following his passing in October, Rob Da Bank filled in for his remaining shows, many featuring sessions also already booked or recorded, and duly took on the responsibility of overseeing the promotion and broadcast of that year's festive fifty. Perhaps understandably, this was approached with a level of enthusiasm and evident excitement by the young DJ that was far removed from the rather dour sense of inevitability with which Peel approached the chart in most years.

Da Bank, it's only fair to recognise, did his best in a situation loaded with potential banana skins and in the wake of the still raw emotion of Peel enthusiasts: his funeral, after all, was taking place as voting commenced. Certainly any attempt to imitate the style of the DJ would have risked embarrassment and a greater level of criticism. The DJ understandably recognised he was only sitting in on a chart that retained the flavour of the Peel show, whose audience were voting for what they understandably believed might be the very last festive fifty and did pretty much what he'd done since filling in from the autumn, presenting the show in a manner that was most natural to him.

It was a pretty good chart too, with far greater variety than that of the previous year. While the word 'grime' was trotted out fairly liberally by Rob Da Bank, as it would be by me in the first edition of this book, what we were hearing would emerge, over time, as stirrings from a genuine range of darker, more intense 'dance' movements in which were mingling elements of dubstep, breakcore and drum and bass, among others. The 2004 festive fifty manages to some extent to encapsulate the spirit of this experimentation in a way that had not been the case with innovative movements in 'dance' inspired subcultures in the past.

Perhaps predictably, many memorable 'Peel' moments were captured in the chart. Among them were two Magic Band entries, culled from the band's live performance that year and another live gem in the shape of Laura Cantrell teaming up with Ballboy from a December 2003 show and subsequently released. Favourites of the late Peel era such as Shitmat, Jawbone and Listen With Sarah also made appearances along with what was then the highest ever appearance for a Half Man Half Biscuit track, with the brilliantly named and executed 'Joy Division Oven Gloves', another session recording and a tune that would return in its official release format the following year.

Other perennial Peel favourites to make the list included PJ Harvey, Bearsuit and The Delgados while, again in a move loaded with presumably unintentional poignancy, Cinerama and The Wedding Present managed to appear in the same chart for the only time. It was also fitting that Calvin Party, a band heavily championed by Peel but one that had enjoyed only one appearance in a festive fifty until now, made a second and final visit here.

The Vaults, a band local to Peel in Suffolk, achieved the rare feat of appearing at number 50 in successive years, their only entries in the chart. Could it be that, like their fellow East Anglians the Dawn Parade in 2002, their position was due to demotion as a result of vote rigging? We don't know, but that the question even gets asked is further evidence of the shadow that was still lurking over the chart due to the events two years earlier.

Some bands that were making that legendary step up from the Peel show to commercial success made their mark on the chart. The duo Black Keys were about to step out of the unfairly imposed shadow of the White Stripes, become the darlings of Uncut and Mojo and be saddled with the unwieldy label of the future of blues-inspired rock, while Bloc Party, one of those guitar bands that down the years have combined commercial potential with enough of an edge to garner interest from Peel, would enjoy three entries in their solitary visit to a festive fifty. Decoration, a band who even at the time always looked to have a great deal more longevity about them, registered a couple of entries on their way to securing more notable successes in the Dandelion years.

There would be a couple of memorable Welsh debuts, with Welsh language titles to boot, from Kentucky AFC and Texas Radio Band, though not for the first time this was a chart very much stamped with a Scottish seal. Aereogramme produced a couple of high entries, with one of these featuring in a run of four top notch Scottish tunes in the top seven: alongside the expected appearance of the Delgados were memorable FF debuts for Sons & Daughters and Sluts of Trust. While a surprise entry at number three gave Caroline Martin her only taste of festive fifty action – with a version of an old song that had warranted this kind of attention before now – the top two appropriately comprised Peel's favourite band of the last thirty years alongside his favourite of more recent times: Bearsuit secured the number two while The Fall, with a new version of a song that had occupied that position the previous year, grabbed themselves a second number one, with Mark E. Smith emulating the feat of the three members of Joy Division/New Order in placing a third track at the top of the chart.

2004 Festive Fifty
Broadcast dates: 28, 29 & 30 December

50. No Sleep No Need – The Vaults (Red Flag CD single)
49. I Don't Have Time to Stand Here With You Fighting About the Size of My Dick – Ballboy (SL CD *The Royal Theatre*)
48. Park Lake Speakers – Ella Guru (Banana CD *The First Album*)
47. Electricity – The Magic Band (Live Peel Session 7.7.04)
46. Your Belgian Things – Mountain Goats (4AD CD *We Shall All Be Healed*)
45. If U Want Me – Aphrodisias (CD *This is a Campaign*)
44. Little Thoughts – Bloc Party (Wichita CD single)
43. Be Nesa – Kentucky AFC (Boobytrap CD *Kentucky AFC*)
42. Cha – Plasticman (Terrorhythm 12")
41. Northern Song – Calvin Party (Probe Plus CD *Never As Black*)
40. Topknot – Cornershop presents Bubbley Kaur (Rough Trade CD single)
39. Joy Adamson – Decoration (Peel Session 13.4.04)
38. Eyeliner – Melys (Sylem CD single)
37. Tale From Black – Tunng (Static Caravan CD *Mother's Daughters & Other Songs*)
36. Interstate 5 – The Wedding Present (Scopitones CD single)
35. International – Jon E. Cash (Black Ops 12")
34. Big Eyed Beans From Venus – The Magic Band (Live Peel Session 7.7.04)
33. There's No Business Like Propa' Rungleclotted Mashup Bizznizz (Planet Mu CD *Full English Breakfast*)
32. I Fought the Angels – The Delgados (Chemikal Underground CD *Universal Audio*)
31. Formed a Band – Art Brut (Rough Trade CD single)
30. Girl is on My Mind – Black Keys (Fat Possum 7")
29. B – Digital Mystikz (CMZ 12" EP *Twisup*)
28. O Superman (Henry Cullen Remix) – Laurie Anderson (X Booty 12")
27. Animal Hop – Listen with Sarah (Womb CD EP *Are You Sitting Comfortably?*)
26. That Man Will Not Hang – McLusky (Too Pure CD *The Difference Between You and Me is That I'm Not on Fire*)
25. Retreat! Retreat! – 65daysofstatic (Monotreme CD single)
24. I Tried It, I Liked It, I Loved It – Decoration (Demo CD EP)
23. Shame – PJ Harvey (Island CD *Uh Huh Her*)
22. 10am Automatic – Black Keys (Fat Possum CD *Rubber Factory*)
21. The Art of Kissing – Ballboy (SL CD *The Royal Theatre*)
20. Banquet – Bloc Party (Moshi Moshi CD single)
19. The Ritual – DJ Distance (Lix Corruptions 12" EP *Closer Than You Think*)
18. Jackrabbit – Jawbone (Self-released CD *Dang*

Blues)
17. I Lost You, But I Found Country Music – Ballboy & Laura Cantrell (Peel Session 23.12.03)
16. The Letter – PJ Harvey (Island CD *Uh Huh Her*)
15. The Unravelling – Aereogramme (Undergroove CD *Seclusion*)
14. It's Not You, It's Me – Cinerama (Go Metric 7")
13. Do Not Underestimate – Martyn Hare (Designer Label 12")
12. Chwareon Bwtleg Pep Le Pew – Texas Radio Band (FF Vinyl V/A CD *The North South Divine*)
11. Helicopter – Bloc Party (Wichita CD single)
10. Hi-De-Hi – Jawbone (Self-released CD *Dang Blues*)
9. Freakin' Out – Graham Coxon (Transcopic/Parlophone CD *Happiness in Magazines*)
8. Joy Division Oven Gloves – Half Man Half Biscuit (Peel Session 16.11.04)
7. Johnny Cash - Sons & Daughters (Domino CD *Love the Cup*)
6. Everybody Come Down – The Delgados (Chemikal Underground CD *Universal Audio*)
5. Leave You Wanting More – Sluts of Trust (Chemikal Underground CD *We Are All Sluts of Trust*)
4. Dreams & Bridges – Aereogramme (Undergroove CD *Seclusion*)
3. The Singer – Caroline Martin (Small Dog CD *I Had a Hundred More Reasons to Stay By the Fire*)
2. Chargr – Bearsuit (Fortuna Pop CD Single)
1. Theme From Sparta FC #2 – The Fall (Action CD Single)

The Post-Peel Festive Fifties

2005 – The One Music Festive Fifty

The BBC's initial response to filling the vacant John Peel slot had a tokenistic feel to it even at the time. The 'One Music' idea entrusted three different DJs with the mantle of taking forward the Peel legacy and that particular element of the move made some sense. The greatest difficulty they faced in facing up to the, let's face it, impossible task of replacing the legendary DJ would have been to identify an individual who not only possessed the kind of idiosyncratic zeal for music that was his forte, but also somebody who prepared and able to devote so much time to the pursuit. In opting to share the task between three people they wouldn't burden any individual with this task and none would be saddled with the impossible tag of 'the new John Peel'.

It soon became, apparent, however that, notwithstanding the clear efforts of two of the DJs to make it work, the initiative was doomed to failure. While Rob Da Bank and Huw Stephens both clearly entered their roles in the appropriate spirit, the third of the trio, Ras Kwarme, clearly had little interest in continuing the legacy. Not only did his show select from a tiresomely narrow range of musical genres, but he committed that most unforgivable of all Peel crimes by repeatedly talking over the intros and endings of records. While in his later years Peel had relaxed his approach in this area when it came, for instance, to the lengthy fade outs of techno tracks, his principle that, if someone had made the track to be that long the DJ ought to pay it the respect of playing the whole thing, had retained a firm commitment down the years. Small issue it might seem to the population in general, nonetheless by failing even to acknowledge the issue, there was a clear stylistic message that the sanctity of the legacy he was a part of continuing held no value or resonance whatsoever.

Stephens and Da Bank were clearly genuine in their efforts, but the initiative as a whole was heavily laden with token gestures and gimmicks. While the tunes the two DJs played managed to a laudable extent to replace the irreplaceable, we really could have done without the strained efforts to link the three shows with joint projects and even more so the particular slots afforded to the promotion of 'new' (and usually British) acts (several of these bands would, somewhat unconvincingly, take up places in the top half of the festive fifty this year). Clearly this was something their BBC overlords saw as an important factor, whereas the most crucial thing about the Peel show was how brilliantly it combined an eye for the new and different with a 'levelling' of musical history that was ultimately the programme's most challenging element: my own cherished musical awakening had, after all, come from tuning in in the late eighties expecting to hear wall to wall punk tunes and being hit, among many sub-three minutes slabs of frenzied guitars, with a healthy dose of reggae and an unanticipated introduction to the wonders of Lightnin' Hopkins.

There had always been a suspicion that the BBC didn't really 'get' Peel and here was its final confirmation, a resurrected 'Evening Session' approach and a narrowing of the concept held dear by the man who will remember, you suspect for ever, as their greatest DJ. It was only due to the fervent respect and commitment to their task that Stephens and Da Bank managed to save the thing from being a complete disaster. While there might be few airings for Lightnin' Hopkins in the offing, it was nonetheless apparent that the pair were prepared to put in the effort to give us something that demonstrated clear respect for the Peel vision and do their utmost to make a decent fist of the job.

Retaining the festive fifty was, thankfully, recognised as a part of that commitment. Initially, the 2005 chart was promoted by all three DJs and part of that promotion told us that the three would collectively present the results. When the time came to reveal the chart, however, only Da Bank and Stephens were present at the microphones. Why Kwarme ultimately didn't take part can only be speculated on, but to the clear stylistic differences between his and the other two shows together with the fact that only one entry in the chart (the entry from Benjamin Zephaniah) emanated from his playlists, it was easy to hazard a guess.

The chart itself, while it contained good tunes in abundance, had a slightly odd look and feel to it, not the least of which was the fact that only one band managed to generate more than a single entry. Although this would be repeated in one of the subsequent Dandelion festive fifties, and despite the welcome variety that it unquestionably helped to generate, there was nevertheless a feeling that a vital element of the festive fifty was missing. Not only that, but the appearance of Arcade Fire and Arctic Monkeys in the top five, albeit bands that had found some favour with two of the One Music DJs, left an impression that many of the Peel audience's most cherished sensibilities had been lost on the road between the last chart and this one. It was also hard to imagine that Peel would have awarded Kate Bush's new work the kind of praise and airplay some of his successors did, either, something that resulted in an entry in a festive fifty some 27 years after the artist's first release.

Despite that, the number one was an absolute delight and a selection that, I suspect, the late DJ would have approved of; ditto the appearance, finally, of The Crimea's modern classic at number two, an appearance for Steveless at number nine and Camera Obscura's memorable 'Burns Night' contribution at number seven. Ollo's remix of an old Dodgems track much loved by Peel in its original version also managed to gatecrash the top ten. It was one of three tracks in the chart to feature a sample of the great man voice, the others being the entries from Cuban Boys and Listen With Sarah.

2005 Festive Fifty
Broadcast: 20 & 22 December

50. The Tunnel – Richie Hawtin (Novamute CD *DE9/Transitions*)
49. Hollywood Bowl – Fleeing New York (White label)
48. Do the Whirlwind – Architecture in Helsinki (Moshi Moshi CD *In Case We Die*)
47. Rong Radio Station – Benjamin Zephaniah (One Little Indian CD *Naked*)
46. Masho Le Fan Star – Stabmaster Vinyl (High Quality Recordings CD *Masho Fe Lan Star*)
45. Green Cosmos – Deerhoof (ATP CD *Green Cosmos*)
44. Imagine This – Wax Audio (Metal Postcard 7")
43. My Babyskull Has Not Yet Flowered – Mugstar (Lancashire & Somerset 7")
42. King of the Mountain – Kate Bush (EMI CD *Aerial*)
41. Me Animal – Suicidal Birds (Transformed Dreams CD *Z-List*)
40. Goddamn – Son of Dave (Kartel Creative CD *02*)
39. Bottle Rocket – Go! Team (Memphis Industries CD *Thunder, Lightning, Strike*)
38. Emily Kane – Art Brut (Fierce Panda CD *Bang Bang Rock & Roll*)
37. Girls of Valour – The Delgados (Chemikal Underground 7")
36. Bowl Me Over – Acid Casuals (Placid Casual Recordings 12")
35. Everything 2 Me – Aluminum Babe (Self-released CD *Dream Dancing*)
34. I Tried It, I Liked It, I Loved It – Decoration (SL CD *Don't Disappoint Me Now*)
33. The Nation Needs You – Cuban Boys (White label Promo CD single)
32. I Can Hear the Grass Grow – The Fall (Sanctuary LP *Fall Heads Roll*)
31. I'm From Further North Than You – The Wedding Present (Scopitones CD *Take Fountain*)
30. Take the Lovers Home Tonight – Mother and the Addicts (Chemikal Underground Promo CD single)
29. What About Us – The Fall (Sanctuary LP *Fall Heads Roll*)
28. Tetris Wonderland – DJ Scotch Egg (AD AAD AT CD *KFC Core*)
27. Pwer Y Fflwer – Radio Luxembourg (Ciwdod 7")

26. Your Love – Kid Carpet (Tired & Lonesome CD *Ideas & Oh Dears*)
25. All I Ever Wanted Was You – Jegsy Dodd and the Original Sinners (Piffle/Cherry Red CD *Wake Up & Smell the Offy*)
24. Drove Through Ghosts to Get Here – 65 Days of Static (Monotreme CD *One Time For All Time*)
23. Break My Heart – Malcolm Middleton (Chemikal Underground CD *Into the Woods*)
22. Hope There's Someone – Antony and the Johnsons (Rough Trade CD *I Am A Bird Now*)
21. Dirty Mind – The Pipettes (Memphis Industries CD single)
20. Little One – Rory McVicar (White Label)
19. Joy Division Oven Gloves – Half Man Half Biscuit (Probe Plus CD *Achtung Bono*)
18. Don't Touch My Neck – Hunting Lodge (White Label)
17. The Last Thing She Ever Said – Autochtone (White Label)
16. The Story of Love – Misty's Big Adventure (There's A Riot Going On CD *The Black Hole*)
15. Whistler's Delight – DJ Riko (Prank Monkey 12")
14. Blindness – The Fall (Sanctuary LP *Fall Heads Roll*)
13. Another Nice Mix – Listen With Sarah (Womb 7")
12. Pig Fucker – Evils (White Label)
11. Movin', Twistin', Groovin' – Paranormal (White Label)
10. Bees – Laura Cantrell (Matador CD *Humming By the Flowered Vine*)
9. Bored – Steveless (Cherryade LP *Popular Music in Theory*)
8. Lord Lucan is Still Missing (The Ask Betty or Freddie Queenspiracy Mix) – Ollo (12 Apostles 12" EP *Lord Lucan Is Missing*)
7. I Love My Jean – Camera Obscura (Elefant CD single)
6. All the Ones and Zeros – Early Years (Beggars Banquet CD single)
5. Rebellion (Lies) – Arcade Fire (Merge CD *Funeral*)
4. Klutz – King Creosote (Domino CD single)
3. I Bet You Look Good on the Dancefloor – Arctic Monkeys (Domino CD single)
2. Lottery Winners on Acid – The Crimea (Warner Bros CD *Tragedy Rocks*)
1. Grumpy Old Men – Jegsy Dodd & The Original Sinners (Piffle/Cherry Red CD *Wake Up & Smell the Offy*)

The Truly Festive Festive Fifty

A footnote, really, to the next chart in this list but placed before it because chronologically that's when it happened, comes in the form of this one-off chart initiated by yours truly who, devastated by the prospect of a future without the festive fifty, sought to canvas the thoughts of like-minded souls on the internet during the autumn of 2006 with a view to putting something together that might fill the gap, however imperfectly.

It soon became apparent that such an endeavour was destined not to succeed so I ditched it in favour of a stop-gap temporary solution. As 2006 would be the year of the thirtieth anniversary of the chart, I decided an appropriate way of commemorating that would be to gather votes for a special one-off chart that restricted voters to tunes with a Christmas theme. My thinking on this was as follows: incoming votes were likely to be restricted to a relatively narrow selection of tunes and therefore, in the event that only 50 or 60 people deigned to take part, we might still be able to cobble something together. In the event, such concerns proved to be unfounded and, via the then still vibrant myspace, various forums, simple e-mails and other outlets, several hundred voters took part, drawing their selections from quite an impressive range of tunes, from the obscure to the traditional.

The Truly Festive Festive Fifty thus came into existence, albeit briefly and, without any broadcasting outlet myself or any knowledge of the means to get one, I revealed the results via my myspace blog, which attracted an increasing number of views each day another chunk of the chart was unleashed into cyberspace. By that point it had already become clear that Dandelion Radio, thankfully, had come to the rescue and the festive fifty's future was secured, so by the time it was announced the chart below stood only as an additional distraction for those who wanted one. I would finally decide to collate and broadcast the chart, mainly because every year people kept asking me to do it, on Dandelion Radio as part of the December 2013 schedule.

Perhaps predictably, all five of The Fall's festive classics found a place, but there were a fair number of surprise entries, perhaps the most significant being a reasonably high showing for Snow Patrol, with one of six entries that featured on Jeepster's *It's a Cool Cool Christmas* compilation, the most placed of the many various artists packages that contributed to the chart. Were I to award it official status, which I'm not going to, we'd also credit this festive fifty with the distinction of recognizing the earliest recordings in chart history. There are four Xmas tunes dating back to the fifties, including a couple from Elvis Presley and cuts from Chuck Berry and The Drifters, both of which made the top ten.

Intriguingly, a number of tunes began the voting process by gathering votes at a cracking rate before running out of steam in the later stages. For reasons I'm not entirely clear about, this included both the Flaming Lips tracks that made the chart, plus their version of 'White Christmas', which ultimately failed to gain a place. Presumably due to greater promotion from sources with Peel credentials, including Dandelion Radio, the latter stages saw enormous surges in the votes for the Captain Beefheart and Wedding Present entries in this list, neither of which would have made the chart had voting ended a week earlier. There was a close scrap for the number one spot. The top two were neck and neck throughout, with the Waitresses track ahead with one day to go, only for it to be pipped by Low, with one of three entries from their celebrated *Christmas* mini-album, at the death.

This results of this chart have not contributed to any of the statistics found elsewhere in this book and I list it here partly for curiosity value, the fact that it was voted for using the established festive fifty formula and because, for

2006 Truly Festive Festive Fifty
Eventually broadcast December 2013

50. Santa Doesn't Cop Out On Dope – Sonic Youth (Hip-O V/A CD *Sleighed: The Other Side of Christmas*)
49. Back Door Santa – Clarence Carter (Atco LP *Soul Christmas*)
48. Feliz Navi-Nada – El Vez (Jeepster CD *It's a Cool Cool Christmas*)
47. Christmas Eve – Gorky's Zygotic Mynci (Mantra CD *Spanish Dance Troupe*)
46. Do You Hear What I Hear? – Copeland (Nettwork V/A CD *Maybe This Christmas Tree*)
45. A Change at Christmas (Say It Isn't So) – Flaming Lips (Warner Bros EP *Ego Tripping at the Gates of Hell*)
44. Everything's Gonna Be Cool This Christmas (Live) – Eels (Dreamworks CD *Electro-Shock Blues Show*)
43. She Came Home for Christmas – Mew (Evil Office/Epic CD single)
42. Christmas is Going to the Dogs – Eels (Interscope V/A CD *The Grinch*)
41. Don't Believe in Christmas – The Sonics (Etiquette split 7" w/The Wailers)
40. Gee Whiz It's Christmas – Carla Thomas (King 7")
39. The Snow Doesn't Fall – The Aislers Set (Fortuna Pop V/A CD *A Christmas Gift From Fortuna Pop*)
38. (We Wish You a) Protein Christmas – The Fall (Action CD single)
37. Jesus Christ – Big Star (Dojo LP *Third/Sister Lovers*)
36. Christmas at the Zoo – Flaming Lips (Warner Bros CD *Clouds Taste Metallic*)
35. Jingle Bell rock – The Fall (Castle CD Box Set *The Complete Peel Sessions*)
34. There Ain't No Santa Claus on the Evening Stage – Captain Beefheart (Reprise LP *The Spotlight Kid*)
33. It's Christmas Time – Yo La Tengo (Ego CD EP *Merry Christmas From Yo La Tengo*)
32. River – Joni Mitchell (Reprise CD *Blue*)
31. 100,000 Turkeys – Chris T-T (Snowstorm V/A CD *The True Meaning of Christmas Vol. 4*)

30. Donna & Blitzen – Badly Drawn Boy (Twisted Nerve/XL CD *About A Boy: Original Soundtrack*)
29. Candy Cane Children – White Stripes (XL 7" *Merry Christmas From The White Stripes*)
28. Christmas Steps – Mogwai (Chemikal Underground CD *Come On Die Young*)
27. Little Drummer Boy – Low (Tugboat CD *Christmas*)
26. Thanks for Christmas – The Three Wise Men (Virgin 7")
25. Santa Claus is Back in Town – Elvis Presley (RCA Victor LP *Elvis' Christmas Album*)
24. Xmas With Simon – The Fall (Cog Sinister 12" *High Tension Line* B-side)
23. Christmas (Baby Please Come Home) – Death Cab for Cutie (Nettwork V/A CD *Maybe This Christmas Tree*)
22. Winter Wonderland – Cocteau Twins (Mercury CD single)
21. It's Cliched to be Cynical at Christmas – Half Man Half Biscuit (Probe Plus CD *Trouble Over Bridgewater*)
20. Alan Parsons in a Winter Wonderland – Grandaddy (Jeepster V/A CD *It's a Cool, Cool Christmas*)
19, Merry Christmas Baby – Otis Redding (Atco 7")
18. Blue Christmas – Elvis Presley (RCA Victor LP *Elvis' Christmas Album*)
17. Christmas Song – The Raveonettes (Nettwork V/A CD *Maybe This Christmas Tree*)
16. When I Get Home for Christmas – Snow Patrol (Jeepster V/A CD *It's a Cool, Cool Christmas*)
15. No Xmas For John Quays – The Fall (Castle CD Box Set *The Complete Peel Sessions*)
14. Hark the Herald Angels Sing – The Fall (Castle CD Box Set *The Complete Peel Sessions*)
13. Frosty the Snowman – Cocteau Twins (Mercury CD single)
12. Santa Claus Go Straight to the Ghetto – James Brown (Spectrum CD *Funky Christmas*)
11. Blue Christmas – Low (Tugboat CD *Christmas*)
10. Step Into Christmas – The Wedding Present (RCA 7" single *No Christmas* B-side)
9. Father Christmas – The Kinks (Arista 7")
8. Run Rudolph Run – Chuck Berry (Chess 7")
7. O Come O Come Emmanuel – Belle and Sebastian (Jeepster V/A CD *It's a Cool, Cool Christmas*)
6. White Christmas – The Drifters (Atlantic 7")
5. A Fairytale of New York – The Pogues (Pogue Mahone LP *If I Should Fall From Grace With God*)
4. Merry Christmas (I Don't Want to Fight Tonight) – The Ramones (Chrysalis CD *Brain Drain*)
3. Christmas in Hollis – Run DMC (A&M V/A CD *A Very Special Christmas*)
2. Christmas Wrapping – The Waitresses (Ze/Island 7")
1. Just Like Christmas – Low (Tugboat CD *Christmas*)

MARK WHITBY

The Dandelion Radio Festive Fifties

2006

Dandelion Radio had barely been in existence for half a year when the opportunity to rescue the festive fifty from potential death presented itself. With Colin Murray now filling the old 10pm Peel slot with utterly bland musical fare played by a man whose only connection with the great man was that he claimed to support the same football team, the BBC clearly had no intention whatsoever in seeking a permanent replacement with a brief to continue in the spirit of the Peel show. Their argument, presumably, was that 6music was offering a whole station-full of the kind of stuff he'd been playing, although even a cursory listen to the station's output revealed it to be doing nothing of the sort, whatever the acknowledged merits of some of their DJs. The festive fifty, like the rest of Peel's legacy, had simply been abandoned. However, Peel's old production team thankfully had both the respect for that legacy and the presence of mind to approach Dandelion Radio with an invitation to continue the chart, and Dandelion readily accepted.

Had they not done so, the Festive Fifty wouldn't have exactly disappeared, but it would have continued in name only, in those personal charts that spring up all over the internet each December, which would have been far worse. These, like The Word magazine's own pitiful attempt to continue something allegedly in its spirit, bear absolutely no resemblance to the historical festive fifty and merely employ the name as a recognisable heading to accompany end of year 'best of' lists. While it was never the case that this end of year chart (with the exception of 1977, of course) ever managed fully to reflect the eclectic zeal of the Peel show itself, Dandelion's first chart was a promising first effort at least to span the range of tastes of its listening audience and reflect the spirit of the original. Understandably, the station's DJs had no idea what voters might come up with, and the selections overall show recognition for some well-established Peel giants, along with some more personal choices and the burgeoning influence of social media and the opportunities it presented to bands and artists to get their stuff out there. Fewer than half of the entries had actually been broadcast on Dandelion, however, much of the chart being a reflection more of the content of the Radio One shows of Rob Da Bank and Huw Stephens, who of course had formerly carried the OneMusic mantle as well as co-presenting the previous year's festive fifty, and who also gave assistance in promoting the chart. In addition to their lingering, and it must be said positive, influence, another factor was that the station itself had been in existence a bare six months by that point.

Things have been moving quickly during the years since Dandelion took up the baton, so much so that it seems odd now to consider how much the 2006 chart was influenced by myspace. Facebook hadn't yet extended its influential grip across cyberspace, and myspace – soon to be bought up by Rupert Murdoch and tampered with to within an inch of its life – was at that time very much the leader among social network sites. In those days bands and artists could offer up their music for free download from their myspace player should they choose to do so, something that established the platform as a firm favourite among musicians who would eventually find a retreat to Soundcloud and Bandcamp in the days after the option's withdrawl. Its influence was certainly evident in those early Dandelion shows, and perusal of these results reveals that significantly more than 50% of the chart was, at the time of broadcast, available via myspace either to stream or to add to ever-growing digital download collections.

New music was becoming far more easy to access than it had been even in the later Peel years, and the days when we listened to the Peel show and then scoured the independent record shops in the often forlorn hope of tracking down something we'd heard were so far behind us it seemed hard to believe we'd ever managed to survive them and still somehow assemble decent record collections. Now, it seemed barely possible that a phenomenon like New Band Things' 'I Suck' – played by Peel and utterly out of range of any other collector in the UK - could happen in the way that it did: it would presumably be whacked up somewhere on the internet and immediately made available for mass circulation.

Because of this, Dandelion Radio DJs faced an entirely different challenge to the one that Peel had faced for years:

how to remain resolutely new and fresh, seeking out and drawing attention to the vibrant and the new in a world in which such things could now be sought and found very easily. That it managed to do this, more or less from its first month of broadcast, was quite a feat. There had been cynical responses all over the internet to news of the station's imminent emergence, carrying with them assumptions that any such station was almost bound to be backward-looking, searching for the spirit of Peel in fond memories of old releases and ultimately descending into a kind of 'Desert Island Discs' like sterility. 'What do they do – play back to back Undertones and Wedding Present records for hours on end?' scoffed one early forum contributor, whose level of cynicism had clearly prevented him from actually tuning in. Had he done so, he'd have had his question answered with a firm and emphatic no.

If the time and circumstances presented Dandelion with a challenge, it was one that carried also the silver lining of opportunity. There were, in truth, two significant barriers to the emergence of a new Peel-instigated show or station. One was how to find someone with the ears and open mind to seek out new music, untrammelled by concerns of taste or established listening habits. Thankfully, Dandelion DJs, with only occasional (and understandable) false starts, were putting this concern to bed with remarkable ease within the first few months of broadcast. The second was how a new DJ could establish him or herself quickly enough to receive the sheer number and frequency of releases acquired by Peel, which had allowed him for so many years to sift through them and put together such great and varied radio shows with such remarkable regularity.

As it turned out, the still increasing openness of the internet did new music and Dandelion a big and very timely favour. While in time enough new bands and labels would begin to discover the station and generate a momentum of fresh-sounding releases to fill their DJs' inboxes, for now there was enough of interest one could find via the occasional browsing and surfing spree on the internet. And because Dandelion was self-funded, reliant neither on advertising nor high listening figures to remain alive, it answered to no one and largely did what the hell it liked, as remains the case today.

How the festive fifty would be broadcast did change, however. Dandelion produced new shows every month, which were then repeated throughout the calendar month until a new cycle began. This first festive fifty would thus have its first airing on 1 January, at the beginning of the new monthly schedule. In future years, it was decided that the festive fifty would be introduced into the final week of the previous month's schedule, allowing for a first broadcast at midnight as Christmas Eve gave way to Christmas Day, then repeated throughout the month and at varying times during the following month. The days of a single one-off broadcast were now over, although it continued to be the case that the most intensive listening would occur within the first few streaming.

Parts of this first chart are a bit of a throwback to those Festive Fifties (of which 1982 remains the paradigm case) where there was much elbow room for the popular and commercially successful alongside the obscure and obtuse. Step forward Gnarls Barkley, The Raconteurs and The Klaxons in particular to lend the chart variety from some perhaps unexpected angles. Morrissey also made an unexpected return to the chart, some 23 years after his first appearance with The Smiths and 16 years after his most recent solo entry. Two bands who'd been big Peel favourites but had never previously featured in a festive fifty also made their belated mark here. The Nightingales, with two entries, and Beatnik Filmstars, who made the top ten, had both recently re-formed and had their merits at last recognized at last among festive fifty voters only in this second phase of their existence. The Nightingales' absence from earlier charts being a particularly curiosity of the Peel years, but easily the most conspicuous absentees here were The Fall. They had made an appearance in every festive fifty since 1983 but, with no new material released in 2006 other than a Monks' cover on a limited edition single, the chart's Dandelion years would begin without them, though this would prove to be only a temporary break from chart duties. Established Peel favourites who did find themselves in the chart were Mogwai, with two entries, Bearsuit and Camera Obscura, while Decoration continued their push from the end of the Peel era and would feature strongly in these early Dandelion charts.

Even after all these years, the chart could still break new ground, albeit in some fairly peripheral ways. The number 47 entry, for instance, was the first ever to feature tap-dancing as a percussion instrument, while Ivor Cutler, having been overlooked by voters through his long and illustrious career, found himself name-checked in titles twice in the same festive fifty. Sweden's Peter, Bjorn & John became the highest non-UK or Ireland European entrants in a festive fifty since the Sugarcubes made it to number one nineteen years earlier. Tall Pony, despite not having been played during the year by any of the station's DJs, grabbed number one, beating off challenges from the well-established Camera Obscura and early Dandelion favourites The Autons. The Tall Pony track would be released the following year on Dandelion DJ Rachel Neiman's Cherryade label, but earned its position here, you suspect, due to championing from Huw Stephens.

2006 Festive Fifty
First broadcast: 1 January 2007

50. You Will With Ivor Cutler – Uke Stanza (Self-Released CD *Pheasants Will Cross The Road*)
49. Willow – Gilbert (Self-Released Download Album *Gilbert*)
48. Mr Whippy – Lost Penguin (Pop Disc 7")
47. Flying – Seize The Day (Wildwood Acoustic CD *The Tide Is Turning*)
46. Reckless – Tilly & The Wall (Trash Aesthetics 7")
45. I Believe I Can Fly – Lost Penguin (Fake Product 7" *Pleasurewood Kills* B-Side)
44. Cheddar Would Be Better – Chalkdust (Self-Released CD *Lover of Ponies, Protector of Men*)
43. So You Think You're Unhappy – Forest Giants (Cherryade CD *Welcome to the Mid-West*)
42. Tolerance – N-Type (Tempa V/A 2x12" *Tempa All-Stars Vol. 3*)
41. Running The World – Jarvis Cocker (Rough Trade CD *Jarvis*)
40. To The Ramones – Dustin's Bar Mitzvah (HungryKid CD Single)
39. The Beeching Report – iLIKETRAINS (Dance To The Radio V/A CD *What We All Want*)
38. Fraud in the 80s – Mates of State (Moshi Moshi 7")
37. In White Rooms – Booka Shade (Get Physical Music CD *Movements*)
36. Crazy – Gnarls Barkley (Warner Bros CD Single)
35. Once & Never Again – The Long Blondes (Rough Trade CD Single)
34. Steady As She Goes – The Raconteurs (XL CD Single)
33. Monster Hospital – Metric (Drowned In Sound CD Single)
32. The Greatest – Cat Power (Matador CD *The Greatest*)
31. Pop The Glock – Uffie (Ed Banger 12")
30. We Share Our Mother's Health – The Knife (Brille CD Single)
29. Life Is A Pigsty – Morrissey (Attack CD *Ringleader of the Tormentors*)
28. Only Skin – Joanna Newsome (Drag City CD *Ys*)
27. Magick – The Klaxons (Because Music CD Single)
26. Black Country – The Nightingales (Cargo CD *Out of True*)
25. Born Again in Birmingham – The Nightingales (Cargo CD *Out of True*)
24. Standing in the Way of Control – Gossip (Backyard CD *Standing in the Way of Control*)
23. It's Not What You Know – Beatnik Filmstars (Track & Field CD *In Great Shape*)
22. Good Posture vs Bad Posture – Mugstar (Sea Records CD *Mugstar*)
21. Fooling Around – Cartridge (Self-Released CD *Class*)
20. We're From Barcelona – I'm From Barcelona (Dolores CD *Let Me Introduce Me Friends*)
19. Pull Shapes – The Pipettes (Memphis Industries CD *We Are The Pipettes*)
18. Steven F***ing Spielberg – Bearsuit (Fantastic Plastic 7")
17. My Baby Skull Has Not Yet Flowered – Mugstar (Lancashire & Somerset 7")
16. Ivor Cutler Is Dead – The Bobby McGees (Cherryade 7" EP *The Bobby McGees...Yes Please!*)
15. Glasgow Mega Snake – Mogwai (Rock Action CD *Mr Beast*)
14. The Orange Shop – Das Wanderlust (Don't Tell Clare 7")
13. The Chronicles of a Bohemian Teenager (Part 1) – Get Cape, Wear Cape, Fly (Atlantic CD Single)
12. You! Me! Dancing! – Los Campesinos (mp3 demo)
11. Candidate – Decoration (13 B Sides 7" Single)
10. Friend of the Night – Mogwai (Rock Action CD *Mr Beast*)
9. Fashion Parade – Misty's Big Adventure (Sunday Best CD Single)
8. Wolf Like Me – TV On The Radio (4AD 7")
7. Hello New World – The Playing Fields (CactiShed CD *Hello New World*)
6. Really Quite Bizarre – Beatnik Filmstars (Track & Field CD *In Great Shape*)
5. Young Folks – Peter, Bjorn & John (Wichita CD Single)

4. Job in London – Decoration (13 B Sides 7" Single *Candidate* B-side)
3. Lloyd, I'm Ready To Be Heartbroken – Camera Obscura (Merge CD *Let's Get Out of This Country*)
2. Snakes – Autons (Bill Badger Recording Co. 7" single)
1. I'm Your Boyfriend Now – Tall Pony (demo CD)

2007

A memorable festive fifty for me as, having joined the Dandelion team in May 2007, I got to reveal the top five. Rather oddly, this also coincided with my own favourite of the year being voted to number one for the first time ever. It also coincided with a festive fifty that had far more of the flavour of Dandelion playlists in its content. While a number of tracks not played on Dandelion during the year made the chart, these were mostly bands who had achieved airplay with other records, though there were exceptions, such as releases from the likes Of Montreal, Editors and The Bees, all of which had a certain appeal in some left-field circles, even if that didn't include Dandelion DJs.

The chart itself shares some of the characteristics of the 2006 Festive Fifty, in so much as it includes several wannabes knocking on the door of mainstream success (Laura Marling, Editors and Bat For Lashes, for example) as well as those already through it (Arcade Fire, Radiohead and The White Stripes). However, if the first Dandelion chart had mainly a kind of Peel favourites/myspace self-releases flavour to it, 2007 had far a much firmer stamp of Dandelion Radio and what it was about. The station was unsurprisingly a more established feature of the post-Peel world now and the bands above found themselves rubbing shoulders with artists and bands for whom airplay on Dandelion represented their best real stab at getting wider attention. This latter category would include a couple of brilliant tracks from the irreverent Trouserdog as well as entries for already well-established station favourites like Uke Stenza and the Bobby McGee's, both of whom had featured in 2006, and newcomers like Manhattan Love Suicides, Horowitz and Pete Green.

That said, there's a fair bit of trite indie rock in here, indeed rather more than had been the case in that inaugural Dandelion chart, and, despite some real highpoints, in retrospect it can certainly be viewed as one of the less remarkable festive fifties, both of the Dandelion period and generally. I suspect, and hope, that the DJ Europe track that made it to number 39 did so as a result of some voters mistaking the nature of the chart and assuming it was all about Christmas-themed tunes. Even so, they might well have chosen better. Ditto the case of Laura Marling, very much on her way to Uncut/Mojo acclaim at this point but another act that Dandelion DJs chose, rightly, to ignore.

However, the number five entry – Paul Rooney's 'Lucy Over Lancashire' - had the unmistakeable hallmarks of one of those records that could find a home towards the top end of the festive fifty while not standing a chance of gaining any such prominence in any other chart in the world. As such, more than any other entry here it truly cemented Dandelion Radio's role as the home of the festive fifty, an idiosyncratic masterpiece that, in garnering sufficient votes to reach such heights, suggested Dandelion was already reaching a lot of the right people. We also had the first Malian entry, courtesy of the masterful Tinariwen

During the Dandelion years, an increasingly varied range of entries would become a feature of the chart, but this one harks back, at least at its top end, to those fifties of old where a small number of heavyweight artists dominated. Beatnik Filmstars and two Mark E. Smith projects snaffled seven of the top eleven places between them, although neither managed to penetrate the top three. Three entries for The Fall overall showed that the previous year's non-appearance had only been a temporary blip, while Smith's appearances with Von Sudenfed saw him establish a record by appearing in festive fifties with a sixth different band.

Smith actually announced his 'sacking' from Von Sudenfed as the festive fifty votes were being collated, adding the band to a sadly lengthy casualty list in these early Dandelion charts. The excellent Electrelane, havjng found themselves overlooked by festive fifty voters until now, played their final gig on 1 December 2007. More positively, Battles capped an extraordinary year by securing a deserved number one spot, with Dan Le Sac & Scroobius Pip runners followed by the more familiar presence of Bearsuit at number three. Beatnik Filmstars became the first band since Pulp in 1995 to place three tracks in the top ten. My Device's 'Eat Lead' at number 23 was the most Dandelion-approved of the entries, having appeared in three different DJs' shows during the year.

2007 Festive Fifty

First broadcast: 25 December

50. (I'm Gonna Follow Your) Star Trail – The Duloks (Art Goes Pop 7")
49. Keep It Coming – The Manhattan Love Suicides (Lost Music 7")
48. All the Rage – The Royal We (Geographic 7")
47. Comfy in Nautica – Panda Bear (Paw Tracks CD *Person Pitch*)
46. Plenty of Spare – The Nightingales (Caroline True CD *What's Not To Love?*)
45. Heimdalsgate Like a Promethean Curse – Of Montreal (Polyvinyl CD *Hissing Fauna, Are You The Destroyer?*)
44. Smokers Outside the Hospital Door – Editors (Kitchenware CD *An End Has A Start*)
43. Black Mirror – Arcade Fire (Merge CD *Neon Bible*)
42. All I Need – Radiohead (Self-Released Download Album *In Rainbows*)
41. The Lesson of The Smiths – MJ Hibbert & The Validators (Artists Against Success CD *The Lesson of The Smiths*)
40. Knots – Pete & The Pirates (Stolen 7")
39. Christmas Bells – DJ Europe (Self-Released mp3)
38. My Manic & I – Laura Marling (Virgin 7")
37. Everything I Do is Gonna Be Sparkly – Pete Green (Atomic Beat 7")
36. Outwards – Kubichek! (30/30 CD *Not Enough Night*)
35. I'm Your Boyfriend Now – Tall Pony (Cherryade CD Single)
34. Listening Man – The Bees (Virgin CD *Octopus*)
33. Lips Are Unhappy – Lucky Soul (Ruffa Lane CD *The Great Unwanted*)
32. Matadjem Yinmixan – Tinariwen (Independiente CD *Aman Iman Water Is Life*)
31. Dashboard – Modest Mouse (Columbia CD *We Were Dead Before the Ship Even Sank*)
30. Steven F***ing Spielberg – Bearsuit (Fantastic Plastic CD *'Oh:Io*)
29. Tonto – Battles (Warp CD *Mirrored*)
28. Apocalypse for Gary Glitter – Trouserdog (Self-Released CD *Eighties Fixation*)
27. Chest Boxing – Skream (Tempa 12" EP *Skreamism Vol. 3*)
26. Horse & I – Bat For Lashes (Parlophone CD *Fur & Gold*)
25. Our Life is Not a Movie or Maybe – Okkervil River (Jagjaguwar CD *The Stage Names*)
24. The Picket Line – Uke Stanza (Self-Released CD *The Very Thin Line*)
23. Eat Lead – My Device (Shifty Disco CD Single)
22. You! Me! Dancing! – Los Campesinos! (Wichita 7")
21. All My Friends – LCD Soundsystem (DFA 12")
20. Fall Sound – The Fall (Slogan CD *Reformation Post-TLC*)
19. When Father Died Ferrets Licked Away the Tears – Bobby McGee's (Cherryade 7" EP *S'Amuser Com Des Fous*)
18. Tracyanne – Horowitz (Glo-Fi 7")
17. Eleven Fingers – The Nightingales (Caroline True CD *What's Not To Love?*)
16. Icky Thump – The White Stripes (XL CD *Icky Thump*)
15. To the East – Electrelane (Too Pure CD *No Shouts No Calls*)
14. What No Blog? – The Nightingales (Caroline True CD *What's Not To Love?*)
13. Intervention – Arcade Fire (Merge CD *Neon Bible*)
12. Taxi For Tit Boy – Trouserdog (Self-Released CD *Eighties Fixation*)
11. Systematic Abuse – The Fall (Slogan CD *Reformation Post-TLC*)
10. Fledermaus Can't Get It – Von Sudenfed (Domino CD *Tromatic Reflexxions*)
9. The Rhinohead – Von Sudenfed (Domino CD *Tromatic Reflexxions*)
8. Inside the Mind of Sam (Breakfast Serial Killer) – Beatnik Filmstars (International Lo-Fi Underground CD *Shenaniganism*)
7. Reformation – The Fall (Slogan CD *Reformation Post-TLC*)
6. Life In The Country, AKA This Civil War – Beatnik Filmstars (Panda CD *Cat Scan Aces*)

5. Lucy Over Lancashire – Paul Rooney (SueMi 12")
4. Curious Role Model – Beatnik Filmstars (Panda CD *Cat Scan Aces*)
3. Foxy Boxer – Bearsuit (Fantastic Plastic CD *Oh:Io*)
2. Thou Shalt Always Kill – Dan Le Sac vs Scroobius Pip (Lex 7")
1. Atlas – Battles (Warp CD *Mirrored*)

2008

The 2007 had contained some significant highlights, but there were too many disappointing moments, particularly in the chart's lower reaches, to allow the Dandelion Radio festive fifty to stand tall in the presence of its illustrious history. There had been too many tracks not broadcast by the station's DJs and a sense that, if the station itself had seized control of the chart's destiny, it hadn't yet fully taken its listeners with it. 2008 offered the clearest sign yet that they were beginning to do so. This year the chart contained few non-Dandelion interlopers: although hindsight might assume the likes of Glasvegas and Fleet Foxes fall into this category, these bands were both played on the station during the year and indeed Fleet Foxes' 'White Winter Hymnal' appeared in the shows of two different DJs. The chart also played host to a couple of newcomers – The Pains of Being Pure At Heart and The Lovely Eggs – who would emerge as festive fifty heavyweights of the new era as well as welcoming the first entries from that expletive adorned duo Fuck Buttons and Holy Fuck, who added a touch of joyful menace to the countdown, not for the last time in the case of the former. Holy Fuck's 'Lovely Allen' also achieved the distinction of being the first festive fifty entry to have appeared on the shows of four different DJs.

There was room here, too, for a couple of the year's finest breakthrough acts. The MIA single now sounds as familiar as the hum of your microwave, but back then it came across as a welcome feaster on the spoils of mainstream success, while the then still fresh-sounding MGMT (who supported MIA, along with several; other high profile bands, during the year), placed a couple of tracks towards the top end of the chart, both of which had achieved hit single status in the UK and elsewhere during the year. Both were indicative of the festive fifty's role down the years in offering occasional timely and reassuring reminders that commercial acclaim did not have to go hand in hand with artistic sterility.

In terms of the chart's development under Dandelion, it was interesting to hear how the relatively new acts gathering appeal across the Dandelion listening audience fared against genuine festive fifty heavyweights. The two greatest festive fifty acts of all time – The Fall and the reformed Wedding Present – both had releases that enjoyed airplay on the station, as did Half Man Half Biscuit, while Portishead put out a cracking and very well-received album after a long period of inactivity. All would figure in the chart, as would those late entries into the Peel pantheon, Decoration. The choices of Rocker and Rachael Neiman particularly prominent, with close to half the chart featuring tracks heard on either, or occasionally both, of those shows. The chart still contained more tracks not heard on the host station than it had at any time in the Peel years, although again, as with last year, these were mostly from artists whose other work had featured on the station at some point in the year.

Among those that hadn't were two entries from the I Blame The Parents label, which indicated that the rise of this fascinating indie was already underway before Dandelion DJs caught onto it. I Blame The Parents would, over the next couple of years, produce a series of releases unmatched in terms of quality by any other small label during the period, some of which would rightly come to grace future charts. The majority of the better entries did find room in Dandelion's tracklists, however. Dandelion Radio's recent recruit Jeff Grainger brought us Wolfram Wire, who in turn brought one of the chart's more idiosyncratic entries; Andy Morrison championed the enigmatically listenable Alex Canasta; Pete Green arrived on the station's playlists courtesy of Rocker and, following his debut in 2007, duly delivered a much-needed punch to the guts to the sponsorship-contaminated 'indie' scene. Perhaps most notably, Rachel Neiman introduced us to the delights of Ste McCabe, who delivered one of the more uncompromising top five entries in festive fifty history.

It was no great surprise that The Fall should secure their third number one, the first band to achieve such a distinction. '50 Year Old Man' was entirely typical of the kind of Fall tune that normally generates festive fifty acclaim: in combining the brashly caustic appeal of 'Hey! Student' with an autobiographical element found in the likes of 'Bill is Dead' and 'Edinburgh Man', it always appeared to possess a lot of the characteristics needed to fuel a serious challenge by the band for the top spot and enough festive fifty voters duly delivered. The Fall's *Imperial Wax Solvent* album produced three entries. Perhaps more surprisingly, Newcastle's Das Wanderlust came in second, with the aforementioned Decoration, McCabe and MGMT making up the rest of the top five.

2008 Festive Fifty

First broadcast: 25 December

50. Superman's Head – The Pocket Gods (Nub Country CD *Lo-Fi Sci-Fi*)
49. Last Summer – Earl Grey & The Legomen (I Blame The Parents CD Single)
48. I Like Birds But I Like Other Animals Too – The Lovely Eggs (Filthy Little Angels 7")
47. Les Artistes – Santogold (Lizard King CD *Santogold*)
46. Clusterfuck – The Manhattan Love Suicides (Squirrel 7" EP *Clusterfuck*)
45. Liverpool 2008 – Jegsy Dodd & The Original Sinners (Self-issued mp3)
44. 1,2,3, Go! – The Parallelograms (Atomic Beat 7" split single w/The Pains of Being Pure at Heart)
43. Swan Lake – Thomas Tantrum (Cool For Cats 7")
42. Don't Take Me Home Until I'm Drunk – The Wedding Present (Vibrant CD *El Rey*)
41. Can Can Summer – The Fall (Sanctuary CD *Imperial Wax Solvent*)
40. Paper Planes – MIA (XL CD Single)
39. Records – Alex Canasta (Artiscope CD *Reborn Tonight*)
38. Festival – Sigur Ros (EMI CD *Meo Suo I Eyrum Vio Spillum Endalaust*)
37. Claire, Are We Safe to Be On Our Own? – The Deirdres (Cloudberry CD EP *Dinosaurs That Can Swim*)
36. Lovely Allen – Holy Fuck (Young Turks CD *LP*, released in 2007. Eligible version was from the 12" EP release)
35. Took Problem Chimp To Ideal Home Show – Half Man Half Biscuit (Probe Plus CD *CSI Ambleside*)
34. Geraldine – Glasvegas (Columbia CD *Glasvegas*)
33. Penetrate – Exhibition Order (I Blame The Parents 7").
32. Armitage Shanks – Wolfram Wire (Self-Released EP *Wiesenmusik*)
31. Grounds For Divorce – Elbow (Polydor CD *The Seldom Seen Kid*)
30. Best British Band Supported By Shockwaves – Pete Green (Lostmusic CD EP *Platform Zero*)
29. Glasshouse – Decoration (Dandelion Radio session recording)
28. Come Saturday – The Pains of Being Pure At Heart (Self-issued mp3)
27. Dougie – Town Bike (Keith 7" EP *When Good Kids Go Bad*)
26. Tommy Shooter – The Fall (Sanctuary CD *Imperial Wax Solvent*)
25. It's My Own Cheating Heart That Makes Me Cry – Glasvegas (Columbia CD *Glasvegas*)
24. Kill Twee Pop! – Sarandon (Slumberland CD *Kill Twee Pop*)
23. Sweet Love For Planet Earth – Fuck Buttons (ATP CD Street *Horrrsing*)
22. The Rip – Portishead (Island CD *Third*)
21. National Shite Day – Half Man Half Biscuit (Probe Plus CD *CSI Ambleside*)
20. The Thing I Like Best About Him Is His Girlfriend – The Wedding Present (Vibrant CD *El Rey*)
19. Cecilie – The Wolfmen (Townsend CD Single)
18. Idiot Foot – Superman Revenge Squad (Self-Released CD Single)
17. Heat & Panic – The Manhattan Love Suicides (Squirrel CD *Burning Out Landscapes*)
16. Let It Slip – The School (Elefant CD Single)
15. White Winter Hymnal – Fleet Foxes (Bella Union CD *Fleet Foxes*)
14. Kids – MGMT (Columbia CD *Oracular Spectacular*)

13. Everything With You – The Pains of Being Pure At Heart (Slumberland 7")
12. Machine Gun – Portishead (Island 12")
11. Have You Ever Heard a Digital Accordian? – The Lovely Eggs (Cherryade 7" *Have You Ever Heard The Lovely Eggs?*)
10. Hospital Ward – Beatnik Filmstars (SRC CD *The Purple Fez 72 Club Social*)
9. Spoon – The Hillfields (Cloudberry V/A CD EP *What's All The Fuzz about*)
8. Milk Is Politics – The Deirdres (Cherryade 7")
7. Wolf Kidult Man – The Fall (Sanctuary CD *Imperial Wax Solvent*)
6. It Must Be The Pipes – The Container Drivers (Topplers CD Single)
5. Huyton Scum – Ste McCabe (Cherryade CD *Hate Mail*)
4. Time To Pretend – MGMT (Columbia CD *Oracular Spectacular*)
3. Square Mile – Decoration (13 B Sides CD *See You After The War*)
2. Puzzle – Das Wanderlust (Don't Tell Clare 7")
1. 50 Year Old Man – The Fall (Sanctuary CD *Imperial Wax Solvent*)

2009

2009 probably had every right to consider itself among the finest pf recent festive fifties, perhaps challenged in the Dandelion years only by 2013. Although the number of tracks here that I'd played in my show was gratifyingly high, what made the chart a particularly pleasurable listening experience for me was the number of great tunes featured in the chart that I hadn't hitherto paid enough attention to, which for me is always one of the most valuable facets of a festive fifty. Mark Cunliffe's championing of the Qwel & Jackson Jones track gave it a deserved push into the 24 slot and, while YouTube undoubtedly played a major part in propelling the Will & Rick tune into the top twenty, the all-too short-lived DJing stint of Ste McCabe at the station certainly had a hand too (Ste would add to his own FF debut in the previous year with another characteristically uncompromising top ten entry). Not that I wasn't also thrilled by the unexpected appearance of French bullier of electronics Llamatron, a firmly established favourite of mine, surprisingly making an appearance too.

The number twenty entry warrants some comments as it constitutes a rare (perhaps unique) occasion of a festive fifty entry actually causing problems for a band. It was Moolah Temple $tringband's correct accreditation for this track here, and in Simon Hickinbotham's broadcast of the track in his November show, that brought them the kind of ridiculous bother than only the so-called music industry appears able to generate. They'd deliberately put out 'Cherry Bed Antique' under the alias of Tuckaseegee Anchorites and its appearance here led to a dispute with the Pimalia label, for whose compilation *Smatterings Volume One* they'd contributed a track. The band's *Chitterlings Volume II* was an attempt to parody the compilation via a series of tracks from fake bands, one of which was this. In the words of the $tringband, 'To add insult to injury, the perception that they were biting the band that feeds arose due to the fact that they were receiving a lot of airplay for a song attributed to a fake band…In addition to offending their benefactors, Moolah Temple $tringband received cease and desist requests from the attorneys of Pimalia artists and *Smatterings Volume One* contributors.' (http://moolahtemplestringband.com) It's an event that illustrates how thoroughly idiotic the mujsic industry can be, arising purely from a situation where people liked a track enough to play it, vote for it and check out its source correctly to identify and give credit to the artists responsible. What's particularly saddening is how other artists, not just the offended record company, decided to join in the action as well. What shouldn't be overlooked in all this is that it's one hell of a great tune, as enough Dandelion listeners clearly recognized.

There will be some who regard any chart that has room in it for the likes of Mumford & Sons, Bat For Lashes and Florence & The Machine to be irretrievably tainted, but in truth the appearance of the first two represents the kind of blip that can afflict even the better festive fifties and in Florence's case I've always had a bit of a soft spot, to be honest, and even played one of her tunes once, though not the one that made the chart. Similarly, Dizzee Rascal's entry provided us with one of those rare instances where a number one single garners enough appeal among festive fifty voters to grab a place.

In any case, the appearance of a few commercial heavyweights is more than adequately compensated for by the wonderful number of self-released oddities here. In addition to those already mentioned, Red Cosmos began their intriguing relationship with the chart with a track from a demo and there were entries with similar origins from Ten Tigers, Apple Rabbits and Alisia Casper. The number of instances of self-released tunes getting into the festive fifty has shown an increase in recent years (though there was a decline in the 2014 chart), unsurprisingly given the phenomenon of on-line releases and the rise of Soundcloud and Bandcamp, building on and extending those earlier myspace options. Combining self-issued releases and those put out on a band or artist's own label, the number of self-released efforts in this chart reached double figures, showing a further increase from the handful of such releases that gained entry the previous year.

Also with a release on their own label, The Chasms made their first appearance of a relatively short but extremely memorable festive fifty career. Recording all their albums in a barn in the Isle of Man, the band went on to release four extraordinary albums, all of which would be represented by at least one track in a festive fifty, before suddenly calling it a day and removing all traces of their back catalogue from the internet. Although their members have gone on to release some fine music with other projects, so far none has featured in the chart.

The intriguing clash between the more innovative established labels and their relatively obscure cousins is perhaps best illustrated by the battle for top record label in this festive fifty. While PJ Harvey added to the entries from Florence and Mumford to give three entries for Island, a number matched by 4AD courtesy of two appearances for Camera Obscura and one for Future of the Left, they were edged out by Wichita, who secured four entries spread neatly between Sky Larkin and Los Campesinos! Not far behind them were such labels of Slumberland, Fortuna Pop! Cherryade and NR One, each of which grabbing two entries while fervently holding up the indie pop banner with some distinction.

At the top end of the chart, the appearance of The Chasms was a welcome surprise, if one that would become more familiar with time, while Fuck Buttons served equally noisy notice of the designs they had on forthcoming festive fifties and Animal Collective, whose name was everywhere that year, predictably made a tilt for the top spot too. In the end, however, it was a relatively straight indie pop fight between Los Campesinos!, a band who already seemed to be seasoned veterans despite having been around for hardly any time at all, and new heavyweights The Pains of Being Pure at Heart. In the event, the former won out and added a further top ten entry to what then appeared a growing festive fifty portfolio, though it hasn't expanded by much since. Curiously, neither of the Los Campesinos! top ten entries had been played on Dandelion Radio during the year and the number one had only been released in November. The track played by most DJs in the chart was Camera Obscura's 'French Navy', which appeared in three different shows during 2009.

2009 Festive Fifty
First broadcast: 25 December

50. Metro Dromedary – Apple Rabbits (Infernal Machine download album *Kilburn State*)
49. Arming Eritrea – Future of the Left (4AD CD *Travels With Myself & Another*)
48. Ginger Pants – Autorotation (TecknoStan CD *Everything Is Everything*)
47. Dancing – Standard Fare (TSPC Split 7")
46. High Infidelity – Crescendo (I Blame The Parents CD EP *Crescendo*)
45. Son of Morris – Red Cosmos (Demo CD)
44. My Boss Was In An Indie Band Once – MJ Hibbett & The Validators (Artists Against Success CD *Regardez, Ecoutex et Repetez*)
43. Antibodies – Sky Larkin (Wichita CD *The Golden Spike*)
42. The Way – The Bumblebees (Self-Released CD EP)
41. Back Up Plan – Beatnik Filmstars (Satisfaction Download Album *Broken Bones*)
40. Superlucky – Ten Tigers (Self-Released download EP *The Honey Badger EP*)
39. Aidy's Girl's A Computer – Darkstar (Hyberdub download single)
38. You Make Milf Ill – Llamatron (Self-issued mp3)
37. Demons Out! – Art Brut (Cooking Vinyl CD *Art Brut Vs Satan*)
36. Are You Dead? – The Humms (Odd Box/Gypsy Farm download single)

35. Space Mountain – Fuck Buttons (ATP CD *Tarot Sport*)
34. My Maudlin Career – Camera Obscura (4AD CD *My Maudlin Career*)
33. Little Lion Man – Mumford & Sons (Island CD *Sigh No More*)
32. Brother Sport – Animal Collective (Domino CD *Merriweather Post Pavilion*)
31. Drumming Song – Florence & The Machine (Island CD *Lungs*)
30. Die Slow – Health (City Slang CD *Get Color*)
29. Matador – Sky Larkin (Wichita CD *Golden Spike*)
28. Black Hand – Atomizer (Dandelion Radio session recording)
27. Daniel – Bat For Lashes (EMI CD *Two Suns*)
26. C C C Cat – Violet Violet (NR One 7" Single)
25. Higher Than The Stars – The Pains of Being Pure at Heart (Fortuna Pop! 7")
24. The CD Exchange – Qwel & Jackson Jones (Galapagos4 download album *Jump The Gun*)
23. The Greatest Light Is The Greatest Shade – The Joy Formidable (Pure Groove CD *A Balloon Called Moaning*)
22. Henry Rollins Don't Dance – Allo Darlin' (Wee Pop! Download Single)
21. Cardiff in the Sun – Super Furry Animals (Rough Trade CD *Dark Days/Light Years*)
20. Cherry Bed Antique – Moolah Temple $tringband (Self-Released Download Album *Chitterlings Volume II*)
19. Keys In The Bowl – Fever Fever (Cherryade 7")
18. Black Hearted Love – PJ Harvey & John Parish (Island CD *A Man A Woman Walked By*)
17. Two Weeks – Grizzly Bear (Warp 12")
16. Hot Dog Man – Will & Rick (Self-issued mp3)
15. Love Is A Wave – Crystal Stilts (Slumberland 7")
14. Mother I Am Free – Alisia Casper (Self-issued mp3)
13. Two Of The Beatles Have Died – Ginger Tom (Helen Llewellyn Product Nineteen Records V/A CD *Two Of The Beatles Have Died*)
12. French Navy – Camera Obscura (4AD CD *My Maudlin Career*)
11. Bonkers – Dizzee Rascal (Dirtee Stank LP *Tongue N Cheek*)
10. Murder Music – Ste McCabe (Cherryade CD *Murder Music*)
9. The Sea Is a Good Place to Think of the Future – Los Campesinos! (Wichita CD *Romance Is Boring*)
8. Cougar – The Brownies (NR One CD *Our Knife Your Back*)
7. Whirring – The Joy Formidable (Pure Groove CD *A Balloon Called Moaning*)
6. I Am Grimaldi – Nightingales (Klangbad CD *Insult To Injury*)
5. I'm Hear To See The Clouds of Blood – The Chasms (Command To Destroy CD *Advance Paranoia, Advance*)
4. Surf Solar – Fuck Buttons (ATP CD *Tarot Sport*)
3. My Girls – Animal Collective (Domino CD *Merriweather Post Pavilion*)
2. Young Adult Friction – The Pains Of Being Pure At Heart (Slumberland/Fortuna Pop! 7")
1. There Are Listed Buildings – Los Campesinos! (Wichita 7")

i

2010

A curious festive fifty, this. For one thing, only a single band managed to register two entries (Allo Darlin'). Although, strangely, no band or artist since then has any more than this in a single chart, normally there are a few that manage the feat, so the 50 tracks spread across 49 artists in this chart remains a conspicuous oddity in a chart that remains the most Dandelion Radio-friendly in the station's relatively brief history. Although every chart after the first one in 2006 had contained a majority of tracks played by the station's DJs, even in 2009 the number of tracks not played on Dandelion had been in double figures: here, however, the chart contained only a single non-Dandelion interloper, the entry from The Radio Dept at number 14.

Several long-established Peel favourites were present. Belle & Sebastian made a return after a seven year gap; in their more prolific earlier days they'd failed to reach only a single festive fifty between the years of 1996 and 2003 but now, with key members having to find room for the band among engagements with other projects, the *Write About Love* album appeared as a rare treat: indeed, the next collection would be almost another five years in coming, meaning an inevitable paucity of festive fifty entries during this period. Meanwhile, the reformed Teenage Fanclub made a return to the chart after a gap of 19 years and Mike Conroy, formerly of the much-loved Superqueens, partly made up for his previous band's failure ever to feature in a chart by making it to number 21 with The Orch and the spoken word brilliance of 'Kenny & The Snake'.

Newer favourites of Dandelion rubbed shoulders with them, including the vibrant I Blame The Parents label, whose two entries both reached the heights of the top twenty, both tracks from a cracking split EP release featuring the twin charms of Joy of Sex and Gindrinker. This established a new record for the highest joint placing of a split release, smashing the previously held best of Miss Black America and Antihero. Incidentally, the sleeve for the release was designed by Anthony Frost who, among other things, had also created the sleeves for The Fall's *Extricate* and *Imperial Wax Solvent* albums, making him a festive fifty veteran of sorts.

Many, including myself, were pleasantly shocked by the appearance of The Venopian Solitude in the top twenty: TVS was the alias of Malaysia's Suiko Takahara and gave her nation its first ever entry in the festive fifty. At that point Takahara was putting out music for free on her bandcamp site and labeled me 'crazy' for even playing it, but I've not played an artist on Dandelion before or since that received so much feedback (all positive) and so many enquiries, so perhaps the high position here shouldn't have seemed such a surprise. The glorious guitar mayhem of 93millionmilesfromthe sun was another surprise entry, and a similarly pleasing one, while the brilliantly irreverent Tingle in the Netherlands and crushingly wonderful noise of The Truth About Frank (with a tune originally recorded in session for Jeff Grainger's February show that year) got even higher, edging into the top ten. .

All of the above edged supposedly more illustrious bands and artists into the chart's lower regions, where here you could find the likes of Bombay Bicycle Club, The National, Beach House and Skream. Gil Scott-Heron joined the very select ranks of those who got their festive fifty breakthrough after more than forty years in the biz, with a very aptly titled entry at number 50, the title track of a fine album which contained his first new material for sixteen years. Sadly, the legendary Scott-Heron would pass away in the following year. Crocodiles added to the still small but growing list of tunes that have appeared courtesy of two different artists when their celebrated cover of Deee-Lite's 'Groove is in the Heart' (which they combined with a slowed down version of The Beach Boys' 'California Girls', which of course hadn't before troubled the festive fifty scorers) made it into the chart. One of the most lauded artists of the year, Gonjasufi, also made it with a track from his *A Sufi & a Killer* album, a collection that you suspect, in different times, might well have generated at least another appearance and perhaps several.

Although The Fall made a familiar appearance higher up the chart (with, of course, their only entry) and there was a second appearance at number five for The Chasms, the rest of the top six is again indicative of the curious nature of this chart. Chris T-T, who may well have been expected to have featured more in festive fifties down the years, made his only appearance so far (apart from the unofficial Truly Festive Festive Fifty, of course) at the lofty position of number 3, while a place below that were Warpaint, a band already by that stage well over the threshold into broader critical appreciation, again with their one and only appearance in a festive fifty. A release on Slumberland from Phil Wilson always made the ex-June Bride a likely entrant in the chart and he appeared lower down as a member of The Granite Shore also, but these remain his only appearances despite his much-loved combo having received so much acclaim in the chart's indie pop heyday back in the mid-eighties.. Those modern day indie pop practitioners Standard Fare nicked the top spot from under the noses of The Fall, with the gorgeous 'Philadelphia', a track whose magnificence more than excuses the impudence of such an act.

2010 Festive Fifty
First broadcast: 25 December

50. I'm New Here – Gil Scott-Heron (XL CD *I'm New Here*)
49. Georgia – Yuck (Fat Possum 7")
48. Fields of Emotion – Skream (Tempa CD *Outside The Box*)
47. Angewandte Muziek – Harmonious Thelonius

THE FESTIVE FIFTY

(Italic CD *Talking*)
46. Genetic – Emeralds (Editions Mego CD *Does It Look Like I'm Here?*)
45. Crocodile Song – Damn Vandals (Self-Released Promo CD)
44. Zebra – Beach House (Bella Union CD *Teen Dream*)
43. Raptor – The Horn The Hunt (WLM Download Single)
42. Ivy & Gold – Bombay Bicycle Club (Island CD *Flaws*)
41. Bloodbuzz Ohio – The National (4AD CD *High Violet*)
40. Take It Down (In Dub) - L.B. Dub Corp (Ostgut Ton 12" EP *Take It Down (In Dub)*)
39. CMYK – James Blake (R&S CD EP)
38. Flood of Fortune – The Granite Shore (Occultation Records 7" Single)
37. Love Love – Ghost Society (Dandelion Radio session recording)
36. Logical Steps – Cygnus X-1 (9 Volt CD *The Next Logical Step*)
35. Crazy For You – Best Coast (Wichita CD Single)
34. Please Don't Take Him Back – Bearsuit (Fortuna Pop! CD Single)
33. Evelyn Waugh – Applicants (Tigertrap Download Single)
32. Haunted Homes – Will & Rick (Self-issued mp3)
31. Treatise – The War Crimes (Demo CD)
30. Sky Lanterns – The Phantom Light (mp3 demo)
29. Only Snow – The Blanche Hudson Weekend (Squirrel CD *Reverence, Severance & Spite*)
28. Reinforced Concrete Monsters – Ryan Hardy (Self-issued mp3)
27. Serra – Mugstar (Important CD EP *Lime*)
26. Straight in at 101 – Los Campesinos! (Wichita CD *Romance Is Boring*)
25. Groove is in the Heart/California Girls – Crocodiles (Fat Possum 7" *Sleep Forever* B-side)
24. Concrete Gold – Wu Lyf (Self-Released 12")
23. Baptism – Crystal Castles (Polydor Cd *Crystal Castles II*)
22. Sun – Caribou (City Slang/Merge CD *Swim*)
21. Kenny & The Snake – The Orch (skinnydog download album *Small Times*)
20. I Didn't See It Coming – Belle & Sebastian (Rough Trade CD *Write About Love*)
19. We Want War – These New Puritans (Domino CD *Hidden*)
18. Mother Nature & Father Man-Made – The Venopian Solitude (Self-Released download EP *Sangfroid*)
17. Ancestors – Gonjasufi (Warp CD *A Sufi & A Killer*)
16. Bob Grainger: Sexual Pervert – Gindrinker (I Blame The Parents Split CD EP *Split Definitives*)
15. Waiting There (Noise) – 93MillionMilesFromTheSun (Dandelion Radio session recording)
14. Heaven's On Fire – The Radio Dept (Labrador CD Single)
13. Baby Lee – Teenage Fanclub (Pema CD *Shadows*)
12. Red Rocket – Joy of Sex (I Blame The Parents Split CD Single *Split Definitives*)
11. Prostitute's Handbag – Tingle in the Netherlands (Nerve Echo download EP *Prostitute's Handbag*)
10. My Heart is a Drummer – Allo Darlin' (Fortuna Pop! CD *Allo Darlin'*)
9. The Headless Rentman – The Truth About Frank (Odd Box, V/A CD *Broadcast One*)
8. Dreaming - Allo Darlin' (Fortuna Pop! CD *Allo Darlin'*)
7. Say No To Love – The Pains of Being Pure At Heart (Fortuna Pop! CD Single)
6. I Own It – Phil Wilson (Slumberland CD *God Bless Jim Kennedy*)
5. Blue Sun, Golden Sky – The Chasms (Command To Destroy Download Album *Index of Spirits*)
4. Undertow – Warpaint (Rough Trade CD *The Fool*)
3. Nintendo – Chris T-T (Xtra Mile CD *Love Is Not Rescue*)
2. Bury Pts 1 + 3 – The Fall
1. Philadelphia – Standard Fare (Thee SPC/Melodic 7" Single)

MARK WHITBY

2011

A couple of very poignant festive fifty goodbyes coincided with further evidence that Dandelion listeners were increasingly crafting a festive fifty in their own image. We said farewell to Bearsuit, who had called it a day during the year and commemorated the event with the title track of their swan song album making the top ten. Even sadder was the death of Broadcast's Trish Keenan earlier in the year, while her band's to date final appearance in a chart came via a collaboration with Wolfram Wire that had featured on the *Five Years* compilation, released during the year to mark the fifth anniversary of Dandelion Radio. It was one of two tracks from the compilation to feature, the other coming from JD Meatyard, aka former Levellers 5 and Calvin Party mainman John Donaldson at number 11, though the version played in the countdown was the one from his self-titled debut album that had appeared later in the year. It wouldn't be JD Meatyard's only visit to the festive fifty, but for now it marked the highest appearance in the chart for a genuine Peel legend whose previous achievements here had amounted to just two entries with Calvin Party.

His Probe Plus label-mates Half Man Half Biscuit were in there too, though surprisingly with only one track from the excellent *90 Bisodol (Crimond)* album: it was, indeed, another year in which even chart legends found it curiously difficult to get beyond a single entry, something that this year was only achieved by the artists in the number one and two positions. The Fall's *Ersatz GB* album had received a release only in the middle of November, by which point the voting period was half-over, presumably explaining why they appeared only once and in a very low position. As far as other former Peel regulars went, Low made a return to the chart after a nine year gap, while Mogwai resumed their association after five years with a track from their Earth Division EP, though surprisingly the very well-received, and much played on Dandelion, *Hardcore Will Never Die But You Will* album failed to generate an entry. Bjork, who quite correctly had never had a sniff of a festive fifty since her days with the Sugarcubes in the late eighties, barged her way up to number sixteen, though this was courtesy of an admittedly rather splendid mix by Omar Souleyman.

Some figures who until now had received airplay from multiple DJs but had never made a festive fifty broke their chart virginity: these included Spidersleg and the other half of their Rejects Club duo Lord Numb, the latter in collaboration with Julien Auroux, a highly prolific French electronic experimenter and vocalist, with a product of one of many liaisons between finely tuned musical minds that had originated in a mutual discovery via Dandelion. Cambodian Space Project became the first visitors to the chart from, you've guessed it, Cambodia via a release on the Metal Postcard label, run by Sean Hocking. It wasn't Hocking's first dalliance with a festive fifty – he'd had the good sense to put out the tracks from Ollo and Wax Audio that had featured in earlier charts – but it was his first since joining the Dandelion roster. The championing by some DJs of the excellent Daddy Tank label resulted in a deserved entry for Twiggy & The K-Mesons, one of many musical vehicles for the extraordinary talents of Michael Valentine West, from his wonderful *Technique* album. The Pains of Being Pure At Heart made, at the time of writing, their last visit to a festive fifty: curiously, although several DJs played their 'Belong' single, it was the single's B-side that made it into the chart.

Another of the year's finest albums that was recognised here but sadly largely ignored elsewhere was Seedhill Bruiser's *Granite Fists*, released on Tingle in the Netherlands' Nerve Echo label, which produced a perhaps unexpected entry with the amazing 'Trees'. Other gratifyingly idiosyncratic entries included tracks from screaming San Francisco threesome Dadfag, the delightful ukulele and vocals set up of Zoe Bestel and, perhaps best of all, Cyclic Freeload Unit's 'Bitch Chicken Flower' which somehow managed to crash the top ten, perhaps the best example of festive fifty voters' ability to thrust one-off uncompromising brilliance towards the business end of an end of year chart since Paul Rooney's 'Lucy Over Lancashire' in 2007. Listeners were, however, allowed a brief period in which to savour the event before Lana Del Ray somehow crawled in at number seven. The festive fifty clearly retained its capacity to deliver surprises, but this was a reminder that they weren't always pleasant ones. Although again the chart gave a home to a number of tracks not broadcast on Dandelion during the year, Del Ray was one of only a few whose music hadn't been played at all.

In the top five, The Lovely Eggs made a serious tilt for the top spot, only to be denied by the title track from PJ Harvey's much-celebrated *Let England Shake* album, which allowed Harvey to pull off the historically implausible feat of achieving best album of the year status in the monthly music mags along with the Mercury Music Prize and a festive fifty number one. The Chasms joined the other Dandelion favourites in the chart with a third top five appearance in a row, this time cranking up their performance up a notch to settle at number three, while also providing the festive fifty track that enjoyed most plays by Dandelion DJs (four) during the year. At five and four respectively, via the kind of accidental scheduling you sense would have delighted Peel, were a tune from Allo Darlin' celebrating the talents of Darren Hayman and a first entry since his brace with The French in 2003 from Darren himself, featuring the aforementioned band's Elizabeth Morris on vocals.

2011 Festive Fifty
First broadcast: 25 December

50. Echoes of Ghosts – The Phantom Light (Self-Released EP *Lighthouse On Fire*)
49. Fly By Night – Kescho (23 Seconds LP *Accountants By Day*)
48. Nate Will Not Return – The Fall (Cherry Red LP *Ersatz GB*)
47. Verstehen 1.8; 3.296.2.1 – Broadcast & Wolfram Wire (Unwashed Territories V/A Download Album *Five Years – Volume One*)
46. Facile – Lord Numb & Julien Auroux (Self-issued mp3)
45. Try to Sleep – Low (Sub Pop CD *C'mon*)
44. Coming Down – Dum Dum Girls (Sub Pop LP *Only In Dreams*)
43. Panic Plants – The Lovely Eggs (Cherryade 7")
42. I Wanna Go All The Way – The Pains of Being Pure At Heart (Slumberland/Fortuna Pop! 7" *Belong* B-side)
41. Ingland Strip – The Orch (skinnydog Download Album *Small Times*)
40. Baby's Arms – Kurt Vile (Matador CD *Smoke Ring For My Halo*)
39. Buy Nothing Day – Go! Team (Memphis Industries CD *Rolling Blackouts*)
38. Salt – Spidersleg (Dandelion Radio session recording)
37. Flight – Wooden Shjips (Thrill Jockey CD *West*)
36. Dreaming – Seapony (Hardly Art CD *Go With Me*)
35. Sleep – The Rosie Taylor Project (Rosie Taylor Project 7")
34. Midnight City – M83 (Naïve CD *Hurry Up, We're Dreaming*)
33. All the Sun that Shines – Peaking Lights (Weird World CD *936*)
32. Candy – Dadfag (Broken Rekids LP *Probably*)
31. Ponzi – Felice Brothers (Fat Possum CD *Celebration, Florida*)
30. Last Known Surroundings – Explosions in the Sky (Bella Union CD *Take Care, Take Care, Take Care*)
29. Trees – Seedhill Bruiser (Nerve Echo CD *Granite Fists*)
28. Drunk & Crazy – Mogwai (Rock Action CD EP *Earth Division*)
27. 35 Missed Calls – Zoe Bestel (Distilled Download Single)
26. The Words That Maketh Murder – PJ Harvey (Island CD *Let England Shake*)
25. Isabel – Baxter Dury (Regal CD *Happy Soup*)
24. Bizness – tUnE-yArDs (4AD CD *Whokill*)
23. I Can See Through You – The Horrors (XL CD *Skying*)
22. Chnam Oum Dop Pram Mouy (I'm Sixteen) – Cambodian Space Project (Metal Postcard CD *2011: A Space Odyssey*)
21. Cop Killer – John Maus (Upset! The Rhythm CD *We Must Become the Pitiless Censors of Ourselves*)
20. Bear Hug – The 2 Bears (Southern Fried Records CD EP *Bear Hug*)
19. Joy In Leeuwarden (We Are Ready) – Half Man Half Biscuit (Probe Plus CD *90 Bisodol (Crimond)*)
18. Silicon Warning – Atomizer (NagNagNag CD *Open Secret*)
17. Split Infinitives – Help Stamp Out Loneliness (Where It's At Is Where You Are CD *Help Stamp Out Loneliness*)
16. Crystalline (Omar Souleyman Version) – Bjork (One Little Indian CD Single)
15. In Dreams Part II – Let's Wrestle (Full Time Hobby CD *Nursing Home*)
14. Preset Love – Twiggy & The K-Mesons (Daddy Tank CD *Technique*)
13. The Wilhelm Scream – James Blake (Atlas CD *James Blake*)
12. Street Halo – Burial (Hyperdub Download Single)

11. Olive Tree – JD Meatyard (Probe Plus CD *JD Meatyard*)
10. Bitch Chicken Flower – Cyclic Freeload Unit (Self-issued mp3)
9. Bad Feeling – Veronica Falls (Bella Union CD *Veronica Falls*)
8. Get Away – Yuck (Fat Possum CD *Yuck*)
7. Video Games – Lana Del Ray (Stranger Download Single)
6. When Will I Be Queen? – Bearsuit (Fortuna Pop! CD *The Phantom Forest*)
5. Darren – Allo Darlin' (Self-Released 7")
4. I Know I Fucked Up – Darren Hayman (with Elizabeth Morris) (Self-Released Download Album *January Songs*)
3. The Occult Soul Review – The Chasms (Command To Destroy CD *Alchemical Postcards*)
2. Don't Look At Me (I Don't Like It) – The Lovely Eggs (Cherryade CD *Cob Dominos*)
1. Let England Shake – PJ Harvey (Island CD *Let England Shake*)

2012

There were a number of statistical breakthroughs in the 2012 festive fifty. Two tracks with the same name made the chart, Django Django and Thom Yorke's Atoms For Peace both making the top twenty with a tune called 'Default'. Having previously appeared with Radiohead and as a guest vocalist with PJ Harvey, Yorke thus joined that elite, and growing, group of artists who have entered with three different bands. He was joined by Malcolm Middleton, who'd previously appeared solo and with Arab Strap and now featured with his Human Don't Be Angry project. Amelia Fletcher trumped this, her appearance with Tender Trap making it six different bands she'd appeared with, equalling Mark E. Smith's record. Smith remains one of the view artists to have appeared in a single chart with more than one band, and indeed he's the only one to manage it with three (back in 1995), but a perhaps unlikely addition to the list came in the form of krautrock/space rock guitar maestro Neil Whitehead, who appeared as a guest with The Chasms at number 15 and then took his own band Vert:x to the dizzy heights of number nine

The Vert:x track was one of three of considerable length in the top ten that made it the longest in duration since the first festive fifty of 1976 and all three tracks secured a place in the top twenty longest festive fifty entries of all time. The other two came from the reformed Godspeed You! Black Emperor, a band who had been largely overlooked in festive fifty terms, having only appeared once before. Their 'Mladic' was the longest track to make a festive fifty since The Orb's 'Blue Room' twenty years earlier. It was their first appearance since 1998, though the length of the gap would seem minuscule compared to the period of dormancy experienced by Neil Young & Crazy Horse, who made a perhaps unlikely return to the chart after 34 years, also with a track of some length. Had it not been for Young's re-appearance after so long, the return of Public Image Ltd, after a mere 29 years of chart inactivity, might have seemed more remarkable, while the 28 year gap between appearances by The Membranes appeared almost unworthy of comment by the time they were revealed at number six. Dead Kennedys also returned after a long period in the shadows, although in their case they didn't have to do much to correct it, their entry coming via a Soundcloud remix of 'California Uber Alles' by Italians 12" Plastic Toys.

Again the number of self-released tracks was in double figures and another Soundcloud entrant, though much lower down the chart, came from Forkeyes, actually a solo project of Bogshed's Mike Bryson, now making a belated entry in the festive fifty after being curiously, and surely wrongly, overlooked with his former band. More often though, the self-released format served the cause of more recent Dandelion favourites: Alisia Casper gained a deserved second appearance, as did Red Cosmos (whose number 16 entry featured a sample of the voice of Dandelion DJ Andy Morrison), while perhaps even more notable was the arrival of Flies On You, who stormed into the chart on a wave of enthusiastic support from several Dandelion and non-Dandelion DJs alike.

The number of festive fifty tracks from film soundtracks down the years received a further boost with the appearance of Christ., an artist much admired by Peel, and a tune from the Cathexis soundtrack. There were two tracks from compilations also, one featuring the heavily charged psychedelia of Blue Giant Zeta Puppies and the other from Pussy Riot, three of whose members were at the time being held in a Russian jail. They duly made their voices heard here with a typically uncompromising ear-shredder and in the process achieved the best ever festive fifty performance for a Russian artist.

At the top end, The Chasms said their goodbyes, having announced their split during the vote-counting period, and made two appearances, the highest at number two, giving them a fourth consecutive year in the top five and their highest entry to boot. Their 'Death's Pony' was played by more DJs than any other in the chart, appearing in three shows, and one of a number of entries towards the top end released and broadcast towards the end of the year. Another band finding a place near the top of the chart were The Lovely Eggs, who continued their festive fifty adventure with a release on their own label at number five, while another single, this time on Cherryade, made it in at number 13. Allo Darlin' continued to enhance their festive fifty pedigree at number three, while the aforementioned GY!BE settled in a place lower. There never seemed much doubt about the number one, however, which came from Savages, the only band in the top seven to be making their chart debut. At the time it put the band in the company of Neko Case and Bang Bang Machine, who made a single festive fifty appearance but had the satisfaction of making it a number one. This wouldn't last, because Savages would make a not unsurprising return to the chart in the following year and indeed again the the year after that.

2012 Festive Fifty
First broadcast: 25 December

50. Class Clown Spots a UFO – Guided By Voices (Fire 7")
49. Lupine Dominus – Thee Oh Sees (In The Red CD *Putrifiers II*)
48. Fell Off the Penalty Spotty Spot – Forkeyes (Self-released mp3)
47. Older Women – Standard Fare (Melodic CD *Out of Sight, Out of Town*)
46. Walk Like a Giant – Neil Young & Crazy Horse (Reprise CD *Psychedelic Pill*)
45. 1978, Smiling Politely – Martha (Odd Box Cassette *Martha*)
44. Goathead – Goat (Universal CD *World Music*)
43. Puts Me to Work – Cate Le Bon (Turnstile CD *Cyrk*)
42. Fitzpleasure – Alt-J (Infectious CD *An Awesome Wave*)
41. The Greater Picture – The Phantom Light (Self-released download single)
40. Crack Whore – Yva Las Vegass (Moniker LP *I Was Born in the Place of Sunshine & the Smell of Ripe Mangoes*)
39. Andrew in Drag – The Metallic Fields (Domino CD *Love at the Bottom of the Sea*)
38. Gold – The Horn The Hunt (Self-released download single)
37. Elephant – Tame Impala (Modular CD *Lonerism*)

36. Lollipop Opera – Public Image Ltd (PiL Official CD *This is PiL*)
35. A Little Bit – MJ Hibbert & The Validators (Self-released download album *Dinosaur Planet*)
34. Frankie – Lulubelle III (Take It Music CD *Foyle Delta Blues*)
33. The House That Heaven Built – Japandroids (Polyvinyl CD *Celebration Rock*)
32. Oblivion – Grimes (4AD CD *Visions*)
31. Robocop 4 (Fuck Off Robocop) – Future of the Left (Xtra Mile CD *The Plot Against Common Sense*)
30. Clouds – Deep Time (Hardly Art CD *Deep Time*)
29. Chug This – 3rd International (Self-released mp3)
28. My Heart Beats – Veronica Falls (Slumberland 7")
27. Zombie – Lord Numb (Self-released mp3)
26. California Uber Alles (12" Plastic Toys Remix) – Dead Kennedys (Self-released mp3)
25. Monologue: River – Human Don't Be Angry (Chemikal Underground CD *Human Don't Be Angry*)
24. Shipmanesque – Flies On You (Self-released download album *Nothing to Write Home About*)
23. Zeroth Law – Christ. (Parallax Sounds CD *Cathexis: Motion Picture Soundtrack*)
22. The Wild Ride of Ichabod Crane – Blue Giant Zeta Puppies (GRGPNK V/A CD *Garage Monsters – The Best of the GaragePunk Hideout Vol. 9*)

21. Beautiful Idea – Big Joan (Self-released CD *The Long, Slow Death of Big Joan*)
20. Unfire – Alisia Casper (Self-released CD *Chronic*)
19. Ten Thousand Years Won't Save Your Life – Hammock (Hammock Music CD *Departure Songs*)
18. Default – Atoms For Peace (XL 12")
17. Devastating Bones – Shrag (Fortuna Pop! CD *Canines*)
16. I Am the Local DJ – Red Cosmos (Self-released CD *There & Back*)
15. Der Eingriff Schulze – The Chasms (Command To Destroy download Album *Winter Arcade*)
14. End Credits – The Wedding Present (Scopitones CD *Valentina*)
13. Food – Lovely Eggs (Cherryade 7")
12. Putin Has Pissed Himself (Putin Zassal) – Pussy Riot (Riot Grrl Berlin V/A download album *This is What Feminism Sounds Like 2*)
11. Default – Django Django (Because download single)
10. Tallulah – Allo Darlin' (Fortuna Pop! CD *Europe*)
9. Full Fathom Five – Vert:x (Unwashed Territories download EP *1947*)
8. MBV – Tender Trap (Fortuna Pop! CD *Ten Songs About Girls*)
7. Mladic – Godspeed You! Black Emperor (Constellation LP *Allelujah! Don't Bend! Ascend!*)
6. If You Enter the Arena, You've Got to be Prepared to Deal with the Lions – The Membranes (Louder Than War 7")
5. Allergies – The Lovely Eggs (Egg CD *Wildlife*)
4. We Drift Like Worried Fire - Godspeed You! Black Emperor (Constellation LP *Allelujah! Don't Bend! Ascend!*)
3. Capricornia – Allo Darlin' (Slumberland 7")
2. Death's Pony – The Chasms (Command To Destroy download album *Winter Arcade*)
1. Husbands – Savages (Pop Noire 12" EP *I Am Here*)

2013

With a couple of Fuck Buttons tracks in the top four, two angry slabs of expletive-ridden polemic from JD Meatyard in the chart and further unrestrained diatribes from, among others, Council Tax Band and Future of the Left, the 2013 festive fifty stands as probably the sweariest of all time. It's also without doubt the most politically charged chart since the mid-eighties, thanks to the aforementioned three artists, a paean to Pussy Riot from the great Jeffrey Lewis (only his second ever entry) and PJ Harvey's one-off release in support of Guantanamo Bay political prisoner Shaker Aamer.

The weren't the number of returns to the chart after long absences that 2012 had given us, although it was probably always likely that My Bloody Valentine, with their hugely well-publicised return to action, should make a return to the festive fifty also, after a 22 year gap unless you count their two appearances in the 1999 all-time chart. A perhaps less predictable return came from Helen Love, who snuck in at number 50 after a period of fifteen years without an appearance. Also perhaps unanticipated was a second entry for the now commercially-embraced Daft Punk, their first having come way back in 1997. Meanwhile, the re-formed Wolfhounds, members of the original C86 pack, found themselves in the chart twice, having waited almost three decades for any festive fifty recognition at all. Beating them all, though, was David Bowie, who returned after a 34 year absence, somehow muscling his way into the top ten and in the process equalling the record for gaps between entries established by Neil Young & Crazy Horse only a year earlier.

Mogwai continued to make the most of their second wind in festive fifty terms and this chart saw them break through into the top ten FF artists of all time, with two tracks from their soundtrack from cult French TV series *Les Revenants*. The Fall's latest album also saw them, if not returning to the multiple-entry triumphs of yesteryear, at least grabbing a couple of places in the top ten.

At the other end of the longevity spectrum, those fascinating purveyors of cut and paste Public Service Broadcasting made an impact with two entries near the top of the chart, although the only other chart debutants in the top ten were

Scottish indie posters The Spook School, who gained an impressive and well-deserved appearance at number nine. Another highly welcome first appearance was secured by Katie Gately, whose extraordinary voice-only cassette release on the excellent Blue Tapes label gave both artist and label their first involvement in a festive fifty. Other favourites of Dandelion DJs gaining an appearance included the extraordinarily prolific Dissolved, with one of two tracks from the Daddy Tank label in the chart (the other was from the also prolific St Helens-based combo The Bordellos), and there were places also for the savage indie pop of Tyrannosaurus Dead and the much-lauded Cloud, whose *Comfort Songs* album had rightly gained much critical praise for both the artist and the Audio Antihero label. Audio Antihero gained a perhaps surprising second entry, courtesy of Paul Hawkins off-shoot band The Count of Chateau Noir, with a tune from a charity album the label put out in aid of Rape Crisis. Although not reaching the heights of 2010, the chart was largely dominated by tracks played on Dandelion Radio during the year, including 21 played on Rocker's show, making this the highest number of chart placings from a single show since Dandelion took up the festive fifty reins. The most played track by Dandelion DJs in the chart was the number 23 entry, Council Tax Band's 'Mentioning No Names', which had featured in the shows of four different DJs during the year.

The welcome sight of that double assault from Fuck Buttons added much lustre to the top five; the also aforementioned Public Service Broadcasting were the only debut act to scale such dizzy heights, slipping in there at number five, while there was the rather more familiar sight of The Fall settling in at number three. All were beaten to the top by The Wedding Present, who finally made it to the number one slot, in the process giving David Gedge the distinction of reaching number one with a second different band (Cinerama having doing it ten years earlier), matching the achievements of the former members of Joy Division/New Order and, inevitably, Smith.

2013 Festive Fifty
First broadcast: 25 December

50. Atomic – Helen Love (Elefant CD *Day-Glo Dreams*)
49. Shaker Aamer – PJ Harvey (Self-released mp3)
48. Joanna – Flowers (Odd Box 7")
47. After the Carnival – The Count of Chateau Noir (Audio Antihero V/A download album *Regal Vs Steamboat*)
46. The Mother We Share – Chvrches (Virgin LP *The Bones of What You Believe*)
45. Shut – Colour Me Wednesday (Discount Horse LP *I Thought It Was Morning*)
44. My Ram is Sick – Cyclic Freeload Unit (Self-released download single *Chronic Svelte*)
43. Divide & Fall – The Wolfhounds (Odd Box 7")
42. Oh My Stars – Ryan Hardy (Wombnet download album *Day*)
41. Buried Alive – Veronica Falls (Slumberland/Bella Union LP *Waiting For Something to Happen*)
40. Wizard Motor – Mogwai (Rock Action LP *Les Revenants*)
39. In ~2 Seconds – Mat Riviere (Self-released download album *Not Even Doom Music*)
38. GMF – John Grant (Bella Union LP *Pale Green Ghosts*)
37. In Another Way – My Bloody Valentine (MBV LP *MBV*)
36. Forgotten Processes – Dissolved (Daddy Tank CD *Surge of the Lucid*)
35. Trapshit V12 – UZ (Boysnoize download EP *Trapshit 12/13*)
34. Sadie – Tyrannosaurus Dead (Odd Box 12" EP *Pure//Apart*)
33. Lost in Light Rotation – Tullycraft (Fortuna Pop! 7")
32. Angry Young Man – The Short Stories (Breaking Down CD single)
31. Dirty Girl Blues – Burning Condors (Snakehand CD *Round Our Way*)
30. Temperature Drop – The Bordellos (Daddy Tank CD *Ronco Revival Sound*)
29. Honey – Teen Canteen (Neu! Reekie! download single)
28. Sunfield – Postcode (Small Bear download EP *The ZebrATP EP*)
27. WWPRD – Jeffrey Lewis & The Rain (Rough Trade 7")
26. A Political Song (Blow It Our Yr Arse) – JD

Meatyard (Probe Plus CD *Northern Songs*)
25. Backwaters – Drenge (Infectious download single)
24. Giorgio By Moroder – Daft Punk (Columbia LP *Random Access Memories*)
23. Mentioning No Names – Council Tax Band (Self-released download EP *Three*)
22. Singing of the Bonesaws – Future of the Left (Prescriptions LP *How to Stop Your Brain in an Accident*)
21. Reflektor – Arcade Fire (Arcade Fire Music download album *Reflektor*)
20. Brains – Mega Emotion (Self-released mp3)
19. Pipes – Katie Gateley (Blue Tape cassette single)
18. Cheer Up – The Wolfhounds (Odd Box 7")
17. What Are They Doing in Heaven Today – Mogwai (Rock Action LP *Les Revenants*)
16. She Will – Savages (Pop Noire LP *Silence Yourself*)
15. Josephine – Flies On You (Dandelion Radio session recording)
14. I Saw the Stars – Diane Marie Kloba (Striped Shirt CD *It Is All An Illusion*)
13. Sugarcrush – Joanna Gruesome (Fortuna Pop! CD *Weird Sister*)
12. Signal 30 – Public Service Broadcasting (Test Card Recordings LP *Inform-Educate-Entertain*)
11. Mother Sea – Cloud (Audio Antihero CD *Comfort Songs*)
10. No Respects rev. – The Fall (Cherry Red CD *Re-Mit*)
9. I'll Be Honest – The Spook School (Fortuna Pop! LP *Dress Up*)
8. Where Are We Now? – David Bowie (ISO/Columbia CD *The Next Day*)
7. Sycamore – Martha (Odd Box 7")
6. Jesse James – JD Meatyard (Probe Plus CD *Northern Songs*)
5. Spitfire – Public Service Broadcasting (Test Card Recordings CD *Inform-Education-Entertain*)
4. Hidden XS – Fuck Buttons (ATP CD *Slow Focus*)
3. Sir William Wray – The Fall (Cherry Red CD *Re-Mit*)
2. Brainfreeze – Fuck Buttons (ATP CD *Slow Focus*)
1. Two Bridges – The Wedding Present (Scopitones 7")

2014

Even with the chart now within spitting distance (if you were a particularly good spitter) of its fortieth birthday, it was still able to throw up new statistical oddities to illuminate the grim post-Christmas period for the likes of me. The question was posed, when Cloud's cover of Benjamin Shaw's 'You & Me' was announced at number 47, as to whether Shaw's own version might make an appearance. The track came from an Audio Antihero EP featuring Shaw's original alongside three covers, one of which was the Cloud version. Shaw duly registered with his rendition at number 17 and thus provided the only instance of two versions of the same track appearing in the same festive fifty since Tim Buckley and This Mortal Coil both appeared with 'Song to the Siren' in the 1999 all-time chart. And of course, as Buckley and This Mortal Coil had recorded their versions more than a decade apart, Shaw and Cloud were able to claim a first of two versions of the same song released in the same year making the same festive fifty.

Two live tracks featured in the countdown for the first time since the Magic Band placed those two nostalgia-infused tracks in the 2004 chart. 'Fuckers', a live single by Savages, gave that band a third consecutive festive fifty appearance. The Fall's live version of 'Amorator' was also played in the countdown: the live album *Uurpop VIII-XII Places in Sun & Winter, Son* was the band's only album release in 2014, although the studio version from 'The Remainderer' EP, which had been released in December 2013, had also been eligible for votes,

Unlikely as it may once have seemed, the first ever festive fifty number provided the subject matter for a track in the chart, albeit via an irreverent source, courtesy of the voiceover on Mogwai's 'Repelish' which, for the second year running, was one of two Mogwai tunes to appear. Perhaps a more likely reference was found in the content of Fat White

Family's entry, which added yet another festive fifty link to the teetering pile against the name of Mark E. Smith. A reference to a figure surely under-represented in festive fifty terms, Julian Cope, gave The Bordellos an entry for the second year running. Billy Bragg teamed up with ex-Dandelion DJ Ste McCabe to chart for the first time for sixteen years, while Close Lobsters became the latest of the many first generation C86 bands to correct their omission from the mid-eighties festive fifty lists by re-forming and making the top twenty. Shellac, meanwhile, returned to the festive fifty after a fourteen year gap with two top twenty entries from their acclaimed *Dude Incredible* album.

Joining that lengthy list in the Dandelion years of bands for whom a festive fifty entry marked the end of their existence were the excellence Ace Bushy Striptease, who finally made it into the chart after announcing that the album from whence the successful track came would be their last. Thankfully in the world of music one fallen star invariably makes way for a rising one and it was great to see an entry for Spain's Deers (who would soon change their name to Hinds, but be just as good), with a track from their debut single, as well as the astonishing Good Throb, whose bluntly titled *Fuck Off* album was certainly one of the highlights of the year. Following the Blue Tapes entry last year, cassettes continued to make a festive fifty comeback (not that they'd featured much in the first place), with Blue Tapes featuring again, this time courtesy of a release by 13-year old prodigy Henry Plotnick, followed in the countdown by another cassette single, this time from Cruising, on the Soft Power label. Curiously, after enjoying a healthy presence in recent festive fifties, the number of self-released tracks in the chart was down to just five. Instead, it was very much a small labels' chart, with the honours pretty much shared out among a bunch of indies (Odd Box, Fortuna Pop!, Shelflife, Unwashed Territories and Slumberland all got two, as did Rock Action, Probe Plus and Touch & Go, with double entries for single artists) but only Audio Antihero gained as many as three entries, although one of them was played in its session version during the countdown, of which more below.

Although all Dandelion festive fifties have, to varying degrees, featured tracks not played by the station's DJs, arguably 2014 was the year in which this brought the greatest negative impact. There were such tracks in all and, while among them they managed to generate the highest ever entry for a track originating from Brazil (courtesy of Postal Blue), there was an unwelcome and dreary conservatism among several of them, alluded to by certain DJs during the countdown, with Jeff Grainger's acerbic and very warranted dismissal of Future Islands the most overt put-down. The festive fifty, of course, remained a listeners' chart and that's how it should be; indeed, there have been many instances over the years of listeners correcting omissions by Peel (his admission, in 1986, that he'd been wrong to overlook the tracks voted in from The The and Elvis Costello, being an example), and there's no doubt that, during the Dandelion years, listeners have voted in tracks that, were it not for time restrictions, would surely have featured in the station's tracklists, and which certainly added something positive to the festive fifty. Several of the tracks featured here had the opposite effect, marring what was otherwise a pretty good, if not vintage, chart with votes that came, you sense, from well outside the admittedly fluent parameters of the Dandelion listening audience.

The highest of the previously unplayed tracks (from War on Drugs) came at number six. Above that point, however, Mogwai and Half Man Half Biscuit provided familiarity and presumably a more accurate representation of Dandelion listeners' tastes, the latter with their highest ever placing and, strangely, a first ever top five appearance. A second entry for Benjamin Shaw saw him occupy the number five slot with one of a number of album title tracks to make the chart, though the version played was actually the one he recorded in session for my show during the year. Slightly embarrassingly, I also had an involvement in the number one: to commemorate the tenth anniversary of John Peel's death, I'd decided to curate an album of tracks featuring many of his favourite bands. The resulting *21 Songs for John* had already yielded one entry when JD Meatyard featured in the lower regions, but the album's opening track made number one. Cuban Boys had submitted a new version of their 'The Nation Needs You' and, of fuller length and featuring even cheekier snippets of Peel broadcast than had the original, it had always seemed a likely festive fifty contender. In the event, it saw off the challenge from much-heralded Canadians Alvvays (surely a festive fifty powerhouse of the future?) to give the Boys a number one a full fifteen years on from the musical phenomenon that was 'Cognoscenti Vs Intelligentsia'.

2014 Festive Fifty

First broadcast: 25 December

50. Your Love is Killing Me – Sharon Van Etten (Jagjaguwar CD *Are We There*)
49. Pale – Young Romance (Banquet 7")
48. Golden Surf II – Pere Ubu (Fire CD *Carnival of Souls*)
47. You & Me – Cloud (Audio Antihero V/A download EP *You & Me*)
46. Entropicalia – The Soundcarriers (Ghost Box CD *Entropicalia*)
45. Go Polski Boy – Ste McCabe (Self-released CD *Brains of Britain*)
44. Digital Witness – St Vincent (Loma Vista CD *St Vincent*)
43. Today, More Than Any Other Day – Ought (Constellation CD *More Than Any Other Day*)
42. Taking the Asylum – JD Meatyard (Unwashed Terriorities V/A download album *21 Songs for John*)
41. Run into the Sea – The Hobbes Fanclub (Shelflife CD *Up at Lagrange*)
40. Acid House – Good Throb (Self-released download album *Fuck Off*)
39. Bamboo – Deers (Lucky Number 7" *Demo*)
38. Class Historian – Broncho (Dine Alone CD *Just Hip Enough to be Woman*)
37. Amorator – The Fall (Cherry Red CD *Uurpop VIII-XII Places in Sun & Winter, Son*)
36. Cockroach – Ste McCabe with Billy Bragg (Self-released CD *Brains of Britain*)
35. Razorblade The Tape – Slum of Legs (Tuff Enuff 7" single *Begin To Dissolve* B-side)
34. Local Bullies – Tyrannosaurus Dead (Odd Box CD *Flying Ant Day*)
33. Wond'ring – The Very Most (My Little Owl 7" EP *Things Too Obvious to Sing*)
32. Repelish – Mogwai (Rock Action CD *Rave Tapes*)
31. Secret Life – ILL (Dandelion Radio session recording)
30. Wapiti – Henry Plotnick (Blue Tapes cassette single)
29. You Made Me Do That – Cruising (Soft Power cassette single)
28. Mad Mary Jones – The Vacant Lots (Sonic Cathedral CD *Departure*)
27. I Am Mark E. Smith – Fat White Family (Without Consent 10")
26. The Last Goodbye – Postal Blue (Jigsaw 7")
25. We Come From the Same Place – Allo Darlin' (Slumberland CD *We Come From the Same Place*)
24. Urge for Offal – Half Man Half Biscuit (Probe Plus CD *Urge for Offal*)
23. Hide from the Sun – Goat (Rocket CD *Commune*)
22. Smash Them Kill Them – Bourbon Somersault the 3rd (Self-released download single)
21. Bright Eyes – Allo Darlin' (Slumberland CD *We Come From the Same Place*)
20. The Gospel According to Julian Cope – The Bordellos (Small Bear download album *Will.I.Am, You're Really Nothing*)
19. Dude Incredible – Shellac (Touch & Go LP *Dude Incredible*)
18. 1997 Passing in the Hallway – Martha (Fortuna Pop! CD *Courting Strong*)
17. You & Me – Benjamin Shaw (Audio Antihero V/A download EP *You & Me*)
16. Now Time – Close Lobsters (Shelflife 7" EP *Kunstwerk in Spacetime*)
15. Lawman – Girl Band (Self-released 7")
14. Riding Bikes – Shellac (Touch & Go LP *Dude Incredible*)
13. Fuckers – Savages (Matador 12")
12. Seasons (Waiting On You) – Future Islands (4AD 7")
11. Young – Flowers (Fortuna Pop! CD *Do What You Want To, It's What You Should Do*)
10. Ibiza Rocks – Ace Bushy Striptease (Odd Box CD *Slurpt*)
9. Talk to God – Goat (Rocket CD *Commune*)
8. Horseshoe – Withered Hand (Fortuna Pop! 7")
7. Minipops 67 [120.1] [source field mix] – Aphex Twin (Warp CD *Syro*)
6. Red Eyes – War on Drugs (Secretly Canadian CD *Lost in the Dream*)
5. Goodbye, Kagoule World (Dandelion Radio

session recording)
4. Remurdered – Mogwai (Rock Action CD *Rave Tapes*)
3. The Unfortunate Gwatkin – Half Man Half Biscuit (Probe Plus CD *Urge for Offal*)
2. Archie, Marry Me – Alvvays (Transgressive CD *Alvvays*)
1. The Nation Needs You (2014 Version) – Cuban Boys (Unwashed Territories V/A download album *21 Songs for John*

MARK WHITBY

ALPHABETICAL LIST OF BANDS & ARTISTS

All Festive Fifty entries are listed below alphabetically by band/artist, with what aims to be a relatively precise breakdown of performers who took part in the recordings. Research since the first edition has enabled me to be more precise in relation to some entries. The suffix 'AT' denotes the all-time charts of 1982 and 1999.

After some soul-searching and a bit of a fight with myself, I decided to include the first fifty from the 1977 chart here and in any subsequent records and statistical information. Although the chart was not voted for, it is largely accepted as a genuine festive fifty by the wider Peel community and it doesn't seem wrong to let Peel himself have his say on the content of one chart. I've limited it to the top fifty to bring it in line with other charts: the remaining eleven entries can be found in Appendix One, along with 'extra' entries from other charts. Entries in the Truly Festive Festive Fifty have not been included here.

A

AC Acoustics
(Paul Campion – vocals; Mark Raine – guitar; Caz Riley – bass; Dave Gormley – drums)

Stunt Girl	26	1996
I Messiah Am Jailer	19	1997

Ace Bushy Striptease
(Eve Phillips – vocals; Basith Uddin – guitar; Paul Stokes – guitar; Simon Lawson – bass; Jeremy Sheppard – drums)

Ibiza Rocks	10	2014

Acid Casuals
(Cian Ciaran – keyboards/vocals; Meilir Gwynedd – guitar; Kevin Tame – producer. For Ciaran, see also Super Furry Animals)

Bowl Me Over	36	2005

Action Pact
(George Chees – vocals; Wild Planet – guitar; Kim Igoe – bass; Joe Fungus – drums)

Suicide Bag	48	1982

Adam & The Ants
(Adam Ant, aka Stuart Goddard – vocals; Marco Pirroni – guitar; Kevin Mooney – bass; Terry Le Miall – drums; Merrick, aka Chris Hughes – drums. For Pirroni, see also The Wolfmen)

Kings of the Wild Frontier	30	1980

Add N to (X)
(Stephen Clayton, Rob Hallum, Ann Shenton and Barry Smith: synthesisers and percussion)

Metal Finger in My Body	37	1999

Aereogramme
(Craig B – guitar/vocals; Iain Cook – guitar/programming; Campbell McNeil – bass; Martin Scott – drums)

Dreams & Bridges	5	2004
The Unravelling	15	2004

Age of Chance
(Steve Elridge – vocals; Neil Hewson – guitar; Geoff Taylor – bass; Jan Perry – drums and percussion)

Motor City	30	1985
Kiss	2	1986
Bible of the Beats	27	1986

Alex Canasta
(Line – vocals; Simon – guitar; Nikolaj – drums)

Records	39	2008

Allman Brothers Band
(Gregg Allman – guitar/vocals; Dickey Betts – guitar/vocals; Lamar Williams – bass; Chuck Leavell – keyboards; Jai Johanby Johanson – drums; Butch Trucks – drums)

Jessica	38	1976

Allo Darlin'
(*Elizabeth Morris – vocals; Paul Rains – guitar; Bill Botting – bass; Michael Collins – drums*. 2009: featured *Terry Edwards – trumpet/sax*. For Edwards, see also *The Higsons*. For Morris, see also *Darren Hayman*)

Henry Rollins Don't Dance	22	2009
Dreaming	8	2010
My Heart is a Drummer	10	2010
Darren	5	2011
Capricornia	3	2012
Tallulah	10	2012
Bright Eyes	21	2014
We Come From the Same Place	25	2014

Altered Images
(*Clare Grogan – vocals; Caeser – guitar; Tony McDaid – guitar; Johnny McElhone – bass; Michael 'Tich' Anderson – drums*. 'Happy Birthday': Joe McKinven replaced *Caeser – guitar*)

Dead Pop Stars	15	1981
Happy Birthday	50	1981
Dead Pop Stars	21	1982AT

Alt-J
(*Joe Newman – guitar/vocals; Gwil Sainsbury – guitar/bass; Gus Unger-Hamilton – keyboards; Thom Green – drums*)

Fitzpleasure	42	2012

Althea & Donna
(*Althea Rose Forrest – vocals; Donna Marie Reid – vocals; Joe Gibbs – producer*)

Uptown Top Ranking	2	1977

Aluminum Babe
(*Anna Liedberg – vocals; Jeff Botta – guitar; George Michael Musa – bass; Darren Fried - drums*)

Everything 2 Me	35	2005

Alvvays
(*Molly Rankin – guitar/vocals; Alec O'Hanley – guitar; Brian Murphy – bass; Kerri Maclellan – keyboards; Phil MacIsaac – drums*)

Archie, Marry Me	2	2014

Amsterdam
(*Ian Prowse – guitar/vocals; Johnny B – bass; Jez Wing – keyboards; Paul Walsham – drums*)

Does This Train Stop on Merseyside?	31	2003

...And You Will Know Us By the Trail of Dead
(*Jason Reece – guitar/drums/vocals; Conrad Keely – guitar/drums/vocals; Kevin Allen – guitar; Neil Busch – bass*)

Mistakes & Regrets	4	2000

Laurie Anderson
(*Laurie Anderson – guitar/drums/vocals*. 2004 remix was by *Henry Cullen*)

O Superman	34	1981
O Superman	49	1982AT
O Superman (remix)	28	2004

Angelica
(*Holly Ross – guitar/vocals; Brigit Colton – keyboards; Claire Windsor – guitar; Rachel Parsons – drums*. For Ross, see also *The Lovely Eggs*)

Teenage Girl Crush	31	1997

Animal Collective
(*Avey Tare, aka David Portner – guitar/keyboards/vocals; Panda Bear, aka Noah Lennox – guitar/keyboards/drums/vocals; Deakin, aka Josh Dibb – guitar/keyboards/vocals; Geologist, aka Brian Weitz – keyboards/percussion/vocals*. See also *Panda Bear*)

My Girls	3	2009
Brother Sport	32	2009

Antihero
(*Pete Hurley – guitar/vocals; Marcus Ratcliff – guitar/vocals; Davo McConville – bass; Jack Hamson – drums*)

Who's Looking Out For Number One?	38	2001
Rolling Stones T-Shirt	5	2002
You Got Nothing	37	2002

Antony & The Johnsons
(*Antony Hegarty – piano/organ/vocals; Jeff Longston – bass; Maxim Moston – violin; Julia Kent – cello; Doug Wieselman – saxophone; Parker Kindred – drums*)

Hope There's Someone	22	2005

Aphex Twin
(*aka Richard D. James – keyboards/computer*)

Girl/Boy	29	1996
Windowlicker	42	1999
Minipops 67 [102.2] (Source Field Mix)	7	2014

The Aphrodisacs
(Stephen McFall – *guitar/keyboards/vocals*; John Cairns – *guitar/bass*; Kevin Carlin – *bass/drums*)

This is a Campaign	49	2002
If U Want Me	45	2004

Apple Rabbits
(aka Jay Fisher – *guitar/bass/keyboards/percussion/vocals*)

Metro Dromedary	50	2009

Appliance
(James Brooks – *guitar/vocals*; Michael Parker – *bass*; David Ireland – *drums/percussion*)

Food Music	44	1999

Applicants
(Fidel Villeneurve – *guitar/vocals*; Paul Blades - *guitar* ; Jeffrey James – *keyboard/ melodica*)

Evelyn Waugh	33	2010

Arab Strap
(Aidan Moffat – *vocals*; Malcolm Middleton – *guitar*; Gary Miller – *bass*; Jason Gow – *drums*. For Middleton, *see also Malcolm Middleton* and *Human Don't Be Angry*. See also *David Holmes*)

The First Big Weekend	2	1996
Hey Fever	16	1997

Arcade Fire
(Win Butler – *guitar/piano/vocals*; Regine Chassagne – *keyboards/drums/accordian/ vocals*; Richard Reed Parry – *guitar*; Tim Kingsbury – *bass*; William Butler – *bass/synthesiser.xylophone*; Sarah Neufield – *violin*; Howard Bilerman – *drums*. 2007: Jeremy Gara replaced Bilerman – *drums*. 2013: also featured David Bowie – *vocals*; Colin Stetson – *horns*; Stuart Bogie – *horns*; Willinson Duprate – *congos*; Verrieux Zile – *congas*. See also *David Bowie*)

Rebellion (Lies)	5	2005
Invervention	13	2007
Black Mirror	43	2007
Reflektor	21	2013

Elizabeth Archer & The Equators
(Elizabeth Archer – *vocals*; The Equators: Dennis Fletcher – *guitar*; Alfonso Redford – *guitar*; Rocky Bailey – *keyboards*; Donald Bailey – *melodica/percussion*; Leo Bailey – *drums*)

Feel Like Making Love	44	1977

Architecture In Helsinki
(Cameron Bird – *guitar/percussion/vocals*; Kellie Sutherland – *keyboards/clarinet/ melodica/horns/vocals*; Gus Franklin – *guitar/trombone/horns/drums/vocals*; Jamie Mildren – *guitar/bass/keyboards/flute/glockenspie/melodica*; Sam Perry – *guitar /bass/keyboards/drums*; Tara Shackell – *keyboards/trombone/tuba*; Isobel Knowles – *trumpet/horns*; James Cecil – *guitar/keyboards/drums*)

The Owls Go	29	2003
Do The Whirlwind	48	2005

Arctic Monkeys
(Alex Turner – *guitar/vocals*; Jamie Cook – *guitar*; Andy Nicholson – *bass*; Matt Helders – *drums*)

Bet You Look Good On The Dancefloor	3	2005

Arcwelder
(Bill Graber – *guitar/vocals*; Rob Graber – *guitar/bass*; Scott McDonald – *drums*)

Favour	32	1992

Archers of Loaf
(Eric Bachmann – *guitar/vocals*; Eric Johnson – *guitar*; Matt Gentling – *bass/vocals*; Mark Price – *drums*)

Web in Front	23	1993

Art Brut
(Eddie Argos – *vocals*; Chris Chinchilla – *guitar*; Ian Catskilkin – *guitar*; Freddie Feedback – *bass*; Mikey Breyer – *drums*. 2009: Jasper Future replaced Chinchilla – *guitar*)

Formed a Band	31	2004
Emily Kane	38	2005
Demons Out	37	2009

Artery
(Mark Gouldthorpe – *guitar/vocals*; Michael Fidler – *guitar/vocals*; Neil MacKenzie – *bass*; Simon Hinkler – *keyboards*; Gary Wilson – *drums*. For Hinkler, see also *The Mission*)

Into the Garden	9	1982

Asa-Chang & Junray
(Asa-Chang – *tabla/vocals*; Hidehiko Urayama – *programming/guitar*; U-Zhaan – *tabla/alto horn*; Kiyoshi Kusaka – *effects*)

Hana	17	2002

Ash
(Tim Wheeler – guitar/vocals; Mark Hamilton – bass; Rick McMurray – drums)

Jack Names The Planets	12	1994
Uncle Pat	28	1994
Petrol	33	1994
Girl From Mars	4	1995
Kung Fu	6	1995
Angel Interceptor	43	1995
Oh Yeah	38	1996

The Assembly
(Feargal Sharkey – vocals; Vince Clarke – keyboards. For Sharkey, see also Undertones. For Clarke, see also Yazoo)

Never Never	23	1983

The Associates
(Billy McKenzie – vocals; Alan Rankine – keyboards/various; Michael Dempsey – bass; John Murphy – drums. For Dempsey, see also The Cure)

Party Fears Two	14	1982

Atari Teenage Riot
(Hanin Elias – vocals; Carl Crack – MC; Alec Empire – programming; Nic Endo – programming)

Revolution Action	39	1999

Atomizer
(Jonny Slut – DJ; Fil OK – DJ)

Black Hand	28	2009
Silicon Warning	18	2011

Atoms For Peace
(Thom Yorke – guitar/piano/vocals; Flea, aka Michal Balzary – bass; Nigel Godrich – keyboards/guitars; Joey Waronker – drums; Mauro Refosco – percussion. For Yorke, see also Radiohead and PJ Harvey)

Default	18	2012

Julien Auroux – see Lord Numb

Autechre
(Sean Booth – keyboards/computer; Rob Brown – keyboards/computer)

fold4, wrap5	48	1998

Autochtone
(Dan Gavin – guitar/keyboards/vocals; Tim Hancock – bass; Alistair Curd – drums)

The Last Thing She Ever Said	17	2005

Autons
(David Auton – voice/guitar/programming; Leon Auton – guitar; Tony Auton – keyboards)

Snakes	2	2006

Autorotation
(Robyn Sellman – vocals; Igor Olejar – guitar/bass/drums)

Ginger Pants	48	2009

J. Ayes & Ranking Trevor
(J. Ayes, aka Errol Wilson - vocals; Ranking Trevor – DJ)

Truly	13	1977

Aztec Camera
(Roddy Frame – guitar/vocals; Campbell Owens – bass; Bernie Clarke – keyboards; Dave Ruffy – drums. For Frame, see also Strawberry Switchblade. For Duffy, see also The Ruts and Zion Train)

Pillar To Post	24	1982
Oblivious	29	1983

B

Eric B. & Rakim
(DJ Rakim, aka William Griffin Jr – MC; Eric Barrier – DJ)

Paid In Full	27	1987
I Know You Got Soul	36	1987

Babes In Toyland
(Kat Bjelland – guitar/vocals; Michelle Leon – bass; Lori Barbero – drums. 1982: Maureen Herman replaced Lean – bass)

House	38	1990
Handsome & Gretel	18	1991
Catatonic	30	1991
Laugh My Head Off	39	1991
Primus	42	1991
Bruise Violet	9	1982
Handsome & Gretel	22	1982

Babybird
(Stephen Jones – guitar/vocals; Luke Scott – guitar; John Pedder – bass; Robert Gregory – drums)

Goodnight	15	1996

Badly Drawn Boy
(aka Damon Gough – guitar/bass/keyboards/vocals)

I Need a Sign	14	1998
Once Around the Block	41	1999

Ballboy
(Gordon McIntyre – guitar/vocals; Nick Reynolds – bass; Katie Griffiths – keyboards; Gary Morgan – drums. 'All the Records...' features David Ward – trumpet. 2003: Now without Griffiths. 2004: Alexa Morrison replaced Griffiths. *Laura Cantrell & Ballboy: Laura Cantrell – vocals; McIntyre – vocals; Jon Graboff – guitar. For Cantrell and Graboff, see also Laura Cantell)

I Hate Scotland	13	2000
They'll Hang Flags From Cranes Upon My Wedding Day	26	2001
I've Got Pictures of You in Your Underwear	41	2001
All the Records on the Radio Are Shite	10	2002
When Do the Nights of Sleep Go When They Do Not Come to Me	24	2002
The Sash My Father Wore	14	2003
I Gave Up My Eyes to a Man Who Was Blind	23	2003
Born in the USA	38	2003
*I Lost You, But I Found Country Music	17	2004
The Art of Kissing	21	2004
I Don't Have Time to Stand Here With You Fighting About the Size of My Dick	49	2004

Bang Bang Machine
(Elizabeth Freeth – vocals; Steve Eagles – guitar; Stan Wood – bass; Lamp – vocals)

Geek Love	1	1992

Barmy Army
(Adrian Sherwood – producer)

Sharp as a Needle	17	1987

Bastro
(David Grubbs – guitar/vocals; Clark Johnson – bass; John McEntire – drums. For McEntire, see also Toroise, Smog and Stereolab)

Nothing Special	45	1990

Bat For Lashes
(2007: Natasha Khan – keyboards/percussion/vocals; Howard Gott – violin; Sophie Sitora – violin; Abi Fry – viola; Emma Ramsdale – harp; Tim Byford – drums. 2009: Khan – synthesiser/drum programming/vocals; Fry – viola; Ben Christophers – pianochord/synthesiser; Caroline Weeks – flute/synthesiser; Adem – wine glasses; Kath Mann – musical saw; Alex Thomas – drums/percussion; David Kosten – drum programming)

Horse and I	26	2007
Daniel	27	2009

Battles
(Tyondai Braxton – guitar/keyboards/vocals; Dave Konopka – bass/guitar; Ian Williams – guitar/keyboards; John Stanier – drums)

Atlas	1	2007
Tonto	29	2007

Bauhaus
(Pete Murphy – vocals; Daniel Ash – guitar; David J, aka David Haskins – bass; Kevin Haskins – drums)

Ziggy Stardust	15	1982
Third Uncle	46	1982
Bela Lugosi's Dead	9	1982AT

Beach Boys
(Mike Love – vocals; Carl Wilson – vocals; Al Jardine – vocals; Bruce Johnston – vocals; Dennis Wilson – voca;s/organ on 'Good Vibrations'. 'God Only Knows' featured 23 session musicians while 'Good Vibrations' similarly drew on several studio musicians, playing instruments as varied as the harpsichord, fuzz-bass, sleigh bells and, most notably, the electro-theramin. Musicians involved were: Glen Campbell – guitar; Ed Carter – guitar; Bill Pitman – guitar; Tommy Tedesco – guitar; Howard Roberts – guitar; Barney Kessell – guitar; Billy Strange – guitar; Carol Kaye – bass; Ray Pohl – guitar/bass; Lyle Ritz – string bass; Al De Lory – keyboards; Larry Knechtel – Hammond organ; Don Randi – piano; Jay Migliori – saxophone; Steve Douglas – saxophone; Alan Robinson – French horn; Sid Sharp – string arrangements; Hal Blaine – drums; Julius Wechter – percussion. It's difficult to ascertain exactly whose contributions featured on the records, given Brian Wilson's tendency to eliminate them at the mixing stage)

God Only Knows	41	1999AT
Good Vibrations	46	1999AT

Beach House
(Victoria Legrand – keyboards/vocals; Alex Scally – guitar)

Zebra	44	2010

Bearsuit
(Iain Ross – guitar/vocals; Lisa Horton – keyboards/vocals; Jan Robertson – guitar/keyboards/percussion/vocals; Matt Moss – bass; Cerian Hamer, aka Cerian Hutchings – keyboards/cornet/violin/percussion; Matt Hutchings – drums. 2004: Richard Squires replaced Moss – bass. 2010: Charlene Katuwawala replaced Squires – bass; Joe Naylor replaced Matt Hutchings – drums; Cerian Hutchings left. For Horton, Ross and Robertson, see also Mega Emotion. For Horton, see also Hyper Kinako)

Hey Charlie, Hey Chuck	4	2001
Drinkink	30	2002
Itsuko Got Married	5	2003
Chargr	2	2004
Steven F***ing Spielberg	18	2006
Foxy Boxer	3	2007
Steven F***ing Spielberg	30	2007
Please Don't Take Him Back	34	2010
When Will I Be Queen?	6	2011

The Beatles
(John Lennon – guitar/vocals; George Harrison – guitar/vocals; Paul McCartney – bass/vocals; Ringo Starr, aka Richard Starkey – drums. 'A Day in the Life' also features Lennon – piano; Harrison – maracas; McCartney – piano; Starr – piano/congas; Mal Evans – piano/alarm clock; John Marston – harp; Cyril MacArther – double bass; Erich Gruenberg – violin; Granville Jones – violin; Bill Monro – violin; Jurgen Hess – violin; Hans Geiger – violin; D. Bradley – violin; Lionel Bentley – violin; David McCallum – violin; Donald Weekes – violin; Henry Datyner – violin; Sidney Sax – violin; Ernest Scott – violin; John Underwood – viola; Gwynne Edwrds – viola; Bernard Davis – viola; John Meek – viola; Francis Gabarro – cello; Dennis Vigay – cello; Alan Delziel – cello; Alex Nifosi – cello; Roger Lord – oboe; Basil Tsaikov – clarinet; Jack Brymer – clarinet; N. Fawcett – bassoon; Alfred Waters – bassoon; David Mason – trumpet; Monty Montgomery – trumpet; Harold Jackson – trumpet; Raymond Brown – trombone; Raymond Premru – trombone; T. Moore – trombone; Clifford Seville – flute; David Sandeman – flute; Alan Civl – french horn; Neil Sanders – french horn; Michael Barnes –tuba; Tristan Fry – timpani.
'Hey Jude' also features McCartney – piano; Starr – tambourine, plus a 36 piece orchestra (unnamed). 'Strawberry Fields Forever' also features Lennon – mellotron; Harrison – svarmandal/timpani/maracas; McCartney – mellotron/bongos/timpani; John Hall – cello; Derek Simpson – cello; Norman Jones – cello; Tony Fisher – trumpet; Greg Bowen – trumpet; Derek Watkins – trumpet; Stanley Roderick – trumpet; Mal Evans – tambourine; Neil Aspinall – guiro; Terry Doran – maracas. 'I Am The Walrus' also features Lennon – piano/mellotron; McCartney – tambourine; Mike Sammes Singers – backing vocals; session musicians (unnamed).

A Day in the Life	9	1976
Hey Jude	14	1976
Strawberry Fields Forever	17	1976
I Am the Walrus	45	1999AT

Beatmasters/Cookie Crew
(Beatmasters: Paul Carter, Amanda Glenfield and Richard Walmsley – producers. Cookie Crew: Debbie Pryce – MC; Susie Q, aka Susan Banfield – MC)

Rock Da House	49	1987

Beatnik Filmstars
(Andrew Jarrett – guitar/vocals; Tim Rippington – guitar; Maurice Roache – keyboards; Geoff Gorton – bass; Tom Adams – drums. For Rippington, see also The Flatmates. For Rippington & Adams, see also Forest Giants. For Rippington and Gorton, see also Short Stories)

Really Quite Bizarre	6	2006
It's Not What You Know	23	2006
Curious Role Model	4	2007
Life In The Country AKA This Civil War	6	2007
Inside the Mind of Sam (Breakfast Serial Killer)	8	2007
Hospital Ward	10	2007
Back Up Plan	41	2009

Beck
(aka Beck Hansen – guitar/various/vocals)

Loser	32	1994

Jeff Beck with Jan Hammer Group
(Jeff Beck – guitar/effects; Steve Kindler – guitar; Fernando Saunders – bass; Jan Hammer – synthesizer; Tony Smith – drums)

Blue Wind	26	1977

The Bees
(Paul Butler – guitar/keyboards/vocals; Kris Birkin – guitar; Aaron Fletcher - bass/guitar; Tim Parkin – piano/bass; Warren Hampshire – hammond organ, guitar/percussion; Michael Clevett – drums/percussion)

Listening Man	34	2007

Belle & Sebastian
(stuart Murdoch – guitqr/vocals; Steve Jackson – guitar/vocals; Stuart David – bass; Chris Geddes – piano/keyboards; Isobel Campbell – violin/cello; Richard Colburn – drums. 1997-2000: added Sarah Martin – saxophone/violin. 'Dog on Wheels' featured Mick Cooke – trumpet. 'Lazy Line…' featured Monica Queen – vocals. 'Sleep the Clock Around' featured Ian MacKay – pipes. 'I'm Waking Up…' featured Fiona Stephen – violin; Elizabeth Edwards – violin; George Cuthbertson – viola; Jacqui Penfold – viola. 2002: Bob Kildea replaced David – bass; Campell left; added Cooke – guitar/trumpet)

The State I Am In	28	1996
Lazy Line Painter Jane	5	1997
Dog on Wheels	12	1997
The Boy with the Arab Strap	3	1998
Sleep the Clock Around	26	1998
Lazy Line Painter Jane	31	1999AT
Fought in a War	49	2000
Jonathan David	17	2001
I'm Waking Up to Us	32	2001
You Don't Send Me	20	2002
Step Into My Office, Baby	11	2003
Stay Loose	43	2003
I Didn't See It Coming	20	2010

The Beloved
(Jon Marsh – vocals; Steve Waddington – guitar; Tim Havard – bass; Guy Gousden – drums)

A Hundred Words	34	1984

Berntholer
(Drita Kotaji – vocals; Simon Rigot – guitar; Pol Fourmois – bass; Manuel Poutte – keyboards)

My Suitor	34	1984

Best Coast
(Bethany Cosentino – guitar/vocals; Bobb Bruno – guitar/bass/drums)

Crazy For You	35	2010

Zoe Bestel
(Zoe Bestel – ukulele/vocals)

25 Missed Calls	27	2011

Bhundu Boys
(Biggie Tembo – guitar/vocals; Rise Kagonga – guitar/vocals; David Mankaba – bass/vocals; Shakie Kangwena – keyboards/vocals; Kenny Chitsvatsva – drums)

My Foolish Heart	30	1987

Big Black
(Steve Albini – guitar/vocals; Melvin Belli – guitar; David Riley – bass. For Albini, see also Shellac)

Colombian Necktie	18	1987
L Dopa	42	1987

Big Joan
(Annette Berlin – vocals; Adam Burrows – guitar; Simon Jarvis – bass; Keith Hall – drums)

Beautiful Idea	21	2012

Big Stick
(Yanna Trance – vocals; John Gill – keyboards/various/vocals)

On the Road Again	43	1992

Birdland
(Robert Vince – vocals; Lee Vince – guitar/vocals; Sid Rogers – bass; Gene Kale – drums)

Hollow Heart	28	1989
Paradise	40	1989

Birthday Party
(Nick Cave – vocals; Roland S. Howard – guitar; Tracy Pew – bass; Mick Harvey – organ/guitar; Phil Calvert – drums. 1983: Harvey replaced Calvert – drums. For Cave and Harvey, see also *Nick Cave & The Bad Seeds*. For Harvey, see also *PJ Harvey* and *John Parish & Polly Jean Harvey*. For Calvert, see also *Psychedelic Furs*)

Release the Bats	19	1981
Release the Bats	18	1982AT
Deep in the Woods	43	1983
Sonny's Burning	46	1983

Bis
(Manda Rin, aka Amanda McKinnon – keyboards/bass/vocals; Sci-Fi Steven, aka Steven Clark – guitar/vocals; John Disco, aka John Clark – guitar)

School Disco	47	1995
Kandy Pop	14	1996
Sweet Shop Avengerz	22	1997
Eurodisco	7	1998

Bjork
(Bjork Guomundsdottir – various/vocals; choir: Asta Aegisdottir, Auour Albertsdottir; Arnheiour Eiriksdottir, Asdis Bjorg Gestsdottir, Erla Run Guomondsdottir, Kristin Anna Guomundsdottir; Gigja Gylfadottir, Gigja Haraldsdottir, Sigrun Osk Johannesdottir, Fifa Jonsdottir, Sigurborg Skuladottir Kaldal, Bergljot Rafnar Karlsdottir, Kristin Einarsdottir Mantyla, Erla Maria Markusdottir, Asdis Eva Olafsdottir, Drifa Olafsdottir, Guoron M. Sigurbergsdottir, Elin Edda Siguroardottir, Unnur Siguroardottir, Vigdis Siguroadottir, Kristin Sveinsdottir, Eyglo Hoskuldsdottir Viborg; Arni Heimer Ingolfsson – choir transcription; Amar Souleyman – producer. For Bjork, see also *Sugarcubes*)

Crystalline (Omar Souleyman Version)	16	2011

Black Keys
(Dan Auerbach – guitar/vocals; Patrick Carney – drums

Have Love Will Travel	34	2003
10am Automatic	22	2004
Girl is on My Mind	30	2004

James Blake
(James Blake - synthesiser/computer/piano/vocals)

CMYK	39	2010
The Wilhelm Scream	13	2011

Blanche Hudson Weekend
(Caroline McChrystal – vocals; Darren Lockwood – guitar; Sasha Delirium – guitar; Chris Shake – bass; Lee Hooper – keyboards; Matt – drums. For McChrystal and Lockwood, see also *Manhattan Love Suicides*)

Only Snow	29	2010

Blancmange
(Neil Arthur – vocals; Stephen Luscombe – keyboards. 'Feel Me' featured David Rhodes – guitar; Steve Lange – backing vocals; Madelaine Lange – backing vocals. 'Living on the Celing' featured Deepak – sitar; Dinesh – tabla; James Lane – drums)

Living on the Ceiling	34	1982
Feel Me	35	1982

Blizzard Boys
(DJ Phospor, aka Dan Hood – DJ; DJ Justrick, aka Rich Garbutt – DJ)

Ain't No Stoppin' This	48	2003

Bloc Party
(Kele Okereke – guitar/vocals; Russeel Lissack – guitar; Gordon Moakes – bass/vocals; Matt Tong – drums)

Helicopter	11	2004
Banquet	20	2004
Little Thoughts	44	2004

Blue Giant Zeta Puppies
(Mr Blue Giant, plus fluent line-up)

The Wild Ride of Ichabod Crane	22	2012

The Bluetones
(Mark Morriss – vocals; Adam Devlin – guitar; Scptt Morriss – bass; Ed Chesters – drums)

Bluetonic	15	1995
Slight Return	21	1995

Blur
(Damon Albarn – vocals; Graham Coxon – guitar; Alex James – bass; Dave Rowntree – drums. 1999: featured the London Community Gospel Choir. For Albarn, see also *Elastica* and *Gil Scott-Heron*. For Coxon, see also *Graham Coxon*)

Song 2	11	1997
Tender	40	1999

B-Movie
(Steve Hovington – vocals; Paul Statham – guitar; Rick Holliday – keyboards; Graham Boffey – drums)

Remembrance Day	36	1981

Boards of Canada
(Mike Sanderson – computer/keyboards; Marcus Eoin – computer/keyboards)

Aquarius	18	1998
Roygbiv	41	1998
In a Beautiful Place Out in the Country	20	2000

Bob
(Richard Blackborow – guitar/keyboards/vocals; Simon Armstrong – guitar/vocals; Jem Morris – bass; Dean Leggett – drums)

Convenience	31	1989

Bobby McGees
(Jimmy – ukulele/glockenspiel/vocals; Eleanor – ukulele/glockenspiel/recorder/melodica/banjolele/vocals; Becca – saxophone/glockenspiel/melodica/recorder; Graeme – bass/drums)

Ivor Cutler Is Dead (No Friends)	16	2006
When Father Died, Ferrets Licked Away The Tears	19	2007

The Bodines
(Mike Ryan – vocals; Paul Brotherton – guitar; Tim Burtonwood – bass; John Rowland – drums)

Therese	19	1986

Bombay Bicycle Club
(Jack Steadman – guitar/vocals; Jamie MacColl – guitar; Ed Nash – bass; Suren de Saram – drums)

Ivy & Gold	42	2010

Bongwater
(Ann Magmusson – vocals; Dogbowl – guitar; Randolph Hudson III – guitar; Mark Kramer – bass; David Licht – drums)

Nick Cave Dolls	50	1991

Boo Radleys
(Simon Rowbottom – guitar/vocals; Martin Carr – guitar; Timothy Brown – bass; Robert Cieka – drums)

Kaleidoscope	21	1990
Finest Kiss	19	1990
Lazarus	39	1992
Barney…and Me	35	1993

Booka Shade
(Walter Merziger – synths; Arno Kammermeier – synths)

In White Rooms	37	2006

Boom Bip & Dose One
(Dose One, aka Adam Drucker – MC; Boom Bip, aka Bryan Hollon – DJ/producer)

Mannequin Hand Trapdoor I Reminder	32	2002

Boomtown Rats
(Bob Geldof – vocals; Gerry Cott – guitar; Garry Roberts – guitar; Pete Briquette – bass; Johnnie Fingers, aka John Peter Moylett – keyboards; Simon Crowe – drums)

Lookin' After Number 1	39	1977

The Bordellos
(Antony Shea – percussion/harmonica/vocals; Brian Shea – guitar/vocals; Daniel Shea – keyboards/vocals; Gary Storey – bass)

Temperature Drop	30	2013
The Gospel According to Julian Cope	20	2014

Bourbon Somersault the 3rd
(aka Tim Tortoise – computer/electronics. See also Cyclic Freeload Unit and Red Cosmos)

Smash Them Kill Them	22	2014

David Bowie
(David Bowie – vocals; Robert Fripp – guitar; Carlos Alomar – guitar; George Murray – bass; Brian Eno – keyboards; Dennis Davis – drums. 2013: Bowie – vocals; Gerry Leonard – guitar; Tony Levin – bass; Tony Visconti – strings; Zachary Alford – drums. For Bowie and Alomar, see also Iggy Pop. For Bowie, see also Arcade Fire)

'Heroes'	36	1977
'Heroes'	16	1978
'Heroes'	34	1979
Where Are We Now?	8	2013

The Boys
(Matt Dangerfield – guitar/vocals; Honest John Plain – guitar; Duncan 'Kid' Reid – bass; Casino Steel – organ/piano; Jack Black – drums. See also The Yobs)

Box Number	20	1977

Billy Bragg

(Billy Bragg – guitar/vocals. 'The Saturday Boy' features Dave Woodhead – trumpet. 'Levi Stubbs' Tears' features Woodhead; Simon Moreton – percussion. 'Greetings to..' features Kirsty MacColl – vocals; Johnny Marr – guitar; John Porter – guitar/bass; Moreton. 1988: Bragg; Martin Belmont – guitar; Bruce Thomas – bass; Cara Tivey – piano; Woodhead; Micky Waller – drums; Tony Maronie – percussion. 1991: Bragg; MacColl; Marr; Wiggy –bass; Cara Tivey –keyboards; Amanda Vincent – keyboards; Woodhead; J.F.T. Hood – drums. 'Brickbat' features Terry Disley – strings; Dierdre Cooper – cello. 'Way Over Yonder': Billy Bragg & Wilco and with Natalie Merchant – vocals. For Marr, see *The Smiths, Electronic* and *Modest Mouse*. For Merchant, see *10,000 Maniacs,* For Thomas, see *Elvis Costello*. See also *Ste McCabe*)

A New England	7	1983
Between the Wars	13	1984
The Saturday Boy	29	1984
Between the Wars	40	1985
Levi Stubbs' Tears	24	1986
Greetings to the New Brunette	41	1986
Waiting for the Great Leap Forwards	25	1988
Sexuality	29	1991
Northern Industrial Town	37	1995
Brickbat	12	1996
Way Over Yonder in the Minor Key	30	1998

The Breeders

(Kim Deal – guitar/vocals; Kelley Deal – guitar/vocals; Jo Wiggs – bass; Jim MacPherson – drums. For Kim Deal, see also *Pixies*)

| Cannonball | 8 | 1993 |

Broadcast

(Trish Keenan – vocals; Tim Felton – guitar; James Cargill – bass; Roj Stevens – keyboards; Steve Perkins – drums. 1999: added Keith York – drums. 2003: Neil Bullock replaced York and Perkins – drums. See also *Broadcast & Wolfram Wire*)

The Book Lovers	34	1996
Living Room	40	1996
Echo's Answer	36	1999
Come On Let's Go	5	2000
Pendulum	40	2002

Broadcast & Wolfram Wire

(Broadcast: Trish Keenan – vocals; Tim Felton – guitar; James Cargill – bass; Roj Stevens – keyboards; Neil Bullock – drums. Wolfram Wire: Dan Werner – various/vocals. See also *Broadcast, Wolfram Wire*)

| Verstehen 1,8; 3.296.2.1 | 47 | 2011 |

Broken Family Band

(Steven Adams – guitar/vocals; Jay Williams – guitar/vocals; Gavin Johnson – bass; Timothy Victory – banjo/keyboards; Mick Roman – drums)

| At the Back of the Chapel | 19 | 2003 |

Broncho

(Ryan Lindsey – guitar/vocals; Ben King – guitar/vocals; Johnathan Ford – bass; Nathan Price – drums)

| Class Historian | 38 | 2014 |

Bronski Beat

(Jimi Somerville – vocals; Steve Bronski – keyboards; Larry Steinbachek – keyboards)

| Small Town Boy | 48 | 1984 |

Jackson Browne

(Jackson Browne – guitar/piano/vocals; David Linley – guitar; Doug Haywood – bass; Jai Winding – keyboards; Larry Zack – drums)

| Late for the Sky | 35 | 1976 |
| Fountain of Sorrow | 43 | 1976 |

The Brownies

(Sophie – vocals; Maxie - guitar; Stevie - bass; Mike – drums)

| Cougar | 8 | 2009 |

Roy Buchanan

(Leroy Buchanan – guitar; Stanley Clarke – guitar; Will Lee – bass; Malcolm Lukens – keyboards; Byrd Foster – drums)

| Green Onions | 48 | 1977 |

Tim Buckley

(Tim Buckley – guitar/vocals; Lee Underwood – guitar/keyboards)

| Song to the Siren | 40 | 1999AT |

Buffalo Tom

(Bill Janovitz – guitar/vocals; Chris Coulborn – bass; Tom Marginnis – drums)

| Tail Lights Fade | 45 | 1992 |

The Bumblebees

(Ellis – guitar; Roz – keyboards; Bert - bass)

| The Way | 42 | 2009 |

Burial
(aka William Bevan – computer)

| Street Halo | 12 | 2011 |

Burning Condors
(Marcus 'Tommy' Thompson – vocals; Matt – guitar; Churchy – bass; James – drums/percussion)

| Dirty Girl Blues | 31 | 2013 |

Burning Love Jumpsuit
(D.F. Dresden; J. Barsetti; Smiley)

| Cheerleader | 41 | 2002 |

Kate Bush
(Kate Bush – keyboards/vocals; Dan McIntosh – guitar; Peter Erskine – bass; Gary Brooker – hammond organ; Rolf Harris – didgeridoo; Eberhard Weber – drums; Bosco D'Oliveira - percussion)

| King of the Mountain | 42 | 2005 |

Butthole Surfers
(Gibby Haynes – vocals; Paul Sneef – guitar; Jeff Pinker – bass; King Koffey – drums. For Haynes, see also *Ministry*)

| 22 Going On 23 | 44 | 1987 |

Buzzcocks
(Pete Shelley – guitar/vocals; Steve Diggle – guitar; Steve Garvey – bass; John Maher – drums. 'Boredom' features Howard Devoto – vocals. Fpr Devoto, see also *Magazine*)

What Do I Get?	8	1978
Boredom	12	1978
Moving Away from the Pulsebeat	30	1978
What Do I Get?	50	1979

C

Camper Van Beethoven
(David Lowery – guitar/vocals; Chris Pedersen – guitar; Greg Lisher – guitar; Victor Krummenacher – bass; Jonathan Segal – violin; Chris Molla – drums)

| Take the Skinheads Bowling | 47 | 1986 |

Laura Cantrell
(Laura Cantrell – guitar/vocals; Robin Goldwasser – vocals; Jay Sherman-Godfrey – guitar; Jon Graboff – guitar/mandolin/pedal steel; Jeremy Chatzky – bass; Will Rigby – drums. 'Too Late...': Doug Wygal replaced Rigby – drums. 2005: Cantrell; Dave Schramm – guitar; Graboff; Joey Burns – bass; Jon Convertino – drums. For Cantrell and Graboff, see also *Ballboy*. For Burns and Convertino, see *Calexico*)

Somewhere, Some Night	21	2000
Two Seconds	27	2000
Queen of the Coast	42	2000
Too Late For Tonight	7	2002
Bees	10	2005

Captain Beefheart & The Magic Band
(Captain Beefheart, aka Don Van Vliet – vocals; Rockette Norton – guitar; Russ Titelman – guitar; Jeff Cotton – guitar; Roy Estrada – Ed Marimba, aka Art Tripp – marimba; Drumbo, aka John French – drums. For Estrada, see also *Little Feat*. For Drumbo, see also *The Magic Band*)

| Big Eyed Beans from Venus | 18 | 1976 |
| Big Eyed Beans from Venus | 13 | 1999AT |

Caribou
(aka Daniel Victor Smith – guitar/synthesiser/bass/drums)

| Sun | 22 | 2010 |

Cartridge
(Catherine Kontz – keyboards/vocals; Henri Vaxby – guitar/vocals)

| Fooling Around | 21 | 2006 |

Neko Case & Her Boyfriends
(Neko Case – vocals; John Ramberg – guitar; Travis Good – guitar; Evan Johns – guitar; Kevin Kane – guitar; Scott Betts – bass; Joel Trueblood – drums)

| Twist the Knife | 1 | 2000 |

Jon E. Cash
(Jon E. Cash – DJ/producer)

| International | 35 | 2004 |

Alisia Casper
(Alisia Casper – guitar/vocals)

Mother I Am Free	14	2009
Unfire	20	2012

Cat Power
(aka Chan Marshall – guitar/piano/vocals. 2003: featured David Campbell – strings. 2006: featured Mabon Hodges – guitar; Leroy Hodges – bass; Doug Easley – guitar/pedal steel; Rich Steff – keyboards; Jim Spake – saxophone; Scott Thompson – trumpet; Roy Brewer – violin; Beth Luscone – viola; Johnathan Kirkscey – cello)

Wonderwall	33	2000
Werewolf	39	2003
The Greatest	32	2006

Catatonia
(Cerys Matthews – vocals; Mark Roberts – guitar; Paul Jones – bass; Clancy Pegg – keyboards; Dafydd Ieuan – drums. For Ieuan, see also Super Furry Animals)

Bleed	18	1995

The Catherine Wheel
(Rob Dickinson – vocals; Brian Futter – guitar; David Hawes – bass; Neil Sims – drums)

Black Metallic	15	1991

Nick Cave & The Bad Seeds
(Nick Cave – vocals; Mick Harvey – guitar/various; Blixa Bargeld – guitar; Barry Adamson – bass; Anita Lane – keyboards; Hugo Race – drums. 1985: Lane had departed; Thomas Wylder replaced Race – drums. 1986: added Roland S.Howard – guitar/keyboards. 1988: Kid Congo Powers, aka Brian Tristan replaced Howard – guitar; Roland Wolf replaced Adamson – bass. 1990: Wolf had departed. For Cave, Harvey and Howard, see also Birthday Party. For Harvey, see also PJ Harvey. For Powers, see also Gun Club)

St Huck	11	1984
Tupelo	35	1985
By the Time I Get to Phoenix	45	1986
The Mercy Seat	10	1988
The Ship Song	19	1990

Chalkdust
(Line-up unknown: included Bill Vine)

Cheddar Would Be Better	44	2006

The Chameleons
(Mark Burgess – bass/vocals; Reg Smithies – guitar; Dave Fielding – guitar/keyboards; Brian Schofield – drums. 1983: added Alistair Lewthwaite – keyboards)

In Shreds	42	1982
Second Skin	31	1983

Chapterhouse
(Andrew Sheriff – guitar/vocals; Stephen Patman – guitar; Simon Rose – guitar; Russell Barrett – bass; Ashley Bates – drums)

Pearl	33	1991

The Charlatans
(Tim Burgess – vocals; Joe Baker – guitar; Martin Blunt – bass; Rob Collins – keyboards; Jon Brookes – drums)

The Only One I Know	17	1990
Polar Bear	28	1990

The Chasms
(Mike Seed – drums/vocals; Richard Quirk – guitar; Simon Pott – bass. 'Der Eingriff Schulze featured Neil Whitehead – guitar. For Whitehead, see also Vert:x)

I'm Here To See The Clouds of Blood	5	2009
Blue Sun, Golden Sky	5	2010
The Occult Soul Review	3	2011
Death's Pony	2	2012
Der Eingriff Schulze	15	2012

China Crisis
(Eddie Lundon – guitar/vocals; Gerry Daly – keyboards/vocals)

African & White	22	1982

Christ.
(aka Christopher Horne – producer)

Zeroth Law	23	2012

Chumbawamba
(Alice Nutter – vocals; Danbert Novacon – vocals; Boff – guitar/vocals; Louise Watts – guitar/vocals; Mavis Dillon – bass/trumpet; Harry Hamer – drums. 1993: added Howard Storey – vocals; Neil Ferguson – guitar/keyboards; Julian Walker – bass; Geoff Slaphead – violin; Dunston Bruce – saxophone/percussion. 'Enough is Enough' was with Credit To The Nation. See also Credit to the Nation)

Revolution	6	1985
Enough Is Enough	1	1993
Timebomb	28	1993

Chvrches
(Lauren Maybury – synthesizers/vocals; Iain Cook – guitar/bass/synthesizers/vocals Martin Doherty – synthesizers/vocals)

The Mother We Share	46	2013

Cinerama
(David Gedge – guitar/vocals; Sally Murrell – keybaards/vocals; Marty Willson-Piper – guitar; Anthony Cooke – bass; Richard Markangelo – drums/percussion; Che Albrighton – drums/percussion. 'Pacific' also fatured Duncan Bridgeman – flute. 2000: Gedge; Murrell; Simon Cleave – guitar; Terry de Castro – bass; Nigel Pearson – drums. 'Health & Efficiency': and for 2002-04: Karl Paavola replaced Pearson – drums. 2002-03 material also featured: Rachel Davies – violin; Teresa Wipple – viola; Abigail Trundl – cello. For Gedge and Cleave, see also The Wedding Present)

Kerry Kerry	15	1998
Pacific	13	1998
Kings Cross	18	1999
Your Charms	16	2000
Wow	17	2000
Manhattan	41	2000
Health & Efficiency	3	2001
Superman	34	2001
Quick, Before It Melts	2	2002
Careless	13	2002
Cat Girl Tights	39	2002
Don't Touch That Dial	1	2003
It's Not You, It's Me	14	2004

Dave Clarke
(Dave Clarke – DJ/producer)

Red Three	46	1995
No-one's Driving	25	1996

The Clash
(Joe Strummer, aka John Mellor: guitar/vocals; Mick Jones – guitar/vocals; Paul Simonon – bass; with Terry Chimes – drums on 'White Riot' & 'Police & Thieves'. Topper Headon – drums on all other entries)

Complete Control	9	1977
White Riot	27	1977
Complete Control	2	1978
(White Man) In Hammersmith Palais	7	1978
White Riot	15	1978
Police & Thieves	23	1978
(White Man) In Hammersmith Palais	3	1979
Complete Control	5	1979
White Riot	26	1979
Police & Thieves	49	1979
(White Man) In Hammersmith Palais	5	1980
Complete Control	15	1980
Armagideon Time	39	1980
Bankrobber	46	1980
White Riot	48	1980
(White Man) In Hammersmith Palais	10	1981
Complete Control	18	1981
Straight To Hell	6	1982
Should I Stay Or Should I Go?	26	1982
Know Your Rights	27	1982
Rock the Casbah	40	1982
(White Man) In Hammersmith Palais	10	1982AT
Complete Control	19	1982AT
Armagideon Time	40	1982AT
(White Man) In Hammersmith Palais	5	1999AT
Complete Control	33	1999AT

Clinic
(Ade Blackburn – guitar/vocals; Hartley – guitar/keyboards; Brian Campbell – bass; Carl Turney – drums)

IPC Subeditors Dictate Our Youth	9	1997
Cement Mixer	13	1998
Monkey on your Back	27	1998
The Second Line	20	1999
The Second Line	28	2000

Close Lobsters
(Andrew Burnett – vocals; Tom Donnelly – guitar; Bob Burnett – bass; Stuard McFadyen – drums)

Now Time	16	2014

Cloud
(aka Tyler Taormina – various/vocals)

Mother Sea	11	2013
You & Me	47	2014

CLSM
(aka Jon Doe – DJ. Version broadcast was a remix from Fergus Mayhem)

John Peel (Not Enough)	9	2003

Jarvis Cocker
(Jarvis Cocker – guitar/vocals; Richard Hawley – guitar/piano; Steve Mackey – bass; Ross Orton – drums. For Cocker, Hawley & Mackey, see also Pulp)

Cunts Are Still Running The World	41	2006

Cocteau Twins
(1982 and 'Peppermint Pig': Elizabeth Fraser – vocals; Robin Guthrie – guitar/programming; Will Heggie – bass. Rest of 1983: Fraser and Guthrie. 1984: Fraser; Guthrie; Simon Raymonde – bass. For Fraser, Guthrie and Raymonde, see This Mortal Coil. For Fraser, see also Felt and Massive Attack)

Wax & Wane	37	1982
Musette & Drums	5	1983
Sugar Hiccup	14	1983
From the Flagstones	16	1983
Peppermint Pig	28	1983
Hitherto	38	1983
Pearly Drewdrops' Drops	2	1984
The Spangle Maker	4	1984
Ivo	16	1984
Domino	22	1984
Pandora	38	1984
Beatrix	40	1984
Pepper Tree	49	1984
Aikea-Guinea	5	1985
Love's Easy Tears	21	1986
Those Eyes, That Mouth	38	1986
Carolyn's Fingers	26	1988

Coin-Op
(Matt Leuw – guitar/vocals; Nick Hills – guitar/keyboards; Craig Robbins – bass; Matt Cooper – drums)

Democracies	19	2002

Colorblind James Experience
(Colorblind James – guitar/vibraphone/vocals; Philip Marshall – guitar; Bernie Heveron – bass; Jim McAvaney – drums)

Considering a Move to Memphis	47	1987

Colour Me Wednesday
(Jennifer Doveton – vocals; Harriet Doveton – guitar; Carmela Pietrangelo – bass; Sam Brackley – drums)

Shut	45	2013

Colourbox
(Steve Young – keyboards; Martyn Young – keyboards. See also M/A/R/R/S)

Official Colourbox World Cup Theme	46	1986

Container Drivers
(Rik – guitar/vocals; Keg – bass/vocals; Dr Bryn Hans – drums)

It Must Be The Pipes	6	2008

Ry Cooder
(Terry Evans – vocals; Ry Cooder – guitar; Henry Ojeda – bass; Pat Rizzo – saxophone; Flaco Jimenez – accordion; Isaac Garcia – drums; Milt Holland – percussion)

The Dark End of the Street	42	1977

Cookie Crew: see Beatmasters/Cookie Crew

John Cooper Clarke
(John Cooper-Clarke – vocals; supported by The Curious Yellows: Eric, aka Anthony McGann – guitar; Middie, aka Phil Middleton – bass; Joe Viality, aka Tony Roberts – drums; Martin Zero, aka Martin Hannett – percussion)

Suspended Sentence	5	1977

Cornershop
(Ben Ayres – guitar/vocals; Avtar Singh – guitar; John Robb – guitar; Tijinder Singh – bass/vocals; Anthony Saffrey – sitar; David Chambers – drums. 1995: without Chambers. 1997: Ayers; Tijinder Singh; Saffrey – keyboards/sitar; Nick Simms – drums; Peter Bengry – percussion. 2002: Ayres; Tijinder Singh; Saffrey – guitar; Alan Gregson – bass; Ian Hooper – keyboards; Simms; Bengry. 2004: as Cornershop presents Bubbley Kaur: Bubbley Kaur – vocals; Ayres – various; Tijinder Singh – bass)

England's Dreaming	17	1993
6am Jullander Shere	36	1995
Brimful of Asha	1	1997
Staging the Plaguing of the Raised Platform	25	2002
Topknot	40	2004

Elvis Costello
(Elvis Costello, aka Declan McManus – guitar/vocals; with The Attractions: Bruce Thomas 0 guitar; Steve Nieve – keyboards; Pete Thomas – drums, except: 'Alison', supported by The Shamrocks, aka Clover: John McFee – guitar; Alex Call – guitar; John Ciambotti – bass; Sean Hopper – keyboards; Michael Shine – drums. For Costello and Naïve, see also Robert Wyatt. See also The Imposter)

Watching the Detectives	25	1978
Alison	37	1978
Shipbuilding	48	1983
I Want You	40	1986

Council Tax Band
(Laura Simmons – keyboards/vocals; Andy Elliot - guitar; Charlie – guitar; James – drums. For Simmons and Elliot, see also Das Wanderlust)

Mentioning No Names	23	2013

The Count of Chateau Noir
(Mary Beoker – vocals; Paul Hawkins – keyboards; Felix Hunt – keyboards)

After The Carnival	47	2013

Cowcube
(aka Paul Simpson – computer/keyboards/various)

The Popping Song	30	2000

Graham Coxon
(Graham Coxon – guitar/vocals. See also Blur)

Freakin' Out	9	2004

The Cranebuilders
(Tommy Roberts – guitar/vocals; Simon Reynolds – guitar; Matt McParttan – bass; Helen Turner – organ; Steve Keast – drums)

Your Song	28	2002

Credit to the Nation
(MC Fusion, aka Matty Hanson – MC. 'Hear No Bullshit' was with Chumbawamba. See also Chumbawamba)

Hear No Bullshit	12	1993
Call It What You Want	24	1993

Crescendo
(Jonson Walker – guitar/keyboards/vocals; Dan Akerman guitar/keyboards)

High Infidelity	46	2009

The Crimea
(Davey McManus – guitar/vocals; Andy Norton – guitar; Jose Blasé, aka Joe Udwin – bass; Andy Stafford – keybaords; Owen Hopkin – drums)

Baby Boom	8	2003
Lottery Winners On Acid	2	2005

Crocodiles
(Brandon Welchez - vocals; Charles Rowell - guitar; Robin Eisenberg – keyboards; James Ford - drums)

Groove Is In The Heart/California Girls	25	2010

Cruising
(Benzedrine Black – vocals; Dick Vortex – guitar/bass; Dan Handle – guitar/bass; Sex Grimes – drums)

You Made Me Do That	29	2014

Crystal Castles
(Alice Glass – vocals; Ethan Kath – producer)

Baptism	23	2010

Crystal Stilts
(Brad Hargett – vocals; JB Townsend – guitar; Kyle Forester – keyboards; Andy Adler – bass; Keegan Cooke – drums)

Love is a Wave	15	2009

Cuban Boys
(Skeen B – synthesizers/samplers; Ricardo Autobahn – synthesizers/samplers; BL Underwood – guitar/samplers; Jenny MacLaren – samplers. From 2005: without Underwood and MacLaren)

Oh My God They Killed Kenny	6	1998
Cognoscenti vs Intelligentsia	1	1999
Flossie's Alarming Clock	28	1999
Vinyl Countdown	29	2000
Theme from 'Prim & Proper'	34	2000
Drink, Drink, Drink	23	2001
The Nation Needs You	33	2005
The Nation Needs You (2014 Version)	1	2014

Cud
(Carl Puttnam – vocals; Mike Dunphy – guitar; William Potter – bass; Steve Goodwin – drums)

You Sexy Thing	20	1987
Only a Prawn in Whitby	15	1989

The Cult
(Ian Astbury – vocals; Billy Duffy – guitar; Jamie Stewart – bass; Lee Warner – drums. For Duffy, see also Theatre of Hate)

Spiritwalker	30	1984
She Sells Sanctuary	4	1985

Culture
(Joseph Hill – vocals; Frederick Thompson – guitar; Ronald Campbell – guitar; Fez Walker – bass; Vincent Morgan – keyboards; Lewis Daley – drums; Harry Powell – percussion)

See Them a Come	17	1977
Lion Rock	48	1999AT

The Cure
(Robert Smith – guitar/vocals; Michael Dempsey – bass; Lol Tolhurst – drums/keyboards. 1980: Smith; Simon Gallup – bass; Mathieu Hartley – keyboards; Tolhurst – drums. 1982:

now without Hartley; Gallup – bass/keyboards. 1983: Smith; Tolhurst – keyboards; joined by Phil Thornalley – bass; Andy Anderson drums on 'Lovecats'. 1985: Smith; Thornalley; Gallup – keyboards/guitar; Tolhurst. For Smith, see also Siouxsie & The Banshees)

10.15 Saturday Night	43	1979
A Forest	5	1980
A Forest	8	1981
The Hanging Garden	25	1982
The Figurehead	28	1982
A Strange Day	33	1982
A Forest	5	1982AT
Lovecats	15	1983
The Walk	49	1983
In Between Days	27	1985

D

Dadfag
(Eva Hannan – guitar/vocals; Danielle Benson – guitar/vocals; Alan Miknis – drums)

Candy	32	2011

Daft Punk
(Thomas Bangatter – keyboards/various; Guy-Manuel de Homem Christo – keyboards/various)

Rollin' & Scratchin'	8	1997
Giorgio By Moroder	24	2013

Dick Dale
(Dick Dale – guitar; Ron Eglit – bass; Scott Mathews – drums; Prairie Prince – drums)

Nitro	26	1995
Nitrus	27	1996

Damn Vandals
(Jack Kansas – vocals; Frank Pick – guitar; Adam Kilemore Gardens – bass; Chris Christianson – drums)

Crocodile Song	45	2010

The Damned
(1977 and 'New Rose': Dave Vanian, aka Dave Letts – vocals;

Curve
(Toni Halliday – vocals; Alex Mitchell – guitar; Debbie Smith – guitar; Dean Garcia – bass/sequencer; Monti – drums)

Ten Little Girls	3	1991
No Escape from Heaven	38	1991

Cyclic Freeload Unit
(aka Bling Porpoise, aka Tim Tortoise – various. See also Red Cosmos and Bourbon Somersault the Third)

Bitch Chicken Flower	10	2011
My Ram Is Sick	44	2013

Cygnus X-1
(aka Martin Craig – computer/keyboards)

Logical Steps	36	2010

Brian James – guitar; Captain Sensible, aka Ray Burns – bass; Rat Scabies, aka Chris Miller – drums. All other material: Vanian; Sensible – guitar; Algy Ward – bass; Scabies)

Neat Neat Neat	41	1977
New Rose	13	1978
New Rose	10	1979
Love Song	22	1979
New Rose	8	1980
Love Song	29	1980
Smash It Up	42	1980
New Rose	12	1981
New Rose	13	1982AT
Love Song	50	1982AT
New Rose	39	1999AT

Dan Le Sac Vs Scroobius Pip
(Scroobius Pip, aka David Meads – vocals; Dan Le Sac, aka Daniel Stephens – keyboards/guitar/programming)

Thou Shalt Always Kill	2	2007

Danse Society
(Steve Rawlings – vocals; Paul Nash – guitar; Tim Wright – bass; Lyndon Scarfe – keyboards; Paul Gilmartin – drums)

Somewhere	42	1983

The Darkness vs SFB
(Justin Hawkins – guitar/vocals; Dan Hawkins – guitar; Frankie Pullain – bass; Ed Graham – drums. SFB: Adam and Russ – producers)

I Believe in a Thing Called Love	20	2003

Darkstar
(James Young – keyboards; Aiden Whalley – keyboards)

Aidy's Girl is a Computer	39	2009

Darling Buds
(Andrea Lewis – vocals; Harley Farr – guitar; Chris McDonough – bass; Bloss – drums)

Shame On You	47	1988

Das Wanderlust
(Laura Simmons – keyboards/vocals; Andy Elliott – guitar/piano; Natalie Boxall – bass/vocals; Ian Thomas – drums; Phil Davies – percussion. For Simmons and Elliott, see also Council Tax Band)

The Orange Shop	14	2006
Puzzle	2	2008

Datblygu
(David R.Edwards – guitar/organ/vocals; Pat Morgan - guitar/bass/piano/organ/melodica; T.Wyn Davies – percussion/cello)

Popeth	29	1992

The Datsuns
(Christian Livingstone – guitar/vocals; Phil Somersvell – guitar; Dolf De. Datsun – bass/vocals; Matt Osment – drums)

In Love	21	2002

Bette Davis & The Balconettes
(Sam – vocals; Brian – guitar; Joe – bass; Eugene – keyboards; Tracy – drums)

Shergar	15	1997

Dawn of the Replicants
(Paul Vickers – synthesizer/vocals; Roger Simian – guitar/keyboards/vocals)

Science Fiction Freak	29	1999

The Dawn Parade
(Greg McDonald – vocals; Nick Morley – guitar; Barney Wade – bass; Benjamin Jennings – drums)

The Hole in my Heart	50	2002

De La Soul
(Kelvin Mercer, aka Posdnous – vocals; David Jolicoeur, aka Trugoy the Dove – vocals; Vincent Lamont Mason Jr, aka Pasemaster Mase – DJ)

Eye Know	34	1989

Dead Kennedys
(Jello Biafra ,aka Eric Boucher – vocals; East Bay Ray, aka Ray Glasser – guitar; Klaus Flouride – bass; Bruce Slesinger – drums. 12" Plastic Toys: Toy#2 – bass; Toy#1 – producer)

California Uber Alles	33	1979
Holiday in Cambodia	6	1980
California Uber Alles	31	1980
Holiday in Cambodia	9	1981
California Uber Alles	42	1981
Holiday in Cambodia	14	1982AT
Holiday in Cambodia	14	1999AT
California Uber Alles (12" Plastic Toys Remix)	26	2012

Decoration
(Stuart Murray – vocals; Steven Dickinson – guitar; Sam Noble – bass; Steve Taylor – drums)

I Tried It, I Tried It, I Loved It	24	2004
Joy Adamson	39	2004
I Tried It, I Liked It, I Loved It	34	2005
Job in London	4	2006
Candidate	11	2006
Square Mile	3	2008
Glasshouse	29	2008

Deee-lite
(Kier Kirby, aka Lady Miss Keir – vocals; Dmitry Brill – DJ; Towa Tei, aka DJ Towa Towa – DJ)

Groove is in the Heart	44	1990

Deep Purple
(Ian Gillan – vocals; Richie Blackmore – guitar; Roger Glover – bass; Jon Lord – keyboards; Ian Paice – drums)

Child in Time	25	1976

Deep Time
(Jadam Mooroney, aka Jennifer Moore – guitar/keyboards/vocals Adifer Jonesglas, aka Adam Jones – drums)

Clouds	30	2012

Deerhoof
(Satomi Matzuzaki – bass/vocals; John Dieterich – guitar; Chris Cohen – guitar; Greg Saunier – drums)

Green Cosmos	45	2005

Deers
(Carlotta Cosials – guitar/bass/vocals; Ana Garcia Perrote – guitar/drums/vocals)

Bamboo	39	2014

The Deirdres
(Gemma Wood; Sophie Barker; Louise Croft; Robert Fairs; Russell Lomas; Keir Thomas; Amy Burchell - various)

Milk Is Politics	8	2008
Claire, Are We Safe To Be On Our Own?	37	2008

Lana Del Rey
(aka Elizabeth Woolridge Grant – vocals; technical production by Robopop, aka Daniel Omelio)

Video Games	7	2011

The Delgados
(Alun Woodward – guitar/vocals; Emma Pollock – guitar/vocals; Stewart Henderson – bass; Paul Savage – drums. 1998 material also featured: Alan Barr, Jennifer Christie and Emily McPherson – strings; Camille Mason – flute/clarinet; Gregor Reid – percussion. 2000 material also featured: Barry Burns – keyboards; Lorne Cowieson – trumpet/flugel horn; Charlie Cross – violin/viola; Barr – cello; Mason – flute/clarinet/piano. Single version of 'No Danger' featured choir: Dario Galcenti, Scott Laird, Natalie Nolan, Donna Marie Quinn and Scott Richardson. 'Coming in...' also featured: Charles Cross – violin/viola; Vuk Krakovic – violin; Greg Lawson – violin; Barr – cello; Diane Clark – double bass; Chris Cruikshank – saxophone; Dominic Farr – trumpet; James Woods – trumpet; Denise Kane – trombone; Mason – flute. 'Mr Blue Sky' also featured: Lewis Turner – keyboards; Cobus Flick – violin; David Laing – violin; Barr – cello)

Under Canvas Under Wraps	3	1996
Pull the Wires from the Wall	27	1997
Pull the Wires from the Wall	1	1998
Everything Goes Around the Water	9	1998
The Actress	38	1998
Pull the Wires from the Wall	26	1999AT
No Danger	9	2000
American Trilogy	10	2000
Accused of Stealing	14	2000
Witness	38	2000
Mr Blue Sky	29	2002
Coming in from the Cold	44	2002
Everybody Come Down	6	2004
I Fought the Angels	32	2004
Girls of Valour	37	2005

Derek & The Dominoes
(Eric Clapton – guitar/vocals; Duane Allman – guitar; Carl Radle – bass; Bobby Whitlock – keyboards; Jim Gordon – drums)

Layla	2	1976
Layla	31	1978

Derrero
(Ashley Cooke – guitar/vocals; David Thirst – bass; Mary Wycherley – keyboards; Andy Fung – drums)

Radar Intruder	42	1998

Detroit Cobras
(Rachael Nagy – vocals; Dante Aliano – guitar; Maribel Restrepo – guitar; Eddie Hawrsh – bass; Damian Lang – drums)

Shout Bama Lama	15	2001

Desperate Bicycles
(Danny Wigley – vocals; Paul LeClerc – guitar; Roger Stephens – bass; Nicky Stephens – keyboards; Mel Oxer – drums)

Smokescreen	6	1977

Dexy's Midnight Runners
(Kevin Rowland – vocals; Billy Adams – banjo; Girgio Kilkenny – bass; Mickey Billingham – piano/accordion; Brian Maurice – alto saxophone; Paul Speare – tenor saxophone; Jim Patterson – trombone; Seb Shelton – drums. Featuring The Emerald Express: Steve Brennan, Jennifer Tobis, Roger MacDuff, aka Roger Huckle and Helen O'Hara – violins)

Come On Eileen	19	1982

The D4
(Dion Palmer – guitar/vocals; Jimmy Christmas – guitar/vocals; Vaughan Williams – bass; Beaver, aka Daniel Pooley – drums)

Get Loose	47	2002

Digital Mystiks
(Mala – producer; Coki – producer)

B	29	2004

Dinosaur Jr
(J. Mascis – guitar/vocals/percussion; Lou Barlow – bass;Murph, aka Emmett Murphy – drums. 1989: Donna Biddell replaced Barlow – bass. 1990 – Don Fleming replaced Biddell – bass; also added Joe Harvard – guitar; Jay Spiegel – drums.percussion. 1993: Mascis:Mike Johnson – bass; Murph. For Barlow, see also Sebadoh)

Freak Scene	5	1988
Just Like Heaven	12	1989
The Wagon	29	1990
Get Me	42	1993

Dire Straits
(Mark Knopfler – guitar/vocals; David Knopfler – guitar; John Illsley – bass; Pick Withers – drums)

Sultans of Swing	28	1978

Disposable Heroes of Hiphoprisy
(Michael Franti – vocals; Charlie Hunter – guitar/bass/keyboards; Rono Tse – percussion)

Language of Violence	30	1992
Television, the Drug of the Nation	38	1992

Dissolved
(aka Paul Daniels – computer/synthesizers/various)

Forgotten Processes	36	2013

Dizzee Rascal
(Dizzee Rascal, aka Dylan Kwabena Mills – vocals; Armand Van Helzen - producer)

Bonkers	11	2009

DJ Distance
(aka John Graham – DJ)

Ritual	19	2004

DJ Europe
(aka Marios Kokkinos – DJ)

Christmas Bells	39	2007

DJ Riko
(DJ Riko – DJ)

Whistler's Delight	15	2005

DJ Scotch Egg
(aka Shigeru Ishihara – DJ/producer)

Tetris Wonderland	28	2005

DJ Shadow
(aka Josh Davis – DJ)

Stem	35	1996

Django Django
(Vincent Neff – guitar/vocals; Tommy Grace – synthesiser; Jimmy Dixon – bass; David MacLean – drums)

Default	11	2012

Dr Devious & The Wisemen – see VR ft Dr Devious & The Wisemen

Dr Feelgood
(Lee Brilleaux, aka Lee Collinson – hamonica/vocals; Wilko Johnson, aka John Wilkinson – guitar; John B. Sparks – bass;The Big Figure, aka John Martin – drums/percussion)

Paradise	33	1977

Jegsy Dodd & the Original Sinners
(Jegsy Dodd – vocals; Andy Gibson – guitar; Patmo Sheeran – guitar; Staunch – bass/keyboards; Carol Bushell – keyboards; Ed Griffiths – drums; Bobby Demers – percussion)

Grumpy Old Men	1	2005
All I Ever Wanted Was You	25	2005
Liverpool 2008	45	2008

Done Lying Down
(Jack Plug – vocals; Frank Art – guitar; Ali Mac – bass; James Sherry – drums)

Just a Misdemeanour	10	1994

The Doors
(Jim Morrison – vocals; Robby Krieger – guitar; Ray Manzarek – keyboards; John Densmore – drums. 'Riders on the Storm' also featured Marc Benno – guitar; Jerry Scheff – bass)

Riders on the Storm	22	1976
Light My Fire	45	1976

D.O.S.E. with Mark E. Smith
(Kier Stuart – keyboards; Simon Spencer – keyboards; Mark E. Smith – vocals. For Smith, see also The Fall, Inspiral Carpets, Long Fin Killie, Elastica and Von Sudenfed)

Plug Myself In	44	1995

Dose One – see Boom Bip & Dose One

Drag Racing Underground – See Big Stick (name wrongly attritubed in broadcast)

Nick Drake
(Nick Drake – guitar/vocals; Richard Thompson – guitar; Dave Mattacks – bass; John Cale – keyboards/celeste; Dave Pegg – dtums. For Thompson, see also Richar & Linda Thompson. For Cale, see also The Velvet Underground)

Northern Sky	43	1999

Dreadzone
(Tim Bran - various; Leo Williams – bass; Dan Donovan – keyboards; Greg Roberts –drums. 'Life, Love & Unity' and 'Zion Youth' featured Earl Sixteen – vocals. 'Little Britain' featured Donna McKevitt – viola)

Zion Youth	5	1995
Maximum	9	1995
Fight the Power	16	1995
Little Britain	23	1995
Captain Dread	35	1995
Life, Love & Unity	48	1995

Dream City Film Club
(Michael Sheehy – guitar/vocals; Alex Vold – guitar; Andrew Park – bass; Laurence Ash – drums)

If I Die I Die	25	1997

Drenge
(Eoin Loveless – guitar/vocals; Rory Loveless – drums)

Backwaters	25	2013

Drop Nineteens
(Greg Ackell – guitar/vocals; Paula Kelley – guitar/vocals; Monohiro Yasue – guitar; Steve Zimmerman – bass; Pete Koeplin – drums)

Winona	28	1992

Dub Sex
(Mark Hoyle – vocals; Chris Bridgett – guitar; Cathy Brooks – bass; Roger Capman – drums)

Swerve	39	1989

The Duloks
(Mira Manga – vocals; Mina – keyboards; Mars Sellars – drums)

(I'm Gonna Follow Your) Star Trail	50	2007

Dum Dum Girls
(Dee Dee Penny – vocals; Jules – guitar; Bambi – bass; Sandy – drums)

Coming Down	44	2011

Baxter Dury
(Baxter Dury – guitar/keyboards/vocals; Adrian Utley – guitar; Billy Fuller – bass; Adam Gammage - drums)

Isabel	25	2011

Ian Dury & The Blockheads
(Ian Dury – vocals; Chaz Jankel – guitar/keyboards/drums)

Sex & Drugs & Rock & Roll	27	1978

Dustin's Bar Mitzvah
(Dave Lazer – guitar/vocals; Dr Robert – guitar/vocals; Baco – bass/vocals; Desmond Wolfe – drums)

To The Ramones	40	2006

Bob Dylan
(Bob Dylan, aka Robert Zimmerman – guitar/harmonica/vocals. 'Like a Rolling Stone' also featured: Paul Butterfield – guitar; Charlie McCoy – guitar; Russ Savakus – bass; Paul Griffin – keyboards; Al Kooper – organ; Bobby Gregg – drums. 'Visions of Johanna' also featured: Jerry Kennedy – guitar; McCoy; Wayne Moss – guitar; Joe South – bass; Hargus Robinson – piano; Kenneth Buttrey – drums. 'Hurricane' also featured: Emmylou Harris – vocals; Ronnie Blakely – vocals; Steven Soles – guitar; Rob Stoner – bass; Scarlet Riviera – violin; Howie Wythe – drums. 'Desolation Row' featured Dylan with McCoy)

Desolation Row	3	1976
Like a Rolling Stone	10	1976
Visions of Johanna	23	1976
Hurricane	44	1976
Like a Rolling Stone	36	1978
Desolation Row	46	1978
Visions of Johanna	44	199

E

Earl Grey & The Legomen
(Earl Grey – vocals; The Gene Machine – guitar; Judgemental Jones – guitar; The Holy Member – bass; Jesus Murphy – keyboards; Jay Lennon – drums)

| Last Summer | 49 | 2008 |

Early Years
(David Malkinson – guitar/vocals; Roger Mackin – guitar; Brendan Kersey – bass; Phil Raines – drums)

| All Ones & Zeros | 6 | 2005 |

Echo & The Bunnymen
(Ian McCulloch – guitar/vocals; Will Sergeant – guitar; Les Pattinson – bass; Pete De Freitas – drums)

Over the Wall	46	1981
The Back of Love	4	1982
Over the Wall	22	1982AT
Never Stop	17	1983
The Cutter	22	1983
The Killing Moon	19	1984
Thorn of Crowns	47	1984
Bring on the Dancing Horses	21	1985

Editors
(Tom Smith – guitar/piano/vocals; Chris Urbanowicz – guitar; Russell Leetch – bass/synthesizer; Ed Lay – drums/percussion)

| Smokers Outside The Hospital Door | 44 | 2007 |

Dave Edmunds
(Dave Edmunds – guitar/vocals; Nick Lowe – bass; Bob Andrews – keyboards; Terry Williams – drums. For Lowe, see also Wreckless Eric)

| I Knew the Bride | 45 | 1977 |

Eggs
(Andrew Beaujan – guitar/vocals; Rob Christiansen – guitar/vocals; Jonathan Rickman – guitar/drums; Evan Shurak – bass)

| Government Administrator | 10 | 1993 |

808 State
(Martin Price – keyboards/programming; Graham Massey – keyboards/programming; Andy Barker – DJ/keyboards/drum programming; Darren Partington – DJ/drum programming)

| Pacific State | 22 | 1989 |

Eighties Matchbox B-Line Disaster
(Guy McKnight – vocals; Andy Huxley – guitar; Marc Norris – guitar; Sym Ghavial - bass; Tom Diamontopoulo – drums)

| Celebrate Your Mother | 46 | 2002 |

Elastica
(Justine Frischmann – guitar/vocals; Donna Matthews – guitar/vocals; Annie Holland – bass; Justin Welch – drums. Also featured Dan Abnormal, aka Damon Albarn – keyboards. 1999: Frischmann; Paul Jones – guitar; Holland; David Bush – keyboards; Mew – keyboards; Welch – drums. *Elastica ft Mark E. Smith. For Smith, see also The Fall, Inspiral Carpets, Long Fin Killie, D.O.S.E. and Von Sudenfed. For Bush, see also The Fall. For Albarn, see also Blur and Gil Scott-Heron)

Stutter	38	1993
Connection	4	1994
Waking Up	7	1994
Line Up	42	1994
All Nighter	20	1995
*How He Wrote Elastica Man	6	1999

Elbow
(Guy Garvey – vocals; Mark Potter – guitar; Pete Turner – bass; Craig Potter – keyboards; Richard Jupp – drums. 1998: also featured Francoise Lemoignan – saxophone 2008: also featured: Prabjote Osahn – violin; Stella Page – violin; Ian Burdge – cello; Ben Parsons – cornet; Nick Smart – cornet/flugel horn; Tim Barber – trumpet; Matt Ball – trombone; Sheona White – E-flat horn)

| Powder Blue | 34 | 1998 |
| Grounds for Divorce | 31 | 2008 |

Electrelane
(Verity Susman – guitar/keyboards/vocals; Mia Clarke – guitar; Ros Murray – bass/keyboards/cello; Emma Gaze – drums)

| To The East | 15 | 2007 |

Electronic
(Bernard Sumner – guitar/programming/vocals; Johnny Marr – guitar/programming. For Sumner, see also Joy Division and New Order. For Marr, see also The Smiths, Billy Bragg and Modest Mouse)

| Get the Message | 40 | 1991 |

Ella Guru
(John Yates – guitar/keyboards/vocals; Kate Walsh – vocals; Nick Kellington – guitar/ukulele; Christian Burwood – guitar/keyboards; Nik Kavanagh – bass; Bob Picken – double bass; Scott Marmion – pedal steel; Brendan Moore – drums)

Park Lane Speakers   48   2004

Emeralds
(Mark McGuire – guitar; Steve Hauschildt – keyboards; John Elliott - keyboards)

Genetic   46   2010

The Equators: see Elizabeth Archer & The Equators

Evils
(Evils – DJ/producer)

Pig F***er   12   2005

Evolution Control Committee
(TradeMark G., aka Mark Gunderson – producer/programming)

Rebel Without a Pause   20   1998

Explosions In The Sky
(Mark Smith – guitar; Munaf Rayani – guitar; Michael James – guitar/bass; Chris Hrasky – drums)

Last Known Surroundings   30   2011

Extradition Order
(Alastair Harper – guitar/vocals; Matthew Bergin – keyboards; Nicholas Boardman – bass; Mark Davies – drums)

Penetrate   33   2008

Extreme Noise Terror: see KLF & Extreme Noise Terror

F

Th' Faith Healers
(Tom Cullinan – guitar/vocals; Roxanne Stephen – vocals; Ben Hopkin – bass; Joe Dilworth – drums. For Cullinan, see also *Quickspace*. For Dilworth, see also *Miss Mend*)

Gorgeous Blue Flower in My Garden   44   1991

The Fall
(Mark E.Smith – vocals; Marc Riley – guitar; Stephen Hanley – bass; Yvonne Pawlett – keyboards; Mike Leigh – drums.
1 Smith; Craig Scanlon – guitar; Riley – guitar/keyboards; Stephen Hanley; Leigh.
2 Smith; Scanlon; Riley; Stephen Hanley; Paul Hanley – drums.
3 Smith; Scanlon; Riley; Stephen Hanley; Paul Hanley; Karl Burns – drums.
4 M.E. Smith; Scanlon; Stephen Hanley; Paul Hanley; Burns.
5 M.E. Smith; Brix Smith – guitar/vocals; Scanlon; Stephen Hanley; Paul Hanley; Burns.
6 M.E. Smith; Brix Smith; Scanlon; Stephen Hanley; Simon Rogers – keyboards; Burns.
7 M.E. Smith; Brix Smith; Scanlon; Stephen Hanley; Rogers; Simon Wolstencroft – drums.
8 M.E. Smith; Brix Smith; Scanlon; Stephen Hanley; Marcia Schofield – keyboards; Wolstencroft.
9 M.E. Smith; Martin Bramah – guitar; Scanlon; Stephen Hanley; Marcia Schofield; Kenny Brady – violin; Wolstencroft.
10 M.E. Smith; Scanlon; Stephen Hanley; Kenny Brady; Wolstencroft.
11 M.E. Smith; Scanlon; Stephen Hanley; Dave Bush - keyboards; Wolstencroft.
12 M.E. Smith; Scanlon; Stephen Hanley; Dave Bush - keyboards; Wolstencroft; Karl Burns – drums.
13 M.E. Smith; Brix Smith – guitar/vocals; Scanlon; Stephen Hanley; Julia Nagle - keyboards; Wolstencroft; Karl Burns – drums.
14 M.E. Smith; Brix Smith – guitar/vocals; Stephen Hanley; Julia Nagle - keyboards; Wolstencroft; Karl Burns – drums.
15 M.E. Smith; Andy Hackett – guitar; Stephen Hanley; Julia Nagle – guitar/keyboards; Wolstencroft; Burns.
16 M.E. Smith; Neville Wilding – guitar; Nagle; Karen Leatham – bass; Tom Head – drums.
17 M.E. Smith; Wilding; Nagle; Adam Helal - bass; Head.
18 M.E. Smith; Ben Pritchard – guitar; JimWatts – guitar/bass;Nagle - keyboards; Spencer Birtwhistle – drums)
19 M.E. Smith; Pritchard; Watts; Elena Poulou – keyboards; Dave Millner – drums.
20 M.E. Smith; Pritchard; Watts; Simon 'Ding' Archer – bass; Poulos; Millner.
21 M.E. Smith; Pritchard; Watts – guitar; Steve Trafford - bass; Poulos; Birtwhistle - drums.
22 M.E. Smith; Tim Presley, aka Tim Baxter – guitar; Pete

Greenway – guitar; Gary Bennett – guitar; Robert Barbato – bass; Dave Spurr, aka The Eagle – bass; Poulou; Orpheo McCord – drums.
23 M.E. Smith; Greenway; Spurr; Poulou; Keiron Melling – drums.

Other featured musicians:
'Dktr Faustus' & 'Living Too Late' featured Paul Hanley – drums.
Line-up 9 – featured Craig Leon – organ; Cassell Webb organ; Charlotte Bill – flute on some tracks.
'Free Range' and 'Birmingham School of Business School' featured Craig Leon – keyboards; Simon Rogers – keyboards.
'Dr Buck's Letter' featured Ben Pritchard – guitar.)

Song	Pos	Year
Rowche Rumble	40	1979
2 Totally Wired	21	1980
2 How I Wrote 'Elastic Man'	26	1980
1 Fiery Jack	38	1980
Rowche Rumble	49	1980
2 How I Wrote 'Elastic Man'	33	1981
3 Lie Dream of a Casino Soul	47	1981
5 Eat Y'self Fitter	8	1983
4 The Man Whose Head Expanded	21	1983
5 Kicker Conspiracy	35	1983
5 Wings	40	1983
5 Lay of the Land	9	1984
5 C.R.E.E.P.	18	1984
5 No Bulbs	44	1984
6 Cruiser's Creek	3	1985
6 Spoilt Victorian Child	23	1985
6 Gut of the Quantifier	33	1985
6 Couldn't Get Ahead	39	1985
6 L.A.	42	1985
7 Mr Pharmacist	3	1986
7 US 80s-90s	10	1986
7 Living Too Late	15	1986
7 Bournemouth Runner	20	1986
7 Realm of Dusk	26	1986
7 Lucifer Over Lancashire	37	1986
7 Dktr Faustus	48	1986
8 Australians in Europe	2	1987
8 Hit the North	9	1987
8 Athlete Cured	26	1987
8 Cab It Up	14	1988
8 Bremen Nacht	16	1988
8 New Big Prinz	24	1988
8 Kurious Oranj	27	1988
8 Jerusalem	36	1988
8 Guest Informant	40	1988
8 Dead Beat Descendent	38	1989
9 Bill is Dead	1	1990
10 White Lightning	15	1990
10 Blood Outta Stone	30	1990
9 Telephone Thing	35	1990
9 Chicago Now!	41	1990
10 Edinburgh Man	4	1991
10 A Lot of Wind	9	1991
10 High Tension Line	24	1991
10 The War Against Intelligence	35	1991
10 The Mixer	41	1991
10 So What About It?	43	1991
11 The Legend of Xanadu	5	1992
11 Free Range	6	1992
11 Ed's Babe	12	1992
11 Kimble	34	1992
11 Birmingham School of Business School	50	1992
12 Why Are People Grudgeful?	11	1993
12 Lost in Music	19	1993
12 Glam Racket	20	1993
12 I'm Going to Spain	22	1993
12 Service	26	1993
12 Ladybird (Green Grass)	29	1993
12 A Past Gone Mad	41	1993
12 Behind the Counter	43	1993
12 It's a Curse	48	1993
12 War	50	1993
12 Hey! Student	2	1994
12 City Dweller	38	1994
12 M5	41	1994
13 Feeling Numb	7	1995
13 Don't Call Me Darling	24	1995
13 Bonkers in Phoenix	30	1995
13 The Joke	49	1995
14 Cheetham Hill	6	1996
14 The Chiselers	13	1996
14 Hostile	16	1996
15 4½ Inch	7	1997
15 I'm a Mummy	17	1997
16 Shake Off	49	1997
17 Touch Sensitive	4	1998
17 F-Oldin' Money	7	1998
2 How I Wrote 'Elastic Man'	24	1999AT
2 Totally Wired	34	1999AT
3 The Classical	38	1999AT
17 Dr Buck's Letter	3	2000
17 Two Librans	23	2000
17 WB	43	2000
18 I Wake Up in the City	30	2001
19 Susan vs Youth Club	22	2002
19 Theme from Sparta FC	2	2003
20 Green-Eyed Loco Mn	26	2003
20 Theme from Sparta FC#2	1	2004

21Blindness	14	2005
21What About Us	29	2005
21I Can Hear The Grass Grow	32	2005
22Reformation	7	2007
22Systematic Abuse	11	2007
22Fall Sound	20	2007
2350 Year Old Man	1	2008
23Wolf Kidult Man	7	2008
23Tommy Shooter	26	2008
23Can Can Summer	41	2008
23Bury Pts 1 + 3	2	2010
23Nate Will Not Return	48	2011
23Sir William Wray	3	2013
23No Respects rev	10	2013
23Amorator	37	2014

Family
(Roger Chapman – vocals; Charlie Witney – guitar; Rick Grech – bass/violin; Jim King – saxophone; Rob Townsend – drums)

The Weaver's Answer	42	1976

Family Cat
(Paul Frederick – guitar/vocals; Stephen Jelbert – guitar; Tim McVey – guitar; John Graves – bass; Kevin Downing – drums)

Tom Verlaine	48	1989

The Farm
(Peter Hooton – vocals; Steve Grimes – guitar; Keith Mullen – guitar; Carl Hunter – bass; Ben Leach – keyboards; Roy Boulter – drums)

Stepping Stone	46	1990
Groovy Train	47	1990

Farmer's Boys
(Baz – vocals; Stan – guitar; Mark – bass; Frog – keyboards/drums)

Whatever is He Like?	21	1982
I Think I Need Help	50	1982

Fat White Family
(Lias Saoudi – vocals; Saul Adamczewski – guitar; Adam J. Harmer – guitar; Joe Pancucci – bass; Nathan Saoudi – organ; Dan Lyons – drums)

I Am Mark E Smith	27	2014

Fatboy Slim
(aka Norman Cook – DJ/producer)

Rockafeller Skank	28	1998

Fatima Mansions
(Cathal Coughlan – vocals; Andrias O'Gruama – guitar; Hugh Bunker – bass; Nick Bunker – keyboards; Nick Allum – drums)

Blues For Ceaucescu	33	1990

The Felice Brothers
(Ian Felice – guitar/piano/vocals; Christmas Clapton – bass; Jams Felice – accordion/organ/piano; Greg Farley – violin; Dave Turbeville – drums)

Ponzi	31	2011

Felt
(Lawrence Hayward – guitar/vocals; Maurice Deebank – guitar; Martin Duffy – keyboards; Gary Ainge – drums. Track also featured Elizabeth Fraser – vocals. For Fraser, see also Cocteau Twins, This Mortal Coil and Massive Attack. For Duffy, see also Primal Scream)

Primitive Painters	7	1985

Fever Fever
(Rosie – vocals; Ellie – guitar; Smit – drums)

Keys in the Bowl	19	2009

The Field Mice
(Bobby Wratten – guitar/vocals; Harvey Williams – guitar; Mark Dobson – drums. 1995: added Michael Hiscock – bass; Annemari Davies – keyboards. For Wratten, see also Trembling Blue Stars)

Sensitive	26	1989
Missing the Moon	45	1991

Wild Man Fischer
(aka Larry Fischer – vocals)

Go to Rhino Records	48	1976

Five Hand Reel
(Dick Gaughan – guitar/vocals; Bobby Eaglesham – guitar/vocals; Barry Lyons – bass; Tom Hickland – keyboards/violin; Dave Tulloch – drums)

Cruel Brother	34	1977

Flaming Lips
(Wayne Coyne – guitar/vocals; Michael Ivins – bass; Steven Drozd – drums)

Race for the Prize	8	1999
Waiting for a Superman	12	1999

Flaming Stars
(Max Descharne – keyboards/vocals; Johnny Jonson – guitar; Mark Hosking – guitar; Paul Dempsey – bass; Joe Whitney – drums. For Descharne, see also Gallon Drunk. For Johnson, see also The Vibes)

Kiss Tomorrow Goodbye	29	1995
Ten Feet Tall	18	1995
The Face on the Bar Room Floor	48	1996

The Flatmates
(Deb Haynes – vocals; Martin Whitehead – guitar; Kath Beach – bass; Rocker, aka Steve Woods – drums. 'Shimmer' added Tim Rippington guitar; Joel O'Bierne replaced Rocker – drums. For Rippington, see also Beatnik Filmstars, Forest Giants and Short Stories)

I Could Be in Heaven	42	1986
Shimmer	42	1986

Fleeing New York
(Russell Marsden – guitar/vocals; Emma Richardson – bass/vocals; Matt Hayward – drums)

Hollywood Bowl	49	2005

Fleet Foxes
(Robin Pecknold – guitar/vocals; Skyler Skjelset – guitar; Craig Curran – bass; Casey Wescott – keyboards; Nicholas Peterson – drums)

White Winter Hymnal	15	2008

Flesh For Lulu
(Nick Marsh – guitar/vocals; Rocco Barker – guitar; Kevin Mills – bass; Derek Greening – keyboards; James Mitchell – drums)

Subterraneans	39	1984

Flies On You
(Doug Aikman – guitar/vocals; Andrew Watkins – guitar/vocals)

Shipmanesque	24	2012
Josephine	15	2013

Florence & The Machine
(Florence Welch – vocals/percussion; Ladonna Harley-Peters – vocals; Victoria Alkinlola – vocals; Tom Monger – harp; Isabella Summers – piano; Ian Burdge – cello; James Ford – bass/keyboards/drums)

Drumming Song	31	2009

Flowers
(Rachel – bass/vocals; Sam – guitar; Jordan – drums)

Joanna	48	2013
Young	11	2014

Flying Lizards
(Deborah Evans – vocals; Daniel Cunningham – guitar/keyboards; Julian Marshall – keyboards/piano)

Summertime Blues	47	1978

Force & Styles
(aka Paul – keyboards/programming; Darren – keyboards/programming)

Fireworks	30	1996

Foreheads in a Fishtank
(Jeff Leahy – guitar/vocals; Gavin Jones – bass; Matt Brewster – keyboards; Jez Watts – keyboards; Julian Beeston – programming; Adrian Leaman – drums)

Happy Shopper	21	1991

Forest Giants
(Tim Rippington – guitar/vocals; Pete Stillman – guitar; Ruth Cochrane – bass; Paula Knight – keyboards/violin; Tom Adams – drums. For Rippington & Adams, see also Beatnik Filmstars. For Rippington, see also The Flatmates and Short Stories)

So You Think You're Unhappy?	43	2006

Forkeyes
(aka Mike Bryson – keyboards/computer)

Fell Off The Penalty Spotty Spot	48	2012

Frank & Walters
(Paul Linehan – bass/vocals; Niall Linehan – guitar; Ashley Keating – drums)

Happy Busman	31	1992

Frank Chickens
(Kazukho Hohki – vocals; Kazumi Taguchi – vocals; Steve Beresfird – keyboards/drum programming)

Blue Canary	42	1984

Frankie Goes to Hollywood
(Holly Johnson – vocals; Paul Rutherford – vocals; Brian Nash – guitar; Mark O'Toole – bass; Peter Gill – drums.

Two Tribes	25	1984

Free
(Paul Rodgers – vocals; Paul Kossoff – guitar; Andy Fraser – bass; Simon Kirke – drums)

Alright Now   6   1976

Freed Unit
(Jonathan Kerry – guitar/keyboards/autoharp/vocals; keyboards; Matt Kerry – keyboards/autoharp/percussion/programming/vocals; Gary Gilchrist – guitar/bass/keyboards)

Widdershins   31   1998

Freiwillige Selbstokontrolle
(Justin Hoffman – guitar/keyboards/accordian/vocals; Wilfried Petzi – guitar/mandolin/banjo/vocals; Michaela Melion – bass/guitar/violin/vocals; Thomas Meinecke – guitar/drums/vocals)

I Wish I Could Sprechen Sie Deutsch   33   1986

The French
(Darren Hayman – vocals; John Morrison – keyboards. For both, see also Hefner. For Hayman, see also Darren Hayman with Elizabeth Morris)

Porn Shoes   27   2003
Gabriel in the Airport   36   2003

Freddy Fresh
(Freddy Fresh – DJ/producer)

You Can See the Paint   49   2003

Fuck Buttons
(Andrew Hung – keyboards/computer; Benjamin John Power – keyboards/computer/percussion)

Sweet Love For Planet Earth   23   2008
Surf Solar   4   2009
Space Mountain   35   2009
Brainfreeze   2   2013
Hidden XS   4   2013

Future Islands
(Samuel T. Herring – vocals; William Cashion – guitar/bass; Gerrit Welmers – keyboards/programming)

Seasons (Waiting On You)   12   2014

Future of the Left
(Andy Falkous – guitar/vocals; Kelson Mathias – bass/vocals; Jack Egglestone – drums. For Falkous & Egglestone, see also McLusky)

Arming Eritrea   49   2009
Robocop 4 (Fuck Off Robocop)   31   2012
Singing of the Bonesaws   22   2013

Future Sound of London
(Garry Cockbain – keyboards; Brian Dougans – keyboards)

Papua New Guinea   11   1992

The Futureheads
(Barry Hyde – guitar/vocals; Ross Millard – guitar; David Craig – bass; Dave Hyde – drums)

First Day   25   2003

G

Galaxie 500
(Michael Wareham – guitar/vocals; Naomi Yang – bass; Damon Krukowski – drums)

Don't Let Our Youth Go to Waste   41   1989

Gallon Drunk
(James Johnston – guitar/vocals; Mike Delanian – bass; Max Descharne – drums; Joe Byfield – percussion. For Descharne, see also Flaming Stars)

Some Fool's Mess   13   1991

Gang of Four
(Jon King – vocals; Andy Gill – guitar; Dave Allen – bass; Hugo Burnham – drums)

Damaged Goods   23   1979
Damaged Goods   50   1980

Garbage
(Shirley Manson – vocals; Steve Marker – guitar; Doug Erikson – guitar/bass/keyboards; Butch Vig – drums)

Vow   45   1995

Katie Gately
(Katie Gately – vocals)

Pipes	19	2013

Gene
(Martin Rossiter – keyboards/vocals; Steve Mason – guitar; Kevin Miles – bass; Matt James – drums)

As Good as it Gets	33	1999

Generation X
(Billy Idol, aka William Broad – vocals; Bob (Derwood) Andrews – guitar; Tony James – bass; Mark Laff – drums)

Your Generation	29	1977
Wild Dub	49	1977

Genesis
(Peter Gabriel – vocals; Steve Hackett – guitar; Mike Rutherford – bass; Matt James – drums)

Supper's Ready	33	1999

Get Cape, Wear Cape, Fly
(aka Sam Duckworth – guitar/vocals)

Chronicles of a Bohemian Teenager (Part One)	13	2006

Ghost Society
(Sara Savery – bass/synthesizer/drums/vocals; Tobias Wilner - guitar/synthesizer/vocals; Lasse Herbst – percussion)

Love Love	37	2010

Gilbert
(aka Matthew Gilbert Linley – keyboards/drums)

Willow	49	2006

Gindrinker
(D. C. Gates – trumpet/vocals; Graf Middleton – guitar/drums)

Bob Grainger: Sexual Pervert	16	2010

Ginger Tom
(George a-go-go – bass/vocals; Lightning Leo – guitar; Michael Knife – guitar; Starz – drums)

Two of The Beatles Have Died	13	2008

Girl Band
(Dara Kieley – vocals; Alan Duggan – guitar; Daniel Fox – bass; Adam Faulkner – drums)

Lawman	15	2014

Glasvegas
(James Allan – vocals; Rab Allan – guitar; Paul Donoghue – bass; Jonna Lofgren – drums)

It's My Own Cheating Heart That Makes Me Cry	25	2008
Geraldine	34	2008

Gnarls Barkley
(Cee-Lo Green, aka Thomas De Carlo Callaway – vocals; Danger Mouse, aka Brian Joseph Burton – producer)

Crazy	36	2006

Go! Team
(Ninja – recorder/vocals; Kaori Tsuchida – guitar/keyboards/recorder/vocals; Ian Parton – guitar/harmonica/drums; Sam Dook – guitar/banjo/drums; Jamie Bell – bass; Chi Fukami Taylor – drums)

Bottle Rocket	39	2005
Buy Nothing Day	39	2011

Goat
(Christian Johansson – various/vocals; with Goatgirl, Fluffan and other members in a fluctuating line-up)

Goathead	44	2012
Talk to God	8	2014
Hide from the Sun	23	2014

Godspeed You Black Emperor!
(Efrim Menuckk – guitar; Dave Bryant – guitar; Roger Terrier – guitar; Mauro Pozente – bass; Thierry Amar – bass/piano; Sophie Trudeau – violin; Norsola Johnson – cello; Bruce Cordran – drums/timpani/glockenspiel. 2012 (now Godspeed You! Black Emperor – Menuck – guitar/hurdy gurdy; Bryant – guitar/dulcimer/Portasound/kemence; Mike Moya – guitar; Amar – bass/double bass/keyboards; Mauro Pezzente – bass; Trudeau – violin; Cawdon – drums/vibraphone/marimba/glockenspiel; Aidan Girt – drums)

Hung Over as the Oven at Maida Vale	21	1999
We Drift Like Worried Fire	4	2012
Mladic	7	2012

Golden Virgins
(Lucas Renney – guitar/vocals; Allan Burnup – bass; David Younger – keyboards; Neil Basset – drums)

Renaissance Kids	42	2003

Gonjasufi
(aka Sumach Ecks – various/vocals)

Ancestors	17	2010

Good Throb
(KY Ellie, aka Ellie Roberts – vocals; BB Thing, aka Bryony Byron – guitar; Ash Tray – bass; L-Hard, aka Louis Harding – drums)

Acid House	40	2014

Gorky's Zygotic Mynci
(Euros Childs – keyboards/vocals; Richard James – guitar; John Lawrence – bass/keyboards; Megan Childs – violin; Euros Rowlands – drums)

If Fingers Were Xylophones	19	1995
Patio Song	8	1996
Sweet Johnny	35	1998
Hush the Warmth	36	1998
Spanish Dance Troupe	5	1999
Fresher than the Sweetness in Water	36	2000

Gossip
(Beth Ditto – vocals; Brace Paine, aka Nathan Howdeshell – guitar; Hannah Blilie – drums)

Standing in the Way of Control	24	2006

Grandaddy
(Jason Lytle – vocals; Jim Fairchild – guitar; Kevin Garcia – bass; Tim Dryden – keyboards; Aaron Burtch – drums)

The Crystal Lake	50	2000

Grandmaster Flash & The Furious Five
(Grandmaster Flash – DJ; The Furious Five: Cowboy, Melle Mel, Kid Creole, Mr Ness and Raheim – vocals)

The Message	3	1982

Grandmaster Gareth
(Grandmaster Gareth, aka Gareth Jones – DJ. See also *Misty's Big Adventure*)

Dr Dre Buys a Pint of Milk	45	2003

The Granite Shore
(Nick Halliwell – vocals; Phil Wilson – guitar; Arash Torabi – bass; Andy Fonda - drums. For Torabi, Fonda and Wilson, see also *Phil Wilson*)

Flood of Fortune	38	2010

John Grant
(John Grant – piano/vocals)

GMF	38	2013

The Grateful Dead
(Jerry Garcia – guitar/vocals; Bob Weir – guitar; Phil Lesh – guitar; Ron 'Pigpen' McKernan – keyboards/vocals; Tim Constanten – keyboards; Bill Kreutzmann – drums; Mickey Hart – percussion)

Dark Star	40	1976

Pete Green
(Pete Green – guitar/vocals)

Everything I Do Is Gonna Be Sparkly	37	2007
Best British Band Supported By Shockwaves	30	2008

Greenskeepers
(Nick Maurer – keyboards; James Curd – electronic percussion)

Low and Sweet	24	2001

Grimes
(aka Claire Boucher – keyboards/vocals)

Oblivion	32	2012

Grinderswitch
(Dru Lombar – guitar; Larry Howard – guitar; Joe Dan Petty – bass; Stephen Miller – keyboards; Rick Burnett – drums)

Pickin' the Blues	27	1976

Grizzly Bear
(Ed Droste – keyboards/omnichord/vocals; Daniel Rossen – guitar/banjo/keyboards/vocals; Chris Taylor – bass; Christopher Bear – drums)

Two Weeks	17	2009

Guided By Voices
(Robert Pollard – guitar/vocals; Tobin Sprout – guitar/vocals; Charles Mitchell – guitar; Greg Demos – bass; Kevin Fennell – drums)

Class Clown Spots a UFO	50	2012

Gun Club
(Jeffrey Lee Pierce – vocals; Nick Sanderson – guitar; Romi Mori – bass; Kid Congo Powers – drums. For Powers, see also Nick Cave & The Bad Seeds)

The Breaking Hands	48	1987

H

H Foundation
(aka James Harrigan – keyboards/programming)

Laika	11	1994

Half Man Half Biscuit
(Nigel Blackwell – guitar/vocals; Simon Blackwell – guitar; Neil Crossley – bass; David Lloyd – keyboards; Paul Wright – drums. 1996: Blackwell; Crossley – guitar; Ken Hancock – bass; Carl Henry – drums. 1998: Blackwell; Hancock – guitar; Crossley – bass; Henry)

The Trumpton Riots	14	1986
Dickie Davies Eyes	39	1986
Paintball's Coming Home	43	1996
Turn a Blind Eye	25	1998
Look Dad No Tunes	11	1999
24 Hour Garage People	30	1999
24 Hour Garage People	32	2000
Irk the Purists	37	2000
Bob Wilson Anchorman	13	2001
Vatican Broadside	16	2001
The Light at the End of the Tunnel (Is the Light of an Oncoming Train)	14	2002
Breaking News	38	2002
Tending the Wrong Grave for 23 Years	7	2003
It Makes the Room Look Bigger	28	2003
Joy Division Oven Gloves	8	2004
Joy Division Oven Gloves	19	2005
National Shite Day	21	2008
Took Problem Chimp To Ideal Home Show	35	2008
Joy in Leeuwarden (We Are Ready)	19	2011
The Unfortunate Gwatkin	3	2014
Urge for Offal	24	2014

Jan Hammer: see Jeff Beck & Jan Hammer

Hammock
(Marc Byrd – guitar; Andrew Thompson – guitar)

Ten Thousand Years Won't Save Your Life	19	2012

Happy Mondays
(Shaun Ryder – vocals; Mark Day – guitar; Paul Ryder – bass; Paul Davis – keyboards; Gary Whelan – drums)

Wrote For Luck	48	1988
WFL	4	1989
Step On	8	1990
Kinky Afro	32	1990

Hard Corps
(Regine Feret – vocals; Paul Davies – keyboards; Robert Doran – keyboards; Hugh Ashton – computers)

Dirty	46	1984

Ryan Hardy
(Ryan Hardy – guitar/drums/vocals)

Reinforced Concrete Monsters	28	2010
Oh My Stars	42	2013

Martyn Hare
(Martyn Hare – DJ)

Do Not Underestimate	13	2004

Harmonious Thelonious
(aka Stefan Schwander – producer)

Angewandte Muziek	47	2010

Roy Harper
(Roy Harper – guitar/vocals; Chris Spedding – guitar; Dave

Cochran – bass; Bill Bruford – drums; with the Grimethorpe Colliery Band, conducted by Elgar Howarth)

When An Old Cricketer Leaves the Crease   47   1976

PJ Harvey
(Polly Jean Harvey – guitar/vocals; Ian Olliver – bass; Rob Ellis – drums. 1992: Harvey; Stephen Vaughan – bass; Ellis. 1995: PJ Harvey; John Parish – guitar/percussion; Joe Gore – guitar; Mick Harvy – bass/keyboards; Jean-Marc Butty – percussion. 1998: PJ Harvey; Gore; Jeremy Hogg – guitar; Parish; Mick Harvey; Eric Drew Feldman – bass/keyboards; Ellis. 2000: PJ Harvey; Mick Harvey – bass/keyboards/drums; Ellis – harpsichord/piano/drums/percussion. 2004: PJ Harvey – guitar/bass/piano.melodica/ accordion/autoharp/vocals; Ellis – drums/percussion. 2011: PJ Harvey – autoharp/saxophone/vocals; Parish – guitar/trombone/thodes/mellotron/xylophone/drums/percussion; Mick Harvey – bass/bass harmonica/ piano/drums/percussion). 'The Mess We're In' featured Thom Yorke – vocals. 'The Letter' featured Head – vocals). For PJ Harvey, Parish, Feldman and Ellis, see also *John Parish & Polly Jean Harvey*.   For Mick Harvey, see also *The Birthday Party and Nick Cave*. For Yorke, see also *Radiohead and Atoms of Peace*)

Dress	2	1991
Sheela-Na-Gig	2	1992
Rid of Me	4	1993
50 Ft Queenie	15	1993
Wang Dang Doodle	18	1993
Naked Cousin	32	1993
Send His Love to Me	11	1995
Down by the Water	17	1995
To Bring You My Love	34	1995
Is This Desire?	50	1998
Sheela-Na-Gig	49	1999AT
Good Fortune	2	2000
Big Exit	6	2000
The Mess We're In	18	2000
The Whores Hustle and the Hustlers Whore	24	2000
This Is Love	36	2001
The Letter	16	2004
Shame	23	2004
Let England Shake	1	2011
The Words That Maketh Murder	26	2011
Shaker Aamer	49	2013

Harvey's Rabbit
(Tim Lyons – vocals; David Thorn – guitar)

Is This What You Call Change?   42   1995

Darren Hayman (with Elizabeth Morris)
(Elizabeth Morris – vocals; Darren Hayman – guitar. For Hayman, see also *Hefner and The French*. For Morris, see also *Allo Darlin'*)

I Know I Fucked Up   4   2011

Richie Hawtin
(Richie Hawtin – computer/DJ)

The Tunnel   50   2005

Health
(Jake Duzsik – guitar/vocals; John Famiglietti – bass/percussion; Jupiter Keyes – keyboards; Benjamin Jared Miller- drums)

Die Slow   30   2009

Heaven 17
(Glenn Gregory – vocals; Ian Craig-Marsh – synthesizers; Martyn Ware – synthesizers)

(We Don't Need This) Fascist Groove Thang   29   1981

Heavenly
(Amelia Fletcher – vocals; Peter Momtchiloff – guitar; Rob Pursey – bass; Matthew Fletcher – drums. For Amelia and Matthew Fletcher and Momtchiloff, see also *Talulah Gosh*. For Amerlia Fletcher, Momtchiloff and Pursey, see also *Marine Research*. For Amelia Fletcher and Pursey, see also *Tender Trap*. For Fletcher, see also *Hefner and The Wedding Present*. For Pursey, see also *Sportique*)

Atta Girl   33   1993

Hefner
(Darren Hayman – guitar/vocals; John Morrison – bass; Jack Hayter – pedal steel/violin/stylophone/theremin; Antony Harding – drums. 'Good Fruit' featured Amelia Fletcher – vocals. 'Greedy Ugly People' featured Matt Evans – guitar. 'The Day That Thatcher Dies' featured James Williams and Owen Hayter – vocals; Mark Bandola – piano. For Hayman and Morrison, see also *The French*. For Hayman, see also *Darren Hayman (with Elizabeth Morris)*. For Hayter, see also *Benjamin Shaw*. For Fletcher, see also *Talulah Gosh, Heavenly, Marine Research, Tender Trap and The Wedding Present*)

Pull Yourself Together	43	1998
Hymn for the Cigarettes	2	1999
Hymn for the Alcohol	3	1999

I Stole a Bride	22	1999
I Took Her Love For Granted	32	1999
Hymn for the Things We Didn't Do	49	1999
Greedy Ugly People	7	2000
The Day That Thatcher Dies	12	2000
Good Fruit	15	2000
Painting & Kissing	44	2000
Alan Bean	31	2001

Help Stamp Out Loneliness
(D. Lucille Campbell – vocals; Bentley Cooke – guitar; Colm McCrory – bass; Katherine McMahon – piano; Ben Ambridge – drums; Louise Winfield – drums)

Split Infinitives	17	2011

Jimi Hendrix Experience
(Jimi Hendrix – guitar/vocals; Noel Redding – bass; Mitch Mitchell – drums. 'Voodoo Chile': featured Steve Winwood – organ; Billy Cox replaced Redding – bass)

All Along the Watchtower	5	1976
Voodoo Chile	16	1976
Hey Joe	37	1976
All Along the Watchtower	37	1999AT

Herman Dune
(David Ivar Herman Dune – guitar/vocals; Andre Herman Dune – guitar/vocals; Ome – drums)

Drug Dealer in the Park	31	2000

MJ Hibbett & The Validators
(Mark John Hibbett – guitar/vocals; Emma Pattison – vocals; Frankie Machine – bass; Tom McClure – violin; Tom Pattison – drums. For Tom Pattison, see also *Prolapse*)

The Lesson of The Smiths	41	2007
My Boss Was In An Indie Band Once	44	2009
A Little Bit	35	2012

The Higsons
(Charlie Higson – vocals; Terry Edwards – guitar/saxophone/trumpet; Stuart McGeachin – guitar; Colin Williams – bass; Simon Charleton – drums)

Conspiracy	47	1982

The Hillfields
(Rob Boyd – guitar/vocals; Grant Wilkinson – bass; Carlos Russell – drums)

Spoon	9	2008

The Hitchers
(Rich Story – guitar/vocals; Greg Thurland – bass; Mike Ayres – drums)

Strachan	21	1997

The Hives
(Pelle Almqvist – vocals; Nicholaus Arson – guitar; Vigilante Carlstroem – guitar; Matt Destruction – bass; Chris Dangerous – drums)

Hate to Say I Told You So	47	2001

Hobbes Fanclub
(Leon – guitar/vocals; Louise – bass/vocals; Adam – drums)

Run into the Sea	41	2014

Hole
(Courtney Love – guitar/vocals; Eric Erlandson – guitar; Jill Emery – bass; Caroline Rue – drums. 1993: Love; Erlandson; Lesley – bass; Patty Schemel – drums. 199$: Kirsten Pfaff replaced Lesley – bass)

Burn Black	7	1991
Teenage Whore	10	1991
Olympia	25	1993
Beautiful Son	47	1993
Miss World	15	1994
Doll Parts	45	1994
Violet	28	1995

David Holmes
(David Holmes – DJ. Remixed by Arab Strap. See also Arab Strap)

The Holiday Girl (Don't Die Just Yet - Arab Strap Mix)	10	1997

Holy Fuck
(Brian Borcherdt – guitar; Graham Walsh – guitar; Kevin Lynn – bass; Owen Pallett – violin; Matt Shulz – drums)

Lovely Allen	36	2008

The Horn The Hunt
(Clare Carter – vocals; Joe Osbourne – bass/sythesizer)

Raptor	43	2010
Gold	38	2012

Horowitz
(Ian Evans – guitar/bass/keyboards/drums/vocals; Pete Bowers – guitar/bass)

Tracyanne	18	2007

The Horrors
(Faris Badwan – vocals; Joshua Hayward –guitar; Tom Cowan – keyboards; Rhys Webb – bass; Joe Spurgeon – drums/percussion)

I Can See Through You	23	2011

House of Love
(Guy Chadwick – guitar/vocals; Terry Bickers – guitar; Chris Groothuizen – bass; Pete Evans – drums)

Destroy the Heart	1	1988
Christine	9	1988
Love in a Car	18	1988
I Don't Know Why I Love You	10	1989

The Housemartins
(Paul Heaton – vocals; Stan Cullimore – guitar/vocals; Ted Key – bass; Hugh Whitaker – drums)

Flag Day	10	1985

Huggy Bear
(Niki Elliot – vocals; Chris – vocals; John – guitar; Jo – bass/vocals; Karen – drums)

Her Jazz	3	1993

Human Don't Be Angry
(Malcolm Middleton – guitar/keyboards/vocals. See also Malcolm Middleton and Arab Strap)

Monologue: River	25	2012

The Humms
(Zeke Sayer – guitar/vocals; Tyler Glenn – bass; John Bleech – drums)

Are You Dead?	36	2009

Hunting Lodge
(Dan Chandler - vocals; Clive Henry - guitar; Dan Bennett - guitar; Seth Cooke - drums)

Don't Touch My Neck (Hero of the Beach)	18	2005

Husker Du
(Bob Mould – guitar/vocals; Greg Norton – bass; Grant Hart – drums/vocals. For Mould, see also *Sugar*)

Makes No Sense At All	46	1985

The Hybirds
(Richard Warren – guitar/vocals; Darren Sheridan – bass; Louis Divito – drums)

Seventeen	29	1997

Hydroplane
(Kerrie Bolton – vocals; Andrew Withycombe – keyboards)

We Crossed the Atlantic	13	1997

Hyper Kinako
(Toko Sanger –penyoliser/ vocals; Phil Archer – guitar; Lisa Horton – bass; Shigeto Wada – dorami/various electronics; Greg MacDermott – drums/melodica. For Horton, see also *Bearsuit* and *Mega Emotion*)

Tokyo Invention Registration Office	44	2003

I

I, Ludicrous
(Will Hung, aka David Rippingdale – vocals; John Proctor – guitar/keyboards)

Preposterous Tales	11	1987

Ikara Colt
(Paul Resende – vocals; Claire Ingram – guitar/vocals; John Ball – guitar; Dominic Young – drums)

One Note	33	2001

iLIKETRAiNS
(David Martin – guitar/vocals; Guy Bannister – guitar/synthesizer; Alistair Bowis – bass/synthesizer; Simon Fogal – drums)

The Beeching Report	39	2006

ILL
(Roseanne Robertson – vocals; Sadie Noble – guitar; Whitney Bluzma – bass; Helen Shanahan – keyboards; Fiona Ledgard – drums)

Secret Life	31	2014

I'm From Barcelona
(Emanuel Lundgren – guitar/vocals; Mathias Alriksson – vocals; Marcus Carlholt – vocals; Julie Witwicki Carlsson – vocals; Micke Larsson – vocals; Johan Martensson – vocals; Cornelia Norgren – vocals; Emma Maata – vocals; Frida Ohnell – vocals; Jonas Tjader – vocals; Tobias Granstand – guitar; Daniel Lindlof – guitar/banjo; Henrik Olofsson – bass; Tina Gardestrand – piano; Christofer Lorin – piano/synthesizers; Matthias Johansson – saxophone; Fredrik Karp – saxophone; Jacob Sollenberg – clarinet; Johan Aineland – accordion/mandolin; David Ljung – trumpet; Jakob Jonsson – trumpet; Erik Ottosson – tuba; Rikard Ljung – omnichord/synthesizers; Martin Lindh – synthesizers/glockenspiel; Olol Gardestrand – drums; Philip Erixon – percussion)

We're From Barcelona	20	2006

The Imposter
(aka – Elvis Costello – vocals; Steve Nieve – piano. See also Elvis Costello)

Pills & Soap	24	1983

Inspiral Carpets
(1988: Stephen Holt – vocals; Graham Lambert – guitar; Dave Swift – bass; Clint Boon – organ; Craig Gill – drums. 1989: Tom Hingley – vocals; Lambert; Martin Walsh – bass; Boon; Gill. *1994 track was by Inspiral Carpets with Mark E. Smith: featuring Smith – vocals. For Smith, see also The Fall, Long Fin Killie, D.O.S.E., Elastica and Von Sudenfed)

Keep the Circle Around	11	1998
Joe	9	1989
Find Out Why	21	1989
So This is How it Feels	35	1989
Directing Traffik	49	1989
She Comes in the Fall	50	1989
The Beast Inside	50	1990
*I Want You	1	1994

J

J Church
(Lance Hahn – guitar/vocals; David DiDonato – guitar; Gardner Maxam, aka Gardner Fusuhara – bass; Aaron Olson – drums)

Good Judge of Character	34	1993

Jah Woosh
(aka Neville Beckford – DJ/producer)

Freedom Connection	24	1977

The Jam
(Paul Weller – guitar/vocals; Bruce Foxton – bass; Rick Buckler – drums)

Away From the Numbers	46	1977
Down in the Tube Station at Midnight	24	1978
In the City	44	1978
Down in the Tube Station at Midnight	4	1979
The Eton Rifles	19	1979
Strange Town	27	1979
Down in the Tube Station at Midnight	4	1980
Going Underground	13	1980
Down in the Tube Station at Midnight	13	1981
Going Underground	23	1981
Town Called Malice	11	1982
The Bitterest Pill (I Ever Had To Swallow)	39	1982
Down in the Tube Station at Midnight	11	1982AT
Going Underground	17	1982AT
Going Underground	35	1999AT

James
(Tim Booth – vocals; Larry Gott – guitar; Jim Glennie – bass; Gavan Whelan – drums. 1989: Added Saul Davis – violin/guitar; Mark Hunter – keyboards; Dave Baignton-Power

replaced Whelan – drums. For Whelan, see also Calvin Party)

Hymn From A Village	28	1985
What For	33	1988
Sit Down	8	1989

Japandroids
(Brian King – guitar/vocals; David Prowse – drums/vocals)

| The House That Heaven Built | 33 | 2012 |

Jawbone
(aka Bob Zabor – guitar/harmonica/bass drum/vocals)

| Hi-de-hi | 10 | 2004 |
| Jack Rabbit | 18 | 2004 |

JD Meatyard
(John Donaldson – guitar/vocals. See also Calvin Party)

Olive Tree	11	2011
Jesse James	13	2013
A Political Song (Blow It Our Yr Arse)	26	2013
Taking the Asylum	42	2014

Jefferson Airplane
(Grace Slick – vocals; Marty Balin – guitar; Paul Kantner – guitar; Jorma Korkonen – guitar; Jack Cassady – bass; Spencer Dryden – drums)

| White Rabbit | 24 | 1976 |

Jesus and Mary Chain
(1984: Jim Reid – guitar/vocals; William Reid – guitar/vocals; Douglas Hart – bass; Murray Dalglish – drums. 1985/86: Jim Reid; William Reid; Hart; Bobby Gillespie – drums. "Just Like Honey" added Karen Parker – vocals. 1987: John Moore – guitar; Hart; James Pinker – drums. "Nine Million..." featured just Jim and William Reid. 1988: Jim Reid; William Reid; Dave Evans – guitar. 1989: Jim Reid; William Reid; Ben Lurie – guitar; Hart; Richard Thomas – drums. 1992: Jim Reid; William Reid; Lurie; Matthew Parkin – bass; Barry Blacker – drums. 1998: Jim Reid; William Reid; Lurie; Nick Sanderson – drums. For Gillespie see also Primal Scream)

Upside Down	37	1984
Never Understand	1	1985
Just Like Honey	2	1985
You Trip Me Up	12	1985
Some Candy Talking	9	1986
April Skies	16	1987
Kill Surf City	39	1987
Nine Million Rainy Days	41	1987
Sidewalking	3	1988
Blues From a Gun	13	1989
Reverence	13	1992
Crackin' Up	11	1998

Jesus Jones
(Mike Edwards – vocals; Jerry de Borg – guitar; Al Jaworski – bass; Barry D.' aka Iain Baker – keyboards; Gen, aka Simon Matthews – drums)

| Info Freako | 32 | 1989 |

Joanna Gruesome
(Lan McArdle – vocals; George Nicholls – guitar; Owen Williams – guitar; Max Warren - bass; David Sandford – drums)

| Sugarcrush | 13 | 2013 |

Johnny Moped
(Paul Halford – organ/vocals; Slimy Toad, aka Simon Fitzgerald – guitar; Fred Berk – bass; Dave Berk, aka Dave Batchelor – drums)

| Incendiary Device | 15 | 1977 |

Sophie & Peter Johnston
(Sophie Johnson – vocals; Peter Johnson – synthesiser/percussion; Tom McLuskey - synthesiser)

| Television/Satellite | 37 | 1983 |

Daniel Johnston
(Daniel Johnston – guitar/keyboards/vocals)

| Dream Scream 1998 | 12 | 1998 |

Joy Division
(Ian Curtis – vocals; Bernard Albrecht, aka Bernard Dicken – guitar/keyboards; Peter Hook – bass; Stephen Morris – drums. For Albrecht - as Bernard Sumner - Hook and Morris see also New Order. For Sumner (Albrecht), see also Electronic)

Atmosphere	2	1980
Love Will Tear Us Apart	3	1980
Transmission	10	1980
Decades	14	1980
New Dawn Fades	20	1980
She's Lost Control	22	1980
Twenty-Four Hours	41	1980
Atmosphere	1	1981
Love Will Tear Us Apart	3	1981
New Dawn Fades	5	1981

Decades	7	1981
Dead Souls	11	1981
Transmission	14	1981
Twenty-Four Hours	43	1981
Isolation	44	1981
Atmosphere	2	1982AT
Love Will Tear Us Apart	3	1982AT
New Dawn Fades	4	1982AT
Decades	7	1982AT
Dead Souls	12	1982AT
Twenty-Four Hours	23	1982AT
Transmission	26	1982
Isolation	38	1982AT
She's Lost Control	41	1982AT
The Eternal	48	1982AT
Atmosphere	1	1999AT
Love Will Tear Us Apart	3	1999AT
New Dawn Fades	15	1999AT
She's Lost Control	20	1999AT
Transmission	28	1999AT

The Joy Formidable
(*Rhiannon Bryan – guitar/vocals; Rhydian Dafydd – bass; Matthew Justin Stahley – drums/percussion*)

Whirring	7	2009
The Greatest Light is the Greatest Shade	23	2009

Joy of Sex
(*Rosie Smith – keyboards/vocals; Max Hicks – guitar/vocals*)

Red Rocket	12	2010

K

Bubbley Kaur – see Cornershop

Kenickie
(*Lauren Le Laverne – vocals; Marie du Santiago – guitar; Emmy-Kate Montrose – bass; X, aka John Le Laverne, aka Johnny Xaverre – drums*)

Come Out 2 Nite	1	1996
Punka	4	1996

Kentucky AFC
(*Endaf Roberts – guitar/vocals; Huw Owen – bass; Gethin Evans – drums*)

Be Nesa	43	2004

Keshco
(*Andy Brain – guitar/bass/keyboards/vocals; Robert Follen – guitar/keyboards/drums/percussion; Luke Sample – guitar/flute/lapsteel*)

Fly By Night	49	2011

The Keys
(*Matthew Evans – guitar/vocals; Gwion Rowlands – guitar/vocals; Sion Glyn – bass. Elliot Jones – drums. For Evans, Rowlands and Glyn see also Murry the Hump*)

Strength of Strings	41	2003

Kid Carpet
(*aka Ed Patrick – keyboards/Fisher-Price guitars; vocals*)

Your Love	26	2005

Killing Joke
(*Jaz Coleman, aka Jeremy Coleman – keyboards/vocals; Geordie, aka K. Walker – guitar; Youth, aka Martin Glover – bass; Paul Ferguson – drums. For Youth, see also The Orb*)

Requiem	35	1980
Pssyche	36	1980
Requiem	27	1981
Follow the Leaders	28	1981
Pssyche	45	1981
Empire Song	20	1982
Requiem	32	1982AT
Pssyche	34	1982AT

King Creosote
(*aka Kenny Anderson – guitar/bass/piano/keyboards/vocals; Gavin Brown – drums*)

Klutz	4	2005

King Short Shirt
(*aka Mclean Emmanuel – vocals, featuring: Junior 'Jagger' Martin – guitar; Tony McIntosh – piano; Frankie McIntosh – organ; Sylvester Brown – drums; Ralph Ropen – congas; Errol Edwards – percussion; Fitsroy Nesbitt - percussion*)

Nobody Go Run Me	30	1977

Klaxons
(Jamie Reynolds – bass/vocals; Simon Taylor-Davis – guitar; James Righton – keyboards/vocals; Steffan Halperin – drums)

Magick	27	2006

KLF and Extreme Noise Terror
(KLF: Bill Drummond; Jim Cauty. Extreme Noise Terror: Phil Vane – vocals; Dean Jones – vocals; Peter Hurley – guitar; Mark Bailey – bass; Tony Dickens – drums. For Cauty see also The Orb)

3am Eternal	44	1992

Diane Marie Kloba
(Diane Marie Kloba – various/vocals)

L

Lab 4
(Lez and Adam – computers/keyboards)

Candyman	35	2000

Ladytron
(Mira Aroyo – keyboards/vocals; Helena Marnie – keyboards/vocals; Reuben Wu – keyboards; Daniel Hunt – keyboards)

Seventeen	31	2002

Yva Las Vegass
(Yva Las Vegass – guitar/vocals)

Crack Whore	40	2012

L'augmentation
(Simon – keyboards/vocals; Jim – bass; Lisa – flute/trumpet; Angela – drums)

Soleil	17	1998

LB Dub Corp
(aka Luke Slater - DJ)

Take It Down (In Dub)	40	2010

I Saw The Stars	14	2013

The Knife
(Karin Dreijer Anderson – vocals; Olof Dreijer – keyboards)

We Share Our Mother's Health	30	2006

Kraken
(Project of Skynet and Stakka, aka Nathan Vinell and Shaun Morris – keyboards/computers)

Side Effects	26	1999

Kubichek!
(Alan McDonald – guitar/vocals; Mark Nelson – guitar; Michael 'Frog' Coburn – bass; Chris McGreevy – drums)

Outwards	36	2007

LCD Soundsystem
(James Murphy – guitar/bass/keyboards/drums/vocals)

All My Friends	21	2007

Cate Le Bon
(Cate Le Bon – guitar/vocals)

Puts Me To Work	43	2012

Led Zeppelin
(Robert Plant – vocals; Jimmy Page – guitar; John Paul Jones – bass; John Bonham – drums)

Stairway to Heaven	1	1976
Whole Lotta Love	19	1976
Kashmir	36	1976
Stairway to Heaven	14	1978
Stairway to Heaven	24	1978

Leftfield
(Neil Barnes – DJ/synthesizers; Paul Daley – samples)

Afro-Left	41	1995

Legendary Stardust Cowboy
(aka Norman Carl Odam – guitar/vocals; T-Bone Burnett – drums)

Paralysed	15	1976

The Lemonheads
(Evan Dando – guitar/vocals; Jesse Peretz – bass; David Ryan – drums)

Different Drum	13	1996

Let's Wrestle
(Wesley Patrick Gonzalez – guitar/vocals; Sam Pillay – bass; Darkus Bishop – drums)

In Dreams Pt II	15	2011

Jeffrey Lewis
(Jeffrey Lewis – guitar/vocals 2013: Jeffrey Lewis & The Rain, featuring Lewis – guitar/keyboards/vocals; Isabel Martin – bass/vocals; Heather Wagner – drums/vocals)

The Chelsea Hotel Oral Sex Song	23	2002
WWPRD	27	2013

Lift to Experience
(Josh Pearson – guitar/vocals; Josh Browning – bass; Andy Young – drums)

These are the Days	27	2001
Falling From Cloud 9	39	2001

Listen with Sarah
(Sarah Nelson – computer)

Animal Hop	27	2004
Another Nice Mix	13	2005

Little Feat
("Willin'": Lowell George – guitar/vocals; Roy Estrada – bass; Bill Payne – keyboards; Richie Hayward – drums. "Long Distance Love": George; Paul Barrere – guitar; Kenny Gradney – bass; Payne; Hayward; Sam Clayton – congas. For Estrada see also Captain Beefheart & the Magic Band)

Long Distance Love	26	1976
Willin'	49	1976

Llamatron
(Llamatron – producer)

You Make Milf III	38	2009

Robert Lloyd and the New Four Seasons
(Robert Lloyd – guitar/vocals; Dave Lowe – guitar; Micky Harris – bass; Mark Tibenham – keyboards; Roger Morton – saxophone; Mark Fletcher – drums. For Lloyd, see also Nightingales)

Something Nice	21	1988

The Long Blondes
(Kate Jackson – vocals; Dorian Cox – guitar/keyboards; Emma Chaplin – guitar/keyboards; Reenie Hollis, aka Kathryn Hollis – bass; Screech Louder, aka Mark Turvey – drums)

Once & Never Again	35	2006

Long Fin Killie with Mark E. Smith
(Luke Sutherland – vocals; Mark E. Smith – vocals; Philip Cameron – guitar; Colin Greig – bass; David Turner – drums. For Sutherland see also Mogwai. For Smith see also Inspiral Carpets, DOSE, Elastica, Von Sudenfed and The Fall)

Heads of Dead Surfers	10	1995

Loop
(Robert Hampton – guitar/vocals; James Endicott – guitar; John McKay – bass; John Wills – drums)

Collision	41	1988

Lord Numb
(aka Alan Castallero – keyboards/guitar/vocals. See also Lord Numb & Julien Auroux)

Zombie	27	2012

Lord Numb & Julien Auroux
(Julien Auroux – computer/keyboards/vocals; Lord Numb, aka Alan Castallero – keyboards/guitar. See also Lord Numb)

Facile	46	2011

Los Campesinos!
(Gareth Paisey – glockenspiel/vocals; Tom Bromley – guitar; Neil Turner – guitar; Ellen Waddell – bass; Aleksandra Berditchevskaia – keyboards/vocals; Harriet Coleman – keyboards/violin; Ollie Briggs – drums. 2009: added Jamie Stewart – vocals; Zac Pennington – vocals; Jherek Bischoff – double bass/trombone; Isaak Mills – saxophone/flute; Samantha Boshnack – trumpet/flugel horn; Kim Palsey – shruti box/piccolo)

You! Me! Dancing!	12	2006

You! Me! Dancing!	22	2007
There Are Listed Buildings	1	2009
The Sea is a Good Place to Think of the Future	9	2009
Straight in at 101	26	2010

Lost Penguin
(Kerry, aka Charleigh Blue – vocals; Kev Soar – guitar; Matt Gilbert – bass)

| I Believe I Can Fly | 45 | 2006 |
| Mr Whippy | 48 | 2006 |

Helen Love
(Helen Love, aka Helen Jones – guitar/vocals; Gary Love – guitar; Mark Hunter – keyboards; Dave Insen – keyboards. 1997 – Sheena replaced Gary Love – guitar; Beth replaced Hunter and Insen - keyboards)

Girl About Town	10	1996
Does Your Heart Go Boom?	3	1997
Long Live the UK Music Scene	10	1998
Atomic	50	2013

Love Cup
(Mark Baldwin – guitar/vocals; T. J. Harrison – bass; Jason Miling – drums)

| Tearing Water | 36 | 1992 |

The Lovely Eggs
(Holly Ross – guitar/vocals; David Blackwell – drums. For Ross, see also Angelica)

Have You Ever Heard a Digital Accordion?	11	2008
I Like Birds But I Like Other Animals Too	48	2008
Don't Look At Me (I Don't Like It)	2	2011
Panic Plants	43	2011
Allergies	5	2012
Food	13	2012

Low
(Alan Sparhawk – guitar/vocals; Zak Sally – bass; Mimi Parker – drums/vocals. "Immune" featured The Triple A Strings: Ada Pearle – violin; Tresa Ellickson – viola; Kera – cello. "Dinosaur Act" featured Bob Weston – trumpet; Mark Di Gli Antoni – piano; Daniel Huffman – flute. "In the Drugs" featured Marc Gartmann – banjo. 2011: Sparhawk; Steve Garrington – bass/piano; Parker; also featuring: Nels Cline guitar/lap steel; David Carroll – banjo; Chris Price – keyboards; Caitlin Moe – violin; Ryland Steen - percussion)

Immune	10	1999
Dinosaur Act	11	2000
In the Drugs	16	2002
Canada	18	2002
This is How You Sing Amazing Grace	36	2002
Try To Sleep	45	2011

LSG
(aka Oliver Lieb – producer)

| Hearts | 6 | 1994 |

Lucky Soul
(Ali Howard – vocals; Andrew Laidlaw – guitar; Ivor Sims – guitar; Russell Grooms – bass; Paul Atkins – drums)

| Lips Are Unhappy | 33 | 2007 |

The Luddites
(Steve McDermott – vocals; Mike Stead – guitar; Lawrence Gill – bass; Dave Stead – drums)

| Doppleganger | 36 | 1983 |

Lulubelle III
(Ronnie Carnwath – guitar/vocals; Christopher Cowan – guitar)

| Frankie | 34 | 2012 |

The Lurkers
(Howard Wall – vocals; Pete Stride – guitar; Arturo Bassick – bass; Pete Haynes, aka Manic Esso – drums)

| Shadow | 12 | 1977 |
| Love Story | 31 | 1977 |

Lush
(Mike Berenyi – guitar/vocals; Emma Anderson – guitar/vocals; Steve Rippon – bass; Chris Acland – drums)

| Sweetness & Light | 27 | 1990 |

Lynyrd Skynyrd
(Ronnie Van Zant – vocals; Gary Rossington – guitar; Allen Collins – guitar; Ed King – bass; Billy Powell – piano; Bob Burns – drums)

| Freebird | 20 | 1976 |
| Freebird | 18 | 1976 |

M

Madder Rose
(Mary Lorson – vocals; Billy Cote – guitar; Matt Verta-Ray; Johnny Kick – drums)

Swim	2	1993
Beautiful John	36	1993
Lights Go Down	44	1993
The Car Song	19	1994
Panic On	35	1994

Magazine
(Howard Devoto – vocals; John McGeogh – guitar; Barry Adamson – bass; Martin Jackson – drums. For Devoto, see also *Buzzcocks*. For McGeogh, see *Siouxsie & The Banshees*. For Adamson, see *Nick Cave & The Bad Seeds*)

Shot By Both Sides	5	1978
Shot By Both Sides	17	1979
Shot By Both Sides	47	1982AT

The Magic Band
(Drumbo, aka John French – drums/vocals; Gary Lucas – guitar; Denny Walley – guitar; Mark Boston – bass; Michael Traylor – drums. For Drumbo, see also *Captain Beefheart & The Magic Band*)

Big-Eyed Beans From Venus	34	2004
Electricity	47	2004

Magnetic Fields
(Stephin Merritt – guitar/keyboards/vocals; John Woo – guitar/banjo; Claudia Gonson – piano; Sam Davol – cello/flute; Shirley Simms – autoharp; Pinky Weitzman – violin/viola/musical saw; Daniel Handler – accordion/organ; Johnny Blood – tuba/flugelhorn/alto horn)

Andrew in Drag	39	2012

Maher Shalal Hash Baz
(aka Tori Kudo – guitar/piano/violin/cello/trumpet/harp/orchestra leader; Naoto Kawate – guitar/bass; Reiko Kudo – vocals; Saya Ueno – keyboards/alto saxophone/drums; Namio Kudo – piano; Hiro Nakazaki – euphonium/percussion)

Open Field	32	2003

Male Nurse
(Keith Farquar – vocals; Ben Wallers – guitar; Andrew Hobson – guitar; Alistair McInvern – bass; Alexander King – keyboards; Lawrence Worthington – drums)

My Own Private Patrick Swayze	32	1998

Manhattan Love Suicides
(Caroline McChrystal – vocals; Darren Lockwood – guitar; Adam Miller – bass; Eddy Lines – drums. 2008: Rachel Barker – drums replaced Lines)

Keep It Coming	49	2007
Heat & Panic	17	2008
Clusterfuck	46	2008

Manic Street Preachers
(James Dean Bradfield – guitar/vocals; Nicky Wire – bass; Sean Moore – drums)

A Design For Life	42	1996

Marine Research
(Amelia Fletcher – vocals; Peter Momtchiloff – guitar; Rob Pursey – bass; Cathy Rogers – keyboards; John Stanley – drums. For Fletcher, Pursey and Momtchiloff, see also *Heavenly*. For Fletcher and Momtchiloff, see also *Talulah Gosh*. For Fletcher and Pursey, see also *Tender Trap*. For Fletcher, see also *The Wedding Present* and *Hefner*. For Pursey, see also *Sportique*)

Parallel Horizontal	47	1999

Bob Marley & The Wailers
(Bob Marley – vocals; Al Anderson – guitar; Aston Barrett – bass; Bernard Harvey – keyboards; Earl Lindo – keyboards; Carlton Barrett – drums. This was the line-up for the studio version of the track, featured on the *Natty Dread* album in May 1975. In August 1975, a live version, released as a single, featured: Marley; Anderson; Junior Murvin – guitar; Aston Barrett; Tyrone Downie – keyboards; Carlton Barrett; Alvin Patterson – percussion. 1977: The previous line-up for the live track, without Anderson)

No Woman No Cry	32	1976
Waiting in Vain	32	1977

Laura Marling
(Laura Marling – guitar/vocals; Pete Roe – keyboards/banjo; Ted Dwayne – double bass; Joe Ichinose – violin; Marcus Mumford – accordian/percussion. For Mumford, see also *Mumford & Sons*)

My Manic & I	38	2007

M/A/R/R/S
(Steven Young, Martyn Young, Rudy Tambala and Alex Ayuli – various; Chris MacIntosh – DJ; Dave Dorrell – DJ. For Steven and Martyn Young, see also Colourbox)

Pump Up the Volume	46	1987

Martha
(Nathan – guitar/vocals; Daniel - guitar; Naomi – bass; Jc – drums)

1978. Smiling Politely	45	2012
Sycamore	7	2013
1997 Passing in the Hallway	18	2014

Caroline Martin
(Caroline Martin – guitar/vocals)

The Singer	3	2004

MASS
(Justine Berry – vocals; Jonny Green – guitar; Andy Miller – guitar; Paul Hegland – bass; Stuart McMillan – drums)

Hey Gravity	6	2002
Live a Little	35	2003

Massive Attack
(3D, aka Robert Del Naia – keyboards; Mushroom, aka Andrew Vowles – keyboards; Daddy G, aka Grant Marshall – keyboards. Also featured: Elizabeth Fraser – vocals; Angela Bruschini – guitar; Andy Gangadeen – drums. For Fraser, see also Cocteau Twins, This Mortal Coil and Felt)

Teardrop	21	1998

Matching Mole
(Robert Wyatt – drums/vocals; Phil Miller – guitar; Bill McCormick – bass; Dave McRae – keyboards; David Sinclair – oboe. For Wyatt, see also Robert Wyatt, Scritti Politti and Working Week)

O Caroline	46	1976

Mates of State
(Kori Gardner – keyboards/vocals; Jason Hammel – drums/percussion/vocals)

Fraud in the 80s	38	2006

John Maus
(John Maus – keyboards)

Cop Killer	21	2011

Fergus Mayhem: see CLSM

Mazzy Star
(Hope Sandoval – vocals; David Roback – guitar)

Fade Into You	25	1994

Ste McCabe
(Ste McCabe – guitar/vocals. 2009: featues David Hoyle – backing vocals. *Ste McCabe & Billy Bragg. For Bragg, see also Billy Bragg.)

Huyton Scum	5	2008
Murder Music	10	2009
*Cockroach	36	2014
Go Polski Boy	45	2014

McCarthy
(Malcolm Eden – vocals; Tim Gane – guitar; John Williamson – bass; Gary Baker – drums. For Gane, see also Stereolab and Tortoise)

Frans Hals	35	1987
Should the Bible Be Banned?	38	1988

McLusky
(Andrew Falkous – guitar/vocals; Jonathan Chapple – bass; Matthew Harding – drums. 2004: Jack Egglestone replaced Harding – drums. For Falkous and Egglestone, see also Future of the Left)

Alan is a Cowboy Killer	35	2002
Down with Good Intentions	40	2002
That Will Not Hang	26	2004

Rory McVicar
(Rory McVicar – guitar/vocals)

Little One	20	2005

Meanwhile, Back in Communist Russia
(Emily Gray – vocals; James Matthews – guitar; Mark Halleren – guitar; Pete Williams – guitar; Ollie Clewitt – bass; Tim Croston – keyboards)

Morning After Pill	11	2001

Mega City Four
(Wiz, aka Darren Brown – guitar/vocals; Daniel Brown – guitar; Gerald Bryant – bass; Chris Jones – drums)

Miles Apart	43	1988

Mega Emotion
(Lisa Horton – keyboards/vocals; Jan Robertson – keyboards/vocals; Iain Ross guitar/vocals. See also Bearsuit)

Brains	20	2013

M83
(Anthony Gonzalez – guitar/keyboards/vocals)

Midnight City	34	2011

The Mekons
(Andy Corrigan – vocals; Mark White – vocals; Kevin Lycett – guitar; Tom Greenhalgh – guitar; Roz Allen – bass; John Langford – drums. For Langford, see also Three Johns)

Where Were You?	41	1979

Melt Banana
(Yasuko Onuki – vocals; Ichiro Agata – guitar; Rika Chang, aka Rika mm', aka Rika Hamamoto – bass; Youichiro Natsumu – drums. 1999: Toshiaki Sudoh replaced Natsumu – drums. 2003: David William Witte replaced Sudoh – drums)

Stimulus for Revolting Virus	37	1998
Plot in a Pot	38	1999
Shield for Your Eyes a Beast in the Well on Your Hand	12	2003

Melys
(Andrea Parker – vocals; Paul Adams – guitar/keyboards; Rich Eardley – bass; Carys Jones – keyboards; Gary Husband – drums)

Lemming	24	1998
Chinese Whispers	1	2001
I Don't Believe in You	35	2001
So Good	43	2002
Eyeliner	38	2004

The Membranes
(John Robb – bass/vocals; Mark Tilton – guitar; Coofy Sid Coulthart – drums. 2012: Robb; Nick Brown – guitar; Peter Byrchmore – guitar; Keith Curtis – bass; Rob Haynes – drums)

Spike Milligan's Tape Recorder	6	1984
If You Enter the Arena, You've Got to be Prepared to Deal with the Lions	6	2012

The Men They Couldn't Hang
(Stefan Cush – vocals; Paul Simmonds – guitar; Swill, aka Phil Odgers – guitar; Shanne Hasler – bass; Jon Odgers – drums)

The Green Fields of France	3	1984
Ironmasters	11	1985

Mercury Rev
(David Baker – vocals; Jonathan Donahue – guitar/vocals; Grasshopper, aka Sean Mackiowiak – guitar; David Fridmann – bass; Suzanne Thorpe – woodwind; Jimmy Chambers – drums. 1998: Baker had by now left; added Adam Snyder – keyboards. 2001: Donahue; Grasshopper; Fridman; Jeff Mercel – drums/piano. For Fridmann, see also Mogwai)

Car Wash Hair	49	1991
Goddess on a Hiway	33	1998
The Dark is Rising	44	2001

Metric
(Emily Haines – guitar/synthesizer/piano/vocals; James Shaw – guitar/synthesizers; Joshua Winstead - bass/synthesizers; Joules Scott-Key – drums/percussion)

Monster Hospital	33	2006

MGMT
(Andrew VanWyngarden – guitar/vocals; Benjamin Goldwasser – keyboards/vocals)

Time To Pretend	4	2008
Kids	14	2008

Malcolm Middleton
(Malcolm Middleton – guitar/vocals; Stuart Braithwaite – guitar; Barry Burns – keyboards; Jenny Reeve – violin; Alan Barr – cello; Paul Savage -drums . For Middleton, see also Arab Strap and Human Don't Be Angry. For Braithwaite, see also Mogwai. For Barr and Savage, see also The Delgados)

Break My Heart	23	2005

MIA
(aka Mathangi Arulpragasam – various/vocals)

Paper Planes	40	2008

Mighty Lemon Drops
(Paul Marsh – guitar/vocals; David Newton – guitar; Tony Linehan – bass; Keith Rowley – drums)

Like an Angel	34	1986

Mighty Math
(aka Robert Shaw – keyboards/programming)

Soul Boy	39	2000

Mighty Mighty
(Hugh Harkin – vocals; Mick Geoghegan – guitar; Russell Burton – bass; Peter Geoghegan – guitar/keyboards; D.J. Hennessy, aka David Hennessy – drums)

Is There Anyone Out There?	44	1986

The Mighty Wah! – see Wah!

Frankie Miller
(Frankie Miller – guitar/vocals; Ray Minhinnet – guitar; Chrissy Stewart – bass; Jim Hall – piano/organ; Graham Deakin – drums)

Be Good to Yourself	10	1977

Million Dead
(Frank Turner – vocals; Cameron Dean – guitar; Julia – bass; Ben Dawson – drums)

I Am the Party	21	2003

Ministry
(Al Jourgensen – guitar/vocals; Mike Scaccia – guitar; Paul Barker – bass; Roland Barker – keyboards; William Rieflin – drums. Guest vocals: Gibby Haynes. For Haynes, see also Butthole Surfers)

Jesus Built My Hotrod	3	1992

Miss Black America
(Seymour Glass – vocals; Gish – guitar; Mickey Smith – bass; Neil Baldwin – drums)

Human Punk	14	2001
Don't Speak My Mind	42	2001
Talk Hard	3	2002
Miss Black America	11	2002
Infinite Chinese Box	45	2002

Miss Mend
(Linda Rosendahl – vocals; Graeme Wilson – guitar/vocals; Dino Gollnick – guitar; Joe Dilworth – drums. For Dilworth, see also Th' Faith Healers)

Living City Plan	48	1999

The Mission
(Wayne Hussey – guitar/vocals; Simon Hinkler – guitar; Craig Adams – bass; Mick Brown – drums. For Hussey and Adams, see Sisters of Mercy. For Hinkler, see Artery)

Serpent's Kiss	49	1986

Misty's Big Adventure
(Grandmaster Gareth, aka Gareth Jones – vocals; Jonathan Kedge – guitar; Matt Jones – bass; Lucy Bassett – keyboards; Lucy Baines – saxophone; Hannah Baines – trumpet; Sam Minnear – drums/percussion. For Jones, see also Grandmaster Gareth)

The Story of Love	16	2005
Fashion Parade	9	2006

The Misunderstood
(Rich Brown – vocals; Tony Hill – guitar/vocals; George Phelps – guitar; Glenn Ross Campbell – steel guitar; Steve Whiting – bass; Greg Treadway – guitar/keyboards; Rick Moe – drums)

I Can Take You to the Sun	30	1976

Modest Mouse
(Isaac K. Brock – guitar/banjo/vocals; Johnny Marr – guitar; Eric Judy – bass; Tom Peloso – double bass/violin/various; Jeremiah Green – drums; Joe Plummer – drums. For Marr, see also The Smiths and Billy Bragg)

Dashboard	31	2007

Mogwai
(Stuart Braithwaite – guitar/occasional vocals; Brendan O'Hare – guitar/keyboards; Dominic Aitchison – bass; Martin Bulloch – drums. 1998: John Cummings replaced O'Hare - guitar. 1999: added Barry Burns – piano/flute/guitar. 'My Father My King' and 2003/2011 material featured Luke Sutherland – violin. 2003: also featured Caroline Barber – cello; Greg Lawson – violin. '2 Rights Make 1 Wrong' featured Dave Fridmann – strings plus Willie Campbell, Charles Clark, Gary Lightbody and Gruff Rhys – backing vocals. For Braithwaite, see also Malcolm Middleton. For Sutherland, see also Long Fin Killie. For Fridmann, see also Mercury Rev. For Rhys, see also Super Furry Animals)

New Paths to Helicon	2	1997
Xmas Steps	2	1998
Cody	14	1999
Stanley Kubrick	25	1999
My Father My King	10	2001
2 Rights Make 1 Wrong	22	2001
Hunted By a Freak	3	2003
Ratts in the Capital	6	2003
Friend of the Night	10	2006
Glasgow Mega Snake	15	2006
Drunk & Crazy	28	2011
What Are They Doing In Heaven Today	17	2013
Wizard Motor	40	2013
Remurdered	4	2014
Repelish	32	2014

Moolah Temple $tringband
(Johnny Favorite, aka Jonathan Wertheim – guitar; Ian Moore – violin/banjolin/percussion)

Cherry Bed Antique	20	2009

Moose
(Russell Yates – vocals; Kevin McKillop – guitar; Lincoln Fong – bass; Damien Warburton – drums)

Suzanne	17	1991

Van Morrison
(Van Morrison – guitar/vocals; Jay Berliner – guitar; Richard Davis – bass; John Payne – saxophone/flute; Connie Kay – drums; Warren Smith Jr – percussion)

Madame George	21	1976
Madame George	21	1978

Morrissey
(Morrissey, aka Steven Morrissey – vocals; Vini Reilly – guitar; Stephen Street – guitar/bass; Andrew Paresi – drums. 'Last of...' and 'Interesting Drug': Morrissey; Neil Taylor – guitar; Street – guitar; Craig Gannon – guitar; Andy Rourke – bass; Mike Joyce – drums. 'Interesting Drug' featured Kirstay MacColl – vocals. 'Ouija Board': Morrissey; Kevin Armstrong – guitar; Matthew Seligman – bass; Paresi – keyboards; Steve Hopkis – drums. 1990: Morrissey; Mary Margaret O'Hara – vocals; Armstrong; Rourke; Paresi – drums. For Morrissey, Rourke, Joyce, Gannon and Maccoll, see also The Smiths. For Maccoll, see also Billy Bragg. 2006: Morrissey; Alain Whyte – guitar; Baz Boorer – guitar; Jesse Tobias – guitar; Gary Day – bass; Michael Farrell – piano/organ/keyboards/trumpet/trombone/percussion; Matt Chamberlain – drums)

Every Day is Like Sunday	12	1988
Suedehead	13	1988
Late Night Maudlin Street	22	1988
Disappointed	23	1988
The Last of the Famous Playboys	18	1989
Ouija Board, Ouija Board	20	1989
Interesting Drug	47	1989
November Spawned a Monster	16	1990
Life is a Pigsty	29	2006

Mother & The Addicts
(Mother, aka Sam Smith - guitar/vocals; Douglas Morland – guitar; Peter Vallely – bass; Tim Dyer – keyboards; Kendall Koppe – synthesizer; Ian Cronan – drums)

Take The Lovers Home Tonight	30	2005

The Motorcycle Boy
(Alex Taylor – vocals; Michael Kerr – guitar; Scottie, aka David Scott – guitar; Eddie Connolly – bass; Paul McDermott – drums. For Taylor, see also Shop Assistants)

Big Rock Candy Mountain	22	1987

The Motors
(Nick Garvey – guitar/vocals; Bram Tchaikovsky – guitar; Andy McMaster – bass; Ricky Slaughter – drums)

Dancing the Night Away	1	1977
You Beat the Hell Out of Me	3	1977
Emergency	18	1977
Dancing the Night Away	35	1978

Mountain Goats
(John Darnielle – guitar/vocals; Peter Hughes – bass; Franklin Bruno – keyboards; Nora Danielson – violin; Chris McGuire – drums)

Your Belgian Things	46	2004

Mudhoney
(Mark Arm – guitar/vocals; Steve Turner – guitar; Matt Lukin – bass; Dan Peters – drums. For Peters, see also Nirvana)

Sweet Young Thing Ain't Sweet No More	31	1988
You Got It (Keep It Outta My Face)	16	1989

Mugstar
(Pete Smyth – guitar/keyboards; Neil Murphy – guitar; Jason Stoll – bass/saxophone; Steve Ashton – drums)

My Baby Skull Has Not Yet Flowered	43	2005
My Baby Skull Has Not Yet Flowered	17	2006
Good Posture Vs Bad Posture	22	2006
Serra	27	2010

Mum
(Gyda Valtysdottir – vocals; Kristin Anna Valtysdottir – vocals; Orvar Smarason – electronics; Ory Tynes – electronics; Eirikur Orri – organ; Samuli Kosminen – drums/percussion)

Green Grass of Tunnel	48	2002

Mumford & Sons
(Marcus Mumford – guitar/mandolin/drums/vocals; Winston Marshall – guitar/banjo/vocals; Ted Dwayne – guitar/bass/drums/vocals; Ben Lovett – keyboards/accordion/drums/vocals. For Mumford, see also Laura Marling)

Little Lion Man	33	2009

Murry the Hump
(Matthew Evans – guitar/vocals; Gwion Rowlands – guitar/vocals; Sion Glyn – bass; Bill Coyne – drums. For Evans, Rowlands and Glyn, see also The Keys)

Thrown Like a Stone	9	1999

Musical Youth
(Dennis Seaton – vocals; Kelvin Grant – guitar/vocals; Patrick Waite – bass; Michael Grant – keyboards; Junior Waite – drums)

Pass the Dutchie	36	1982

My Bloody Valentine
(Kevin Shields – guitar/vocals; Bilinda Butcher – guitar/vocals; Debbie Goodge – bass; Colm O'Closoig – drums)

You Made Me Realise	6	1988
Feed Me With Your Kiss	17	1988
Soon	2	1990
To Here Knows When	37	1991
Soon	16	1999AT
You Made Me Realise	27	1999AT
In Another Way	37	2013

My Device
(Todd Jordon – guitar/vocals; Russell Eke – bass; Alex 'Doogle' Uren – drums)

Eat Lead	23	2007

N

Nina Nastasia
(Nina Nastasia – guitar/vocals; Gerry Leonard – guitar; Dave Richards – bass; Dylan Willemsa – viola; Stephen Day – cello; Joshua Carlebach – acordian; Gonzalo Munoz – musical saw; Jay Bellarose – drums. 2003: Nastasia; Leonard; Richards; Anne Mette Iversen – bass; Day; Wilemsa; Carlebach; Jim White – drums)

Ugly Face	4	2002
You Her & Me	13	2003

The National
(Matt Berninger – vocals; Bryce Dressner – guitar; Aaron Dressner – guitar/keyboards; Scott Devendorf – bass; Bryan Devendorf – drums)

Bloodbuzz Ohio	41	2010

Naturalites & The Realistics
(Ossie Sams – vocals; Neil Foster – vocals; Percy McLeod – guitar/vocals. The Realistics: Paul Prince – guitar; Lenry Guist – bass; Marcus Hodges – keyboards; Willie Williams – keyboards; Hugh Duffus – saxophone; Albert 'Eitico' Barnes – trumpet; Chester Marzink – drums; Alton Ricketts – drums)

Picture on the Wall	10	1983

Ned's Atomic Dustbin
(John Penney – vocals; Rat, aka Gareth Pring – guitar; Matt Cheslin – bass; Alex Griffin – bass; Dan Warton – drums)

Kill Your Television	26	1990

Neulander
(Korinna Knoll – vocals; Adam Peters – keyboards)

Sex, God & Money	33	2003

New Bad Things
(Matthew Hattie Hein – guitar/vocals; Luke Hollywood – guitar/vocals; Mattie Gaunt – bass; Lars Holmstrom – trumpet; Nayl Rhinestone – drums/fire extinguisher; David French, aka Sticky Dave Friendly – drums/wheelbarrow)

I Suck	16	1993

New Fast Automatic Daffodils
(Andy Spearpoint – vocals; Dolan Hewison – guitar; Justin Crawford – bass; Perry Sanders – drums; Icarus Wilson-Wright – percussion)

Big	14	1990

New Model Army
(Slade the Leveller, aka Justin Sullivan – guitar/vocals; Stuart Morrow – bass; Robb Heaton – drums)

Vengeance	43	1984

New Order
(Bernard Sumner – guitar/vocals; Peter Hook – bass; Gillian Gilbert – keyboards; Stephen Morris – drums. 'Ceremony' –

without Gilbert. For Sumner, Hook and Morris, see Joy Division. For Sumner, see Electronic)

Ceremony	4	1981
Procession	48	1981
Temptation	1	1982
Hurt	17	1982
Ceremony	6	1982AT
Temptation	18	1982AT
Procession	30	1982AT
Blue Monday	1	1983
Age of Consent	3	1983
Your Silent Face	19	1983
Leave Me Alone	25	1983
The Village	45	1983
Thieves Like Us	7	1984
Lonesome Tonight	12	1984
Murder	20	1984
Perfect Kiss	9	1985
Love Vigilantes	16	1985
Sub-culture	18	1985
Sunrise	24	1985
Face Up	45	1985
True Faith	7	1987
1963	43	1987
Fine Time	44	1988
Vanishing Point	27	1988
Regret	13	1993
Blue Monday	6	1999AT
Ceremony	17	1999AT
Temptation	19	1999AT
True Faith	32	1999AT
Brutal	26	2000
Crystal	9	2001

Joanna Newsom
(Joanna Newsom – harp/vocals; Bill Callahan – vocals; Emily Newsom – vocals; Grant Geissman – guitar; Lee Sklar – bass; Matt Cartsonis – banjo/mandolin; Van Dyke Parks – accordion; Don Heffington – percussion. For Callahan, see also Smog)

Only Skin	28	2006

The Nightingales
(2006 :Robert Lloyd – vocals; Alan Apperley – guitar; Pete Byrchmore – guitar; Eamonn Duffy – bass; Aaron Moore – drums. 2007: Lloyd; Apparley; Matt Wood – guitar; Stephen Lowe – bass; Daren Garratt – drums. 2009: John Roberts replaced Lowe – bass. For Lloyd, see Robert Lloyd & The New Four Seasons)

Born Again in Birmingham	25	2006
Black Country	26	2006
What No Blog?	14	2007
Eleven Fingers	17	2007
Plenty of Spare	46	2007
I Am Grimaldi	6	2009

93MillionMilesFromTheSun
(Nick Mainline – guitar/vocals; Rob Hogg – bass)

Waiting There (Noise)	15	2010

Nirvana
(Kurt Cobain – guitar/vocals; Kris Novoselic – bass; Dan Peters – drums. 1991: Dave Grohl replaced Peters – drums. 1994: acoustic line-up added Pat Smeat – guitar; Lori Goldston – cello. For Peters, see also Mudhoney)

Sliver	23	1990
Smells Like Teen Spirit	1	1991
Drain You	16	1991
Lithium	25	1991
Breed	48	1991
Scentless Apprentice	40	1993
Rape Me	45	1993
The Man Who Sold the World	27	1994
Where Did You Sleep Last Night?	40	1994
About a Girl	44	1994
Smells Like Teen Spirit	8	1999AT

Novak
(Adele Williams – vocals; Jeremy Hepburn – guitar; Jane Smith – guitar; Kirsten Morley – bass; David Gerard – keyboards; Tasmin Snell – flute; Phillip Robinson – drums)

Rapunzel	6	1997

N-Type
(aka Mark Newton – DJ/producer)

Tolerance	42	2006

Nurse With Wound: see Stereolab

O

Of Montreal
(Kevin Barnes – various/vocals; Bryan Poole – guitar; James Huggins, aka James Husband – guitar/various; Nina Twin, aka Nina Grottland – bass)

Heimdalsgate Like a Promethean Curse	45	2007

Okkervil River
(Will Sheff – guitar/piano/vocals; Brian Cassidy – guitar; Jonathan Meiburg – guitar/piano; Patrick Pestorius – bass; Scott Brackett – synthesizers/coronet/hammond organ/percussion; Zachary Thomas – mandoloin; Scott Jackson – violin; Kathleen Pittman – violin; Sarah Pizzicheni – violin; Tammy Vo – violin; Katie Nott – viola; Will Thothong – viola; Caitlin Bailey – cello; Frances Smith – French horn, clarinet; Travis Nelsen – drums/percussion)

Our Life Is Not a Movie or Maybe	25	2007

Ollo
(Alex Crowfoot – various; Lars Chresta – various. Remix of The Dodgems: Doug Potter – guitar/vocals; Gary Turner – bass/vocals; Paul Birchall – keyboards; Charlie Zuber - drums)

Lord Lucan Is Still Missing	8	2005

One Thousand Violins
(Vincent Keenan – vocals; Colin Gregory – guitar; Darren Swindells – bass; David Warmsley – keyboards; Ian Addie – drums)

Like One Thousand Violins	49	1985

The Only Ones
(Peter Perrett – guitar/vocals; John Perry – guitar; Alan Mair – bass; Mike Killie – drums)

Another Girl, Another Planet	17	1978
Another Girl, Another Planet	20	1979
Another Girl, Another Planet	28	1980
Another Girl, Another Planet	41	1981
Another Girl, Another Planet	24	1982AT
Another Girl, Another Planet	18	1999AT

The Orb
(Alex Patterson and Jim Cauty – producers, with Andy Falconer, Youth, aka Martin Glover and Thrash, aka Kristian Weston. 1992: Thrash – synthesizers; Aisha, aka The High Priestess – vocals; Steve Hillage – guitar; Jah Wobble, aka John Wardle – bass. For Cauty, see also KLF. For Wobble, see also Public Image Ltd and Primal Scream. For Youth, see also Killing Joke)

Loving You	10	1990
Little Fluffy Clouds	42	1990
Blue Room	20	1992

Orbital
(Paul Hartnoll – keyboards; Phil Hartnoll – keyboards. *Orbital & Angelo Badalamenti, with vocals – Leonardo DiCaprio)

Are We Here?	31	1994
The Box	7	1996
Out There Somewhere	47	1996
Style	15	1999
*Beached	45	2000

The Orch
(Michael Conroy, aka Michael Conroy Harris – vocals; Phil Hayes – guitar; Damian Ashcroft – keyboards)

Kenny & The Snake	21	2010
Ingland Strip	41	2011

Ought
(Tim Beeler – guitar/vocals; Matt May – keyboards; Ben Stidworthy – bass; Tim Keen – drums/violin)

Today, More Than Any Other Day	43	2014

P

The Pains of Being Pure at Heart
(Kip Berman – guitar/vocals; Peggy Wang – keyboards/vocals; Alex Naidus – bass; Kurt Feldman – drums)

Everything With You	13	2008
Come Saturday	28	2008
Young Adult Friction	2	2009
Higher Than The Stars	25	2009
Say No To Love	7	2010
I Wanna Go All The Way	42	2011

Palace Brothers
(Will Oldham – guitar/vocals; Brian McMahan – guitar; Todd Brashear – bass; Britt Walford – drums. For Oldham, see also Bonnie 'Prince' Billy. For McMahan, Brashear and Walford, see also Slint)

Ohio River Boat Song	9	1993

Pale Saints
(Ian Masters – bass/vocals; Graeme Naysmith – guitar; Chris Cooper – drums)

Sight of You	11	1989
She Rides the Waves	25	1989

Panda Bear
(aka Noah Lennox – guitar/synthesizer/piano/drums/vocals. See also Animal Collective)

Comfy in Nautica	47	2007

The Parallelograms
(Meriel – vocals/glockenspiel; Markie – guitar; Tonieee – bass; Ian – drums)

1, 2, 3, Go!	44	2008

Paranormal
(aka Angela – various/vocals)

Movin' Twistin' Groovin'	11	2005

Paris Angels
(Rikki Turner – vocals; Jayne Gill – percussion/vocals; Paul Wagstaff – guitar; Mark Adge – guitar; Scott Carey – bass; Steven Blake – programming; Simon Worrall – drums)

(All On You) Perfume	6	1990

John Parish & Polly Jean Harvey
(Polly Jean Harvey – guitar/vocals; John Parish – guitar/percussion; Jeremy Hogg – guitar; Rob Ellis – drums. 2009 (released as PJ Harvey & John Parish: Harvey; Parish; Giovani Ferrario – guitar; Eric Drew Feldman – bass; Carla Azar – drums. For Harvey, Parish, Feldman and Ellis, see also PJ Harvey)

That Was My Veil	17	1996
Taut	23	1996
Black Hearted Love	18	2009

Party of One
(Eric Fifteen – guitar/vocals; Terrika Kleinknecht, aka Thunder Goddess 666 – bass; Geoff McCusick – drums)

Shotgun Funeral	24	2003

The Passage
(Dick Witts – keyboards/percussion/vocals; Andrew Wilson – guitar; Paul Mahoney – drums)

XOYO	41	1982

The Pastels
(Stephen Pastel, aka Stephen McRobbie – guitar/vocals; Aggi Pastel, aka Annabel Wright – vocals; Brian Taylor – guitar; Martin Hayward – bass; Bernice Simpson – drums)

Truck Train Tractor	23	1986

Pavement
(Stephen Malkmus – guitar/vocals; Spiral Stairs, aka Scott Kanberg – guitar; Gary Young – drums; Bob Nastanovich – percussion. 1994: added Mark Ibold – bass; Steve West replaced Young – drums. 1999: Young returned alongside West)

Summer Babe	34	1991
Trigger Cut	8	1992
Here	10	1992
In the Mouth of a Desert	35	1992
Summer Babe (Winter Version)	37	1992
Circa 1762	42	1992
Conduit For Sale	47	1992
Range Life	14	1994
Gold Soundz	22	1994
Cut Your Hair	34	1994
Father to a Sister of Thought	40	1995
Major Leagues	31	1999
Carrot Rope	45	1999
Here	50	1999AT

Peaking Lights
(Indra Dunis - keyoards/vocals; Aaron Coyes – keyboards/vocals)

All the Sun that Shines	33	2011

Pere Ubu

(David Thomas – vocals; Keith Moline – guitar; Michele Temple – guitar; Daryl Boon – guitar/piano/clarinet/saxophone; Tom Herman – bass; Robert Wheeler – synthesizers/theremin; Gagarin – electronic percussion/synthesizers; Steven A. Mehlman - drums)

Golden Surf II	48	2014

Period Pains
(Chloe Alper – bass/vocals; Felicity Aldridge – guitar; Laura Warwick – bass; Magda, aka Magdalena Przbylski - drums)

Spice Girls (Who Do You Think You Are?)	4	1997

Pete & The Pirates
(Thomas Sanders – vocals; Pete Hefferan – guitar/vocals; David Thorpe – guitar; Peter Cattermoul – bass; Jonny Sanders – drums)

Knots	40	2007

Peter, Bjorn & John
(Peter Moren – guitar/vocals; Victoria Bersman – vocals; Bjorn Yttling – bass/keyboards; John Eriksson – drums)

Young Folks	5	2006

The Phantom Light
(Anthony Jones – vocals; Aisha Chaouche – vocals; Jason Jones – guitar; Simon Jones – guitar; Ed Purcell – bass; Shaun Moseley – keyoards; Matty James – drums/percussion)

Sky Lanterns	30	2010
Echoes of Ghosts	50	2011
The Greater Picture	41	2012

Pico
(Lianne Hall – vocals; Boo – various)

Chard	50	2001

Pigbag
(James Johnstone – guitar/keyboards; Simon Underwood – bass; Ollie Moore – saxophone; Chip Carpenter – drums; Roger Freeman – percussion)

Papa's Got a Brand New Pigbag	39	1981

Pinhole
(Matt McManaman – guitar/vocals; Ben Gordon – guitar; Charlie Turner – bass; Bryan Johnson – drums)

So Over You	8	2002

Pink Floyd
(Roger Waters – bass/vocals; David Gilmour – guitar; Richard Wright – keyboards; Nick Mason – drums)

Echoes	4	1976
Shine On You Crazy Diamond	8	1976
Pigs	14	1977
Shine On You Crazy Diamond	29	1978
Shine On You Crazy Diamond	30	1978

Pipettes
(Rosay, aka Rose Elinor Doughall – vocals; Gwenno Saunders - vocals; RiotBecki, aka Rebecca Stephens – vocals; backed by The Cassettes: Monster Bobby, aka Robert Barry – guitar; Jon Falcone – bass; Seb Falcone – keyboards; Robin of Loxley, aka Joe Van Moyland – drums)

Dirty Mind	21	2005
Pull Shapes	19	2006

Pixies
(Black Francis, aka Charles Thompson – guitar/vocals; Joey Santiago – guitar; Kim Deal, aka Mrs John Murphy – bass/vocals; David Lovering – drums. 'Monkey Gone to Heaven' also features: Corine Metter – violin; Karen Karlsrud – violin; Ann Rorich – cello; Arthur Fiacco – cello. For Deal, see also The Breeders)

Gigantic	7	1988
Where is My Mind?	30	1988
River Euphrates	39	1988
Bone Machine	45	1988
Debaser	3	1989
Monkey Gone to Heaven	5	1989
Wave of Mutilation	36	1989
Here Comes Your Man	37	1989
Dead	43	1989
The Happening	24	1990
Velouria	31	1990
Allison	48	1990
Dig For Fire	49	1990
Planet of Sound	26	1991
Motorway to Roswell	46	1991
Bird Dream of the Olympic Mons	47	1991
Debaser	30	1999AT

Placebo
(Brian Molko – guitar/vocals; Stefan Olsdal – guitar/bass/keyboards; Robert Schultzberg – drums)

Teenage Angst	39	1996

Plasticman
(Chris Reed – DJ/producer)

Cha	42	2004

The Playing Fields
(Steve Bland – guitar/vocals; Mike Bland – guitar/vocals; Jeff Baskett – bass; Hannah Sless – violin; Ron Rosenblum – drums)

Hello New World	7	2006

Plone
(Mike 'Billy' Bainbridge – keyboards; Mark Cancellara – keyboards; Michael Johnston – keyboards)

Plock	16	1998
Be Rude to Your School	34	1999

Henry Plotnick
(Henry Plotnick – keyboards/vocals)

Wapiti	30	2014

The Pocket Gods
(Mark Christopher Lee – guitar/vocals; Annie Moeke – guitar/vocals; Claire Lee – bass; Nigel Ewer – drums)

Superman's Head	50	2008

Poco
(Paul Cotton – guitar/vocals; Timothy Schmit – bass/vocals; Rusty Young – pedal steel; Al Garth – saxophone/violin)

Rose of Cimarron	11	1976

The Pogues
(Shane McGowan – vocals; Spider Stacey, aka Peter Stacey – tin whistle/percussion/vocals; Jem Finer – guitar/banjo; Cait O'Riordan – bass; James Fearnley – accordian; Andy Ranken, aka The Clobberer – drums. 'I'm a Man…' featured O'Riordan – vocals. 1985 (except 'A Pair of…'): added Philip Chevron – guitar)

Dark Streets of London	45	1984
Sally Maclennane	13	1985
A Pair of Brown Eyes	20	1985
I'm a Man You Don't Meet Every Day	25	1985
The Body of an American	50	1986

Pond
(Charlie Campbell – guitar/vocals; Chris Brady – bass/vocals; Dave Triebwasser – drums)

Young Splendor	27	1992

Pooh Sticks
(Hue Williams – vocals; Paul – guitar; Alison – bass; Trudi Tangerine – piano/keyboards/tambourine; Stephanie Bass – drums)

On Tape	34	1988

Iggy Pop
(Iggy Pop, aka James Osterberg – vocals; Carlos Alomar – guitar; Ricky Gardiner – guitar; Tony Sales – bass; David Bowie – keyboards; Hunt Sales – drums. For Bowie and Alomar, see also David Bowie)

Success	28	1977

Pop Off Tuesday
(Minori Odaira – guitar/vocals; Hiroki Miyauchi – keyboards/programming)

Unworldly	5	1998

Popguns
(Wendy Morgan – vocals; Simon Pickles – guitar; Greg Dixon – guitar; Pat Walkington – bass; Shaun Charman – drums. For Charman, see also The Wedding Present)

Landslide	46	1989

Portishead
(Beth Gibbons – vocals; Adrian Utley – guitar; Neil Solman – keyboards; Geoff Barrow – programming. 2008: now without Solman)

Sour Times	8	1994
Machine Gun	12	2008
The Rip	22	2008

Postal Blue
(Adriano C. Ribeiro – guitar/vocals; Francinalto Lacerda – guitar; Ismael Braz – bass; Andre Costa - drums)

The Last Goodbye	26	2014

Postcode
(Marie Reynolds – vocals; Mikie Daugherty – guitar; Kieran Ball – guitar; Steve Halsall – bass; Jonny Peacock – drums)

Sunfield	28	2013

Prefab Sprout
(Paddy McAloon – guitar/vocals; Wendy Smith – vocals; Martin McAloon – bass; Neil Conti – drums)

Faron Young	38	1985

Primal Scream
(Bobby Gillespie – vocals; Jim Beattie – guitar; Robert Young – bass; Tom McGurk – drums; Martin St John – tambourine. 1991: Gillespie; Andrew Innes – guitar; Young – guitar; Henry Olsen – bass; Martin Duffy – keyboards; Paul Taylor – programming; guest appearance from Jah Wobble, aka John Wardle – vocals. For Gillespie, see also *Jesus & Mary Chain*. For Duffy, see also *Felt*. For Wobble, see also *Public Image Ltd* and *The Orb*)

It Happens	44	1985
Velocity Girl	4	1986
Higher than the Sun	11	1991

The Primitives
(Tracy Tracy – vocals; Paul Court – guitar/vocals; Steve Dullagon – bass; Pete Tweedie – drums)

Really Stupid	23	1986
Stop Killing Me	19	1987
Crash	46	1988

Prince
(aka Prince Rogers Nelson – guitar/various/vocals)

Sign 'O' the Times	32	1987

The Prodigy
(Keith Flint – vocals; MC Maxim Reality, aka Keith Palmer – vocals; Leroy Thornhill – synthesizer; Liam Howlett – keyboards/programming/percussion)

Firestarter	37	1996

Prolapse
(Mick Derrick – vocals; Linda Steelyard – vocals; Pat Marsden – guitar; David Jeffreys – guitar; Mick Harrison – bass; Donald Ross-Skinner – keyboards; Tim Pattison – drums)

Autocade	24	1997
Slash/Oblique	30	1997

Propaganda
(Claudia Brucken – vocals; Susanne Freytag – keyboards; Ralf Dorper – keyboards; Michael Mertens – percussion)

Dr Mabuse	31	1984

Propellerheads
(Alex Gifford – producer; Will White – producer)

Velvet Pants	28	1997

Psychedelic Furs
(Richard Butler – vocals; John Ashton – guitar; Roger Morris – guitar; Tim Butler – bass; Duncan Kilburn – keyboards; Phil Calvert – drums. For Calvert, see also *Birthday Party*)

Love My Way	29	1982

Public Enemy
(Chuck D, aka Carlton Ridenhour – vocals; Flavor Flav, aka William Drayton – vocals; Terminator X, aka Norman Lee Rodgers – DJ. 1987: featured Bill Stephney – guitar/bass. For Chuck D, see also *Sonic Youth*)

Rebel Without a Pause	14	1987
You're Gonna Get Yours	38	1987
Night of the Living Baseheads	50	1988

Public Image Ltd
(John Lydon – vocals; Keith Levene – guitar; Jah Wobble, aka John Wardle – bass; Jim Walker – drums. 'Death Disco': Dave Crowe replaced Walker – drums. 1983: Lydon; Levene; Pete Jones – bass; Martin Atkins – drums. 2012: Lydon; Lu Edmonds – guitar/banjo; Scott Firth – bass/synthesizer; Bruce Smith – drums)

Public Image	9	1978
Public Image	9	1979
Death Disco	28	1979
Public Image	11	1980
Poptones	33	1980
Careering	34	1980
Public Image	26	1981
Public Image	20	1982AT
This is Not a Love Song	12	1983
Lollipop Opera	36	2012

Public Service Broadcasting
(J. Willgoose Esq – guitar/compter/sampling; Wrigglesworth – drums)

Spitfire	5	2013
Signal 30	12	2013

Pulp
(Jarvis Cocker – vocals; Russell Senior – guitar; Stephen Mackey – bass; Candida Doyle – keyboards; Nick Banks – drums. 1995: added Mark Webber – guitar/piano. 1998: now

without Senior. 'Trees' featured Scott Walker – keyboards. 'Sunrise' featured Richard Hawley – guitar/lap steel; Julian Poole – percussion. For Cocker, Mackey and Hawley, see also Jarvis Cocker)

Razzamatazz	14	1993
Lipgloss	46	1993
Do You Remember the First Time?	13	1994
Common People	21	1994
Babies	23	1994
Common People	1	1995
Sorted for E's & Whizz	2	1995
I-Spy	8	1995
Mis-Shapes	12	1995
Disco 2000	27	1995
Underwear	31	1995
This is Hardcore	8	1998
Common People	12	1999AT
Sunrise	19	2001
Trees	29	2001

Pussy Riot
(Nadezhda Tolokonnikova; Maria Alyokhina; Yekaterina Samutsevich; Fara; Shaiba; plus others. Band identities remain anonymous during performance)

Putin Has Pissed Himself (Putin Zassal)	12	2012

Q

Qwel & Jackson Jones
(Qwel, aka Adam Vincent Schreiber – vocals; Dallas Jackson, aka Jeff Kuglich – DJ; Dr Jones – DJ)

The CD Exchange	24	2009

Quickspace
(Tom Cullinan – guitar/vocals; Nina Pascale – guitar/vocals; Sean Newsham – bass; Paul Shilton – keyboards; Chin – drums. 1998: Steve Denton replaced Chin – drums. For Cullinan, see also Th' Faith Healers)

Friend	24	1996
If I Were a Carpenter	39	1998

R

Racing Cars
(Morty, aka Gareth Mortimer – vocals; Graham Headley-Williams – guitar/vocals; Ray Ennis – guitar/vocals; David Land – bass/vocals; Geraint Watkins – keyboards; Roy Edwards – keyboards; Bob Wilding – drums)

They Shoot Horses Don't They?	7	1976

The Raconteurs
(Jack White – guitar/vocals; Brendan Benson – guitar; Jack Lawrence – bass; Patrick Keeler – drums. For White, see also White Stripes)

Steady As She Goes	34	2006

The Radio Dept
(Johan Duncanson – guitar/vocals; Martin Larsson - guitar; Daniel Tjader – keyboards; Matthias Olden – saxophone)

Heaven's On Fire	14	2010

Radio Luxembourg
(Meilyr Jones – bass/vocals; Alun Gaffey – guitar; Dylan Hughes – keyboards; Gwion Llewellyn – drums)

Pwer Y Fflwe	27	2005

Radiohead
(Thom Yorke – guitar/vocals; Ed O'Brien – guitar; Jon Greenwood – guitar; Colin Greenwood – bass; Phil Selway – drums. For Yorke, see also PJ Harvey)

Creep	31	1993
Kid A	25	2000
Idioteque	48	2000
Pyramid Song	40	2001
There There	37	2003

| All I Need | 42 | 2007 |

Railway Children
(Gary Newby – guitar/vocals; Brian Bateman – guitar; Stephen Hull – bass; Guy Keegan – drums)

| Brighter | 28 | 1987 |

Ramones
(Joey Ramone, aka Jeffrey Hyman – vocals; Johnny Ramone, aka John Cummings – guitar; Dee Dee Ramone, aka Douglas Covin – bass; Tommy Ramone, aka Thomas Erdelyi – drums)

| Pinhead | 23 | 1977 |

Red Cosmos
(Kim Tortoise, aka Tim Tortoise: various/vocals. 2012: features Junior Tortoise – vocals. See also Bourbon Somersault the 3rd and Cyclic Freeload Unit)

| Son of Morris | 45 | 2009 |
| I Am The Local DJ | 16 | 2012 |

Red Guitars
(Jeremy Kidd – vocals; Hallam Lewis – guitar; John Rowley – guitar; Louise Barlow – bass; Matt Higgins – drums)

| Good Technology | 11 | 1983 |

Redskins
(Chris Dean – guitar/vocals; Martin Hewes – bass; Nick King – drums)

Peasant Army	31	1982
Lean On Me	30	1983
Keep On Keepin' On	10	1984

Rezillos
(Eugene Reynolds, aka Alan Forbes – vocals; Fay Fife, aka Sheila Hynde – vocals; Luke Warm, aka Jo Callis – guitar; Mark Harris – guitar; D.K.Smythe – bass; Alan Patterson – drums)

| I Can't Stand My Baby | 4 | 1977 |
| I Can't Stand My Baby | 20 | 1978 |

Jonathan Richman & The Modern Lovers
(Jonathan Richman – guitar/vocals; Ernie Brooks – bass; Jerry Harrison – keyboards; Dave Robinson – drums)

| Roadrunner | 33 | 1976 |

Ride
(Mark Gardener – guitar/vocals; Andy Bell – guitar/vocals; Stephen Queralt – bass; Laurence Colbert – drums)

Dreams Burn Down	3	1990
Like a Daydream	4	1990
Taste	25	1990
Leave Them All Behind	40	1992

Mat Riviere
(Mat Riviere – keyboards/vocals)

| In ~2 Seconds | 39 | 2013 |

Tom Robinson
(Tom Robinson – bass/vocals; Richard Mazda – guitar; Steve Laurie – drums)

| War Baby | 50 | 1983 |

ROC
(Karen Sheridan – vocals; Fred Browning – guitar; Patrick Nicholson – programming)

| Girl with a Crooked Eye | 46 | 1994 |

Rock of Travolta
(Handsome Dave Travolta – guitar; John Travolta – bass; Phil Travolta – bass/keyboards; Deadly Dave Travolta – keyboards; Ros Travolta – cello; Stumpy Joe Travolta – drums)

| Giant Robo | 48 | 2001 |

Rolling Stones
(Mick Jagger – vocals; Keith Richards – guitar; Brian Jones – guitar; Bill Wyman – bass; Charlie Watts – drums. 'Brown Sugar': Mick Taylor replaced Jones – guitar)

| Brown Sugar | 13 | 1976 |
| Jumping Jack Flash | 39 | 1976 |

Paul Rooney
(Paul Rooney – various/vocals. 1998 as Rooney – Paul Rooney – guitar/vocals; Ian Jackson – bass; Colin Cromer – keyboards/drums/percussion)

| Went to Town | 44 | 1998 |
| Lucy Over Lancashire | 5 | 2007 |

Rose of Avalanche
(Phillip Morris – vocals; Paul Berry – guitar; Glenn Schultz – guitar; Alan Davis – bass; Nicol Mackay – drums)

| L.A. Rain | 26 | 1985 |

The Royal We
(Jihae Simmons – vocals; Roxanne Clifford – guitar; Patrick Doyle – guitar; Graeme Ronald – bass; Joan Sweeney – violin;

Colin Kearney – drums. For Clifford and Doyle, see Veronica Falls)

| All The Rage | 48 | 2007 |

The Ruts
(Malcolm Owen – vocals; Paul Fox – guitar; John Jennings – bass; Dave Ruffy – drums. For Ruffy, see also *Aztec Camera* and *Zion Train*)

In a Rut	11	1979
Babylon's Burning	47	1979
In a Rut	19	1980
In a Rut	31	1981
In a Rut	35	1982AT

S

Sabres of Paradise
(Andy Weatherall, Gary Burns. Jugs Kooner and Nina Walsh – producers. Track features Wonder Schneider – vocals; Tom Baeppler – guitar)

| Wilmot | 19 | 1994 |

Safe Deposit
(aka P.-A. Aeschlimann – keyboards/programming)

| You Can't | 50 | 1995 |

St Vincent
(aka Anne Erin Clark – guitar/vocals; with Daniel Mintseris – keyboards; Bobby Sparks – minimoog; Ralph Carney – horns; Homer Steinweiss – drums)

| Digital Witness | 44 | 2014 |

Saints
(Chris Bailey – vocals; Ed Kuepper – guitar; Kym Bradshaw – bass; Ivor Hay – drums)

| (I'm) Stranded | 35 | 1977 |

Salako
(James Waudby – guitar/vocals; David Langdale – guitar; Luke Barwell – bass; Stu – keyboards; Tommy Spencer – drums. Track also features choir of 200 people)

| Look Left | 19 | 1999 |

Saloon
(Amanda Gomez – vocals; Matt Ashton – guitar; Michael Smoughton – bass; Alison Cotton – viola; Adam Cresswell – drums)

Impact	12	2001
Freefall	49	2001
Girls are the New Boys	1	2002
Have You Seen the Light?	26	2002

Salt Tank
(Malcolm Stanners – keyboards/programming; David Gates – keyboards/programming)

| Charged Up | 36 | 1994 |

Santogold
(aka Santi White – vocals; Chris Feinstein – guitar; J. Salamao – guitar; John Hill – bass/keyboards; Alex Lipsen – keyboards; John Morrical – keyboards; Alfonzo Hunter – horns; J. Louis – horns; L. Benjamin – horns; Chuck Treece – percussion; Mike Dillon – percussion)

| L.E.S. Artistes | 47 | 2008 |

Sarandon
(Crayola, aka Simon Williams – guitar/vocals; Alan Brown – bass; Tom Greenhalgh - drums)

| Kill Twee Pop! | 24 | 2008 |

Savages
(Jenny Beth, aka Camille Berthomier – vocals; Gemma Thompson – guitar; Ayse Hassan – bass; Fay Milton – drums)

Husbands	1	2012
She Will	16	2013
Fuckers	13	2014

Schneider TM KPT.michi.gan
(Schneider TM, aka Dirk Dresselhaus – producer; JPT.michi.gan, aka Michael Beckett – guitar/keyboards)

| The Light 3000 | 8 | 2000 |

The School
(Liz Hunt – vocals; Harri Davidson – guitar; Ivan Moult – guitar; Ryan Cox – bass; Kay Russant – violin; Fran Dimech – trumpet; Steph Doble – strings; Rich Chitty – drums)

| Let It Slip | 16 | 2008 |

Gil Scott-Heron
(Gil Scott-Heron – piano/ vocals; Pat Sullivan – guitar; Chris Cunningham – guitar/synthesiser; Damon Albarn – keyboards; Kim Jordan – piano; Christiana Liberis – strings; Mary Jo Stilp – strings. For Albarn, see also *Blur* and *Elastica*)

| I'm New Here | 10 | 2010 |

Scritti Politti
(Green Gartside – guitar/vocals; Nial Jinks – bass; Mike MacEvoy – synthesizers; Matthew K. – pgoramming; Tom Morley – linn drum. 'The Sweetest Girl' also featured: Mgotse Mothle – double bass; Robert Wyatt – piano. For Wyatt, see also *Matching Mole*, *Working Week* and *Robert Wyatt*)

The Sweetest Girl	22	1981
Faithless	13	1982
Asylums in Jerusalem	18	1982
The Sweetest Girl	27	1982AT

Seapony
(Jen Weidl – guitar/vocals; Danny Rowland - guitar; Ian Brewer – bass)

| Dreaming | 36 | 2011 |

Sebadoh
(Lou Barlow – guitar/vocals; Jason Loewenstein – bass; Eric Gaffney – drums. For Barlow, see also *Dinosaur Jr*)

| Soul & Fire | 7 | 1993 |
| Rebound | 16 | 1994 |

Secret Goldfish
(Kate McCullars – vocals; John Morose – guitar; Steven McSeveney – bass; Paul Turnbull – drums)

| Dandelion Milk Summer | 23 | 1997 |

Seedhill Bruiser
(aka Tim Wilson – guitar/bass/keyboards/mandolin/violin/percussion/vocals)

| Trees | 29 | 2011 |

Seedling
(Marg Van Eenbergen – guitar/vocals; Bas Jacobs – bass; Susanne Linssen – violin/vocals; Mariken Smit – drums)

| Sensational Vacuum | 37 | 2001 |

Seize The Day
(Shannon Smy – guitar/vocals; Theo Simon – hand-drums/vocals; David Williams – guitar/strings; Dan Hayward – bass; Elizabeth Gray – fiddle/harp; Faith Rhodes – saxophone; Rich Whistance – didgeridoo/hand-drums; Ali Blackburn – percussion)

| Flying | 47 | 2006 |

Senseless Things
(Mark Keds – guitar/vocals; Morgan Nicholls – bass; Cass Browne – drums)

| Too Much Kissing | 42 | 1989 |

Senser
(Heitham Al-Sayed – percussion/vocals; Nick Michaelsen – guitar; James Barrett – bass; Haggis – bass/engineer; Andy Awe, aka Andy Clinton – DJ; Kersten Haigh – flute; John Morgan – drums)

| Eject | 21 | 1993 |

Serious Drinking
(Martin Simon – vocals; Eugene – vocals; Andy – guitar; Jem – bass; Lance – drums)

| Love on the Terraces | 38 | 1982 |

70 Gwen Party
(Vicctor N'Dip – guitar/vocals; Lurgin Pin – bass/keyboards/vocals)

| Auto Killer UK | 28 | 1991 |

Sex Pistols
('Anarchy in the UK'- Johnny Rotten, aka John Lydon – vocals; Steve Jones – guitar; Glen Matlock – bass; Paul Cook – drums. Other material: Jones replaced Matlock – bass. For Lydon, see also *Public Image Ltd*)

Holidays in the Sun	11	1977
Anarchy in the UK	1	1978
God Save the Queen	3	1978
Pretty Vacant	6	1978
Holidays in the Sun	18	1978
EMI	45	1978
Anarchy in the UK	1	1979
God Save the Queen	13	1979
Holidays in the Sun	14	1979
Pretty Vacant	16	1979
Anarchy in the UK	1	1980
Holidays in the Sun	12	1980
Pretty Vacant	23	1980
God Save the Queen	25	1980

Anarchy in the UK	2	1981
Holidays in the Sun	17	1981
God Save the Queen	38	1981
Anarchy in the UK	1	1982AT
God Save the Queen	25	1982AT
Holidays in the Sun	37	1982AT
Pretty Vacant	44	1982AT
Anarchy in the UK	4	1999AT
Pretty Vacant	29	1999AT

Shalawambe
(Emmanuel Kabwe – guitar/vocals; Ricky Chote – guitar/vocals; Claudie Kabwe – bass; Gerlad Bwalande – keyboards; Julian Chande Kabwe – drums)

| Samora Machel | 37 | 1988 |

Sham 69
(Jimmy Pursey – vocals; Dave Parsons – guitar; Albie Maskell – bass; Mark Cain – drums)

| I Don't Wanna | 22 | 1977 |

Benjamin Shaw
(Benjamin Shaw – guitar/vocals; Jack Hayter – pedal steel; Lieven Scheerlinck – piano/trumpet; Uncle Rico – percussion. For Jack Hayter, see also *Hefner*.

| Goodbye Cagoule World | 5 | 2014 |
| You & Me | 17 | 2014 |

Shellac
(Steve Albini – guitar/vocals; Rob Weston – bass; Todd Trainder – drums. For Albini, see also *Big Black*)

Crow	18	1994
The Dog & Pony Show	24	1994
Prayer to God	19	2000
Riding Bikes	14	2014
Dude Incredible	19	2014

The Shins
(James Mercer – guitar/vocals; Neal Langford – bass; Marty Crandall – keyboards; Jessie Sandoval – drums)

| New Slang | 43 | 2001 |

Shitmat
(Henry Collins – DJ/producer)

| There's No Business Like Propa' Rungleclotted Mashup Bizznizz | 33 | 2004 |

Shop Assistants
(Alex Taylor – vocals; David Keegan – guitar; Sarah Kneale – bass; Laura MacPhail – drums/percussion. For Taylor, see also *The Motorcycle Boy*)

All That Ever Mattered	17	1985
All Day Long	50	1985
Safety Net	8	1986
I Don't Want to Be Friends With You	43	1986

Short Stories
(Tim Rippington – guitar/vocals; Stephen Miles – guitar/vocals; Geoff Gorton – bass; Kay Farnell – keyboards; Simon Harrison – drums, For Rippington, see also *Beatnik Filmstars, Forest Giants* and *Flatmates*)

| Angry Young Man | 32 | 2013 |

Shrag
(Helen King – keyboards/vocals; Steph Goodman – keyboards/vocals; Bob Brown – guitar/vocals; Russell Warrior – bass; Helen – keyboards; Andy Pyne – drums)

| Devastating Bones | 17 | 2012 |

Sigur Ros
(Jon Thor Birgisson – guitar/vocals; Georg Holm – bass; Kjartan Sveinsson – keyboards; Orri Pall Dyrason – drums)

| Svefn G Englar | 47 | 2000 |
| Festival | 38 | 2008 |

Simple Minds
(Jim Kerr – vocals; Charlie Birchall – guitar; Derek Forbes – bass; Mick McNeill – keyboards; Kenny Hyslop – drums. 'Glittering Prize': Mike Ogletree replaced Hyslop – drums. 'Someone...': Mel Gaynor replaced Ogletree – drums)

Promised You a Miracle	30	1982
Someone, Somewhere in Summertime	32	1982
Glittering Prize	45	1982

Siouxsie & The Banshees
(Siouxsie Sioux, aka Susan Dallion – vocals; John McKay – guitar; Steve Severin – aka Steven Bailey – bass; Kenny Morris – drums, except: *McGeogh replaed McKay – guitar; Budgie, aka Peter Clark, replaced Morris – drums. 1983: Robert Smith replaced McGeogh – guitar. For McGeogh, see also *Magazine*. For Smith, see also *The Cure*)

Hong Kong Garden	22	1978
Helter Skelter	34	1978
Overground	38	1978

Switch	41	1978
Mirage	42	1978
Jigsaw Feeling	43	1978
Metal Postcard	50	1978
Love in a Void	21	1979
Icon	35	1979
Switch	38	1979
Jigsaw Feeling	42	1979
Playground Twist	44	1979
Helter Skelter	46	1979
Hong Kong Garden	48	1979
Jigsaw Feeling	37	1980
Switch	44	1980
Icon	45	1980
Hong Kong Garden	47	1980
Jigsaw Feeling	35	1981
*Israel	37	1981
Icon	40	1981
Switch	49	1981
*Fireworks	16	1982
*Slowdive	23	1982
*Melt	49	1982
*Israel	15	1982AT
Jigsaw Feeling	39	1982AT
Switch	42	1982AT
Icon	45	1982AT
Hong Kong Garden	46	1982AT
Dear Prudence	20	1983

Sisters of Mercy
('Alice': Andrew Eldritch, aka Andrew Taylor – vocals; Gary Mars, aka Mark Pearman – guitar; Ben Gunn, aka Benjamin Matthews – guitar; Craig Adams – bass. Other material: Wayne Hussey replaced Gunn – guitar. For Hussey and Adams, see also The Mission)

Temple of Love	19	1983
Alice	27	1983
Walk Away	8	1984
Emma	15	1984
Marian	36	1985
Some Kind of Stranger	43	1985

Six By Seven
(Chris Okey – guitar/vocals; Sam Hempton – guitar; Paul Douglas – bass; James Flower – keyboards; Chris Davis – drums)

| Helden | 43 | 1999 |

65 Days of Static
(Joe Shrewsbury – guitar; Paul Wolinski – guitar/programming; Simon Wright – bass; Rob Jones – drums)

| Retreat! Retreat! | 25 | 2004 |
| Drove Through Ghosts To Get Here | 24 | 2005 |

The Skids
(Richard Jobson – guitar/vocals; Stuart Adamson – guitar; Bill Simpson – bass; Tom Kellechan – drums)

| Into the Valley | 37 | 1979 |

Skream
(aka Oliver Dene Jones – DJ/producer)

| Chest Boxing | 27 | 2007 |
| Fields of Emotion | 48 | 2010 |

Sky Larkin
(Katie Harkin – guitar/keyboards/vocals; Doug Adams – bass; Nestor Matthews – drums)

| Matador | 29 | 2009 |
| Antibodies | 43 | 2009 |

Sleeper
(Louise Wener – guitar/vocals; Jon Stewart – guitar; Diid Osman – bass; Andy MacClure – drums)

| Delicious | 20 | 1994 |
| Swallow | 48 | 1994 |

Slowdive
(Rachel Goswell – guitar/vocals; Neil Halstead – guitar/vocals; Brook Savill – guitar; Nicholas Chaplin – bass; Neil Carter – drums)

| Catch the Breeze | 20 | 1991 |

Slum of Legs
(Tamsin – vocals; Kate – guitar; Alex – bass; Emily – keyboards; Maria – violin; Michelle – drums)

| Razorblade the Tape | 35 | 2014 |

Sluts of Trust
(John McFarlane – guitar/vocals; Anthony O'Donnell – drums)

| Piece of You | 16 | 2003 |
| Leave You Wanting More | 5 | 2004 |

Smashing Pumpkins
(Billy Corgan – guitar/vocals; James Iha – guitar; D'Arcy

Sretsky – bass/vocals; Jimmy Chamberlain – drums)

| Siva | 27 | 1991 |

Marc Smith vs Safe N Sound
(Mark Smith – DJ; Safe N Sound: Jon, aka Sharkey – DJ; Pete, aka K-Komplex – DJ)

| Identify the Beat | 9 | 2002 |

The Smiths
(Morrissey, aka Steven Morrissey – vocals; Johny Marr, aka John Maher – guitar; Andy Rourke – bass; Mike Joyce – drums. 'Ask' and 'Panic' featured Craig Gannon – guitar. 'Sheila...' featured Kirsty Maccoll – vocals. Marr also featured on mandolin on 'Please Please Please...', on piano on 'Meat is Murder' and harmonica on 'Hand in Glove'; Morriseey featured on piano on 'I Won't Share You'. For Morrissey, Rourke, Joyce, Gannon and Maccoll, see also Morrissey. For Marr, see Billy Bragg, Electronic and Modest Mouse)

This Charming Man	2	1983
Reel Around the Fountain	6	1983
Hand in Glove	9	1983
Handsome Devil	22	1983
How Soon is Now?	1	1984
Nowhere Fast	14	1984
What Difference Does It Make?	17	1984
William, It Was Really Nothing	23	1984
Heaven Knows I'm Miserable Now	24	1984
Please Please Please, Let Me Get What I Want	28	1984
Reel Around the Fountain	36	1984
The Boy with the Thorn in His Side	8	1985
The Headmaster Ritual	29	1985
That Joke Isn't Funny Anymore	31	1985
Meat is Murder	32	1985
Well I Wonder	41	1985
There is a Light That Never Goes Out	1	1986
Panic	5	1986
I Know It's Over	6	1986
The Queen is Dead	7	1986
Ask	11	1986
Bigmouth Strikes Again	12	1986
Cemetry Gates	35	1986
Last Night I Dreamt That Somebody Loved Me	5	1987
Stop Me if You Think You've Heard This One Before	12	1987
Girlfriend in a Coma	15	1987
Paint a Vulgar Picture	21	1987
Sweet & Tender Hooligan	23	1987
Half a Person	24	1987
Death of a Disco Dancer	25	1987
I Won't Share You	29	1987
Sheila Take a Bow	34	1987
I Started Something I Couldn't Finish	40	1987
Shoplifters of the World Unite	45	1987
How Soon is Now?	7	1999AT
There is a Light That Never Goes Out	9	1999AT
This Charming Man	22	1999AT

Smog
(aka Bill Callahan – guitar/vocals. 2000: also featured Jeff Parker – guitar; Matt Lux – bass; John McEntire – drums. For McEntire, see also Bastro, Tortoise and Stereolab)

| Cold Blooded Old Times | 35 | 1999 |
| Dress Sexy at My Funeral | 40 | 2000 |

Snatch
(Patti Palladin – vocals; Judy Nylon – guitar/vocals)

| I.R.T. | 50 | 1977 |

Snuff
(Simon Crighton – guitar/vocals; Andy Wells – bass; Duncan Redmonds – drums/vocals)

| Not Listening | 44 | 1989 |

Sodastream
(Karl Smith – guitar/vocals; Pete Cohen – bass/double bass/piano)

| Turnstyle | 45 | 1998 |

Solar Race
(Eilidh Bradley – guitar/vocals; Andrew Holland – bass; Carl Rogers – drums)

| Not Here | 39 | 1995 |

Solex
(aka Eliabeth Essenlink – various/vocals)

| All Lickety Split | 19 | 1998 |
| One Louder Solex | 23 | 1998 |

Some Chicken
(Ivor Badcock – vocals; Jess Chicken – guitar; Terry Bull, aka Mike Nowicki – bass; Galway Kinnel, aka Bob – drums)

| New Religion | 16 | 1977 |

Son of Dave

(aka Benjamin Darvill – guitar/harmonica/percussion/vocals)

Goddamn   40   2005

Sonic Subjunkies
(Holger Phrack – vocals; Thaddeus Herrman – producer/programming; Rob Marvin - programming)

Do You Even Know Who You Are?   16   1999

Sonic Youth
(Thurston Moore – guitar/vocals; Lee Ranaldo – guitar; Kim Gordon – bass/vocals; Steve Shelley – drums. 'Kool Thing' featured Chuck D – vocals. 'Youth Against Fascism' featured Ian MacKaye – guitar. For Chuck D, see also Public Enemy)

Schizophrenia	13	1987
(I Got A) Catholic Block	37	1987
Teenage Riot	19	1988
Silver Rocket	29	1988
Tunic (Song For Karen)	5	1990
Kool Thing	40	1990
Youth Against Fascism	7	1992
Sugar Kane	17	1992
100%	23	1992
Theresa's Sound World	26	1992
Superstar	47	1994

Sons & Daughters
(Scott Paterson – guitar/vocals; Adele Bethel – guitar/keyboards; Ailidh Lennon – bass; Dave Gow – drums)

Johnny Cash   7   2004

Soul Bossa
(Peter Jones – guitar/vocals; Tracey Bellaries – bass; Michael Ford – drums)

Sore Loser   44   1996

The Soundcarriers
(Carly Collingwood – keyboards/vocals; Dorian Conway – guitar; Pish, aka Paul Isherwood – bass; Adam Cann – drums)

Entropicalia   46   2014

Soup Dragons
(Sean Dickson – guitar/vocals; Jim McCulloch – guitar; Sushil K. Dade – bass; Ross Sinclair – drums)

Hang Ten!	17	1986
Whole Wide World	25	1986

Spacemen 3
(Sonic Boom, aka Pete Kember – vocals; Jason Pierce – guitar; Will Carruthers – bass; Jon Mattock – drums. For Pierce, Carruthers and Mattock, see also Spiritualized)

Hypnotised   33   1989

Spare Snare
(Jan Burnett – guitar/vocals; Alan Cormack – guitar; Paul Esposito – bass; Barry Gibson – guitar/drums)

Bugs   32   1995

The Specials
(Terry Hall – vocals; Neville Staples – vocals; Lynval Goulding – guitar/vocals; Roddy Radiation, aka Roderick Byers – guitar; Horace Gentleman, aka Horace Painter – bass; Jerry Dammers, aka Gerald Dankin – keyboards; Brad, aka John Bradbury – drums. *As Special AKA. 1983: Stan Campbell – vocals; Rhoda Dakar – vocals; Egidio Newton – vocals; John Shipley – guitar; Radiation; Gary McManus – bass; Dammers; Brad. For Golding and Dammers, see also Robert Wyatt)

*Gangsters	7	1979
Too Much Too Young	36	1979
*Gangsters	32	1980
Ghost Town	21	1981
Ghost Town	43	1982AT
*Nelson Mandela	41	1983

Jon Spencer Blues Explosion
(Jon Spencer – guitar/vocals; Judah Bauer – bass; Russell Simins – drums)

2 Kindsa Love   22   1996

Spidersleg
(aka Rob Johnson – guitar/keyboards/programming/vocals)

Salt   38   2011

Spiritualized
(Kate Radley – vocals; Jason Pierce – guitar; Mark Refoy – guitar; Will Carruthers – bass; John Mattock – drums. 1997: Pierce – guitar/vocals; Radley; Sean Cook – bass; Damon Reece – percussion. 1998: Pierce; Cook; Reece; also featured Paul Bernard – vocals; Tony Clarke – vocals; Janice Whyne – vocals; Denise Seally – vocals; Jason Thompson – vocals; Thighpaulsandra – piano; Dinah Beamish – strings; Sally Herbert – strings; Jocelyn Pook – strings; John Singleton – strings; Kevin Brown – horn; Rob Charles – horn; Tony Robinson – horn; Raymond Dickaty – flute. For Pierce, Carruthers and Mattock, see also Spacemen 3. For Dickaty, see also Stereolab)

Any Way That You Want Me	37	1990
Ladies & Gentlemen We Are Floating in Space	18	1997
Oh Happy Day	22	1998

Spit
(Vinnie Spit – guitr/vocals)

| Road Pizza | 32 | 1988 |

Spizz Energi
(Spizz, aka Kenneth Spiers – guitar/vocals; Dave Scott – guitar; Jim Solar, aka James Little – bass; Mark Coalfield – keyboards; Brian B. Benzine – drums)

| Where's Captain Kirk? | 40 | 1980 |

SPK
(Sinan Leong – percussion/vocals; Oblivion, aka Derek Thompson – guitar/bass/synthesizers/percussion; Graeme Revell – electronics)

| Metal Dance | 39 | 1983 |

The Spook School
(Nye Todd – guitar/vocals; Adam Todd – guitar; Anna Cory – bass; Niall McCamley – drums)

| I'll Be Honest | 9 | 2013 |

Sportique
(Gregory Webster – guitar/vocals; Mark Flunder – guitar; Rob Pursey – bass. For Pursey, see also Heavenly and Tender Trap)

| Kids are Solid Gold | 46 | 1998 |

Bruce Springsteen & The E Street Band
(Bruce Springsteen – guitar/vocals; Steve Van Zandt – guitar; Garry Tallent – bass; Danny Federici – keyboards; Roy Bittan – piano; Clarence Clemens – saxophone; Max Weinberg – drums)

| Born to Run | 26 | 1978 |

Squarepusher
(aka Tom Jenkinson – keyboards/programming)

| My Red Hot Car | 20 | 2001 |

Stabmaster Vinyl
(aka Geraint Ffrancon – producer/DJ)

| Masho Fe Lan Star | 46 | 2005 |

Standard Fare
(Emma Kupa – bass/vocals; Danny How – guitar/vocals; Andy Beswick – drums)

Dancing	47	2009
Philadelphia	1	2010
Older Women	47	2012

Uke Stanza
(aka Colin Shaddick – guitar/vocals)

| You Will With Ivor Cutler | 50 | 2006 |
| The Picket Line | 24 | 2007 |

Status Quo
(Francis Rossi – guitar/vocals; Rick Parfitt – guitar; Alan Lancaster – bass; Andy Bown – keyboards; John Coghlan – drums)

| Can't Give You More | 25 | 1977 |

Stereolab
(Laetitia Sadier – vocals; Mary Hansen – guitar/percussion/vocals; Tim Gane – guitar/keyboards; Sean O'Hagan – guitar/keyboards; Duncan Brown – guitar/bass; Andy Ramsay – keyboards/percussion. 1994: added Katherine Gifford – keyboards. 'Les Yper Sound': Sadier; Hansen; Gane; Brown; Morgane Lhote – guitar/keyboards; Ramsay. 'Cybele's Reverie: as previous, plus O'Hagan; John McEntire; Raymond Dickerty. 1997/'Fluorescences': Sadier; Hansen; Gane; Richard Harrison – bass; Ramsay. 1999: Sadier; Hansen; Gane: Lhote; Simon Johns – bass; Ramsay; McEntire; O'Hagan; Kevin Hopper – musical saw. 2001: Sadier; Hansen; Gane; O'Hagan; McEntire; Johns; Jim O'Rourke – keyboards/percussion. *Stereolab & Nurse with Wound, aka Simon Stapleton. For Gane, see McCarthy. For Gane, Sadier and McEntire, see Tortoise. For McEntire, see Smog and Bastro. For Hopper, see Stump. For Dickerty, see Spiritualized)

French Disko	5	1993
Jenny Ondioline	39	1993
Ping Pong	9	1994
Pop Quiz	33	1995
Cybele's Reverie	11	1996
Fluorescences	20	1996
Les Yper-Sound	50	1996
*Simple Headphone Mind	14	1997
Fluorescences	20	1997
Miss Modular	26	1997
The Free Design	46	1999
French Disko	36	1999AT
Captain Easychord	45	2001

Steveless

(Dan Newman – guitar/vocals; Simon Peter Jarvis – guitar; Rhys Herman – keyboards; Matt Williams – drums)

| Bored | 9 | 2005 |

Rod Stewart
(Rod Stewart – vocals; Ron Wood – guitar; Sam Mitchell – guitar; Andy Pyle – bass; Ian McLagan – organ; Mickey Waller – drums)

| Maggie May | 34 | 1976 |

Stiff Little Fingers
(Jake Burns – guitar/vocals; Henry Cluney – guitar; Ali McMordie – bass; Brian Faloon – drums)

Suspect Device	4	1978
Alternative Ulster	11	1978
Alternative Ulster	6	1979
Suspect Device	8	1979
Johnny Was	15	1979
Wasted Life	18	1979
Alternative Ulster	9	1980
Johnny Was	16	1980
Suspect Device	24	1980
Wasted Life	27	1980
Alternative Ulster	16	1981
Johnny Was	24	1981
Suspect Device	32	1981
Alternative Ulster	16	1982AT
Johnny Was	29	1982AT
Suspect Device	31	1982AT

Stone Roses
(Ian Brown – vocals; John Squire – guitar; Mani, aka Gary Mounfield – bass; Reni, aka Alan Wren – drums)

I am the Resurrection	6	1989
She Bangs the Drums	7	1989
Made of Stone	17	1989
Fool's Gold	23	1989
I Wanna Be Adored	29	1989

The Stranglers
(Hugh Cornwell – guitar/vocals; Jean-Jacques Burnel – bass; Dave Greenfield – keyboards; Jet Black, aka Brian Duffy – drums)

London Lady	21	1977
Hanging Around	32	1978
No More Heroes	33	1978
London Lady	40	1978
No More Heroes	45	1979

Strawberry Switchblade
(Jill Bryson – guitar/vocals; Rose McDowell – guitar/vocals; Roddy Frame – guitar; Mark Bedford – bass; Kate St John – oboe. For Frame, see also *Aztec Camera*. For Bedford, see also *Robert Wyatt*)

| Trees & Flowers | 47 | 1983 |

The Strokes
(Julian Casablancas – vocals; Nick Valensi – guitar; Albert Hammond Jr – guitar; Nikolai Fraiture – bass; Fab Moretti – drums)

Last Nite	5	2001
Hard to Explain	7	2001
The Modern Age	18	2001
New York City Cops	28	2001
Someday	46	2001

Stump
(Mick Lynch – vocals; Chris Salmon – guitar; Kevin Hopper – bass; Rob McKahey – drums. For Hopper, see also *Stereolab*)

| Charlton Heston | 35 | 1988 |

Suburban Studs
(Eddy Zipps – guitar/vocals; Keith Owen – guitar; Paul Morton – bass; Steve Poole – drums)

| Questions | 43 | 1977 |

Suede
(Brett Anderson – vocals; Bernard Butler – guitar/keyboards; Matt Osman – bass; Simon Gilbert – drums)

| The Drowners | 15 | 1992 |

Sugar
(Bob Mould – guitar/vocals; Dave Barbe – bass; Malcolm Travis – drums. For Mould, see also *Husker Du*)

Changes	16	1992
A Good Idea	21	1992
Helpless	48	1992

Sugarcubes
(Bjork Gudmundsdottir – vocals; Einar Orn Benediktsson – vocals; Thor Eldon Jonson – guitar; Bragi Olafsson – bass; Einar Mellas – keyboards; Siggi Baldursson – drums)

| Birthday | 1 | 1987 |
| Deus | 20 | 1988 |

Birthday	23	1999AT

Suicidal Birds
(Jessie – guitar/vocals; Chay – bass/vocals)

Me Animal	41	2005

The Sundays
(Harriet Wheeler – vocals; David Gavurin – guitar; Paul Brindley – bass; Patrick Hannan – drums)

Can't Be Sure	1	1989
Here's Where the Story Ends	37	1990
Can't Be Sure	47	1999AT

Super Furry Animals
(Gruff Rhys – guitar/vocals; Huw Bunford – guitar/vocals; Guto Pryce – bass; Cian Ciaran – keyboards; Dafydd Ieuan – drums. For Ieuan, see also Catatonia. For Rhys, see also Mogwai. For Ciaran, see also Acid Casuals)

God Show Me Magic	49	1996
Ice Hockey Hair	29	1998
Fire in My Heart	17	1999
Northern Lites	24	1999
The Turning Tide	27	1999
(Drawing) Rings Around the World	21	2001
Slow Life	46	2003
Cardiff in the Sun	21	2009

Supergrass
(Gaz Coombes – guitar/vocals; Mickey Quinn – bass; Danny Goffey – drums)

Caught by the Fuzz	5	1994
Alright	13	1995

Superman Revenge Squad
(aka Ben Parker – guitar/vocals)

Idiot Food	18	2008

The Sweeney
(Murray Torkildsen – guitar/vocals; Sid – bass; Adam Batterbee – drums)

Why?	9	1996

T

June Tabor
(June Tabor – vocals; Jon Gillespie – piano/synthesizer)

No Man's Land	40	1977

Tall Pony
(Paul Towey – keyboards/vocals; Tony Gate – keyboards/vocals)

I'm Your Boyfriend Now	1	2006
I'm Your Boyfriend Now	35	2007

Tame Impala
(Kevin Parker – guitar/bass/keyboards/vocals; Dominic Simper – bass/percussion; Jay Watson – guitar/keyboards/ drums)

Elephant	37	2012

Teen Canteen
(Carla Easton – keyboards/vocals; Amanda Williams – guitar/vocals; Sita Pierrachini – bass/vocals; Deborah Smith – drums/vocals)

Honey	29	2013

Teenage Fanclub
(Norman Blake – guitar/vocals; Raymond McGinley – guitar/vocals; Gerard Love – bass; Brendan O'Hare – drums)

Everything Flows	11	1990
God Knows It's True	43	1990
Star Sign	5	1991
The Concept	6	1991
Like a Virgin	36	1991
Baby Lee	13	2010

Ten Tigers

(M – guitar/flute/saxophone/clarinet/bass./vocals; Manda – guitar/vocals; CK – bass/vocals; PK – drums/percussion)

| Superlucky | 40 | 2009 |

Tender Trap
(Amelia Fletcher – vocals; Emily Bennett – guitar/vocals; Rob Pursey-guitar; John Stanley – bass; Katrina Dixon – drums. For Fletcher, see also Hefner and The Wedding Present. For Fletcher and Pursey, see also Talulah Gosh, Heavenly and Marine Research For Pursey, see also Sportique)

| MBV | 8 | 2012 |

Thee Oh Sees
(John Dwyer – guitar/vocals; Brigid Dawson – vocals; Chris Woodhouse – bass/drums/percussion; Mikal Cronin – saxophone; Heidi Alexander – trumpet; K. Dylan Edrich – viola)

| Lupine Dominus | 49 | 2012 |

These New Puritans
(Jack Barnett – various/vocals; Thomas Hein – keyboards/bass/drums; Sophie Sleigh-Johnson – keyboards; George Barnett – drums)

| We Want War | 19 | 2010 |

Thomas Tantrum
(Megan Thomas – guitar/vocals; David Miatt – guitar/vocals; Jimmy Shivers – bass; Ken Robshaw – drums)

| Swan Lake | 43 | 2008 |

Rosie Taylor Project
(Johnny – guitar/vocals; Jon – guitar/vocals; Nick – bass; Sam – keyboards; Sophie – trumpet; Shakey – drums)

| Sleep | 35 | 2011 |

Tilly & The Wall
(Neely Jo Jenkins – vocals; Kianna Alarid – bass/vocals; Derek Pressnall – guitar; Nick White – keyboards; Jamie Lynn Pressnall. Aka Jamie Williams – tap dancing)

| Reckless | 46 | 2006 |

Tinariwen
(Ibrahim Ag Alhabib – guitar/vocals; Hassan Ag Touhami – guitar/vocals; Abdallah Ag Alhousseyni – guitar/vocals; Elaga Ag Hamid – guitar; Abdallah Ag Lamida, aka Intidao – guitar; Eyadou Ag Leche – bass; Said Ag Ayad – percussion; Mohammad Ag Tahada – percussion)

| Matadjem Yinmixan | 32 | 2007 |

Tingle in the Netherlands
(Helen T – vocals; Owen J – keyboards/various)

| Prostitute's Handbag | 11 | 2010 |

Town Bike
(Sarah Maher – vocals; Morgan Brown – guita/vocals; Jane Slavin – bass; Peter Charles – drums)

| Dougie | 27 | 2008 |

Trouserdog
(Woz, aka Warren Trousers – vocals; Rich – guitar; Jim – bass; James – synthesizer; Aidan – drums)

| Taxi For Tit Boy | 13 | 2007 |
| Apocalypse for Gary Glitter | 28 | 2007 |

The Truth About Frank
('Frank' & 'Frank' – keyboards/vocals)

| The Headless Rentman | 9 | 2010 |

Chris T-T
(Chris T-T, aka Christopher Thorpe-Tracey – guitar/piano/vocals; Owen Turner – guitar/cornet; Andrew Raynor – drums)

| Nintendo | 3 | 2010 |

Tullycraft
(Sean Tollefson – bass/vocals; Jenny Mears – percussion.vocals; Chris Munford – guitar/vocals; Corianton Hale – guitar/vocals; Jeff Fell – drums)

| Lost in Light Rotation | 33 | 2013 |

tUnE-yArDs
(Merrill Garbus – ukulene/percussion/vocals; Nate Brenner – bass/ukulele/vocals)

| Bizness | 24 | 2011 |

TV on the Radio
(Tunde Adebimpe – vocals; Kyp Malon – guitar/bass/vocals; Katrina Ford – vocals; Jaleel Bunton – guitar/drums; Dave Sitek – guitar/synthesizer; Martin Perna – baritone saxophone)

| Wolf Like Me | 8 | 2006 |

Twiggy & The K-Mesons
(aka Michael Valentine West – producer/various)

Preset Love	14	2011

The 2 Bears
(Joe Goddard – producer/DJ; Raf Rundell – producer/DJ)

Bear Hug	20	2011

U

Uffie
(Uffie, aka Anna-Catherine Hartley – vocals; Feadz, aka Fabien Planta – DJ)

Pop The Glock	31	2006

Undertones
(Feargal Sharkey – vocals; John O'Neill – guitar; Damian O'Neill; Mike Bradley – bass; Billy Doherty – drums. 2003: Paul McLoone replaced Sharkey. For Sharkey, see The Assembly. For John & Damian O'Neill, see That Petrol Emotion)

Teenage Kicks	10	1978
Teenage Kicks	2	1979
Get Over You	12	1979
You've Got My Number	29	1979
Jimmy Jimmy	31	1979
Teenage Kicks	7	1980
Get Over You	17	1980
Teenage Kicks	6	1981
Get Over You	20	1981
Teenage Kicks	8	1982AT
Get Over You	36	1982AT
Teenage Kicks	2	1999AT
Thrill Me	4	2003
Oh Please	22	2003

Underworld
(Rick Smith – keyboards/vocals; Karl Hyde – keyboards/vocals; Darren Emerson – keyboards)

Tyrannasaurus Dead
(Eleanor Rudge – vocals; Billy Lowe – guitar/vocals; Martin Edwards – guitar; Thomas Northam – bass; Rupert Willows – drums)

Sadie	34	2013
Local Bullies	34	2014

Dirty Epic	43	1994
Born Slippy	5	1996

Unknown Cases
(Reebop Kwaku Baah – percussion/vocals; Helmutt Zerlett – keyboards; Stefan Krachten – drums)

Masimba Bele	26	1984

Urusei Yatsura
(Graham Kemp – guitar/vocals; Fergus Lawrie – guitar/vocals; Elaine – bass; Ian Graham – drums)

Kewpies Like Watermelon	45	1996

The Users
(Phil James – vocals; Chris Free – guitar; Bobby Kwock – bass; Andrew Bor – drums)

Sick of You	37	1977

U2
(Bono Vox, aka Paul Hewson – vocals; The Edge, aka David Evans- guitar; Adam Clayton – bass; Larry Mullen – drums)

New Year's Day	41	1983

UZ
(UZ, more accurately ΩZ – producer)

Trapshit	35	2013

V

The Vacant Lots
(Jared Artaud – guitar/vocals; Brian McFadyen – percussion/vocals)

Mad Mary Jones   28   2014

Van Basten
(Van Basten – producer)

King of the Death Posture   38   1995

Sharon Van Etten
(Sharon Van Etten – guitar/organ/vocals; Heather Woods Broderick – vocals; David Hartley – guitar/bass; Jacob C. Morris – organ/piano. For Hartley, see also War On Drugs)

Your Love is Killing Me   50   2014

The Vaults
(Beaz Harper – vocals; Jimmy Vandel – guitar; Richie Kicks – bass; Eddy Treasure – drums)

I'm Going   50   2003
No Sleep, No Need   50   2004

The Velvet Underground
(Lou Reed – guitar/vocals; Sterling Morrison – guitar; John Cale – electric viola; Maureen Tucker – drums, For Cale, see also Nick Drake)

Heroin   42   1999AT

The Venopian Solitude
(Suiko Takahara – guitar/vocals)

Mother Nature & Father Man-Made   18   2010

Veronica Falls
(Roxanne Clifford – guitar/vocals; James Hoare – guitar/vocals; Mario Herbain – bass; Patrick Doyle – drums. For Clifford and Doyle, see also The Royal We)

Bad Feeling   9   2011
My Heart Beats   28   2012
Buried Alive   41   2013

Vert:x
(Neil Whitehead – guitar/bass/keyboards/drums. See also The Chasms)

Full Fathom Five   9   2012

Veruca Salt
(Nina Gordon – guitar/vocals; Louise Post – guitar/vocals; Steve Lack – bass; Jim Shapiro – drums)

Seether   3   1994

Verve
(Richard Ashcroft – guitar/vocals; Nick McCabe – guitar; Simon Jones – bass; Peter Salisbury – drums)

All in the Mind   49   1992

The Very Most
(Jeremy Jensen – all instruments; featuring Vinnie Ransome – vocals)

Wond'ring   33   2014

Very Things
(The Shend, aka Chris Shendo, aka Chris Harz – vocals; Sir Robin Dalloway, aka Nibbs, aka Robin Raymond – guitar; Fudger O'Mad, aka Budge – bass; Gordon Disneytime, aka Robin Holland – drums. 1986: now without O'Mad)

The Bushes Scream While My Daddy Prunes   27   1984
This is Motortown   30   1986

The Vibes
(Gaz Voola, aka Gary Boniface – vocals; Johnny 'Mother' Johnson, aka Johnny 'Tub' Johnson – guitar; Fuzz Fung – guitar; Lloyd – bass; Johnny J. Beat – drums. For Johnson, see also Flaming Stars)

I'm in Pittsburgh (and it's Raining)   37   1985

Kurt Vile
(Kurt Vile – guitar/vocals; Meg Baird – vocals; Mike Polizze – bass; Rob Laasko – keyboards; Lea Cho – keyboards; Mike Zanghi – drums)

Baby's Arms   40   2011

Violet Violet
(Cheri Violet – guitar/vocals; Violet Fliss – drums/vocals)

C C C Cat	26	2009

Vive La Fete
(Els Pynoo – tapes/vocals; Danny Mammens – guitar)

Noir Desir	15	2003

Von Bondies
(Jason Stollsteimer – guitar/vocals; Marcie Bolan – guitar/vocals; Anjula Basker – bass; Rajni Bhatia – keyboards; Stefania – drums)

It Came From Japan	33	2002

Von Sudenfed
(Mark E. Smith - vocals; Jan St Werner – keyboards/computer; Andi Tona – keyboards/computers. For Smith, see also *The Fall, Inspiral Carpets, Long Fin Killie, D.O.S.E. and Elastica*)

The Rhinohead	9	2007
Fledermaus Can't Get It	10	2007

Voodoo Queens
(Anjali Bhatia – guitar/vocals; Ella Drauglis – guitar; Anjula Basker – bass; Rajni Bhatia – keyboards; Stefania – drums)

Supermodel Superficial	6	1993

VR ft Dr Devious & The Wisemen
(Dr Devious, aka Paul Walden – producer)

Cyberdream	25	1992

W

Wah!
(Pete Wylie – guitar/vocals; Carl Washington – bass; Charlie Griffiths – keyboards; Jay Naughton – piano; Chris Joyce – drums. 'Remember' (as Shambeko! Say Wah!) : Wylie; Washington; Henry Priestman – keyboards; Paul Barlow – drums. 'Come Back' as The Mighty Wah!)

The Story of the Blues	7	1982
Remember	44	1982
Come Back	5	1984

Joe Walsh
(Joe Walsh – guitar/vocals; supported by *Barnstorm*: Kenny Passarelli – bass; Rocke Grace – keyboards; Joe Vitale – drums; Joe Lala – percussion)

Rocky Mountain Way	28	1976

The War Crimes
(Edward S. Dodd - vocals; Owen Gaffney - guitar)

Treatise	31	2010

The War On Drugs
(Adam Granduciel – guitar/vocals; Anthony LaMarca – guitar; David Hartley – bass; RJon obbie Bennett – keyboards; Jon Natchez – saxophone; Charlie Hall – drums. For Hartley, see also *Sharon Van Etten*)

Red Eyes	6	2014

Warpaint
(Emily Kokal – guitar/vocals; Theresa Wayman – guitar/vocals; Jenny Lee Lindberg – bass; Stella Mozgawa – keyboards/drums)

Undertow	4	2010

Wax Audio
(aka Tom Compagnoni – guitar/percussion/computer; Benson Graham – bass; Hamish Ford – drum embedding)

Imagine This	44	2005

Weather Prophets
(Pete Astor – guitar/vocals; Oisin Little – guitar; Greenwood Golding – bass; Dave Morgan – drums)

Almost Prayed	13	1986

Marlene Webber
(Marlene Webber – vocals; Lloyd Campbell – producer)

Right Track	7	1977

The Wedding Present
(David Gedge – guitar/vocals; Pete Salowka – guitar; Keither Gregory – bass; Shaun Charman – drums. 1988: Simon Smith replaced Charman – drums. 1992: Paul Dorrington replaced Salowka - guitar. 1994: Darren Belk replaced Gregory – bass.

1995/96 material: Gedge; Belk; Smith, except '2, 3, Go': Gedge; Simon Cleave - guitar; Jayne Lockey – bass; Smith. 2004: Gedge; Cleave; Terry de Castro – bass; Kari Paavola – drums. 2008: Gedge; Christopher McConville – guitar; de Castro; Graeme Ramsay – drums. 2012: Gedge; Ramsay – guitar/piano/harmonium; Pepe le Moko – bass; Charles Layton – drums/percussion. 2013: Gedge; Patrick Alexander – guitar; Katharine Wallinger – bass; Layton – drums. 'Everyone Thinks He Looks Daft' featured Amelia Fletcher – vocals. For Gedge, Cleave, de Castro and Paavola, see also *Cinerama*. For Fletcher, see also *Talulah Gosh, Heavenly, Marine Research, Tender Trap* and *Hefner*)

Go Out & Get 'Em Boy	15	1985
Once More	16	1986
This Boy Can Wait	18	1986
You Should Always Keep in Touch with Your Friends	28	1986
Everyone Thinks He Looks Daft	3	1987
My Favourite Dress	6	1987
A Million Miles	8	1987
Anyone Can Make a Mistake	10	1987
Getting Nowhere Fast	31	1987
Nobody's Twisting Your Arm	2	1987
Take Me (I'm Yours)	4	1987
Why Are You Being So Reasonable Now?	8	1988
I'm Not Always So Stupid	15	1988
Don't Laugh	49	1988
Kennedy	2	1989
Take Me	14	1989
Brassneck	19	1989
Bewitched	24	1989
What Have I Said Now?	45	1989
Make Me Smile (Come Up & See Me)	7	1990
Corduroy	9	1990
Don't Talk, Just Kiss	18	1990
Heather	20	1990
Crawl	22	1990
Dalliance	39	1990
Dalliance	8	1991
Dare	12	1991
Fleshworld	16	1991
Rotterdam	22	1991
Octopussy	32	1991
Come Play with Me	4	1992
Flying Saucer	14	1992
Silver Shorts	18	1992
Love Slave	19	1992
Blue Eyes	24	1992
Sticky	41	1992
Falling	46	1992
Swimming Pools Movie Stars	15	1994
Click Click	30	1994
So Long Baby	37	1994
Spangle	39	1994
Sucker	3	1995
2, 3, Go	36	1996
Go Man Go	46	1996
Brassneck	21	1999AT
My Favourite Dress	25	1999AT
Interstate 5	36	2004
I'm From Further North Than You	31	2005
The Thing I Like Best About Him Is His Girlfriend	20	2008
Don't Take Me Home Until I'm Drunk	42	2008
End Credits	14	2012
Two Bridges	1	2013

Weekend

(Alison Statton – bass/vocals; Spike – guitar; Harry Beckett – trumpet/flugelhorn; Larry Stabbins – saxophone; Simon Booth – drums. For Stabbins and Booth, see also *Working Week*)

A View From Her Room	43	1982

We've Got a Fuzzbox & We're Gonna Use It

(Maggie Dunne – guitar/vocals; Vickie Perks – vocals; Jo Dunne – bass; Tina O'Neill – drums/saxophone)

Rules & Regulations	31	1986

Wheat

(Scott Levesque – guitar/vocals; Ricky Brennan – guitar; Brendan Harvey – drums)

Don't I Hold You?	50	1999

White Stripes

(Jack White – guitar/vocals; Meg White – drums/percussion. For Jack White, see also *The Raconteurs*)

Hotel Yorba	2	2001
Fell in Love with a Girl	6	2001
Dead Leaves and the Dirty Ground	25	2001
Dead Leaves and the Dirty Ground	15	2002
Fell in Love with a Girl	27	2002
Seven National Army	10	2003
Black Math	17	2003
Icky Thump	16	2007

White Town

(aka Jyoti Prakash Mishra – producer/vocals)

Your Woman	31	1996

The Who
(Roger Daltry – vocals; Pete Townshend – guitar; John Entwhistle – bass; Keith Moon – drums)

Won't Get Fooled Again	29	1976
My Generation	39	1978
My Generation	32	1979

Wild Swans
(Paul Simpson – vocals; Jerry Kelly – guitar; Alan – bass; Ged Quinn – keyboards; Alan Willis – drums)

Revolutionary Spirit	10	1982

Will & Rick
(Will Youds & Rick Cavers - various)

Hot Dog Man	16	2009

Phil Wilson
(Phil Wilson – guitar/vocals; Arash Torabi – bass; Jon Hunter – trumpet; Frank Sweeney – viola; Andy Fonda – drums. For Wilson, Torabi and Fonda, see also *The Granite Shore*)

I Own It	6	2010

Wire
(Colin Newman – guitar/keyboards/vocals; Bruce Gilbert – guitar/vocals; Graham Lewis – bass; Robert Gotobed, aka Mark Field – drums)

99.9	34	2002

Withered Hand
(aka Dan Willson – guitar/vocals)

Horseshoe	8	2004

The Wolfhounds
(David Callahan – guitar/vocals; Andy Golding – guitar/vocals; Richard Golding – bass; Peter Wilkins – drums)

Cheer Up	18	2013
Divide & Fall	43	2013

The Wolfmen
(Chris Constantinou – bass/vocals; Marco Pirroni – guitar; Zelig Preston Heyman – percussion. For Pirroni, see also *Adam & The Ants*)

Cecilie	19	2008

Wolfram Wire
(aka Dan Werner – producer/various. See also *Broadcast & Wolfram Wire*)

Armitage Shanks	32	2008

Wooden Shjips
(Erik 'Ripley' Johnson – guitar/vocals; Dusty Jermier – bass; Nash Whalen – organ; Omar Ahsanuddin – drums)

Flight	37	2011

Woodentops
(Rolo McGinty – guitar/vocals; Simon Mawby – guitar; Frank De Freitas – bass; Alice Thompson – keyboards; Benny Staples – drums)

Move Me	19	1985
Well Well Well	48	1985

Working Week
(Tracy Thorn – vocals; Robert Wyatt – vocals; Simon Booth – guitar; Larry Stabbins – saxophone. For Wyatt, see also *Matching Mole*, *Scritti Politti* and *Robert Wyatt*. For Booth and Stabbins, see also *Weekend*)

Venceremos (We Will Win)	50	1984

Would Be's
(Julie O'Donnell – vocals; Matthew Finnegan – guitar; Eamonn Finnegan – bass; Brendan McCahey – keyboards; Paul Finnegan – drums)

I'm Hardly Ever Wrong	12	1990

Wreckless Eric
(aka Eric Goulden – guitar/vocals; Nick Lowe – guitar/bass; Steve Goulding – drums. For Lowe, see also *Dave Edmunds*)

Whole Wide World	47	1977

Wu Lyf
(Ellery Roberts – vocals; Evans Kati – guitar; Tom McClung – bass; Joe Manning – drums)

Concrete Gold	24	2010

Robert Wyatt
(Robert Wyatt – vocals; keyboards/percussion on 'Biko'. Also featuring - 1982: Elvis Costello – backing vocals; Mark Bedders, aka Mark Bedford – bass; Clive Langer – organ; Steve Nieve – piano; Martin Hughes – drums. 1985 (Robert Wyatt & the SWAPO Singers): Richard Muzira – vocals; Ben

Mendelsohn – guitar; Lynval Golding – guitar; Mgotse Mothle – double bass; Jerry Dammers – keyboards; Claire Hurst – saxophone; Mark Lockheart – saxophone; Dick Cuthell – cornet; Annie Whitehead – trombone; Roy Dodds – drums; the SWAPO Singers: Bience Gawanas, Vaino Shivute, Lohmeier Angula, Theo Angula and Clarina Simbwayi – vocals. For Costello and Nieve, see also *Elvis Costello*. For Bedford, see also *Strawberry Switchblade*. For Golding and Dammers, see also *The Specials*. For Mothle, see also *Scritti Politti*. For Wyatt, see also *Matching Mole, Scritti Politti* and *Working Week*)

Shipbuilding	2	1982
Biko	35	1984
The Wind of Change	47	1985
Shipbuilding	11	1999AT

X

X Ray Spex
(Poly Styrene, aka Marianne Elliot-Said – vocals; Jak Airport, aka Jack Stafford – guitar; Paul Dean – bass; Lora Logic, aka Susan Whitby – saxophone; Paul Hurding – drums)

Oh Bondage Up Yours!	38	1977

Xmal Deutschland
(Anja Howe – vocals; Manuela Rickers – guitar; Wolfgang Ellerbrock – bass; Fiona Sangster – keyboards; Manuela Zwingmann – drums)

Incubus Succubus	13	1983
Qual	32	1983

Y

Yazoo
(Alison Moyet – vocals; Vince Clarke – keyboards. For Clarke, see also *The Assembly*)

Only You	12	1982

Yeah Yeah Noh
(Derek Hammond – guitar/vocals; John Grayland – guitar/vocals; Tom Slater – guitar/vocals; Adrian Crossan – bass; Sue Dorey – drums)

Bias Binding	32	1984

Yeah Yeah Yeahs
(Karen *O – vocals; Nick Zinner – guitar; Brian Chase – drums)

Bang	12	2002
Maps	18	2003

Yes
(Jon Anderson – vocals; Steve Howe – guitar; Chris Squire – bass; Rick Wakeman – keyboards; Bill Bruford – drums)

And You and I	50	1976

The Yobs
(Matt Dangerfield – guitar/vocals; Honest John Plain – guitar; Duncan 'Kid' Reid – bass; Casino Steel – organ/piano; Jack Black – drums. See also *The Boys*)

The Worm Song	19	1977

Neil Young & Crazy Horse
(Neil Young – guitar/vocals; Crazy Horse: Frank Sampedro – guitar/organ; Billy Talbot – bass; Ralph Molina – drums)

Cortez the Killer	12	1976
Like a Hurricane	8	1977
Like a Hurricane	48	1978
Walk Like a Giant	46	2012

Young Romance
(Claire – drums/vocals; Paolo – guitar)

Pale	49	2014

Yuck
(Max Bloom – guitar/vocals; Daniel Blumberg – guitar/vocals; Mariko Doi – bass; Jonny Rogoff – drums)

Georgia	49	2010
Get Away	8	2011

Z

Benjamin Zephaniah
(Benjamin Zephaniah – vocals; Dennis Bovell – guitar)

Rong Radio Station   47   1994

Zion Train
(Molora – vocals; Colin Cod – melodica; Neil Perch – bass/DJ; Dave Hake, aka David Tench – trumpet; Chris Hetter – trombone. 1996: also featured Dave Ruffy – drums. For Ruffy, see also The Ruts and Aztec Camera)

Dance of Life   14   1995
Babylon's Burning   32   1996

TOP FESTIVE FIFTY BANDS & ARTISTS

In the original book, I compiled a chart of the fifty most successful bands or artists in the history of the festive fifty. There are now significant changes to this list, mostly as a result of course of the Dandelion Radio festive fifties, but to some degree because I've decided the 1977 statistics also ought to make a contribution. In most cases, this has had little effect, but in the case of The Jam and The Damned – both of which placed a track in that chart which didn't feature subsequently – it's made a fairly substantial difference to their position here.

The scoring system is the same as previously, taking the total Gedge points for each act (based on the system devised by David Gedge, who awarded the number one 50 points and the number 50 one point, with everything that follows in between) and then multiplies this by the number of *different* tracks that this act placed in festive fifties. This allows us to include the pre-1982 festive fifties, without allowing them sizeable total marks that would be denied later entrants.

The reconfigured chart means that there is now no room for bands whose entire festive fifty career was based on a single productive year (Dreadzone, Stone Roses and The Strokes), while there are eight new entries from artists who have figured strongly during the Dandelion years. Again, data from the Truly Festive Festive Fifty has not been included.

Just outside the chart are now a number of bands who were previously in the fifty and have been edged out, in addition to others that have generated recent entries and are knocking on the door. There are also inevitably a few others that were just outside then and are still just outside now. Before listing the top fifty in detail, I thought it might be worth a look at those that are 'bubbling under'. After the 2013 festive fifty, Helen Love made a brief appearance at 75, only to be dislodged this year following the entry of Shellac at number 60.

Bubbling Under

75. Orbital (550)
74. Melys (570)
73. Madder Rose (595)
72. Killing Joke (604)
71. Bob Dylan (604)*
70. Broadcast (624)
69. Chumbawamba (628)**
68. Clinic (632)
67. House of Love (664)
66. Nick Cave & The Bad Seeds (675)
65. Cornershop (680)
64. Dead Kennedys (699)
63. Miss Black America (700)
62. Los Campesinos! (740)
61. The Strokes (775)
60. Shellac (805)

59. Stone Roses (865)
58. Fuck Buttons (935)
57. Sisters of Mercy (948)
56. Gorky'z Zygotic Mynci (1002)
55. Low (1020)
54. Dreadzone (1020)*
53. The Nightingales (1032)
52. My Bloody Valentine (1035)
51. Laura Cantrell (1092)***

*Where scores are tied, the artist with the highest single festive fifty entry has been placed higher as is the case with the list below.
**Includes points from collaborations with Credit to the Nation
***Includes points from collaboration with Ballboy

The Top Fifty

50. The Lovely Eggs
1104 pts

Singer Holly Ross cut her festive fifty teeth way back in 1997 with Angelica, but it was through her collaboration with David Blackwell as The Lovely Eggs that she truly entered the realms of the chart's heavyweights. The tunefully anarchic duo from Lancaster made a splash back in 2008 with two entries released on Rachael Neiman's Cherryade label, their highpoint coming three years later when the rabidly infectious 'Don't Look At Me (I Don't Like It)' made it to number two.

49. The Chasms
1125 pts

In years to come it may be that this abrasive yet enigmatic Isle of Man three piece finally get the recognition they deserve but, for now, it's festive fifty voters who've helped to secure for them some kind of position in the annals of recent musical history. The band released four albums, all available for free and all now sadly unavailable, and each yielded a top five festive fifty entry, the last in 2012 producing their highest placed track – 'Death's Pony' at number two. Sadly, during the countdown of that chart, it emerged that the band had split and, though there have been many interesting spin-off projects from their former members, nothing has come close to matching the majesty of their collaborative output, either from them or anyone else.

48. Elastica
1134 pts

To many, Elastica were no more than brazen rip-off merchants, riding other people's Britpop wave largely due to the company they kept and whose most applauded offerings were nothing more than blatant imitations of new wave classics. They cite 'Connection', a shameless steal from Wire, and 'Waking Up', an even less subtle heist from The Stranglers. Others cynically regarded vocalist Justine Frischmann as little more than an indie Patsy Kensit, ascending the ladder of fame on the back of well-publicised relationships with Brett Anderson and Damon Albarn.

Yet it wasn't as if Elastica were concealing or disguising their pillaging; instead they unashamedly sucked in punk and new wave influences, spraying them back at a generation who'd been unlucky enough to miss out on them first time round. Peel loved bands whose record collections remained a mystery, but the case of Elastica shows that, sometimes, an equally productive creed can be that, if you're going to steal, do it from all the right places and sound like you're enjoying it.

47. The Pains of Being Pure At Heart
1134 pts

If it's true, and for me it is, that indie pop enjoyed something of a renaissance towards the end of the first decade of the 21st century, then The Pains of Being Pure At Heart deserve credit for being one of the most important reasons for it happening.

After announcing their arrival via a split release with The Parallelograms in 2008, the band then went on to place their first four singles in the festive fifty, gaining plaudits along the way for a fresh and unpretentious approach that breathed life into their chosen genre and did much to rescue its reputation from the cynics. Especially championed by Rocker, they became one of the most played bands on Dandelion Radio, although their festive fifty star seems to have declined of late.

46. The Damned
1136 pts

The Damned were assured of their legendary status from the moment they released 'New Rose', and nothing that they did during the early eighties was going to detract from it, though a fair bit of it had a damn good try. The single enjoyed six appearances in festive fifties, still there in the 1999 all-time chart, long after the band had degenerated into an unfortunate parody of themselves, little more than a music hall act, mock-gothic anthems dished out from behind a Vanian-fronted vaudeville punk freakshow.

Captain Sensible of course added to the novelty by claiming a national number one with his cover of 'Happy Talk', a track that had the temerity to almost to make the festive fifty in that conspicuously commercial year of 1982. It did, I admit, have some cultural value in that it prompted an entirely new audience to go and check out the band, many of whom were alarmed when they then witnessed the captain appearing, as was his custom of the time, bollock-naked on stage.

The Damned would have tumbled out of this top fifty had it not been for the discovery of that 1977 chart, Peel having had the excellent taste to include the hitherto unrecognised (in festive fifty terms) speed anthem 'Neat Neat Neat' among his selections that year.

45. Teenage Fanclub
1152 pts

Like The Damned, Teenage Fanclub managed to stave off elimination from this top fifty and have actually edged up a few places since the first edition of this book, though in their case it was as one of a number of bands whose reinvigoration was well-received by the Dandelion Radio voting audience who placed their 'Baby Lee' single at number 10 in the 2010 festive fifty,

Many years earlier, they'd enjoyed a brief but highly productive flirtation with the chart, with five entries over the years of 1990 and 1991: in the initially non-broadcast chart of the latter year they had two tracks in the top ten in addition to an entry for their memorable rendition of Madonna's 'Like A Virgin' further down. Although there was a nineteen year gap before their next entry, the band weren't inactive in the period in between though their festive fifty entry followed the release of their first album for five years (*Shadows*) and further critical acclaim.

44. Babes In Toyland
1246 pts

Although Peel championed them from a very early stage and named their *Spanking Machine* album his favourite of 1990, their festive fifty career was slow getting off the ground. Subsequent releases, however, afforded Babes In Toyland multiple entries and *To Mother* and *Fontanelle* saw them take their place briefly among FF heavyweights before a disappointing decline set in at the same time as mainstream success knocked at the door, reflected in bizarrely incongruous namechecks on *Roseanne* and *Absolutely Fabulous* and their identification as godmothers of the high profile riot grrrl fad by a music media typically hell-bent on trivialisation and pigeon-holing.

To Mother remains an especially powerful example of what made this band so vital, post-*Zen Arcade* about as close as the descendents of old school American hardcore could get to a bona fide concept album. A seven-track mini-album, It's one of the few collections to manage to place more than half its tracks in a single chart, albeit the initially abandoned festive fifty of 1991.

43. Hole
1260 pts

If cynics labelled Justine Frischmann the Patsy Kensit of her time, they made Courtney Love its Yoko Ono. And those who disputed this tended to do so out of fairness to Yoko.

Like Babes In Toyland, Hole carried the largely unwanted banner of riot grrrl godmothers, slashing, aggressive guitars proceeding with the ongoing redefinition of women in rock music without, for me, the urgent thrill of the former. Love, of course, gained much notoriety as a result of her marriage to Kurt Cobain, although Peel's support for her and the band was considerable, with apparently a genuine affection prevailing between the two.

There were suggestions that Cobain's vocals had been carefully edited out of *Live Through This*, Hole's crowning glory and a record that contained as many as four festive fifty entries. I'll not comment, save to reflect that, post-Cobain, Hole's recording output became unrelentingly trite.

42. Echo & The Bunnymen
1260 pts

On reflection, it's surprising the Bunnymen didn't make even more of an impact on the festive fifties of the early eighties. It was understandably difficult for them to score heavily in the Joy Division-dominated charts of 1980-81, in which they managed to feature only with the remarkable 'Over The Wall' from their *Heaven Up Here* album, but few bands bestrode the years immediately after that with the singular power of these Liverpudlians, who managed both to capture much of the spirit of the age as well as remaining defiantly aloof from it.

Fighting off their own mythology as a result of the music media's lazy preoccupation with their genesis from the semi-mythical Crucial Three, and utterly defiant in their refusal to be pigeon-holed along with U2 and Simple Minds however much the lure of stadium rock might have remunerated them as a result, the Bunnymen were right in the vanguard of the fight, fought by Peel and very few others, against the Melody Maker, NME and Sounds and their dull efforts at categorisation during the period.

It wasn't admitted by many Bunnymen purists of the time, and many still dispute it now, but 1984's *Ocean Rain* put much of even their highly lauded earlier work into a very dark shade and, after it, the band perhaps understandably appeared to have nowhere else to go. The slick attention to production put off many, but the album's eclectic creativity has truly stood the test of time, as exemplified by its two festive fifty entries, the gorgeously poetry and sublime Will Sergeant riff of 'The Killing Moon' and the disjointed majesty of 'Thorn of Crowns'.

41. Decoration
1278 pts

Decoration's one and only Peel session was broadcast in April 2004, only months before the DJ's untimely passing, and they would place two entries in that year's festive fifty before going on to become one of the early heavyweights of the Dandelion period.

They featured in the following year's One Music chart and then gained the distinction in the first Dandelion Radio chart of 2006 of placing both sides of their 'Candidate'/'Job in London' single in the top eleven of the chart, emulating the long-standing achievement of Joy Division's 'Atmosphere'/'Dead Souls' in 1981.

Predictably, Decoration become firm Dandelion favourites, particularly of Andy Morrison's show, their classic indie guitar and drums set up finding much room within for a musical and lyrical ingenuity that set them apart from most of their contemporaries.

40. Ash
1351 pts

Ash's position at the spikily commercial end of the Peel spectrum always made them an easy target for some, as did their unabashed enjoyment for what they did, so heavily evident in the pop-punk of their 1994 debut *Trailer* that many snootily observed that it was as if they'd caught the bus 16 years too late, largely because they were travelling by pram first time round. A band of sincere teenage music lovers offering unpretentious melodies purely off the back of loving what they do can find it hard going in a cynical world.

Even those who were prepared to be positive often pointed to the fresh naivety of their sound, dismissing any possibility that a group of such tender years could be in possession of anything of great depth. A closer look at their back catalogue soon puts that theory into perspective. Their talent has been in the knowing utilisation of pop sensibilities that always stayed the right side of retro. Their craft both in terms of songwriting and promotion has since been more properly acknowledged – best exemplified in the choice of the infamous Cantona kick for the cover of their 'Kung Fu' single – and the path straddling commercial fulfilment and genuine artistic integrity is one they've walked with considerable, and in many respects surprising, dexterity. Their peak came with the top five entry of 'Girl From Mars' in the much-lauded festive fifty of 1995.

39. Super Furry Animals
1392 pts

Super Furry Animals' festive fifty life got off to a modest enough start with the vibrant 'God Show Me Magic' in 1996, an excitable, infectious piece of angular pop that hinted at the melodic strength that would be more fully realised in 1999's *Guerilla* album.

Three tracks from that album suggested a consummation of their relationship with the festive fifty that would lead to something more durable but in fact it's been a fitful affair since then, a single entry in 2001 followed by an appearance for the cascadingly brilliant 'Slow Life' in 2003 and a one-night stand with the Dandelion chart that followed six years later. While the anticipated communion with the heavyweights never happened for them, an on-off career spanning fourteen years tells something of a revealing story of a band whose longevity has surpassed the observations of those who viewed them as little more than a mid-nineties flavour of the month.

38. Inspiral Carpets
1456 pts

Conventionally regarded as third in the accepted 'Holy Trinity' of the 'Madchester' scene, behind Happy Mondays and Stone Roses, in festive fifty terms Inspiral

Carpets comfortably eclipsed the achievements of the other two. Building their distinctive sound from Clint Boon's mesmeric keyboard riffs, the Inspirals took their lead from the brooding drones of Ray Manzarek in the Doors, combining them with the playful farfisa sounds of sixties garage bands.

The Inspirals were at their best, and certainly produced many of their most prominent festive fifty moments, when Boon's sound took the lead in the recording, as in the mighty rush of 'Directing Traffik', while the band worked best lyrically when, as with the much loved 'Joe', they dealt in small obsessions and where social commentary was inferred rather than explicit. Less effective (though many festive fifty voters clearly disagreed) was the approach to a song like 'This Is How It Feels', which veers dangerously close to cliché and occasionally collides.

Their partnership with Mark E. Smith yielded one of the more predictable of festive fifty number ones and, although the band's well-received comeback in 2014 garnered much Dandelion Radio airplay but, perhaps surprisingly, it hasn't yet resulted in a return to the chart.

37. Camera Obscura
1512 pts

Although their recent output and direction probably make it unlikely that Camera Obscura will be troubling the festive fifty scorers in the future, they enjoyed a period among the chart heavyweights during the late Peel and early Dandelion years, unquestionably taking their place in the pantheon of great Scottish indie performers..

While national and regional characteristics are too often rudely exaggerated, the Caledonian pedigree of this band has always been to the fore. Their early work – including first festive fifty entry Eighties Fan – was produced by Belle & Sebastian's Stuart Murdoch and they were one of a number of Scottish bands invited by Peel to record versions of Robert Burns' poems for successive Burns' Days in the DJ's later years, achieving the distinction of becoming the only band to place their rendition in a festive fifty when 'I Love My Jean' became temporarily the band's highest placed entry in the One Music chart of 2005. When considered against the fact that The Delgados' wonderful version of 'Parcel of Rogues' never appeared in spite of that band's considerable festive fifty pedigree, the nature of the achievement is given further emphasis.

It didn't remain their highest placing for long, however. The first Dandelion Radio chart saw a top three placing for their perky response to Lloyd Cole's 'Are You Ready To Be Heartbroken?' and the band returned to the chart three years later with two entries, one of which – 'French Navy' – was adopted by Echo Falls for an ad and recent evidence suggests that from there the band's ascent/decline into more commercial territory has been secured.

36. White Stripes
1560 pts

I've always found it slightlyworrying that a band like the White Stripes could exist largely unnoticed for some time prior to Peel discovering their releases in a Dutch record shop, unearthing a body of work, most of which was by that point ineligible for the festive fifty, arguably better than anything else that came out either side of the cusp of the millennium. Even worse, it makes you wonder just how many great bands have, before or since, failed to enjoy such a discovery.

Jack and Meg White pillaged an ancient seam with remarkable originality and freshness and Peel's discovery of them led very quickly to a highly gratifying level of success. Ditching the bass was only a very small part of it, of course: for a spell this encouraged an almost novelty interest in the band from sections of the media, but nonetheless one that opened a door that would let in the likes of the Yeah Yeah Yeahs and Black Keys among others.

Anticipation at the arrival of their *Elephant* album in 2003, by which point the band had turned three tracks into five festive fifty entries, was peaking and Peel was inevitably as excited as anyone but, when he played three tracks from the album one night in his programme and announced his intention to play three more the following night, and carry on doing so, XL records and their lawyers became alarms and instructed him to cease forthwith.

Having broken the band to a wider audience – and in this caae there is no doubt that is what he did – Peel was understandably disappointed by this and had further salt rubbed into the wound when, just prior to its release, XL grandly informed him he was now permitted to play the 'Seven Nation Army' single. In the circumstances the aforementioned track, plus 'Black Math', still made the festive fifty but the episode illustrated, perhaps more than any other in the history of the Peel show, the gulf between the values of the Peel show and those of the record industry.

Jack White was, by this point, well on the way to megastardum, but his visibly upset appearance at the Peel funeral left no doubt that he was an artist who hadn't been about to join the ranks of those set to establish a Bolanesque distance between himself and the DJ as soon as wider success started rolling in. As a postscript, White's successful offshoot band The Raconteurs recorded an appearance in a Dandelion festive fifty, as did the title track from the White Stripes' *Icky Thump* album.

35. Public Image Ltd
1704 pts

Following his departure from the Sex Pistols, their only truly creative force, Johnny Rotten, returned to his real name and, forming this new outfit with ex-guitarist from the early Clash Keith Levene, wasted little time in turning music on its head again. 'Public Image' became a central element in a second push to reinvigorate a music scene that had barely had time even to miss him, as the Pistols' new material, bereft of Lydon's incisive lyrics and piercing delivery, quickly entered the depths of shameful self-parody.

'Public Image', an ever-present in the festive fifty until the all-time format was abandoned in 1982, gave immediate notice that Lydon, unrestrained by the colossal spectre of his former band, intended to carry on ploughing an entirely individualistic furrow, but this time within a format that allowed him far more room to breathe artistically. Like the best material of the time, it still sounds entirely convincing now, and yet it gave only a glimpse of what was to come from the new venture.

The appearance of 'Death Disco', a twisted take on 'Swan Lake' with unvarnished and highly personal lyrical content, on Top of the Pops remains one of the most jarring and memorable moments of the late seventies. The album on which it would appear, *Metal Box*, would, despite being renowned intially for the awkwardness of its packaging, become one of the great and most influential works of the period. Although The Clash, Stiff Little Fingers and others had long since added more space into their material via the incorporation of reggae, no punk band had ever hinted at the rhythmic diversity found here, duly recognised in the festive fifty, though only fleetingly, by the appearance of 'Poptones' and 'Careering'.

After the appearance of 'This Is Not a Love Song' in the 1983 chart, that appeared to be it as far as the festive fifty was concerned. But we ought to have known not to write Lydon off and, remarkably, he returned triumphantly with the *This Is PiL* album in 2012, returning to the chart with the track 'Lollipop Opera' after a gap of twenty-nine years.

34. Beatnik Filmstars
1813 pts

Beatnik Filmstars recorded five Peel sessions between 1995 and 1997 but never registered an entry in the festive fifty. When the band split in 1998, it seemed they never would; however their reformation in 2004 saw them become a firm favourite of early Dandelion Radio listeners, fellow Bristolian Rocker's show, and they began to see to see their legendary Peel status reflected in festive fifty voters' selections.

While many reformed bands would benefit from this in future festive fifties, none would match the kind of splash the Beatnik Filmstars made, recording two entries in the first Dandelion chart of 2006 before, in the following year, placing three tracks in the top ten of a single chart, the last band at the time of writing to achieve such a feat.

While a second split in 2008 brought the curtailment of a promising long-term engagement with the chart, that hasn't prevented long-time member Tim Rippington continuing his involvement with an entry for The Short Stories in 2013 that would place him among a very elite group who've appeared in the chart with four different bands, following his earlier appearance with The Flatmates and a further entry in 2006 with spin-off band Forest Giants.

33. Cuban Boys
2024 pts

One of the freshest and most enjoyable acts to appear in the late nineties and one that perhaps more than any other illustrates 'mainstream' music's baffled attempts to come to terms with the possibilities of the digital age, as well as its pitiful endeavours to tame the untameable that recalled, for once with some accuracy, its earlier tussles with punk.

Cuban Boys are also one of those bands that will always be inseparable from the Peel programme; there was something mischievously cute about them, but also something unpredictable, menacing even, in their gleeful carving up, sampling and pure desecration of multifarious and sometimes remote elements of popular culture.

From their first offering, 'Oh My God, They Killed Kenny', that took early seventies novelty record 'The Bump' and sampled, among other things, a South Park catchphrase that had already by that point long become a cliché, they gave notice of what would emerge as a prevailing ability to work with thoroughly suspect material, recycle it and turn it into something wonderful.

Now pared down to a duo of Skreen B and Ricardo Autobahn, their entry with brilliantly observed Peel tribute 'The Nation Needs You', in the OneMusic chart of 2005 appeared to signal the end of their relationship with the festive fifty. Nine years later, however, they responded to a request to submit a track to the 21 Songs for John compilation, released to commemorate the tenth anniversary of the DJ's untimely death, by recording a new, longer version of the track. It captured so well what they and John Peel were about that it stormed to number one, given the band a second appearance in the top spot fifteen years on from the legendary 'Cognoscenti Vs Intelligentsia'.

32. The Cure
2036 pts

Far more eclectic and innovative that they're given credit for, including by me, incidentally: I'll admit to having found myself surprised at the quality of their late seventies and early eighties work when encountering it again many years on. Possibly they're a band who suffered from being too influential, with so many of the imitations pallid and lacking in substance, qualities that have unfairly reflected back on the band whose ideas they nicked. Robert Smith, it's said, could walk through the front door of a Cure gig, past lines of fans who didn't notice him because the queue was crammedl with back-combed men in black who looked more like Smith than he did himself.

The Cure always lacked the claustrophic intensity of Joy Division, but were a band who influenced early eighties music to a comparable degree, signalling one of the many routes beyond punk and towards a less public, more introspective music with dark, bleak overtones that many loved but others reacted to with tribal repulsion.

As eighties Gothic Rock attitudes – if attitude is the right word – came to prominence, The Cure were understandably hailed as forefathers. Consciously or not, it was as the canonisation was taking place that Smith and Lol Tolhurst took the band in a completely new direction, unashamedly drawing on New Order's influence for 'The Walk' and embracing a poppiness they'd hitherto only cautiously flirted with on 'The Lovecats': both tunes made the festive fifty of 1983, though Peel distanced himself somewhat from the latter when announcing its number 15 position.

While unquestionably setting them up for the greater commercial success that was to come, in many ways it was the band's most fertile period artistically. The pervasive spirit of gloom gave way to a kind of kitsch quirkiness that set them well apart from their more rigidly rooted wannabe gothic peers. In festive fifty terms, however, their crowning achievement remains the earlier brooding masterpiece 'A Forest', which provided an emblematic template that became so badly abused by later imitators: however, to criticise The Cure for that is a bit like holding the creator of Nelson's Column responsible for all the pigeon shit.

31. Nirvana
2040 pts

Nirvana were fortunate, or perhaps unfortunate, to be at the forefront of new attitudes in American music just as they passed from the so-called underground into the commercial pop marketplace. They can claim an attribute that very few in this list, however great, truly share: they changed music. And if you don't believe me take a look, if you can bear it, at Kerrang! magazine in pre-1989 and post-1991 phases. Heavy metal would, thankfully, never entirely be the same again, though that's not to say that what it became was any better.

Of course, to lump Nirvana in with the Kerrang! crowd is a gross under-representation, at best, of what they did, another example of the music media's contemptuous need for pigeonholes. Forced to widen that particular pigeonhole and let Nirvana in, *Nevermind* went global and Cobain became understandably pissed off and, allegedly, killed himself. But whatever the circumstances surrounding his death, Cobain clearly wasn't built for fame in the same way that Dave Grohl, who has gone on to build a stellar career on these foundations, was.

Rock and roll ennui wasn't new, of course, but Cobain used it to shape his music in a way that no one else ever has, before or since. While the musical landmark that was their debut for Geffen understandably took the bulk of the plaudits, his bleakest and most enigmatic hour is *In Utero*, an album that also produced some spectacular festive fifty moments. The *MTV Unplugged* stuff that so closely preceded his death managed to indicate vast, untapped avenues of creativity and yielded three posthumous FF moments in its own right. Sad that the legacy should be a suspicious suicide note in two different styles of handwriting, a shotgun that, somehow, a guy with his veins full of heroin managed to operate and somehow hold upright after his death, and the Foo Fighters.

30. Stiff Little Fingers
2044 pts

Along with the Undertones, SFL made Northern Ireland a vital territory on the map of late seventies music and gained a very special place at the heart of the Peel programme while doing so. While the former, at least in their earlier period, stayed deliberately away from what were then euphemistically termed the 'troubles' in their lyrics, SLF drew on the intrinsic fury of punk to articulate the struggles of the individual against a political backdrop which, whatever side you were supposed to be on, left you feeling distant and disenfranchised.

The festive fifty did a pretty good job of capturing their finest moments. 'Wasted Life' blasts back with rage at the only prospect of 'heroism' held out during those times, that of becoming a paramilitary, for whatever cause. 'Suspect Device' and 'Alternative Ulster', arguably the best ever one-two punch of a pair of debut singles outside the Pistols, were anthemic diatribes in the battle between individual and state. 'Johnny Was', although never a favourite of Peel, thrilled enough of the band's audience to secure it ever-present status in the chart during the years 1979-82, a recasting of Jamaican street violence in modern Ulster.

Stiff Little Fingers' early music exudes anger and defiant individualism in a form that not even the very best British punk bands could emulate. Perhaps it was the result of existing even closer to the sharp end of the problems a political machine could create. A revelatory Clash gig brought them into existence, and a very limited edition release of the 'Suspect Device' single yielded a copy that received relentless airplay from Peel. If later offerings never matched the ferocity of this and other early material, it was still bloody good by any recognisable standards. Their festive fifty legacy, however, lies in those early blasts of energy that contain a thrill that remains undiminished with time, despite the band being overlooked when votes were cast for the 1999 all-time chart.

29. Morrissey
2331 pts

Morrissey wasted little time getting his highly anticipated solo career off the ground after the break up of The Smiths. Predictably, he carried with him a loyal fan base, though one whose expectations didn't always square with Morrissey's chosen direction which, given the nature of the man, was always going to be somewhat idiosyncratic. It was also inevitable that he would soon encounter a backlash from a music press that had long since decided it preferred the more conventional rock and roll image cast by Johnny Marr to the celibate vegetarian whom, you sensed, they'd kind of reluctantly gone along with only as a result of his band being so damn good.

Morrissey, cerebral and reclusive, had always been a more difficult figure to pin down and his solo material would take this to sometimes deliberately provocative extremes. However, although the critics' knives were, you suspect, already being sharpened, they took a while to be put to any significant use and the early phase of his individual career produced artistic highs that ranked not too far behind the best moments of his previous band. The slickly simulated orchestration of 'Every Day is Like Sunday' wasn't a million miles from what was so richly celebrated in 'There is a Light...', while 'Disappointed' reached new heights of brilliant self-mockery. 'Late Night Maudlin Street' continued his penchant for litery references that stretched back to the earliest days of The Smiths and brought to the surface the pain that always lay behind that irony.

The critics really lunged in around the time of 'Ouija Board, Ouija Board', but the relative crassness of that effort still worked on at least a couple of levels and was much liked by Peel. His last appearance in a Peel festive fifty was 'November Spawned a Monster', a painful listen in many respects but a further manifestation of that artistic flair for exposing the all too easily hidden, dealing frankly with subject matter more easily cloaked in euphemism. Bafflingly, Morrissey appeared to assume Peel disliked the song, though the quote from the DJ he cited as evidence appears very much open to interpretation and Peel was very quick to play the single as the opening track in his show as soon as he received a copy.

Although, for me, his finest solo album – *Vauxhall & I* – failed to trouble the festive fifty scorers, we hadn't heard the last of him: there were rumours of an ill-fated vote canvassing campaign to get him into the chart in 2004 (by that point, his loyal audience would do anything for him, to the extent that vote-rigging would, you suspect, produce barely an ethical murmur among a number of them), but he eventually succeeded in doing in returning, with the emblematic 'Life is a Pigsty', in the first Dandelion chart, without, so far as we can make out, any similar shenanagins.

28. Allo Darlin'
2432 pts

Fortuna Pop! has emerged as the most successful festive fifty label in the early years of the second decade of the twenty-first century and the demise of Bearsuit has left Allo Darlin' as unquestionably their most prominent band. Five of their eight festive fifty entries thus far have made the top ten and lead singer Elizabeth Morris can also add a vocal contribution to a Darren Hayman top five entry to those achievements.

Formed in 2008, the band quickly surged to the forefront of a great new wave of indie pop bands during the period, and certainly the most prominent in festive fifty terms. Morris formed the band after moving from her native to Australina from London, its name coming from the greeting she heard from Soho market traders.

Both of their first two albums produced two top ten entries and while a third in 2014 also saw a couple of appearances, if lower down the chart. Three albums producing a brace of entries, in a period in which multiple entries have become much rarer, is a feat no one else can match. In the Dandelion Radio years, only The Fall have recorded more festive fifty appearances.

27. Bearsuit
2776 pts

John Peel bestowed on Bearsuit a comment he reserved for only the very best: they sounded, he said, like no one else. Lest you consider that fairly faint praise, remember that this is a man who once said that, in the whole of the seventies, only Roxy Music were worthy of such a commendation. To those in the know, such a statement supplied unequivocal proof of the prominent place that this Norwich band had secured very quickly in the DJ's affections.

Bearsuit were still some way off a position in this top fifty at the time of this first edition of this book and have become the highest placed of the 'new entries' here as a result of Dandelion loving them just as much, especially Rachel Neiman, who declared them her favourite band. By then, of course, they were already FF regulars, having appeared in every one of the final four years of John Peel's life, with three of those entries in the top five. Although 'Hey Charlie, Hey Chuck' will perhaps always be remembered as their finest Peel moment, its number four placing was actually beaten by a number two entry for the brief and energetic 'Chargr' in the chart revealed by Rob Da Bank in 2004.

They'd only return to the top five once more, with 'Foxy Boxer', but nonetheless the band remained regular visitors to the festive fifty during the Dandelion years. They remain perhaps the finest example in the modern era of a band of people who couldn't play getting together and, in learning how to make noises, producing something that no one armed with a bunch of Bert Weedon books could ever hope to get close to. Although they've now sadly called it a day, three of their members live on in Mega Emotion, who made their festive fifty debut in the 2013 chart.

26. Undertones
3048 pts

'The ultimate Peel band' according to Dave Cavanagh in the sleeve notes to their *Peel Sessions* album. In the late seventies, Peel took an almost paternal shine to them and their sound reflects, more than anything else, the spirit of the Peel shows in that vintage era. When, during those shows, the DJ announced that he considered them the best band in the world, that delivered a final, decisive uppercut to any rock traditionalists still hanging around, the kind who'd spluttered on their late night Horlicks, or whatever it is rock traditionalists drink, on their first exposure to The Ramones.

Yet they enjoyed relatively few festive fifty entries and their position here is, of course, largely due to those persistent reappearances of 'Teenage Kicks', one of many songs capable of reducing Peel to tears, but the one he took to the grave as his all-time favourite.

While the Pistols spat and The Clash agitated, it was left to the Undertones to attend to more immediate adolescent concerns, specifically failed romance, unachieved romance, missed opportunities for romance and all-night masturbation. Later the

O'Neill brothers – the band's chief songwriters – would talk of a deliberate lyrical strategy (in contrast with their peers Stiff Little Fingers) rooted in avoidance of the political concerns relevant to anyone in Northern Ireland at the time. This stance altered somewhat in their later work, by which point the various members were looking to move in different directions, with That Petrol Emotion, who also scored with a clutch of festive fifty entries, a more receptive vehicle for their political views.

When That Petrol Emotion faded and Feargal Sharkey, having appeared once in collaboration with Vince Clarke as The Assembly, went off into sub-cabaret territory, that appeared to be it. However, in 2003, the Undertones, minus Sharkey, returned. Nothing surprising about that: reformed bands from the punk era was cropping up all over the place. But, unlike the reformed Buzzcocks and SLF, Undertones returned with a freshness that clearly excited the hell out of their former mentor and which saw them back in the festive fifty after a gap of 23 years. 'Thrill Me' even managed to lodge itself in the top five, ground that had only previously been occupied by their celebrated debut release. The 'ultimate Peel band' had, briefly, returned to reclaim some of their former territory though those early gems ('Get Over You' joined 'Teenage Kicks' in every all-time chart between 1979 and 1982) remain the band's most treasured moments.

25. Ballboy
3135 pts

As was more than hinted at in their 2000 festive fifty debut, there is a perceptive quality to the lyrics of Gordon McIntyre that, while often rooted in the everyday, always stays triumphantly aloof from the trite and dull. The band can lay claim to some of the finest song titles in festive fifty history, but when you happen across a title like 'I've Got Pictures of You in Your Underwear', you're going to be disappointed if what lies beneath the surface is any sense than brilliant, and Ballboy never disappointed. They stayed clear of fellow Scots Arab Strap's savagery, but still poked at life with the rusty sharpness of a used hypodermic needle. And on the rare occasions when they came away from that approach, as on the heart-rending 'I Gave Up My Eyes to a Man Who Was Blind', the effect was just as startling.

By 2003, they'd become one of the genuine festive fifty heavyweights of the period, cementing this by becoming the year's most placed band with three entries that revealed more than ever the panoramic span of McIntyre's writing, from the aching humanity of 'I Gave Up...', to the direct savagery of 'The Sash My Father Wore' (although it must be said that, though Peel delighted in the Manchester United putdown, any true hardline Rangers bigot would regard United as inherently Catholic and Tim sympathisers). The brilliance with which they transformed Springsteen's 'Born in the USA' was stunning: had the 'Boss' set it to vinyl in such a manner you suspect he would have avoided a lot of the misinterpretation that dogged the original.

They repeated the achievement of most placed band in 2004. Although it was little short of sinful that *The Royal Theatre*, surely their most consistently brilliant album, only managed two entries, they did include the brilliant, and brilliantly titled, 'I Don't Have Time to Stand Here With You, Fighting About the Size of My Dick', which became the longest title ever to appear in the festive fifty.

2008's *I Worked On The Ships* became the first Ballboy album to fail to produce an entry and that appeared to be it until the band resurfaced with a self-released EP at the end of 2013, too late to put any sort of dent in that year's festive fifty but raising the prospect of a return in the future.

24. Billy Bragg
3278 pts
Includes points with Ste McCabe

When Billy Bragg, formerly of Riff Raff, shot to our attention as a have-guitar-will-play-anywhere solo artist in 1983, many were inclined not to take him seriously, as if he were merely a street busker, voice rough as a bear's arse, who'd made it onto record via a combination of brash self-belief and sheer luck despite being no more than some bastard offspring of punk and skiffle with hilariously misguided singer-songwriter aspirations.

Beneath the raw exterior, it quickly became apparent that Bragg possessed the musical and lyrical skills to face down such criticisms and quickly render them ridiculous. By the end of the year, *Life's a Riot With Spy vs Spy*, a cut price album in both production and retailing terms, had made a significant commercial impact and a track from it, 'A New England' – still his highest place track - gave Bragg the first of many festive fifty entries. By the time the session track 'Between

The Wars' made it in the following year, Bragg's immense observational spectrum was already apparent..

He would soon expand beyond his rudimentary beginnings, adding musicians and exploring broader avenues of sound before a wiser, older observer emerged around the undiminished central core. There was still an admiration for the human spirit and, of course, he still deplored the materialism, false values and easy conformity of the Thatcher era, but 'Brickbat' was the writer of 'A New England' grown up and married, reflecting on how the personal had a power to eclipse the political, which still nonetheless loomed powerfully in the background, the lost inclination to plant bombs on the Last Night of the Proms not signifying anything like a descent into political apathy.

His last entry in a Peel-presented chart came from the adaptation of a lost Woody Guthrie lyric, from an album of such gems that could only have been pulled off with any success by a genuine kindred spirit. Guthrie had always remained an honest figure with a raw blue collar heart who lived his life aloof from commercial capitulation: Bragg followed the model flawlessly, and continues to do so, returning to the chart briefly in 2014 with a typically forthright comment on the times in collaboration with Ste McCabe.

23. Sonic Youth
3278 pts

As the 1980s began, quivering from the onslaught of punk, many American fans took their lead from the crossover success of Blondie and the buoyant danceability of the B52s and headed for the accessible climes of pop punk or else happily weaved their way, led by Springsteen, back into the cultural dead end of guitar hero territory. Meanwhile, in a different America, 'no wave' declared the ultimate musical nihilism, paradoxically producing a non-movement that refused to be defined by any such thing, or anything.

While much of what emerged remained inevitably obscure, Sonic Youth took no wave's legacy and moulded it brilliantly into something that went well beyond these raw statements of intent. Several albums into their existence, festive fifty voters began belatedly recognising that some American bands had been filtering what The Velvet Underground had started through their amps long before the Jesus & Mary Chain and My Bloody Valentine had happened upon the idea and that Thurston Moore and his colleagues were arguably doing it far better than anyone else. They were among a clutch of US bands that finally barged open the door of the festive fifty in 1987; quite why it had taken voters so long to admit them is something that might be an appropriate topic for lengthy discussion elsewhere, but here it's enough to note that it was as Sonic Youth were moving decisively way from their earlier sub-avant garde guitar stylings that they caught up. Those no wave roots were increasingly disguised behind tracks like 'Teenage Riot', which contained something discernible as a groove and managed to catch the indie crowd just as it became prepared to dance, and the masterful *Daydream Nation* album, a release that continues to reveal further layers of brilliance as the decades roll by.

Sonic Youth left their mark on much of the best American music of the eighties and early nineties. Along with Husker Du, they provided a lasting artistic blueprint and a path along which many other great bands have blazed. Babes in Toyland came to prominence after touring with them, Kim Gordon was instrumental in the formation of Hole and Moore even forcefully argued Nirvana's corner in their negotiations over their deal with Geffen. During the period, Sonic Youth entered the playground with some of the most innovative music of their existence, producing a body of work that played within a framework located somewhere between the accessible and the experimental. It was to their credit that they remained on that creative tightrope for far longer than most before, it must be admitted, eventually succumbing to gravity, their final festive fifty entry, a cover of The Carpenters' 'Superstar', offering a thematic link to their highest chart placing, the haunting 'Tunic (Song for Karen)' an evocative and portrait of Karen Carpenter's life and death, having squeezed into the top five in 1990.

22. Hefner
3333 pts

If great bands are so often rooted in one person's obsessions. then it's hardly surprising that Hefner were such a great band. Vocalist Darren Hayman's often roots his subject matter in the fertile soil of relationships gone wrong and those relationships tend to draw in everything around him: cigarettes, booze, Thatcher, the third man on the moon; often there's a subdued social commentary that clashes with moments of lost intimacy, often an angle, a perspective that casts brilliant light on the mundane. He's not a writer of the personal-political song in the mannter of Billy Bragg, more a carver of personal compositions out of the rock of a broader environment from which they can only be extracted with meticulous care. If the lyrics are to be believed, Hayman doesn't love very successfully, but nor does he love in a cocoon.

The albums *The Fidelity Wars* and *We Love The City* both stand as masterpieces from around the cusp of the twentieth/twenty-first century, rewarded with nine festive fifty entries between them, and largely responsible for the band's position in this list. Yet in some ways the two festive fifty entries that came from elsewhere tell us most about Hefner's appeal: the almost audacious simplicity of their debut entry, 'Pull Yourself Together' and 'Alan Bean', their final festive fifty appearance, the story of a figure gaining solace for a single great achievement in his life, unperturbed in the knowledge that no one else remembers it. By that point, Hayman was already singing to a keyboards-dominated backdrop that provided him with the setting for his next, albeit brief, musical adventure, with The French, who registered two entries in 2003.

Hayman returned as a solo artist in the Dandelion years with 'I Know I Fucked Up', a track that featured Allo Darlin's Elizabeth Morris on vocals. While the other members of Hefner haven't made the chart without him, ANT and Jack Hayter's many subsequent releases have demonstrated the considerable talent and depth of ideas that swam around that deceptively simple central vision.

21. Stereolab
3399 pts

The Stereolab project provided some of the most fertile and consistently brilliant music of the nineties, involving an ever-changing group of musicians gathered around the central partnership of Tim Gane and Laetitia Sadier. Their influence is discernible in the work of the many very fine bands who emerged later, including multiple festive fifty entrants such as Broadcast and Saloon. There were significant links to the past also, with the line-up that made their chart debut in 2003 possessing an unmistakeable stamp of Peel heritage, featuring as it did Sean O'Hagan, who had remarkably failed to appear in a festive fifty with Microdisney, and Gane himself, who'd been there twice before with McCarthy.

The sound ranged from wonky experimentalism to innovative takes on classic pop arrangements. The latter has proved their richest source of festive fifty entries, exemplifed by top ten appearances for 'French Disko' and 'Ping Pong'. Their most accessible offering to date, *Emperor Tomato Ketchup*, along with the first of two outings (both, oddly, in the same position) for 'Fluourescences', saw them running neck and neck with The Fall for the title of most featured band in 1996 before securing the accolade for themselves in 1997. Their use of technology often happily tended towards conscious anachronism at times, a happy contravention of a potentially stale agenda that we were all so much better for.

By 1999, they'd veered back towards left field with the avant-jazz influences on *The Free Design*, while their return in 2001 saw them once again reclaiming more familiar ground, the influence of Tortoise's John McEntire prominent in helping to make the *Sound Dust* album one of their very best, though it only scratched the surface of the festive fifty with a single entry, 'Captain Easychord'. Sadly, the death of long-standing member Mary Hansen and the end of the Gane-Sadier relationship eventually brought the core of the band to an untimely end.

20. Pavement
3455 pts

Pavement were that most remarkable thing: the American 'rock' band with a distinctly semi-detached relationship with American rock. Great bands that preceded them tended to mix, swap and engage with influences that were then woven into an often appealing patchwork of sound. Nothing wrong with that: Sonic Youth, The Pixies and Nirvana basically adopted this very broad template and did some great things with it.

But Pavement didn't fit the rest of that quilt. They came along at a time when a lot of people were prepared to consider guitar music, even the best of it, as essentially formulaic and something from which nothing inventive would ever again ensue and very helpfully forced such people to reevaluate their opinions. The simplest (too simple) reference point was The Fall: like Mark E. Smith, Stephen Malkmus could engage in sonic fisticuffs with the guitars or sing on the note, often with impressive disregard for convention (witness the 1997 session cover of 'The Classical' to witness this approach at its ramshackle best). Having thrilled us with the cacophonous delights this brought to our ears – brilliantly showcased in the six tracks that made it into the 1992 festive fifty – the same band returned to the chart in 1994 with a marriage of the off-kilter and something more conventional, though not by anyone else's standards, something that was a big step away from the dischordant brilliance of their earlier work but nonetheless working brilliantly, exemplified best by their highest entry that year, the caustically irreverent 'Range Life'.

The band's casual approach to rehearsal – allegedly because they lived too far apart to do it very often – lent that earlier material an amateurish charm and distinctively messy edge that thankfully wasn't sacrificed as Pavement developed through the nineties. Those who baulked at Malkmus' vocal limitations missed the point: his constant, occasionally painful straining against these limitations gave the band much of their appeal. Like Will Oldham, he viewed such constraints as yet another challenge to be met and defeated as innovatively as possible. An ideal at the heart of punk, perhaps: indeed, it's hard to think of a band who came closer than Pavement to realising that other treasured late seventies ideal of breaking down all barriers between artist and audience with whatever tools were at their disposal.

19. The Jam
3480 pts

First of all, The Jam produced a run of singles between 1979 and 1982 that is unrivalled by any band in any period, and that includes their contemporaries The Clash. Secondly, while others among that generation of punk bands saw 1976 as the starting point for everything, setting a standard for British music that proclaimed that to be good was to be uncontaminated by what came before, viewing only reggae as worthy of interest, The Jam happily and defiantly embraced sixties beat and soul within their sound, and never apologised for doing so.

They are one of a few bands to benefit in this chart from their appearance in 1977 with 'Away From The Numbers', the subsequent recognition of which has allowed them an anachronistic leap of six places up this chart. Festive fifty voters would ignore the song, however, preferring instead the raw 'In The City' which, like the latter and much of their first album, was most notable for its energy and proclamation of intent, though it does include one of the truly classic punk riffs, stolen by the Pistols for the far better 'Holidays in the Sun'.

Later, however, the album would be reevaluated as a launching pad for some of the most stirring moments in late seventies music. Top of the list in festive fifty terms is 'Down in the Tube Station at Midnight', a single that fused narrative and format brilliantly and with a meticulous craft that brought a sophistication of form that took the band well away from their raw beginnings and into other realms entirely. Although it only appeared once in a festive fifty, 'Strange Town' is only slightly behind in terms of its determination to cram enough melodic ideas into one song to see most bands through an entire career.

'Going Underground', a song that combined both the rawness of that early material and the brilliant craft of their later work, has since outstripped it in festive fifty terms, securing an appearance in the 1999 all-time chart from which 'Tube Station' was curiously excluded.

The band would go on to record three more UK number ones, one of which, 'Town Called Malice' would at the time set a record for the highest placed number one UK single in a festive fifty (number 11 in 1982), a record that stood throughout the Peel years, only eventually beaten by Arctic Monkeys in the OneMusic chart of 2005. Acknowledging their final appearance in the countdown of 1982, Peel applauded the courage of Weller in breaking up the band at that stage: though the quality of his later efforts would fall well short of what he achieved with The Jam, having the conviction to plot their own path and gain success on their own terms was very much the hallmark of this great band and the comments served as a highly appropriate epitath.

18. Sex Pistols
3935 pts

There's little of interest that hasn't already been said, really. It is, of course, to the credit of festive fifty voters that only tracks from that one real Pistols album ever made the listings: Eddie Cochran covers and Ronnie Biggs contributions rightly never stood a chance. There were some of us who continued to believe in the legend long after it has shot its bolt and now rightly feel embarrassed about it. I plead youthful naivety.

Five tracks from that album made the fifty, and four of them continued to do so repeatedly, until the all-time format was suspended in 1982. The current format makes it very close to impossible for a single track to be number one on four occasions, so the status of 'Anarchy in the UK' as the only track ever to achieve this seems confirmed for eternity. Then again, it seems difficult to imagine that anything like 'Anarchy in the UK' could ever happen again. For the record, Peel preferred 'Holidays in the Sun', arguing that it was likely to gather greater appreciation over time among Pistols aficionados, though it's non-appearance in the 1999 all-time chart suggests otherwise.

There remain issues to sort out, or more likely never sort out because inevitably they'll persist. The McLaren version of the Rotten version. But then McLaren was the one who claimed it was all a scam, a hoax, which renders his version of events unpalatable to anyone who could see there was far more to it than that. Post-Rotten that's what it became, because Rotten was the band's only real creative force, at least after Glen Matlock had been shunted aside. They were his lyrics, his vocals; it was his stance, not to mention his darting rat-like stare that raised the Sex Pistols high above the level of a mundane and predictable pub rock band That's what they became without him, but the rest of music moved on, and that is their true legacy.

Rotten escaped with his artistic legacy intact, as Public Image Ltd occupied the crucial place vacated by the Pistols, while his former colleagues continued, smothered by McLaren's narrowed vision, warped by the concept that the ultimate rock and roll band could be that facile and insisting, against all evidence, that it could go on. What happened made Elvis' death on the toilet seem a fairly dignified end.

Vicious's death allowed him to become what, in truth, he'd always been, a symbol, nothing more. Always a myth without substance, by that point he was little more than a circus act: the bass line from Bowie's 'Hang on to Yourself' resonating down through history amid a pile of used needles and useless dreams. 'Anarchy in the UK' remained number one in the hearts, and more importantly the heads, of festive fifty listeners long after these events had been played out to their tiresome conclusion. Quite simply, it's still impossible to remember any song, or any band, or any time in history quite like it.

17. Belle and Sebastian
4392 pts

In 1996, Belle & Sebastian released a limited number of copies of their first album T*igermilk* via a college label. In time-honoured fashion it was picked up by Peel and the band's songcraft and pleasing-on-the-ear stylings allowed them to cut through the invisible line that in those days divided the Evening Session from the John Peel show and bewitch us with tunes that scratched at the grimy underbelly of the world and did so in an immaculately tuneful manner.

Fortunately, band leader Stuart Murdoch's well-documented affection for Felt didn't lead them into the sometimes disappointing artistic cul-de-sacs that were often the destination of that band: beneath the slick arrangements and enchanting melodies lay considerable substance, layers of meaning and a lyrical dexterity that lifted them well beyond the so-called 'chamber pop' bands of the time, with which they were often lazily linked. Belle & Sebastian work in forms of classic songs and songwriting, the defiantly innovative coming as naturally to them as the commercial forms in which such ideas found a home.

The best material – 'Lazy Line Painter Jane', 'Dog on Wheels', 'Jonathan David' and pretty much everything else that's been recognised in a festive fifty – combines the slick grace of the unabashed pop performer with an at times enhanced literary observational zeal. Where 'Jonathan David' offers Old Testament text to provide an angle on highly secular, and sexual, concerns, 'Dog on Wheels' weaves images from Samuel Beckett into a brilliantly conceived expression of everyday angst. One path leads to an emotionally shattered sense of resignation, the other to near-madness. Such are the themes that beat within the heart of such eminently hummable tunes. It's entirely fitting that their highest placing in a festive fifty to date came with the title track from their album *The Boy with the Arab Strap*, a jaunty tune allowing lyrics to peep through that veer between the desperate, the socially paralysed and the semi-obscene.

Belle & Sebastian took huge strides towards wider commercial recognition in 2003 with the Trevor Horn-produced *Dear Catastrophe Waitress* album, but the leap in accessibility left no dent in the quality of the band's material as Stevie Jackson continued to emerge as a songwriting force to complement the ever-dependanble Murdoch. The album became the first and so far only album by the band to register three festive fifty entries ('You Don't Send Me' having appeared a year earlier as a session track) despite on this occasion receiving only minimal airplay from Peel. Their output has slowed down considerably, partly due to the involvement of band members in other projects (such as Murdoch's production on the excellent first album from Camera Obscura), though they returned to the festive fifty after a seven year haitus in 2010 with 'I Didn't See It Coming'.

16. Jesus and Mary Chain
4980 pts

As punk faded further and further into nostalgic, and sometimes reconfigured and over-romanticised, memory, the music press, then as now obsessed with movements and tribes, sought with increasing desperation for the 'new Sex Pistols', an inevitably futile search as, should such a definitively singular event ever truly be repeated, its impact would be lessened to the point where it would scarcely register even among those who missed it first time round. The Jesus and Mary Chain, from East Kilbride, became thus saddled with the identity: early gigs became infamous for violent exchanges and the connections were cranked up as the band began to risk action from the authorities that recalled those banned Pistols concerts from the late seventies. Adding fuel to the flames were the suggestions that the band had instigated the violence in some cases, certainly in the case of the legendarily truncated 20-minute set in Liverpool to which the band responded with 'we don't like long sets' shrugs.

Their name obviously caused some offence too, though in this post-'Da Vinci Code' world it would probably register recognition rather than even a flicker of concern. There were obvious drug references: Radio One DJ Mike Smith, one of a group of individuals at the station clearly bloated by their own sense of self-importance, followed the lead of future UKIP spokesman Mike Read's 'banning' of Frankie Goes To Hollywood by stating his refusal to play 'Some Candy Talking'. It was partly because of such 'moral guardians' that the world needed bands like the Jesus and Mary Chain, whose folk devil notoriety was further compounded by the fact that their early work, such as festive fifty debut 'Upside Down', were soaked in a wall of feedback that, if it didn't delight, could only irritate the hell out of people.

By the time 'Never Understand' appeared in 1985, the legend was already fully formed and the track duly made number one in the festive fifty that year, apparently by some distance, though an entry for the far more melodic 'Just Like Honey' at number two was already suggesting far greatet depth to the band's sound than many had anticipated. Statistically, the band had done what even Joy Division had failed to do – gain the top two places in a festive fifty, a feat since only emulated by Pulp.

'Just Like Honey' emphasised the carefully plotted artistic vision at work within the band, something that suggested a longevity that the thrill of their earliest singles, magnificent though they were, had barely hinted at. The extraordinary *Psychocandy* album illustrated the brilliant dichotomy within their sound and emphasised that what was truly fascinating about this band was not the drenching feedback per se, but that mesmerising corridor of uncertainty where a pop tune ends and white noise begins. This was their undoubted peak, but the future would still bring a succession of triumphant moments, and continued festive fifty recognition, from a band that simply refused ever to lie down and become dull.

15. Pixies
5370 pts

One of the most enduring and pleasing aspects of what might broadly still be termed rock and roll is when it digs right back into its own heart and presents you with something you feel you ought to have heard before, but haven't, and you can't imagine how you ever got by without it. The Pixies drew on punk, surf, folk, beat music, latin elements and almost everything else over four albums, all of which produced multiple festive fifty entries, before imploding almost inevitably due to the same clash of artistic sensibilities that was so central to what was great about them. They've reformed since, of course, but it was perhaps inevitable that the new Pixies would be forced eventually to get along without the crucial Black Francis-Kim Deal axis and so it has proved with, dare I suggest, fatal consequences for their imperious vision.

While Joey Santiago's lead guitar and the rhythm guitar, plus harsh vocals, of Francis were the rudimentary building blocks of the Pixies sound, Deal's bass and far less caustic vocal appeal added an important further dimension. Their appearances in the 1988 and 1989 festive fifties undoubtedly reflect the band at their creative peak. Deal rose to prominence during this period despite being on the receiving end of the imposition of restricted songwriting duties, her contribution to the phenomenon recognised by a quickly assembled and rapidly growing collection of devotees. But then, the rise to eminence of the band as a whole in the UK in particular was steep and, perhaps like man bands before them (The Specials would be a pertinent example), it sent them into the living legends bracket before they'd completely had a chance fully to sort out what was what within the band. They were, after all, a collection of individuals that came together after an advertisement in the small ads, and not a group of people who'd grown together as an organic collective.

When the band returned to Britain for their second tour in the wake of *Doolittle*'s release, they seemed visibly shocked in early gigs at the mass adulation that greeted them: understandably so, because I'd never seen anything like it either. Black Francis was inclined to come across almost Mark E. Smith-like in interviews of the time and perhaps there was a sense of his wishing to assert a similar level of artistic control over the project, something that was clearly apparent in the band's next two albums, both of which saw Deal marginalised. The result was a sound that certainly lacked the abrasiveness of *Surfer Rosa* – although Francis had, anyway, derided Steve Albini's production of that album even though to most ears it sounded utterly masterful – and indulged the singer and chief songwriter's love for more melodic arrangements.

While Deal has since scored a solitary entry with The Breeders, Black Francis' solo work – as Frank Black – failed to register with festive fifty voters. It will be intriguing to see whether anything from the reformed band gets a look-in. Whether it does or not, Peel once said that Pixies records had probably been played in his house more than those of any other band: and that's some achievement, I would think.

14. Cinerama
5681 pts

From the ashes of The Wedding Present, one of the greatest of all festive fifty phenomena, rose Cinerama, a band initially conceived to indulge David Gedge's love for movie-style arrangements, but which quickly came to produce work of much greater breadth and a stylistic variety that went beyond the work of his much-lauded first band. They continued their remarkable festive fifty legacy to ensure that, up to the end of the Peel era, the magnificent Mr Gedge had only failed to appeal in two charts since 1985, a feat only surpassed, inevitably, by Mark E. Smith.

In contrast to the case of the Fall frontman – Peel was always having to remind people that he really didn't have much of a connection with him aside from loving his music – you sensed his relationship with Gedge was rooted in a strong mutual appreciation and respect. Lyrically, there is a Peel-esque eye for the humorous and bizarre that was given free rein in Cinerama's work. Indeed, for those who found that The Wedding Present's later work (at the time, because obviously they've since reformed) lacked something of the charm of their earlier efforts, Cinerama's development came as a welcome breath of fresh air. Rooted in stylish pop arrangements rather than frantic guitars, their flexibility allowed Gedge far greater freedom to explore and the most successful of these explorations invariably found festive fifty recognition easy to secure.

Like Half Man Half Biscuit, it seemed at one stage they'd be confined to regular appearances just outside the top ten, the effortless beauty of 'Pacific' – with its flute interjections that Peel initially found unappealing but grew to love – their crowning festive fifty achievement, while the plaintive and wonderful 'Superman' and 'Cat Girl Tights' had to settle, criminally, for places well down the chart. However, in the early years of the new century, 'Health & Efficiency' and 'Quick Before It Melts' returned Gedge to the once familiar territory of the top three before finally, after eighteen years of trying, 'Don't Touch That Dial' edged out The Fall to give him his first number one. As Peel pointed out at the end of the broadcast, this was a rare example of a festive fifty artist for whom it could be guaranteed that the moment would mean something. It was also guaranteed that said artist would be listening in as eagerly as any other FF devotee.

However, that career-defining achievement was followed by the news that Gedge had split with long-time partner and fellow Cinerama founder Sally Murrell, a parting that let to the sudden demise of the band and the equally sudden rebirth of The Wedding Present, albeit initially with a group of musicians who'd spent the previous three years working on the Cinerama project. Although there has been a recent reflowering of activity under the moniker, it warrants comment that in this first phase Cinerama claimed the unique feat of placing at least one track in each of the seven festive fifties that spanned their existence.

13. The Delgados
5746 pts

The Delgados progressively added layers of sound to the elementary four-piece set-up that released their first single back in 1995, those same four members eventually becoming a central part of an increasingly sophisticated sea of arrangements as the band secured a position among the true greats of the later Peel era.

By 1998 the band had already achieved the double distinction of being the year's most placed band in the festive fifty and the number one slot, with 'Pull the Wires from the Wall', which had charted as a session track a year earlier and would appear again a year later, with the distinction of the most recent release to secure a place in the 1999 all-time festive fifty. The string arrangements were already beginning to stir in the *Peloton* album on which the song appeared, a richly developing sound that had already come a long way from the raw and frantic 'Under Canvas Under Wraps', which had rudely assaulted the number three position to give the band their first appearance in 1996.

It would have been easy, if not forgiveable, for a band in this position to slide away from what sound distinctly like a creative peak and into crude pathos or cliché, but thankfully The Delgados avoided this fate and in 2000 *The Great Eastern* made an even bigger impact on the festive fifty, placing four tracks and cementing its identity as the most complete expression of the band's memorable artistic journey.

Some critics suggested that, by 2002's *Hate*, the band had run out of ideas. That seemed an unfairly negative response, although it was true that there was no easily discernible great leap forward on this occasion and festive fifty voters only gave the collection a single entry, and that in a low position, with 'Coming in From the Cold'. New ground wasn't broken, perhaps, but these ears certainly didn't pick up any diminishing quality and there was enough to suggest an extremely fruitful future in their Peel session of that year, which consisted entirely of cover versions, with the Emma Pollock-led version of 'Mr Blue Sky' a particular highlight and one that gave the band a further festive fifty entry that year.

Universal Audio similarly only yielded one entry and following that release the band chose to bring the curtain down on a highly fruitful existence, their end coinciding, sadly, with that of their great champion. Their time is remembered, rightly, not purely for their own output, but for the excellence of their Chemikal Underground label, which gave a platform for a whole range of other fine Scottish talent, including many who made an impact on the festive fifty themselves, including Bis, Arab Strap, Mogwai, Aereogramme, Mother & The Addicts and Sluts of Trust.

12. Siouxsie & The Banshees
5992 pts

Siouxsie & The Banshees were the band of choice for much of Peel's listening audience in the late seventies, as even a short glance at the festive fifties of 1978 and 1979 will confirm. Though Siouxsie Sioux and Steve Severin began their association with the punk scene as members of the Pistols' inner circle, their early work placed them stylistically well apart from other punk bands. They nurtured a proto-gothic aesthetic and even had the courage to go against the prevailing 'year zero' tide and include a Beatles cover on their debut album (although a song given much darker undertones since Charles Manson's bloody adoption of it).

Perhaps it was a difficulty in pigeonholing the band that initially delayed the interest of major labels who at that point were already busy attempting to buy up the most prominent proponents of revolutionary spirit in order to package it and sell it back to us. Whatever, it led to a massive 'Sign the Banshees' graffiti campaign in London that became a graphic feature of the punk movement as it moved into its second phase. Airplay on the Peel programme accompanied the wider aural stimulation unleashed when Polydor signed the band and put out their debut album *The Scream* in 1978. By this point they'd amassed a huge following that led, unsurprisingly, to more tracks from the Banshees in that year's festive fifty than from any other band.

Severin's name was a clear nod to the artistic debt the band owed to the Velvent Underground; they weren't the only band of the period to owe such a debt, but they were one of the few to own up to it, further enhanced by Siouxsie's adoption of an aesthetic at least partly borrowed from Nico. Changes in the band's personnel led to the recruitment of Budgie on drums and it was his greater rhythmic variety that fostered their development away from the earthy, teutonic thud that accompanied their earlier work.

There were fewer entries for the Banshees as the eighties began. Joy Division had moved the sub-Gothic urge stirring in the underbelly of punk into new areas, in the process seizing the vacated crown of festive fifty darlings. The rising gothic rock genre the Banshees had helped nurture had become artistically passé in many circles while the number of Siouxsie clones still knocking about gave the band an association with gothic sterility they didn't deserve, though this probably wasn't helped when they recruited Robert Smith, someone who spawned even more back-combed imitators than Siouxsie, as a guitarist.

In truth, they retained a creative power that peers like The Damned, sucked almost completely into self-parody by this stage, lacked. Their festive fifty life ended in 1983 with a second cover of a track from the Beatles' White Album, a quasi-psychedelic interpretation of 'Dear Prudence'.

11. Pulp
6487 pts

We're lucky to have Pulp. Having made a tentative first album back in 1983 and getting absolutely nowhere with it, it's frankly astonishing that nine years later they were still plugging away hoping something would happen.

And then it's 1993 and Pulp are, if not exactly huge, then at least prominent enough to confirm that suspicion you'd always had that, if they just moved a little in that direction, you could really grow to love them. And as well as that slight move towards the something indefinable that makes a good band truly great, it can also be about sticking around for long enough for good taste to assert itself as opposed to attempting to follow the fame bus in however many contrived and unpleasant directions it might take you. Suddenly Suede were getting noticed for writing semi-androgynous love songs that others were copying and, bizarrely, people started saying that, you know, there was this band called Pulp and they were a bit late that.

As Peel himself noted in the 1993 countdown, that wasn't true at all, but the association produced a happy accident that we all benefited from, because fortune had dictated that the attention would hit them just as they were peaking artistically with, conveniently, vogueish ruminations on lower class sexual adventures gone wrong. There were reflections on what happened when you loved too much, such as in 'Lipgloss', a yearning romantic underbelly beneath the dysfunctional teenage sex fantasy of 'Babies', and Razzamatazz, which showed that even those who believed themselves slightly ahead of the pack were headed towards a future they should realistically comtemplate with trepidation and fear.

And one day it became clear that, all along, Pulp had been building towards the masterpiece that was *Different Class*, a triumph whose festive fifty legacy is bettered only by a couple of Smiths albums.

Cocker's songs went elsewhere after that. After all, as he commented himself, it was difficult to carry on writing convincingly about how crap your life was when it wasn't anymore. *This is Hardcore* and the strangely upbeat, if only on the surface, *We Love Life* both appeared after lengthy periods of hibernation with festive fifty entries and Cocker himself would appear solo in the first Dandelion Radio festive fifty with the blunt but no less brilliantly observed 'Cunts Are Still Running the World'.

10. The Clash
7730 pts

It's hard to know what to add really Punk was the way forward, decided Joe Strummer, walking away from the 101ers to change the direction of his life and everyone else's. Strummer suddenly had the obsession he needed to fuel his artistic direction and from this The Clash quickly evolved, through early line-up changes, to become the most important punk band, and for a time the most important band of any sort, in the world.

From their supercharged eponymous debut, both 'White Riot' and 'Police & Thieves' pointed a couple of stunningly prescient ways forward and both, in another example of how well those festive fifty voters of the late seventies judged the content of the new musical canon that was emerging, became early festive fifty staples. However well he hid his influences in The Clash's music, Strummer knew his musical roots as well as anyone active in that late seventies scene and he took the spirit, not just of the Notting Hill riots, but of those blues singers who stuck their necks out and lamented the apathy of their peers. 'Police & Thieves' dug the anti-authority stance out of the ganja haze surrounding roots reggae and added it to the punk armoury, fully ripe for development once they got Topper Headon on board as drummer.

From that relatively small but vital starting point, we got the Lee Perry production of 'Complete Control' and the timeless punk-reggae hybrids of '(White Man) in Hammersmith Palais' and 'Armagideon Time'. Crucially, it wasn't just an acute political sensibility that empowered The Clash, but an artistic restlessness that released them from the largely self-imposed restrictions of those early statements to give birth to one of the most vibrant musical manifestos in history.

In festive fifty terms, the number of Clash tracks that featured was almost certainly restricted by the all-time format. It was telling that, after the classic *London*

Calling had failed to generate any chart action at all, *Combat Rock*, whose release coincided with the introduction of the first annual chart in 1982, racked up four entries, making it easily the highest performing Clash album in festive fifty terms.

If Headon was one of the great late seventies drummers, Jones was certainly one of its finest guitarists and, just as important for the group's development, an eager student of production techniques. Anything raw and crude The Clash produced was not a product, as it was with, say, the early Ramones, of a lack of ability to produce anything more sophisticated: it was that way because they wanted it that way and Jones in particular was willing to bury his guitar virtuosity in the interests of getting it to sound just right. It remains one of the period's great ironies that the ultimate punk band's only attempt at a Peel Session never reached the radio: it was aborted half-way through as the band complained about the lack of the sophistication of the BBC studio's equipment.

9. Cocteau Twins
7956 pts

A few years on, it was astonishing to think that many had dismissed the Twins' early work as the mere dabbling of Banshees copyists. Soon those early critics would have their words forcibly rammed back down their throats as Cocteau Twins summoned from that nascent template a sound that defied attempts at description among even more sensitive critics and that made those who attempted such a thing look irredeemably foolish. In doing so they produced a body of work that appeared to have come from nowhere and that pretty much defied imitation. While purveyors of shoegaze and dream pop often attempted to integrate elements of the band into their sound, it's hard to think of anyone who did so overtly with any success.

The duo of Robin Guthrie and Liz Fraser now joined by by Simon Raymonde, the band emblazoned a path across 1984 with a series of projects that may well stand as the best year's work of any band ever. Guthrie and Fraser had contributed a version of Tim Buckley's 'Song to the Siren' to the first This Mortal Coil project – in doing so setting new standards for cover versions everywhere – and the resultant album was injected with the creative influence of all three members. To this they added their masterpiece *Treasure* album and 'Pearly Dewdrops' Drops' single, all three tracks from which made the festive fifty, the first time this had happened, with the title track and the majestic 'The Spangle Maker' both featuring in the top four.

Although only represented by 'Aikea-Guinea' in the festive fifty, 1985 saw them continue their astonishingly prolific workrate. Guthrie also found time to produce Felt's *Ignite the Seven Cannons* album. Although there were conflicting opinions about the results, he added further layers of sound to a band's sound that had often been accused of whimsy and would be again. Bringing in Fraser as guest vocalist, the album's 'Primitive Painters' would give Felt their only festive fifty entry, though the single failed to find favour with Felt or indeed Peel.

Guthrie would ultimately emerge as a producer of some note, although the Twins' relationship with the festive fifty came to an end in 1987 with 'Carolyn's Fingers'. Perhaps it all went wrong festive fifty-wise when they began releasing material in which you could identify the words among Fraser's once majestically elusive vocals. Her voice would be heard again in a festive fifty 1998, however, on Massive Attack's 'Teardrop', which narrowly failed to make the top twenty.

8. Mogwai
8175 pts

Mogwai were at number 26 in this list at the end of the Peel festive fifty era and their rise to these heights might suggest how seamless for them was the move to finding favour with Dandelion Radio voters. In truth, while the presence of two Mogwai tracks in the top fifteen of the first Dandelion chart suggested nothing much had changed, there would be a five year gap until their next entry, after which the band have been as prolific as ever.

I was never a great lover of the term 'post-rock' in describing such bands, but the extent to which Mogwai's festive fifty performance trumps that of luminaries of the alleged genre such as Tortoise and GY!BE is startling. All of these bands re-engaged with unfinished musical business from the post-punk and indeed pre-punk period, Mogwai in particular drawing brilliantly from the Velvet Underground school of alternating soft melody and extreme noise and taking it into entirely new places. Little surprise that they bemused and bewildered those weaned on a diet of Britpop as the movement, such as it was, began to fade and Mogwai caught onto the arse end of it, gave it a hefty tug and left the entrails for others to clean up.

Their 'New Paths to Helicon' served notice of their potential longevity when it gave the band their festive fifty debut at number 2 in 1997, an achievement matched by 'Xmas Steps' a year later, though arguably their musical peak came in 2001, particularl in the case of 'My Father My King', a stunning re-working of a Jewish hymn.

In 2003, Mogwai placed two tracks in the top six, offering a startling contrast to everything else in that year's top ten. Despite that five year gap between 2006 and 2011(their 2008 album *The Hawk is Howling* failed to generate any entries, as indeed was the case, even more surprisingly, with *Hardcore Will Never Die But You Will)*, Mogwai reengaged with the festive fifty with the entry of 'Drunk & Crazy' in 2011 and they placed two tracks in both the 2013 and 2014 charts, the former coming via two tunes from the soundtrack to French drama series *Les Revenants*, while 'Remurdered' returned them to the top five in 2014 following an eleven year gap. With the band continuing to tap into even higher levels of sonic exploration, the Mogwai festive fifty juggernaut has gathered renewed momentum and shows no signs of stopping yet.

7. Joy Division
10190 pts

Although since the first edition of this book they've dropped down a place in this list, a good case could be made for Joy Division being the greatest ever festive fifty band. After all, they appear this high despite a recorded output that amounted to just two albums and a clutch of singles, plus two extraordinary Peel sessions recorded in 1979.

But to get a real sense of the significance of Joy Division in musical history we need to go back a little further than that. The rock vocalist as shaman had been accepted uncritically even among many of those who should have known better and often by those to whom the term referred: the lives and deaths of Hendrix, Morrison and others bear out how poorly a gifted mortal can support the burden of imposed immortality. Obviously this was one of the many bloated concepts against which punk railed but, perhaps unconsciously, similar demands came to be made on figures like Sid Vicious and certainly on the frail body and personality of Ian Curtis. Shortly before his suicide, Curtis had informed the NME of how happy he'd been as a factory maker before the band took off, simply working in a mechanical role while daydreaming about music. He wasn't a man who'd ever wanted to live the dream and his transformation into one of the age's reluctant new gods emerged as a simple extension of his love for music, before becoming perhaps the defining case of natural inability to carry an unnatural burden.

Presumably, had Ian Curtis lived, Joy Division would have gone on to leave an even greater musical legacy. There's certainly no evidence they were anything like a spent force. Cynics will claim that their domination of the 1980 festive fifty would not have occurred were it not for Curtis' death earlier that year. History has surely debunked such a claim: in 1982, in the last all-time chart for 17 years, the band placed ten tracks from their short back catalogue and, when it resumed briefly in 1999, five of them would still be there (more than any other band), with two in the top three.

Unknown Pleasures continues to resonate as a work of fractured genius, combining the creative and destructive strands inherent in the punk make-up and applying them across a practically faultless selection of songs whose clinical perfection was, in their hands, just one of several elements that came together to create its chilling emotional landscape. Tony Wilson's claim that the band influenced the direction of music just as much as the Pistols was not, in this instance, merely a case of well-judged Wilsonic overstatement

After Curtis' death, it became perhaps inevitable that his position as the band's guiding genius and visionary would be enhanced still further. However, behind that vision, there is a musical mastery and intensity that begins with the first track on *Unknown Pleasures* and doesn't waver for a moment throughout their brief existence. The contribution of Hook's brooding bass lines often receive due acknowledgement also but the creation and abolition of musical structures wrought by Albrecht's guitar was always a crucial element of their nihilistic soundscapes, while Morris' drums, often unusually pronounced in the mix largely thanks to the highly significant influence of Martin Hannett's ground-breaking production techniques, do much to enforce the eerie, off-centre feel of the whole work. It was something Morris and Hannett had already taken to extraordinary heights in their contributions to 'Transmission', one of four Joy Division tunes to have graced the festive fifty on as many as four separate occasions.

The forces of creation and the consequent demolition contained within their sound were what Joy Division were essentially about, summed up in so many oxymoronic titles: new dawns fade and love tears apart. There is no irony in Joy Division. There is no hope without inevitable despair. The only end is death. The stuff of existential philosophy brilliantly and uniquely manifested in music, in illustration of how far music can go, how vast can be its conceptual embrace. It was, and remains, anathema to those who see the territory of popular music as consisting only of the trivial and frivolous. In their uncompromising refusal to inhabit such territory, Joy Division staked out the shifting boundaries of an entire new musical world that would allow for so much fascinating sonic exploration that has taken place since.

6. Half Man Half Biscuit
11305 pts

It always seemed likely that the enduring appeal of Half Man Half Biscuit, who were at number 11 in this list when the first edition came out, would eventually see them attain a position more befitting their place in the Peel universe. Dandelion Radio voters have duly obliged, and quite rightly, given that in recent years this remarkable band have, perhaps against expectations, produced much of their best work.

Emerging from a conceptual base that bracketed the too often under-used musical influences offered by football and daytime TV, their classic debut album *Back in the DHSS* was eagerly picked up on by Peel back in 1985, its laconic commentaries and dour wordplay standing out in an era where the anorak, the long fringe and the obtuse lyric often held sway. Half Man Half Biscuit wore their anoraks as they'd presumably always done, characteristically apathetic towards their potential as fashion accessories.

Remarkably, despite reaching number one in the then vibrant indie charts, the album failed to generate any festive fifty entries, a wrong that was righted the following year with what, at the time, amounted to a posthumous debut, two tracks appearing, the second accompanied by the earnest appeal from Peel that he hoped they'd continue in some form.

They didn't at that point, but thankfully the split did prove a temporary one and from the mid-nineties onward the band became festive fifty regulars. Since their *Voyage to the Bottom of the Road* album in 1997, all eight HMHB albums have registered at least one festive fifty entry, while the most recent two even fulfilled the wider promise of Back in the DHSS by scraping into the lower reaches of the UK album charts.

They continue to provide crucial commentaries on such crucial features of contemporary existence as the over-stated significance to humanity of Slipknot, the paucity of a television culture that saw fit to employ Bob Wilson and the curious life forms that inhabit the backwaters of an all-night garage. Strangely, it wasn't until 2003 that the band reached the top ten, with 'Tending the Wrong Grave for 23 Years'. They repeated this the following year with 'Joy Division Oven Gloves', a typical triumph of comic juxtaposition that became the first session-only track to make the top ten for sixteen years.

Presumably, the band had little knowledge of or interest in the fact that they would soon go on to overhaul the festive fifty total of the track's subject. The tune would feature again in its official version in the One Music chart of 2004 and, though the excellent *90 Bisodol (Crimond)* album would only generate a single entry, 2014's *Urge for Offal* improved on this with an appearance for the title track and, with the much-celebrated 'The Unfortunate Gwatkin', a first ever place in the top three.

To the unfamiliar, their art – if they'd permit me to call it that, and I'm sure they wouldn't – could appear little more than a cynical cultivation of popular culture in search of a cheap laugh at even cheaper targets, underpinned by luddite artistic values. Conversely, to those who know them, few bands have seemed less contrived throughout an, albeit briefly interrupted, existence of thirty years.

5. PJ Harvey
16422 pts
Total includes collaborations with John Parish

One of the true giants of music over more than two decades, PJ Harvey can justify such a label while attaining something like a deserved level of respect in much wider circles, resulting in an MBE and a couple of Mercury music prizes among many other accolades, all achieved entirely without compromise.

Thankfully, despite such adulation, her music has remained refreshingly untainted by any overly commercial tendencies and, among the many remarkable things about this artist, the most remarkable is that throughout all this time her distinctly idiosyncratic outlook has never wavered for a moment.

Aided by some of the period's finest multi-instrumentalists (most notably mentor John Parish, ex-Birthday Party member and Bad Seed Mick Harvey and Rob Ellis, whose involvement, like that of Parish, goes back to the late eighties and Automatic Dlamini days), the PJ Harvey project has been moulded and re-fashioned constantly; yet, despite its artistic fluidity and changes of direction, it's hard to think of a PJ Harvey recording that hasn't had something remarkable about it.

Both 'Dress' and 'Sheela-Na-Gig' gave early indications of a healthy individualism, as Harvey defiantly distanced herself from the emerging riot grrrl fad while fending off ludicrous accusations of anti-feminist elements in her music. The singles both made number two in the festive fifty and establishied a fascinating template that has been repeatedly re-invented and re-interpreted to the point where, as with all great art, any early attempts at categation have come with time to appear all the more crude and trite. Like Patti Smith, with whom she was inevitably compared, she remained aloof from any easy associations, although frankly even Smith's breadth of artistic vision fails to withstand scrutiny against the variety and longevity achieved by Harvey.

From the Albini-produced Rid of Me, through the first post-Automatic Dlamini project with John Parish and throughout the remainder of the nineties, Harvey's music embraced further levels of complexity, continuing to pose questions concerning sexuality, romance and the nature of humanity with unflinching honest. If such subject matter kept her away from broader appreciation for a while, it was no less fascinating for all that and, in 2000, she emerged as if from a sewer into the wider ocean with the astonishing Stories of the City, Stories of the Sea.

From there it became possible to begin to contextualise Harvey's history as a recording artist: seven years of artistic struggle after the appearance of the, in retrospect, much cleaner (though it had scarcely seemed so at the time) debut *Dry*, had mined the personal element in her work to extremes, veering from the experimental to the maudlin to the plain difficult. *Stories...* contained all those elements too, but the serenity of the album as a whole was the work of a mature artist, its vision more clear and complete and it was this, rather than any deliberate nod to commercialism, that brought the album its broader appeal;

With the, by turns, brutal and melodic *Uh Huh Her* in 2004, Harvey took us back into the storm, playing all instruments except drums on the album, while White Chalk, her only album to date not to yield a festive fifty entry, sacrificed even the involvement of Ellis in its pursuit of a quieter, more ethereal sound.

If by that point we were to assume that a decline, both artistically and in festive fifty terms, had set in, we were to be loudly awakened from any such inane speculations by *Let England Shake*, a masterpiece that returned her to the festive fifty and, at last, the number one spot, courtesy of the album's title track. Her brilliant examination of war and conflict in the early twenty-first century was universally hailed as a masterpiece, while the self-released track 'Shaker Aamer', a timely paean to the Guantanamo Bay prisoner that later scraped into the festive fifty, dismissed any notions arising from the album that Harvey wasn't prepared to take a firm side on the subject matter it explored.

4. New Order
23400 pts

When Curtis' death brought the end of Joy Division, its remaining members made it known fairly quickly that they intended to change both their name and direction. The phenomenon of Curtis was far too great for them to given any serious consideration simply to carrying on without him. So Albrecht became Sumner and took on vocal duties; the keyboards that had begun to establish a presence in Joy Division's later work were embedded into the new plans when Gillian Gilbert was brought into the band.

'Ceremony', the first recorded output of New Order, was already established as a Joy Division song; similarly 'Procession' was created very much in the shadow of their former band. However, by 1982 New Order were already moving firmly, startlingly away from that shadow. Partly as a result of the introduction of new rhythms, and new chemicals imbibed, during trips to America, their entire musical output from then could be read subsequently as a prefiguring of the direction of Mancunian music, pre-dating the Madchester scene by a good six years after a breaking of their mould that introduced elements that, at that time, were regarded as dangerous to know for any 'serious' band.

What New Order retained, crucially, were the enigmatic lyrics and wavering mystique that helped them to retain a certain post-new wave credibility while literally giving their audience a musical education. Astonishingly, the band that were once Joy Division had, in the space of just two years since Curtis' death, changed music again.

It's difficult to assess the claim that, had Curtis lived, the band would probably have taken this direction anyway. New Order would certainly come to challenge those early perceptions of themselves as po-faced and introspective. Given the nature of the music they were now playing, this wasn't too great a task; but then, the band were now keen to assert, it wasn't as if Ian Curtis had been an especially miserable or introspective human being. While Joy Division had probed emotional disintegration further than any band before, New Order were taking music forward in a very different direction – in many ways exploring the antithesis of what their former band had been about – but then the members of Joy Division had probably all been shrewd enough to know that their original project probably only had a certain amount of mileage anyway and, indeed, many of the hinted changes of musical direction, could be picked up on Closer by anyone with a well-tuned ear and open mind.

New Order continued for some time to make new departures and wrong-foot the wrong-headed: I now recall with disbelief the number of people who dismissed 'Truth Faith' as insubstantial froth, and I wonder how many of them do also. As such, they remained through a 'Peel band', the excellent 'Regret' featuring in the festive fifty after a long break in 1993 and the band would then apparently disappear before re-forming to score a gain with 'Brutal' in 2000 and 'Crystal', which reached the heights of the top ten a year later. They remain the only band to have made number one in the festive fifty with two different tracks in consecutive years.

3. The Smiths
41745 pts

Only Joy Division can rival the kind of impact made by The Smiths over such a short period of time. During an extremely prolific five year period, they achieved two festive fifty number ones, ten top ten appearances (at least one in each of those five years) and, in their final year as a band, secured more tracks in a single chart than any other act, a record that seems unlikely ever to be beaten.

Their arrival in 1983 was roaringly heralded by elements of the music press, aided by already legendary live performances and Morrissey's provocative eloquence in interviews. As one of the truly great runs of singles commenced with the extraordinary 'Hand In Glove', four stunning radio sessions – two for Peel and a further two for David Jensen – revealed the depth of material that was already there.

Opinions were polarised from the outset, with the band's stance and musical approach clearly intent of making it that way. The music press had all along been preoccupied with the search for a ground-breaking band to shake up music in the manner of the Sex Pistols and The Smiths confirmed that they were, and always had been, looking in all the wrong places. The controversy that could be engendered by outrageous antics and televised swearing may have breathed live into the music scene via the agency of the Pistols, but it had rendered itself a tired cliché in the process. Morrissey claimed a life of celibacy and extolled the merits of a night in stroking the cat. When the rest of the band partied after a gig, he strolled back to his room and got out a good book. As if finding such a way of life inevitably bogus, early critics twisted his lyrics to reveal alleged references to child molestation and, later, bizarre claims that the 'Hang the DJ' refrain in 'Panic' was a call for racial violence were aired.

The Smiths were already the most significant band of the eighties by the time their first album was released in 1984. That year 'How Soon is Now?' became festive fifty number one after appearing on the B-side of a 12" single. As a slew of releases made the national charts, opinions remained rudely split between those who hailed them as the first genuine post-new wave phenomenon and those who just didn't get the music or the joke.

Where much of the chilling power of Joy Division had lain in an entire lack of irony, The Smiths had it sprouting from every orifice. While, bafflingly, some couldn't see it, the rest of us delighted in the perverse humour of 'Heaven Knows I'm Miserable Now' and 'William, It Was Really Nothing' and the provocative jibes of 'Nowhere Fast' and 'The Queen is Dead'. And when The Smiths stripped away the irony and gave us bare, naked emotion, as in tracks like 'I Know It's Over', they did that better than anyone else too.

It wasn't just about the lyrical content, either. The clash that lay within the meeting of minds of Morrissey and Marr was vital to the unique conflict at the heart of the band's musical manifesto. Marr rocked where Morrissey popped for much of the time; uplifting guitar riffs provided the backdrop for the most outrageous declarations of misery. Although there was an acknowledged necessity for Marr to curb any excessive rockist urges he might have been tempted to bring along, he could still inject something as brilliantly irreverent as Status Quo guitar motif into 'What Difference Does It Make?' and made it work, while creating the stunning riff around which 'How Soon is Now?' whirled and the sprawling, almost orchestrail sweep of 'The Queen is Dead'.

In 1986 they emulated Joy Division's achievement of placing four tracks in the top seven, before beating the same band's record of ten records in a chart the following year. Of the band's singles, only 'Shakespeare's Sister' failed to make the festive fifty. When the band's light finally did go out, it always seemed unlikely that the individual members could sustain the legacy in festive fifty terms, although there followed a run of entries for Morrissey's solo singles. Marr would return only sporadically, but has now joined that small group of artists to have appeared with four bands or more, adding entries with Electronic, Billy Bragg and Modest Mouse to the remarkable legacy he left after the demise of The Smiths.

2. The Wedding Present
95472 pts

The Wedding Present grew up on the festive fifty. From their lovingly amateurish beginnings on 'Go Out & Get 'Em Boy' in 1985, to their fascinating attempts to diversify throughout the nineties, they matured, developed, alienated a few listeners, gained a few more, and rarely but a foot wrong if festive fifty votes are anything to go by.

By 1986, their guitar-based sound and David Gedge's reflective lyrics saw them roughly rammed into a C86 pigeonhole and, for a spell, it seemed to many in the game that they'd go the way of most bands who'd been thus classified, but by 1989 the band were still offering brilliant variations on those early themes, apparently unaffected by the taste upheavals of the period and the indie/dance experiments embraced by many of their peers. In a sense, they'd already peaked in a festive fifty sense by then when, in 1987, they'd gatecrashed The Smiths' farewell party, impudently placing four tracks from their debut *George Best* album in the top ten.

Seasoned contenders by this point, even by this stage their remained something homely about The Wedding Present. They were already part of the furniture of the Peel show and of the festive fifty. Gedge was a regular listener, contacting the show during broadcasts with accounts of the yearly records he was keeping. His own band were creeping up his lists, a further three tracks having made the festive fifty in 1988. In that year the band registered the highest ever entry for a session track that was, at that stage, unavailable in any other form when 'Take Me (I'm Yours)' made the top five. It would return again the following year in a different form, as one of a bunch of festive fifty entries from the masterful *Bizarro* album.

1990, however, saw a distinct move away from the familiar Wedding Present sound template. The new approach would be augmented by the shrewd choice of Steve Albini as producer on Seamonsters. Of course, there comes a time when you have to get rid of that comfortable old pair of slippers or that tub of Greek yoghurt in the fridge that has just edged past its sell-by date. With bands, you have to judge the timing of such a move perfecgtly, at the time where your previous format appears to have peaked but where ideas are creeping in that just don't have the right consistency for the old mix. New Order had achieved this with deft regularity and now The Wedding Present emulated them.

The album was certainly a success with festive fifty voters, with tracks from it appearing all over the 1991 Phantom Fifty and when, in 1993, they announced their intention to release a single every month, a number of these did pretty well in the end of year chart too, as well as allowing the band, somewhat bizarrely, to equal Elvis Presley's record of most top thirty singles in the UK charts in a single year. By now, original guitarist Pete Salowka had left the band and eventually Gedge would be left as their only original member. Festive fifty entries did begin to fall off before the band called it a day, with the new vehicle of Cinerama again allowing Gedge to inject new vitality at just the right point.

Out of nowhere, however, The Wedding Present re-appeared in 2004 and it was only fitting that the return should be commemorated with a festive fifty entry. And it was even more fitting, perhaps, that in 2013, their 'Two Bridges' should finally give them their first number one.

1. The Fall
269990 pts

There's an old edition of the Guinness Book of Hit Singles that seems to sum of the music industry's bewilderment when it comes to The Fall. It reads: 'Mark E. Smith – male vocalist and multi-instrumentalist.'

Now, I hold what Smith has achieved down the years in extremely high regard, but one thing he ain't is a multi-instrumentalist (a few tweaks on a keyboard here and there and some occasional guitar work surely doesn't qualify). What the writers of the aforementioned work struggled with was the concept of a band with a central visionary, around whom have circulated a large number of talented musicians and songwriters, who has managed to maintain a position at the centre of his musical universe for an extraordinary length of time. In this sense, Smith can onl be compared with Frank Zappa and Captain Beefheart, neither of whom the Guinness writers had much cause to trouble themselves with, and, even to approach an understanding of the phenomenon of The Fall, that is where we must begin.

I once witnessed a live performance of The Fall in which Smith, during a particular song – I forget which 0 began turning his microphone on and off, clearly creating confusion among the band members behind him, but not to the audience who were merrily involved in his mischief. I was also in attendance at another gig where he left the band playing for several minutes before appearing onstage, then proceeded to mess with their instruments and amplifiers as they gamely strove to maintain their groove. To remain the central figure in a shifting line-up of musical innovators, to keep people on their toes who themselves are more than capable of making a significant contribution in their own right, you need a few tricks up your sleeve, perhaps. The guys behind him were performing their tasks immensely well, but Smith could still lead them anywhere he wanted, whether they knew where he was going or not.

Marc Riley. Craig Scanlon. Stephen Hanley. Brix Smith. Julia Nagle. And, more recently, Elena Poulou, Smith's third wife and someone who, from an outsider's perspective anyway, seems as well-balanced a figure in anchoring and complementing Smith's vision as anyone. And indeed most of the people listed among Fall line-ups in this book. Signficant individuals, not just in terms of what they've brought to The Fall musically, but often as songwriters and as architects of the band's sound. Beefheart notoriously kept his bands on a tight leash, often naming them himself and even at times dictating what they could eat. Smith has gained a not dissimilar reputation, but his control of The Fall hasn't been anything like as eccentric nor as obsessively singular. He's been more than happy to draw on the contributions of other members, to allow them to play a large part in forging the sound, which is surely a major component in allowing The Fall, as John Peel famously remarked, to remain somehow always different yet always the same.

There have been individuals who've been crucial at various times in holding the band together to allow space for the creative relationships at the heart of The Fall to flourish. Craig Scanlon and Stephen Hanley were vital at the time of Brix Smith's influentail period, while Ben Pritchard later performed brilliantly in a later period, performing a particularlry necessary role given the elastic nature of the Smith/Jim Watts relationship.

To infuse this proficiency with the spark that brings into being the unique artistic phenomenon that is The Fall requires a unique individual, which is of course what Smith is. Not a genius, not a shaman (those who make these claims on his behalf are very silly and I suspect he'd regard them similarly), and certainly not a rock star in any conventional sense. The impact of Riley was evident in the early Fall, and in long-standing classics like 'Totally Wired' and '(How I Wrote) Elastic Man'. It was inevitable, then, that there would be an identity shift when Riley left and Brix Smith brought her considerable influence to the band of the mid-eighties. And of course there are Fall fans who will tell you it fell apart at this point, exemplified by the 1999 all-time festive fifty, which contained only material from the pre-Brix days. Yet the mid-eighties was a time in which The Fall, jostling for eminence with The Smiths and The Wedding Present, became a truly dominant festive fifty force.

When Brix and Mark split up in the late eighties, Craig Scanlon stepped out from the long shadows to cast even more of his influence across the band's music, once again bringing a new vision to sit alongside that of MES. Brix returned in the nineties, briefly, then left again for Julia Nagle to succeed in the position, only for Jim Watt then to fill the gap, albeit in an apparently fractious way.

This presents a very vague pattern, but it's a pattern nonetheless. To retain freshness and originality, Mark E. Smith has always had the sense to find a partner figure who can drive the band forward and, when necessary, to have a further anchor figure during periods where creative volatility prevailed. I suspect it is this, and not simply that Smith doesn't get on with people, that lies at the heart of The Fall's often frequent line-up changes and the legendarily swift and harsh manner in which some band members have been dropped.

The approach has left us with something remarkable. A band for whom a new release is instantly recognisable yet more often than not surprising and, more frequently than we have any right to expect, brilliant. Only rarely has a Fall album failed to gain any recognition at all from festive fifty voters and only three charts since the band's first appearance in 1979 have failed to feature them. Their three number one have been spaced well apart. 'Bill is Dead', a selection that only seems even more surprising with time, gave them their first some eleven years after their debut, while the subsequent achievements of 'Sparta FC' and '50 Year Old Man' have been more predictable, if no less welcome, number ones.

In terms of dominating the festive fifty, The Fall don't look like they'll ever get near the number of tracks they managed to place back in 1993, but then nor does anyone else. Since then, there have been years in which they managed to place no more than a single entry, while in 1998 they only just managed to sneak in at the bottom end, albeit with a session track in a year of no official releases. *Are You Are Missing Winner* became the first Fall album for donkey's years to fail to produce a single entry, but every album since has managed to do so and, after that, the 'Sparta FC' phenomenon – two versions of the track appeared at numbers two and one in successive years – confirmed The Fall's unique relationship with the chart, re-establishing The Fall, beyond Joy Division, Half Man Half Biscuit and even Beefheart, as the band that remains most perfectly synonymous with the spirit of both the John Peel show and the festive fifty. Fittingly, even in the Dandelion Radio years, they've had more appearances in the chart than any other band.

TOP FESTIVE FIFTY ALBUMS

If John Peel had ever canvassed his listeners' opinions on their favourite albums of all time, it's a safe bet that the list would be very different from the one that follows, and would presumably have featured LPs that failed to produce even a single festive fifty entry.

It would be fatuous to attempt to guess what such a chart would look like, but what we are able to do is take the points process from the previous section and apply it to albums. In other words, the two most crucial questions here are: how many festive fifty entries did the album generate (whether in the year of the album's release or not)? And how many combined 'Gedge' points did those tracks accumulate? The former figure is then multiplied by the latter, as in the previous section, to produce overall points scores that produce the resulting top fifty. In the case of songs that appeared in more than one festive fifty, the highest placing achieved by that track in the one that counts, and the others are disregarded. Whether the version of the track played in the countdown is the one from the album or not is considered irrelevant for our purposes here. Where scores are tied, the album with the highest placed single track is awarded the higher position.

Compilation albums are excluded, otherwise it would just become a fairly meaningless list of Greatest Hits compilations alongside the likes of The Smiths' *Hatful of Hollow* and The Wedding Present's *Hit Parade* and any number of Peel Sessions collections. Albums put together in the studio are the only ones to make this list. I've also decided that mini-albums like Ash's *Trailer* and Babes In Toyland's *To Mother* shouldn't be included, although neither of these examples would have gained enough points to make the top fifty in any case.

Because of the nature of the scoring system, albums that failed to produce at least three festive fifty entries can't mathematically qualify, which means the exclusion, for instance, of PJ Harvey's *Dry*, even though it produced two number two entries. Similarly, there can be no place for classic albums like *The Clash*, Joy Division's *Unknown Pleasures* or Dylan's *Highway 61 Revisited*, all of which failed to register that crucial third track.

A number of albums produced three festive fifty entries, and one even managed four, but failed to gain enough points to make the top fifty. Before the countdown, here's a rundown of those albums:

Four tracks:

Bossanova – Pixies (4AD, 1990)

Three tracks:

Metal Box – Public Image Ltd (Virgin, 1979)
Pornography – The Cure (Fiction, 1982)
Songs To Remember – Scritti Politti (Rough Trade, 1982)
New Gold Dream (81/82/83/84) – Simple Minds (Virgin, 1982)
This Nation's Saving Grace – The Fall (Beggars Banquet, 1983)
It'll End in Tears – This Mortal Coil (4AD, 1984)
First & Last & Always – Sisters of Mercy (Merciful Release, 1985)
Rum, Sodomy & The Lash – The Pogues (Stiff, 1985)
Shop Assistants – Shop Assistants (Blue Guitar, 1986)
Extricate – The Fall (Cog-Sinister, 1990)
Life – Inspiral Carpets (Cow, 1990)
Trompe Le Monde – Pixies (4AD, 1991)
Copper Blue – Sugar (Creation, 1992)
Bring It Down – Madder Rose (Seed, 1993)

The First Tindersticks Album – Tindersticks (This Way Up, 1993)
Crooked Rain, Crooked Rain – Pavement (Big Cat, 1994)
To Bring You My Love – PJ Harvey (Island, 1995)
Guerrilla – Super Furry Animals (Creation, 1999)
Disco Volante – Cinerama (Scopitones, 2000)
Not the Tremblin' Kind – Laura Cantrell (Spit & Polish, 2000)
The Unutterable – The Fall (Eagle, 2000)
Trouble Over Bridgewater – Half Man Half Biscuit (Probe Plus, 2000)
Trust – Low (Rough Trade, 2002)
Dear Catastrophe Waitress – Belle & Sebastian (Rough Trade, 2003)
The Sash My Father Wore & Other Stories – Ballboy (SL, 2003)

It's curious that, during the course of the post-Peel festive fifties, only three albums have recorded three entries or more in a chart (incidentally, two are by The Fall, bringing the number of their albums in this list to ten).

Therefore, the chart below is, with those three exceptions, pretty much a repeat of the top fifty in the first edition of this book. As a simple repeat of the full commentary from that first chart seems unnecessary, I've concentrated instead on much briefer comments this time, alongside factual details, assuming that there is somebody out there interested in such details. Apologies if that person isn't you.

Tracks listed are those that appeared across different versions of the releases. Any tracks that appeared purely as exclusives on the vinyl, CD or cassette version or on any subsequent reissues are not included, nor do they contribute points to the total.

50. The Fall
The Marshall Suite (Artful, 1999)
279 pts

Touch Sensitive/F-'Oldin' Money/Shake-Off*/Bound/This Perfect Day/(Jung Nev's) Antidotes/Inevitable/Anecdots + Antidotes in B#/Early Life of the Crying Marshall/Birthday Song/Mad Men-End Dog/On My Own

*Appeared as a session track in 1998

Producers: Mark E. Smith and Steve Hitchcock

Performers:
Mark E. Smith – guitar/keyboards/vocals
Julia Nagle – guitar/keyboards/programming
Neville Wilding – guitar
Adam Helal – bass
Karen Leatham – bass
Tom Head – drums

An album that confirmed that, after a period of disruption that was extreme even for The Fall, Mark E. Smith was still very much alive and kicking in a musical sense. 'Touch Sensitive', following its high festive fifty placing, would go on to achieve an unusually wide audience after its use in a TV car commercial.

49. The Delgados
Peloton (Chemikal Underground, 1998)
315 pts

Everything Goes Around the Water/The Actress/The Arcane Model/Clarinet/**Pull the Wires from the Wall**/Repeat Failure/And so the Talking Stopped/Don't Stop/Blackpool/Russian Orthodox/The Weaker Argument Defeats the Stronger

Producers: The Delgados

Performers
Alun Woodward – guitar/vocals
Emma Pollock – guitar/vocals
Stewart Henderson - bass
Paul Savage – drums

Additional musicians:
Alan Barr – strings
Jennifer Christie – strings
Emily MacPherson – strings

More musically complex that their debut, The Delgados' second album sees the band adding extra musicians and adding the layers of sound that would instigate the beginnings of the growth of a musical template that would continue on future albums. In festive fifty terms, it's most notable for containing the number one track 'Pull the Wires from the Wall', while 'Everything Goes Around the Water' remains one of the finest examples of the band's dual vocal interplay.

48. Morrissey
Viva Hate (HMV, 1988)
318 pts

Alsatian Cousin/Little Man, What Now?/**Everyday is Like Sunday**/Bengali in Platforms/Angel, Angel, Down We Go Together/**Late Night, Maudlin Street/Suedehead**/Break Up the Family/The Ordinary Boys/I Don't Mind if You Forget Me/Dial-A-Cliche/Margaret on the Guillotine

Producer: Stephen Street

Performers:
Morrissey – vocals
Vini Reilly - guitar
Stephen Street – guitar/bass
Andrew Paresi – drums

Additional musicians:
Richard Korster – violin
Fenella Barton – violin
John Metcalf – viola
Rachel Maguire – cello
Mark Davies – cello
Robert Woolhard – cello

The album's two singles had already demonstrated that, following the break-up of The Smiths, Morrissey was likely, at least for a while, to remain a significant figure in festive fifty terms. In addition to those singles, there was also a place for 'Late Night, Maudlin Street', which remains one of the singer's finest post-Smiths moments.

47. Undertones
The Undertones (Sire, 1979)
324 pts

Family Entertainment/Girls Don't Like It/Male Model/I Gotta Getta/**Teenage Kicks***/Wrong Way/Jump Boys/Here Comes the Summer/**Get Over You***/Billy's Third/**Jimmy Jimmy**/True Confessions/ She's a Runaround/I Know a Girl/Listening In/Casbah Rock

*Not included on intial pressings of the LP, but a second version released later in the year did include 'Teenage Kicks'

Producer: Roger Bechirian

Performers:
Feargal Sharkey – vocals
John O'Neill – guitar
Damian O'Neill – guitar
Michael Bradley – bass
Billy Doherty – drums

Peel had already upset many of his older listeners by decreeing that the Undertones were the best band in the world and this debut album gives plenty of evidence as to why he felt that way. 'Teenage Kicks' and 'Get Over You' were the serial festive fifty entrants, of course, but 'Jimmy Jimmy' – which brilliantly combined multiple hooks, a hummable chorus and the band's rough charm – gave the album a third entry in its year of release.

46. The Wedding Present
Watusi (Island, 1994)
332 pts

So Long, Baby/**Click, Click**/Yeah Yeah Yeah Yeah Yeah/Let Him Have It/Gazebo/Shake It/**Spangle**/It's a Gas/**Swimming Pools, Movie Stars**/Bit Rat/Catwoman/Hot Pants

Producer: Steve Fisk

Performers:
David Gedge – guitar/vocals
Paul Dorrington – guitar
Darren Belk – bass
Simon Smith – drums

Additional musicians on festive fifty tracks:
Heather Lewis – vocals on 'Click Click' and 'Swimming Pools, Movie Stars'
Steve Fisk - piano
Greg Powers – trombone

By this point only David Gedge remained from the band's original line-up and the early template of one-sided conversational lyrics and frantically strummed guitars were long gone by now. 'Swimming Pools, Movie Stars' stands comparison with teh band's best work but the spirit of Cinerama is lurking in the background and ultimately the album comes across as one of constrained exploration that wouldn't find its fullest expression until Gedge plunged headlong into his new project.

45. Pixies
Surfer Rosa (4AD, 1988)
332 pts

Bone Machine/Break My Body/Something Against You/Broken Face/**Gigantic**/**River Euphrates**/**Where is My Mind?**/Cactus/Tony's Theme/Oh My Golly!/Vamos/I'm Amazed

Producer: Steve Albini

Performers:
Black Francis – guitar/vocals
Joey Santiago – guitar
Mrs John Murphy, aka Kim Deal – bass/vocals
David Lovering – drums

Although Surfer Rosa is undoubtedly the Pixies at their most abrasive, the tempo changes, occasional Latin elements and tension between melody and noise gave this full debut an impressive depth. Black Francis welds an artfulness learned from Brian Wilson to harsh walls of sound borrowed from Husker Du and, with Steve Albini's production (later criticised by Francis), noise just about wins.

44. The Smiths
The Smiths (Rough Trade, 1984)
342 pts

Reel Around the Fountain*/You've Got Everything Now/Miserable Lie/Pretty Girls Make Graves/The Hand That Rocks the Cradle/Still Ill/**Hand In Glove***/**What Difference Does It Make?**/I Don't Owe You Anything/Suffer Little Children

Both appeared in the 1983 chart., although 'Reel Around the Fountain' also featured in a lower position in 1984, though again the track played in the countdown was the original session version rather than the version on this album.

Producer: John Porter

Performers
Morrissey – vocals
Johnny Marr – guitar/harmonica
Andy Rourke – bass
Mike Joyce – drums

Few debut albums have been so keenly awaited and, following the already legendary Peel sessions and singles from the previous year along with the production problems that had bedevilled it from the beginning, the disappointment that ensued was probably inevitable. Even so, there's not a bad song on here and the soon to be familiar lyrical spectrum of Morrissey is splendidly apparent, ranging from romantic failure and embittered social despair to that quirky sense of irony.

43. The Fall
Reformation Post-TLC (Slogan, 2007)
345 pts

Over! Over!/**Reformation/Fall Sound**/White Line Fever/Insult Song/My Door is Never/Coach & Horses/The Usher/The Wright Stuff/Scenario/Das Boat/the Bad Stuff/**Systematic Abuse**

Producers: Mark E. Smith and Tim Presley, aka Tim Baxter, credited as Tim 'Gracielands'

Performers:
Mark E. Smith – vocals
Tim Presley – guitar
Gary Bennett – guitar
Peter Greenaway - guitar
Dave Spurr – bass.
Robert Barbato - bass
Elena Poulou – keyboards
Orpheo McCloud – drums

One of the most triumphant Fall achievements of recent times: although the moody experimentation of 'Das Boat' would alienate many, the rest of the album is an unmitigated triumph. In interviews, Smith would teasingly suggest that 'TLC' stood for 'treacherous lying cunts' (or 'traitors, liars and cunts' in some versions), a reference to the break-up of the previous line-up, and there are numerous musical and lyrical references to rebirth and renewal, all of which combine to make Reformation both a delight to listen to and a fascinating manifesto for the recent Fall.

42. Los Campesinos
Romance is Boring (Wichita, 2010)
351 pts

In Media Res/**There Are Listed Buildings***/Romance is Boring/We've Got Your Back (Documented Minor Emotional Breakdown #2)/Plan A/200-102/**Straight in At 101**/Who Fell Asleep In/I Warned You: Do Not Make An Enemy of Me//HeartSwells/100-1//I Just Sighed, I Just Sighed, Just so You Know/A Heat Rash in the Shape of the Show Me State; or, Letters From Me to Charlotte/**The Sea is a Good Place to Think of the Future***/This is a Flag. There is No Wind/Coda: A Burn Scar in the Shape of the Sooner State

*Appeared in the 2009 chart

Producer: John Goodmanson

Performers:
Gareth Paisley – glockenspiel/vocals
Aleksandra Berditchevskaia – keyboards/vocals
Jamie Stewart - vocals
Zac Pennington – backing vocals
Tom Bromley - guitar
Neil Turner - guitar
Ellen Waddell – bass
Jherek Bischoff – double bass/trombone
Samantha Boshnack – trumpet/flugel horn
Izaak Mills – saxophone/flute
Harriet Coleman – violin/keyboards
Kim Paisley – shruti box/piccolo
Ollie Briggs – drums

At the time of writing, this collection is the last to register as many as three festive fifty entries. It comes from a band whose almost banner-waving position in the worlds of indie and tweecore announced itself in the very first Dandelion Radio chart, although by now their sound was diversifying and there is a conceptual and musical complexity here that was absent in the band's earlier work.

41. Cocteau Twins
Treasure (4AD, 1984)
352 pts

Ivo/Lorelei/**Beatrix**/Persephone/**Pandora**/Amelia/Aloysius/Cicely/Otterly/**Domino**

Producers: Cocteau Twins

Performers:
Elizabeth Fraser – vocals
Robin Guthrie – guitar
Simon Raymonde – bass

An album that catches the Cocteau Twins at their peak, *Treasure* is a beautifully manicured collection of material, perfectly utilising the larynx of Elizabeth Fraser to its devastating potential. Perhaps it's not surprising that the festive fifty entries weren't particularly high: for one thing, they were battling for attention tracks from the equally astonishing P*early Dewdrops' Drops* single and the album is very much one that demands to be heard and appreciated as a whole.

40. Joy Division
Closer (Factory, 1980)
352 pts

Atrocity Exhibition/**Isolation***/Passover/Colony/A Means to an End/Heart & Soul/**Twenty Four Hours/The Eternal***/Decades

*Highest placing was in the 1982 all-time chart

Producer: Martin Hannett

Performers:
Ian Curtis – vocals
Bernard Sumner – guitar
Peter Hook – bass
Stephen Morris – drums

The second of their two masterpieces is a chillingly perfect depiction of a bleak, nihilistic world. The triumph of *Closer* lies not just in how well it presents an eerie sense of the inevitability of self-destruction but also its astonishing musical cohesion. Rarely, if ever, has a collection of songs sounded so tightly managed, yet carried such a sense of danger and an intrinsic sense of being close to falling apart.

39. The Fall
The Light User Syndrome (Jet, 1996)
354 pts

D.I.Y. Meat/Das Vulture Aus Ein Nutter-Wain/He Pep!/**Hostile**/Stay Away (Old White Train)/Spinetrak/Interlude/**Chilinism***/Powder Keg/Oleano/ **Cheetham Hill**/The Coliseum/Last Chance to Turn Around/The Ballard of J. Drummer/Oxymoron/ Secession Man

*Appeared under the title of 'The Chisilers'

Producers: Mike Bennett and Mark E. Smith

Performers:
Mark E. Smith – vocals
Brix Smith – vocals
Stephen Hanley – bass

Julia Nagle - keyboards
Simon Wolstencroft – drums
Karl Burns – drums

Additional musicians:
Lucy Rimmer – vocals
Mike Bennett – vocals

Among The Fall's best albums of the nineties, although by that point they'd been bettering previous efforts and exceeding expectations for so long you'd kind of got used to it. It's an album borne of Brix Smith's brief second phase in the band, but also one of the band's greatest team efforts, with songwriting credits shared all over the place and even vocal contributions passed around, leading to one of the band's most diverse and fascinating collections.

38. Dreadzone
Second Light (Virgin, 1995)
372 pts

Life, Love & Unity/Little Britain/A Canterbury Tale/**Captain Dread**/Cave of Angels/**Zion Youth**/One Way/Shining Path/Out of Heaven

Producers: Dreadzone

Performers:
Tim Bran – various
Leo Williams – bass
Greg Roberts – drums

Additional musicians on festive fifty tracks:
Earl Sixteen – vocals on 'Life, Love & Unity', 'Zion Youth'
Dan Donovan - keyboards
Donna McKevitt – viola on 'Little Britain'

An album hailed by Peel as a masterpiece and one of his favourites of all time, he was understandably delighted when it made such an impact on the celebrated 1995 chart, to which it brought so much quality and diversity. When 'Zion Youth' made the top five, it became the most successful reggae-inspired track in the chart's history, some twelve years after Naturalites & The Realistics had breached the top ten.

37. The Fall
Cerebral Caustic (Permanent, 1995)
376 pts

The Joke/Don't Call Me Darling/Rainmaster/**Feeling Numb**/Pearl City/Life Just Bounces/I'm Not Satisfied/The Aphid/**Bonkers in Phoenix**/One Day/North West Fashion Show/Pine Leaves

Producers: Mike Bennett and Mark E. Smith

Performers:
Mark E. Smith – guitar/vocals
Brix Smith – guitar/vocals
Craig Scanlon – guitar
Stephen Hanley – bass
Dave Bush - keyboards
Simon Wolstencroft – drums
Karl Burns – drums

The album that heralded Brix Smith's temporary return to the Fall ranks and she duly left her mark, appearing as a songwriting partner on half the tacks. Although Peel expressed reservations about it, 'Bonkers in Phoenix' made the festive fifty and stands very much as an extended metonym for the album, its short-wave radio like intrusions a fine example of Mark and Brix's artistic sparring, his spoken vocals jarring with Brix's melodic contributions against a backdrop of dischordant noise.

36. White Stripes
White Blood Cells (Sympathy for the Record Industry, 2001)
360 pts

Dead Leaves & The Dirty Ground*/Hotel Yorba/I'm Finding It Harder to Be a Gentleman/**Fell in Love with a Girl**/Expecting/Little Room/The Union Forever/The Same Boy You've Always Known/We're Going to Be Friends/Offend in Every Way/I Think I Smell a Rat/Aluminum/I Can't Wait/Now Mary/I Can Learn/This Protector

*Highest entry was in 2002 when released as a single.

Producer: Jack White

Performers:

Jack White – guitar/vocals
Meg White – drums

The album that confirmed the White Stripes as the band of 2001 and took them well beyond the nurturing environs of the John Peel show surprisingly only managed to place three tracks in the festive fifty that year. Perhaps this had something to do with both the challenge from The Strokes, more of which later, and the fact that two of the entries are right up at the top end, suggesting a large number of votes were spliced between them. 'Dead Leaves & The Dirty Ground' gained a higher entry the following year, perhaps providing further evidence of the competitive nature of the 2001 chart.

35. The Fall
Middle Class Revolt (Permanent, 1994)
405 pts

15 Ways/The Reckoning/**Behind the Counter***/ M5/Surmount All Obstacles/Middle Class Revolt!/You're Not Up to Much/Symbol of Mordgan/**Hey! Student**/Junk Man/The $500 Bottle of Wine/**City Dweller/War***/Shut Up!

*Featured as tracks on the Behind the Counter EP in 1993.

Producer: Rex Sergeant

Performers:
Mark E. Smith – vocals
Craig Scanlon – guitar
Stephen Hanley – bass
Dave Bush - keyboards
Simon Wolstencroft – drums
Karl Burns – drums

An album of inevitabilities, perhaps: exclamation marks in titles, an extract from a conversation on football between Peel and Craig Scanlon and, in 'Hey! Student' a track that surely The Fall seemed destined to make one day. Indeed, its origins go back to the late seventies and an unreleased song called 'Hey Fascist'; it's the undisputed highlight of the album, a bitter but entertaining rant that alternates between cynical humour and snarling threats that was Peel's favourite track of the year.

34. The Fall
I Am Kurious Oranj (Beggars Bqt, 1988)
412 pts

New Big Prinz/Overture From 'I Am Curious Orange'/Dog is Life/**Jerusalem/Kurious Oranj**/Wrong Place, Right Time/Win Fall CD 2080/ Yes, O Yes/Van Plague?/Bad News Girl/**Cab It Up**

Producers: Ian Broudie and Mark E. Smith

Performers:
Mark E. Smith – vocals
Brix Smith – guitar/vocals
Craig Scanlon – guitar
Stephen Hanley – bass
Marcia Schofield – keyboards
Simon Wolstencroft – drums

Featuring music from a ballet made in collaboration with Michael Clark's Dance Company, the venture inspired the band to some significant creative heights, Smith achieving combination of surreal lyrics and bombast that he's matched elsewhere, but rarely with such consistency. In Smith's hands, the so-called 'quiet revolution' of William of Orange's ascent to the throne is robbed of its historical significance in terms of the establishment of a constitutional monarchy and instead sucked dry of its bizarre potential. If the idea of a concept album hadn't been so badly abused, this might happily have regarded itself as one.

33. Siouxsie & The Banshees
The Scream (Polydor, 1978)
414 pts

Pure/**Jigsaw Feeling/Overground**/Carcass/ **Helter Skelter/Mirage/Metal Postcard (Mittageisen)**/ Nicotine Stain/Suburban Relapse/**Switch**

Producers: Steve Lilywhite/Siouxsie & The Banshees

Performers:
Siouxsie Sioux – vocals
John McKay – guitar
Steve Severin – bass
Kenny Morris - drums

The Banshees' debut was a landmark in festive fifty terms: until the days of The Smiths it would stand as the only album to yield as many as six entries and only their relatively low positions prevent The Scream from reaching greater heights in this list. In retrospect, however, it stands as an album of great material rather than a great album: on the one hand a firm statement of intent on behalf of an already celebrated band, one the other a strange lightness of impact in places that belies Steve Lilywhite's production and is debilitating in places.

32. Jesus and Mary Chain
Psychocandy (Blanco y Negro, 1985)
414 pts

Just Like Honey/The Living End/Taste the Floor/The Hardest Walk/Cut Dead/In a Hole/Taste of Cindy/**Never Understand**/Inside Me/Sowing Seeds/My Little Underground/**You Trip Me Up**/Something's Wrong/It's So Hard

Producers: The Jesus and Mary Chain

Performers:
Jim Reid – guitar/vocals
William Reid – guitar
Douglas Hart – bass
Bobby Gillespie – drums

One of the key albums of the age, redefining the guitar music of its age and a triumph of intuitive genius and careful process behind what at first, to the casual listener, may sound like a noisy mess. Closer inspection reveals *Psychocandy* to be brilliantly executed and anything but messy, the Reid brothers' then obsessive search for the perfect song yielding a full fourteen candidates for the tag. The pure pop songs lurk beneath a layer of noise: bubblegum and surf, yes, but you're getting close still if you think the Shangri-Las and the White Boots played in a cement mixer.

31. The Clash
Combat Rock (CBS, 1982)
420 pts

Know Your Rights/Car Jamming/**Should I Stay or Should I Go?**/Rock the Casbah/Red Angel Dragnet/**Straight to Hell**/Overpowered By Funk/Atom Tan/Sean Flynn/Ghetto Defendant/Inoculated City/Death is a Star

Producers: The Clash and Glyn Johns

Performers:
Joe Strummer – guitar/vocals
Mick Jones – guitar/vocals
Paul Simonon – bass/vocals
Topper Headon – drums/bass on 'Rock the Casbah'

Additional musicians on festive fifty tracks:
Joe Ely – backing vocals on 'Should I Stay or Should I Go?'

If this is not first choice as the album to remember The Clash by, it's a damn fine selection of songs that has, if anything, improved with age. 'Straight to Hell' is rightly given prominence in festive fifty terms, but there was room in the 1982 chart also for the still rampant punk idealism of 'Know Your Rights', the international smash hit 'Rock the Casbah' and 'Should I Say or Should I Go', with its brilliantly conceived beat band undertones.

30. Ash
1977 (Infectious. 1996)
452 pts

Lose Control/Goldfinger/**Girl From Mars***/I'd Give You Anything/Gone the Dream/**Kung Fu***/Oh Yeah/Let It Flow/Innocent Smile/**Angel Interceptor***/Lost in You/Darkside Lightside

Featured when released as singles in 1995

Producers: Ash and Owen Morris

Performers:
Tim Wheeler – guitar/vocals
Mark Hamilton – bass
Rick McMurray – drums

Ash's marketing prowess gives such a thing a good name. Obviously they claimed the title was taken from the year of birth of two of their members, but you always felt there was more shrewdness at work than that. There's nothing wrong with clever packaging, especially where it doesn't mask an inferior product, which is certainly the case here. It's topped off with top festive fifty top ten entrants: 'Kung Fu', which gets away with its undisguised take on The Ramones simply because it's so damn good, and 'Girl On Mars', one of those rare songs that gives the overtly commercial a good name.

29. New Order
Power, Corruption & Lies (Factory, 1983)
452 pts

Age of Consent/We All Stand/**The Village**/5-8-6/**Your Silent Face**/Ultraviolence/Ecstasy/**Leave Me Alone**

Producers: New Order

Performers:
Bernard Sumner – guitar/synthesizers/vocals
Peter Hook – bass
Gillian Gilbert – guitar/synthesizers
Stephen Morris – drums/synthesizers/programming

It's Joy Division/New Order's *Rubber Soul*, capturing the band in a transitional period and crackling with creativity and a desire to experiment, while remaining very much the work of the band that used to be Joy Division. Given that completion for places in the remarkable festive fifty of 1983 were so tight, it's quite an achievement to have placed four of the album's eight tracks in there as well as '5-8-6', the clearest nod in a future direction and the origins of what would eventually become 'Blue Monday'.

28. Hole
Live Through This (City Slang, 1994)
456 pts

Violent*/**Miss World**/Plump/Asking For It/Jennifer's Body/**Doll Parts**/Credit in the Straight World/Softer, Softest/She Walks on Me/I Think That I Would Die/Gutless/**Rock Star****

*Featured in the 1995 chart, when released as a single.
**Appeared in 1993 as 'Olympia'.

Producers: Paul Q. Kolderie and Sean Slade

Performers:
Courtney Love – guitar/vocals
Eric Erlandson – guitar
Kristen Pfaff – bass/piano
Patty Schemel – drums

Additional Musicians on festive fifty tracks:
Dana Kletter – backing vocals

Released just after Kurt Cobain's death, much of the album seemed loaded with self-parody and weirdness, particularly among those who claimed to detect Cobain's vocals buried within the mix. Those with an interest in such things may also wish to note that, here, the album gains the same number of points as the next one in this list. It's certainly Hole's most finely tuned collection of material too, while those who subscribe to the claim that traces of Cobain's contributions were cynically edited out legitimately point to the evidence that the band never took their music anywhere remotely interesting after this.

27. Nirvana
Nevermind (Geffen, 1991)
456 pts

Smells Like Teen Spirit/In Bloom/Come As You Are/**Breed**/Lithium/Polly/Territorial Pissings/**Drain You**/Lounge Act/Stay Away/On a Plain/Something in the Way

Producer: Butch Vig

Performers
Kurt Cobain – guitar/vocals
Chris Novoselic – bass
Dave Grohl – drums

Aside from its extraordinary commercial impact, *Nevermind* blurred the lines of acceptability between those who traced the ancestry of their musical tastes through punk and those who did so through heavy metal to such an extent that it redefined the debate like no release since the late seventies. Its guitar heavy sound belies a stunning fragility and this is the feature that most strikingly sets it apart and has ensured its longevity. So many imitators went for the quiet-loud thing, usually in a pretty ham-fisted way. Here's it simply provides a structure that holds together, brilliantly but with difficulty, the temporal and emotional extremes central to Cobain's music and life.

26. Hefner
We Love the City (Too Pure, 2000)
504 pts

We Love the City/**Greedy Ugly People/Good Fruit/Painting & Kissing**/Hold Me Close/Don't Go/Greater London Radio/As Soon As You're Ready/She Can't Sleep No More/Cure For Evil/**The Day That Thatcher Dies**/Your Head To Your Toes

Producers: Hefner

Performers:
Darren Hayman – guitar/vocals
John Morrison – bass
Jack Hayter – various
Antony Harding – drums

Additional musicians on festive fifty tracks:
Matt Evans – guitar/backing vocals on 'The Greedy Ugly People'
Amelia Fletcher – backing vocals on 'Good Fruit'
Mark Bandola – piano on 'The Day That Thatcher Dies'
James Williams – vocals on 'The Day That Thatcher Dies'
Owen Hayter – vocals on 'The Day That Thatcher Dies'

Following their magnificent debut, of which more later, *We Love the City* saw Hefner coming of age, but thankfully not too much. Darren Hayman's observational sharpness and humour, but he sounds vastly more assured and the result was probably the best album in a particularly good year for them. The album strengthened the feeling many of us already had that, when it came to the use of simple strong structures and arrangements to say something far more complex, Hefner were in a class of their own. The extra political dimension provided by 'Day That Thatcher Dies' and the emotional weight of 'Greedy Ugly People' enforce an underlying message that runs through the entire collection: that those who live for exploitation of others and material gain miss out on life's essential pleasures, and also its essential pains.

25. The Fall
Imperial Wax Solvent (Sanctuary, 2008)
516 pts

Alton Towers/**Wolf Kidult Man/50 Year Old Man**/I've Been Duped/Strangetown/Taurig/**Can Can Summer/Tommy Shooter**/Latch Key Kid/Is This New/Senior Twilight Stock Replacer/Exploding Chimney

Producers: Andi Toma, Grant Showbiz, Mark E. Smith and Tim Presley, aka Tim Baxter, credited as Tim 'Gracielands'

Performers:
Mark E. Smith – vocals
Peter Greenaway – guitar
Dave Spurr – bass
Elena Poulou – keyboards/vocals
Keiron Melling – drums

The most successful album since Dandelion took over responsibility for the festive fifty comes from a predictable source. The album gave The Fall their third festive fifty number one and built on the previous year's Reformation Post-TLC in terms of praise from established fans and new ones alike: it was the first Fall album since 1993 to break into the UK Top 40 Albums chart. '50 Year Old Man' seemed a likely number one for the FF from the moment it made itself heard, a mixture of curmudeonly griping and irrepressible humour the high point of a collection that brimmed with a discernible sense of abandon and enjoyment.

24. Sonic Youth
Dirty (Geffen, 1992)
524 pts

100%/Swimsuit Issue/**Teresa's Sound World**/Drunken Butterfly/Shoot/Wish Fulfillment/**Sugar Kane**/Orange Rolls, Angel's Spit/**Youth Against Fascism**/Nice Fit/On the Strip/Chapel Hill/JC/Purr/Creme Brulee

Producers: Butch Vig and Sonic Youth

Performers:
Thurston Moore – guitar/vocals
Lee Ranaldo – guitar/vocals
Kim Gordon – bass/vocals
Steve Shelley – drums

Additional musicians:
Ian MacKaye – guitar on 'Youth Against Fascism'

Dirty was derided in some quarters as Sonic Youth's final capitulation to more conventional song structures and formats. Dimissed in some circles as a record by a band that had lost its balls, to these ears it's always come across more as the entirely logical, and highly pleasing, culmination of a process that had begun at least as early as the mid-eighties. The most interesting thing about the band in this period was how they blended their awareness of such conventions with their avant-garde inclinations. Some of the most notable results of this were duly given festive fifty recognition: the sub-psychedelic 'Teresa's Sound World', for example, or the blunt brutality of 'Youth Against Fascism', one of the most perfect attacks on the far right ever delivered.

23. The Delgados
The Great Eastern (Chemikal Underground, 2000)
532 pts

The Past That Suits You Best/**Accused of Stealing/American Trilogy**/Reasons For Silence (Ed's Song)/Thirteen Guiding Principles/**No Danger**/Aye Today/**Witness**/Knowing Where to Run/Make Your Move

Producer: Dave Fridmann

Performers:
Alun Woodward – guitar/vocals
Emma Pollock – guitar/vocals
Stewart Henderson – bass
Paul Savage – drums

Additional musicians:
Barry Burns – keyboards
Lorne Cowieson – trumpet/flugel horn
Charlie Cross – violin/viola
Alan Barr – cello
Camille Mason – flute/clarinet/piano

The Delgados' third album was their most assured offering, which isn't necessarily to say their best: certainly it was more consistent than Peloton and a further movement away from their brash debut. By now their sound had graduated to a point of highly manicured instrumentation. Strings, brass, keyboards and, overall, meticulous attention to detail make The Big Eastern a sophisticated success and to have achieved such sophisticated without losing what had made the band so wonderful in the first place is a feat that deserves much credit.

22. The Smiths
Meat Is Murder (Rough Trade, 1985)
540 pts

The Headmaster Ritual/Rusholme Ruffians/I Want the One I Can't Have/What She Said/**That Joke Isn't Funny Anymore/Nowhere Fast*/Well I Wonder**/Barbarism Begins At Home/**Meat Is Murder**

*Appeared as a session track in 1984.

Producers: The Smiths

Performers:
Morrissey – vocals
Johnny Marr – guitar/piano on 'Meat Is Murder'
Andy Rourke – bass
Mike Joyce – drums

Although there are some who consider this the band's masterpiece, it lacks the overall coherence of their final two albums and there is a sense of the band over-reaching themselves in trying to fit the album around a prepared political message, most obviously in the title track. 'Nowhere Fast', originally intended as a single, has a stab at the monarchy that would be more fully realised in the next album. And perhaps that's the best way to understand *Meat Is Murder*: as an anything but tentative step towards what would be achieved far more successfully in *The Queen is Dead*.

21. Stone Roses
The Stone Roses (Silvertone, 1989)
580 pts

I Wanna Be Adored/She Bangs the Drums/ Waterfall/Don't Stop/Bye Bye Badman/Elizabeth My Dear/(Song For My) Sugar Spun Sister/**Made of Stone**/Shoot You Down/This is the One/**I Am the Resurrection**

Producer: John Leckie

Performers:
Ian Brown – vocals
John Squire – guitar
Mani, aka Gary Mounfield – bass
Reni, aka Alan Wren – drums

Peel notoriously wasn't keen on it and, when a poll towards the end of the centry placed it only behind *Sgt Pepper* in a list of the nation's favourite ever albums, Bob Geldof labelled the verdict 'preposterous'. It's a record that captured a spirit of a time that had become more open to paying homage to our sixties forefathers and wanted something to add to the legacy itself. We knew there was nothing particularly original in the naive experimentation of 'Don't Stop' or 'I Am the Resurrection': it was pulled so majestically that it really didn't matter. The results remain a delight, perhaps because, as much as anything, of the simple and unpretentious enthusiasm contained within for the sources it so unabashedly plunders.

20. Hefner
The Fidelity Wars (Too Pure, 1999)
580 pts

Hymn for the Cigarettes/May God Protect Your Home/**Hymn for the Alcohol**/**I Took Her Love for Granted**/Every Little Gesture/Weight of the Stars/**I Stole a Bride**/We Were Meant To Be/Far Kelly's Teeth/Don't Falke Out on Me/I Love Only You

Producers: Hefner

Performers:
Darren Hayman – guitar/vocals
John Morrison – bass
Jack Hayter – pedal steel/violin/stylophone/theremin
Antony Harding – drums

Prior to the relative musical sophistication of We Love the City, Hefner's debut finds Darren Hayman rawly wearing his heart on his sleeve through what were apparently still more turbulent emotional times. The two 'hymns' appearing at two and three meant the album became only the fourth in history to achieve such a feat in the same year, Hefner duly joining the Sex Pistols, Jesus and Mary Chain and Pulp in a very elite club. Those two tracks, although the undisputed highlights of this collection, are only glimpses into the album's brilliant pathos, while another festive fifty entry 'I Stole a Bride' is emblematic of the, at times, selfish introspection at play here. The fidelity wars, it appeared, could only be fought continuously, or lost.

19. Cinerama
Torino (Scopitones, 2002)
588 pts

And When She Was Bad/Two Girls/Estrelle/**Cat Girl Tights**/Airborne/**Quick, Before it Melts**/Tie Me Up/**Careless**/Close Up/Starry Eyed/Get Up & Go/Get Smart/**Health & Efficiency***

**Appeared when released as a single in 2001*

Producers: Andy 'Dare' Mason, David Gedge, Simon Cleave and Steve Albini

Performers:
David Gedge – guitar/vocals
Simon Cleave – guitar
Terry de Castro – bass
Sally Murrell – keyboards
Kari Paavola – drums

Such is the prolific nature of the David Gedge songwriting pen, it seemed only a matter of time before a Cinerama album appeared with enough festive fifty material to enter this list. Three of the successful tracks were already well-establshed, having existed as three quarters of a session the band had recorded in 2001, while 'Health & Efficiency' had graced the chart of that year, giving the band their first appearance in a top three, with 'Quick Before It Melts' going one better in the following year. In retrospect, the wonderful 'Cat Girl Tights' seems unfairly placed as the lowest of the album's four entries.

18. Stiff Little Fingers
Inflammable Material (Rough Trade, 1979)
644 pts

Suspect Device*/State of Emergency/Here We Are Nowhere/**Wasted Life**/No More of That/Barbed Wire Love/White Noise/Breakout/Law & Order/Rough Trade/**Johnny Was**/**Alternative Ulster**/Closed Groove

**Highest placing was in 1978, when released as a single.*

Producers: Geoff Travis, Mayo Thompson and Doug Bennett

Performers:
Jake Burns – guitar/vocals
Henry Cluney – guitar/vocals
Ali McMordie – bass
Brian Faloon – drums

A great collection of songs, but only a very good album. While the material can't be faulted, the sometimes wooden production can. If SLF's debut surprised some with its diversity, it disappointed others in the way it was presented. That's not to say listening to it isn't an exhilarating experience: 'Suspect Device' and 'Alternative Ulster', both with multiple festive fifties to their name, remain classics of the period. 'Johnny Was' was not a favourite of Peel but clearly appealed to many festive fifty voters. However, the version they recorded in session was much better and that's indicative of the problem here: comparison with the rush of exhilaration present in those session recordings reveals something to be missing in this collection. The eventual release of those sessions by Strange Fruit was probably more welcome than any in that series and, for the best introduction to what made this band so special, the interested beginner would be better directed there.

17. Pixies
Doolittle (4AD, 1989)
655 pts

Debaser/Tame/**Wave of Mutilation**/I Bleed/**Here Comes Your Man**/**Dead**/**Monkey Gone to Heaven**/Mr Grieves/Crackity Jones/La La Love You/Number 13 Baby/There Goes My Gun/Hey/Silver

Producer: Gil Norton

Performers:
Black Francis – guitar/vocals
Joey Santiago – guitar
Kim Deal – bass/vocals
David Lovering – drums

Additional musicians on 'Monkey Gone to Heaven':
Corine Metter – violin
Karen Karlsrud – violin
Ann Rorich – cello
Arthur Fiacco – cello

Steve Albini's rock hard production on the first album was replaced by Gil Norton's rounder edges and the result was probably the band's best. If later collections would be largely dominated by Black Francis, here Kim Deal's vocals provide a softer focus while Francis' more raucous tones offer a violent contrast at times. The balance works brilliantly and the all-band focus even allows drummer Lovering a vocal outing on one track. The album's at its best, however, when there's that wonderful, edgy balance between the two main vocalists. 'Debaser' came within a guitar string's width of making number one and would return as an entry in the all-time chart of 1999.

16. The Fall
Shift-Work (Cog Sinister, 1991)
655 pts

So What About It?/Idiot Joy Showland/**Edinburgh Man**/Pittsville Direct/The Book of Lies/**The War Against Intelligence**/Shift-Work/You Haven't Found It Yet/**The Mixer/A Lot of Wind**/Rose/Sinister Waltz

Producers: Craig Leon, Grant Showbiz and Robert Gordon

Performers:
Mark E. Smith – vocals
Craig Scanlon – guitar
Stephen Hanley – bass
Kenny Brady – violin
Simon Wolstencroft – drums

The second Fall album to appear after Brix Smith's first departure is similar to the first (Extricate) it that it finds Mark E. Smith finding some direction in the Madchester indie-dance scene, but this time savagely parodying it in 'The Mixer' and 'Idiot Joy Showland'. In many ways, this made it far more of a classic Fall album than its much-loved, but often surprising, predecessor: with the benefit of hindsight, *Shift-Work* now stands as one of the band's best, and often most under-valued, collections. Its highest entry, 'Edinburgh Man', was, like 'The Mixer' and 'The War Against Intelligence', co-written by Smith and Craig Scanlon, who was developing an even greater influence on the band at this stage. Both in the role of guitarist and songwriting partner, the album seems Scanlon beginning to fill the essential Fall role of second visionary after several years of service and to highly positive effect.

15. Miss Black America
God Bless Miss Black America
(Integrity, 2002)
700 pts

Human Punk*/Strobe/Car Crash for a Soul/**Infinite Chinese Box**/Roadkill/Personal Politics/**Talk Hard**/Scream For Me/**Don't Speak My Mind*/Miss Black America**/Montana

*Appeared in 2001 when released as singles.

Producer: Gavin Monaghan

Seymour Glass – guitar/vocals
Gash – guitar
Mickey Smith – bass
Neil D. Baldwin – drums

A band who looked destined to go on take the world, or at least a portion of it, by storm, were disbanded by leader Seymour Glass after this first album, which delivered five festive fifty entries over two years and remains a highly intoxicating collection. It's Glass's voice that gives the band and the album much of its distinctiveness, straining against its limitations to unleash an extraordinary power. The lyrics are superb throughout: highlights include the strangled animal cry of 'Human Punk' and the new angle on the retort of the downtrodden offered in 'Talk Hard', both of which were correctly recognised in the festive fifty. Sometimes those lyrics can teeter on the edge of ludicrousness but that only adds to the album's charm.

14. The Wedding Present
George Best (Reception, 1987)
708 pts

Everyone Thinks He Looks Daft/What Did Your Last Servant Die Of?/Don't Be So Hard/**A Million Miles**/All This & More/**My Favourite Dress**/Shatner/Something & Nothing/It's What You Want That Matters/Give My Love to Kevin/**Anyone Can Make a Mistake**/You Can't Moan Can You?

'Getting Nowhere Fast', which made the festive fifty, only appeared on CD and cassette versions of the album, and therefore contributes no points. Had it been included, the extra points would have moved the album up to number six.

Producer: Chris Allison

Performers:
David Gedge – guitar/vocals
Pete Solowka – guitar
Keith Gregory – bass
Shaun Charman – drums

Additional musicians on festive fifty tracks:
Amelia Fletcher – vocals on 'Everyone Thinks He Looks Daft'

The album that honed their trademark sound to something intoxicatingly close to perfection produced four top ten festive fifty entries, an achievement no other album has equalled. It seemed almost unfair that someone's unhappy love live could be so entertaining, and possibly only Hefner's The Fidelity Wars has ever approached the standard of David Gedge's work here in dealing with such subject matter. He re-writes Tennyson's 'Maud' for the late twentieth century but throws away any unnecessary formal complexity, leaving frank and at times gently humorous explorations of everyday life. Crucially, there's an artistic flair added by both Gedge's lyric touches and those rushing, chiming guitars to add a vital extra dimension. Emotional integrity on its own is, after all, not enough. Gedge, like Hayman, understood this and still does, and it's those deft touches that transform the ordinary into the fascinating that make this album a work of brilliance.

13. New Order
Low-Life (Factory, 1985)
715 pts

Love Vigilantes/**Perfect Kiss**/This Time of Night/**Sunrise**/Elegia/Sooner Than You Think/**Subculture**/Face Up

Producers: New Order

Performers:
Bernard Sumner – guitar/synthesizers/vocals
Peter Hook – bass

Gillian Gilbert – synthesizers
Stephen Morris – drums/programming

Following the step towards a new direction by *Power, Corruption & Lies*, *Low-Life* saw New Order confidently securing their post-Joy Division identity of dance music pioneers, as brilliantly illustrated by the album's 'Perfect Kiss' and 'Sub-culture' singles, while continuing to maintain distance and contrast through enigmatic lyrics and Sumner's detached vocals. They occupied this new territory not to become part of it, however, but to transform it, as is brilliantly illustrated by the choice of 'Love Vigilantes' as the opening track. Essentially a mock-folk song with tongue-in-cheek lyrics and a harmonica intro, it stands conspicuously opposed to everything else here. It's emblematic of a band fully confident in taking bold new steps, eagerly embracing unexpected new directions and simply seeing where they would take them.

12. Elastica
Elastica (Deceptive, 1995)
720 pts

Line Up/Annie/Connection/Car Song/Smile/Hold Me Now/S.O.F.T./Indian Song/Blue/All-Nighter*/Waking Up/2:1/Vaseline/Never Here/Stutter**

Producers: Marc Waterman and Elastica

*Appeared when released as a single in 1996
**Appeared when released as a single in 1994

Performers:
Justine Frischmann – guitar/vocals
Donna Matthews – guitar
Annie Holland – bass
Justin Welch – drums

Additional musicians:
Dan Abnormal, aka Damon Albarn – keyboards

All but one of Elastica's festive fifty entries appear on this album and it's a collection that emulated the achievement of Hole's Live Through This in featuring entries from three different years. Leaving aside all those tired accusations of plagiarism, let it be recorded that Elastic revived the spirit of new waave better than anyone else linked with what was known as Britpop. Through the collection, there's a freshness that makes the listener happily put to one side Elastica's infamy as musical shoplifters. Given that so many others who've attempted such a thing rarely sound anything more than embarrassing, that's a notable achievement.

11. The Fall
Bend Sinister (Beggars Banquet, 1986)
740 pts

R.O.D.*/Dktr Faustus/Shoulder Pads/Mr Pharmacist/Gross Chapel – British Grenadiers/U.S. 80s-90s/Terry Waite Sez/Bournemouth Runner/Riddler/Shoulder Pads 2

*Appeared as 'Realm of Dusk'

Producer: John Leckie

Performers:
Mark E. Smith – vocals
Brix Smith – guitar/keyboards/vocals
Craig Scanlon – guitar
Stephen Hanley – bass
Simon Rodgers – keyboards/programming
Simon Wolstencroft – drums/percussion

If the artistic peak of the Brix Smith era was still to come – I *Am Kurious Oranj* was already being worked on as a parallel project – this album revealed that The Fall were getting very close to it. It's a great body of work from beginning to end, properly rewarded in festive fifty terms. Admittedly, given that the album was released at the height of the period of domination of The Fall and The Smiths, this was always likely to happen, but it's difficult to know how voters could have resisted anyway. The highest placing rightly goes to their version of 'Mr Pharmacist' – Peel said it would have been his number one – but the other four entries all stand as classics of the period in their own right, while a perfectly good case could also be made for the neglected 'Riddler!' and 'Gross Chapel – British Grenadiers'. Those who, at this time, continued to argue that Brix was a debilitating influence were finding the evidence piling up against them.

10. The Strokes
Is This It (Rough Trade, 2001)
755 pts

Is This It/**The Modern Age**/Sonia/Barely Legal/**Someday**/Alone. Together/**Last Nite/Hard to Explain/New York City Cops**/Trying Your Luck/Take It or Leave It

Producer: Gordon Raphael

Performers:
Julian Casablancas – vocals
Albert Hammond Jr – guitar
Nick Valensi – guitar
Nikolai Fraiture – bass
Fabrizio Moretti – drums

If festive fifty votes are anything to go by, only two bands in history have produced a better album than this. Garage punk attitudes and sensibilities were due a makeover and those who complained that it had all been done before were missing the point, as indeed were those who conversely proclaimed The Strokes the future of music. The album revisits the past but puts all the pieces together so lovingly, the rare work of obsessives who choose to channel that obsession into making music as opposed to merely collecting it or, heaven help us, writing about it. Sadly, the second Strokes album would lose this focus completely and, despite the band continuing to score points with punters and critics alike, they never again got close to this masterpiece: the work of a highly adept group of musicians using their expertise to create something close th perfection within a set of expertly imposed limitations.

9. Pavement
Slanted & Enchanted (Big Cat, 1992)
780 pts

Summer Babe/Trigger Cut/No Life Singed Her/**In the Mouth of a Desert/Conduit For Sale**/Zurich is Stained/Loretta's Scars/**Here**/Two States/Perfume V/Fame Throwa/Jackals, False Grails: The Lonesome Era/Our Singer

Producers: Pavement

Performers:
Stephen Malkmus – guitar/vocals
Spiral Stairs, aka Scott Kannberg – guitar
Gary Young – drums/percussion

What Stephen Malkmus and Pavement had openly borrowed from The Fall and others they more than paid back on this first album, which blends rawness with creative genius ruggedly throughout, placing five tracks in the 1992 chart to make it the most successful debut album in festive fifty terms since *Never Mind the Bollocks*. It's the work of a band who'd been working together for some time by now, yet had retained a certain lopsided awkwardness in spite of that. This endearing feature would never be lost throughout their existence, but unquestionably it's presented here in its purest form which is why *Slanted & Enchanted* will always remain the definitive Pavement album. Most remarkable is the manner in which Malkmus' vocal restrictions strain and jar against material that offers him few concessions. Neither he nor the band gave himself a script they would find it easy to perform and this lack of an easy control over what they were performing is what gives both album and band a unique charm.

8. The Wedding Present
Bizarro (RCA, 1989)
805 pts

Brassneck/Crushed/No/Thanks/**Kennedy/What Have I Said Now?**/Granadaland/*Bewitched*/Take Me*/Be Honest

*Highest position was as a session track in 1988, as 'Take Me I'm Yours'.

Producer: Chris Allison

Performers:
David Gedge – guitar/vocals
Pete Solowka – guitar
Keith Gregory – bass
Simon Smith – drums

For those who questioned how far The Wedding Present's original template could take them before they faced accusations of staleness, the answer came in the form of this album. *Bizarro* took the creative possibilities within those boundaries to their highest point; in doing so they managed both to craft something entirely different from their celebrated debut album while still retaining many of its most cherished characteristics. In addition, then, to brilliant dramatic monologues like 'What Have I Said Now?' and 'Brassneck', we get tracks like 'Kennedy', which drafts very different subject matter onto a familiar musical framework, and 'Bewitched', which takes the reverse tack and even gets away with incorporating a Doris Day sample. 'Take Me', already a favourite following its session appearance the previous year, almost parodies itself with its elongated guitar attack, as if Gedge and Salowka are allowing themselves a final stylistic tour de force before taking the band and those guitars into new places.

7. PJ Harvey
Stories from the City, Stories from the Sea (Island, 2000)
845 pts

Big Exit/Good Fortune/A Place Called Home/One Line/Beautiful Feeling/**The Whores Hustle & The Hustlers Whore/The Mess We're In**/You Said Something/Kamikaze/**This is Love*** /Horses in My Dreams/We Float

*Appeared in 2001, when released as a single.

Producers: Rob Ellis, Mick Harvey and Polly Jean Harvey

Performers:
Polly Jean Harvey – vocals/guitar/keyboards/piano
Mick Harvey – bass/organ/percussion/drums and harmonium on 'Big Exit'/keyboards on 'The Mess We're In' and 'This is Love'
Rob Ellis – drums/piano/tambourine on 'Big Exit' and 'This is Love'/synthesizer on 'Good Fortune'

Additional musicians on festive fifty tracks:
Thom Yorke – vocals on 'The Mess We're In'

In her tenth year as a recording artist, PJ Harvey produced her most celebrated work to date with an album that drew together much of the finer elements of her previous work and mixed them with more candid, ane penetrative, personal reflections than had been in evidence before. While Hefner's We Love the City drew expertly on the mood of London, Harvey, developing the setting of New York, offers a vision that's inevitably very different. Her vocals range characteristically from the plaintive and melancholic to the angry and desperate, even stepping back at one point to allow guest vocalist Thom Yorke prominence on 'The Mess We're In', ending with the resigned 'We Float', which finds Polly Jean absorbing the experiences delineated elsewhere on the album and building a life around whatever debris there is. It probably doesn't need to be said that this was the first of her two Mercury Prize winning albums, nor that it achieved platinum status in the UK, but it remains a feat characteristic of Harvey that she could achieve a highpoint among festive fifty voters while at the same time crafting something that gained so much critical and commercial recognition.

6. Sex Pistols
Never Mind the Bollocks (Virgin, 1977)
945 pts

Holidays in the Sun/Bodies/No Feelings/Liar/**God Save the Queen**/Problems/Seventeen/**Anarchy in the UK**/Submission/**Pretty Vacant**/New York/**EMI**

All featured tracks achieved their highest entries in 1978, with the exception of 'Holidays in the Sun, which scored its highest position in the Peel-selected chart of 1977. 'Anarchy in the UK' went on to repeat its 1978 position on three further occasions, of course.

Producer: Chris Thomas

Performers:
Johnny Rotten, aka John Lydon – vocals
Steve Jones – guitar and bass
Glen Matlock – bass on 'Anarchy in the UK'
Paul Cook – drums

The soundtrack of a generation, of course; conceptually and musically as important as anything that's been released in the whole, sprawling history of rock and roll. Rightly, festive fifty voters offered confirmation that the first three singles formed the greatest ever debut triumvirate in the history of the world. There are insistent, also, that the fourth shouldn't be forgotten, and Peel for one certainly concurred, going so far as to claim that 'Holidays in the Sun' was even better than its three illustrious predecessors. Rotten was right when he said the Pistols had ended rock and roll but, as usual, people were often too lazy to interpret the remark correctly. After this rock and roll couldn't be the same, couldn't be viewed in the same way, and certainly couldn't rebel in the same way. The album rendered all attempts to do so in its wake fatuous and dull, at the same time energising other artists to unprecedented levels of creativity. Paradoxically, music that on the surface concerned itself with destruction and negativity, kickstarted music's most unpredictable and innovative period.

5. The Fall
The Infotainment Scan (Permanent, 1993)
1064 pts

Ladybird (Green Grass)/Lost in Music/Glam Racket/I'm Going to Spain/It's a Curse/Paranoid Man in Cheap Sh*t Room**/Service/**The League of Bald Headed Men**/A Past Gone Mad/**Light/Fireworks

'Why Are People Grudgeful' appeared on the CD version but not the vinyl release. Because of this, its points do not contribute to the total: were they to do so, it would make this album number one in the list.

Producers: Rex Sergeant, Simon Rogers and Mark E. Smith

Performers:
Mark E. Smith – vocals
Craig Scanlon – guitar
Stephen Hanley – bass
Dave Bush – keyboards/programming
Simon Wolstencroft – drums

The only album in history to present us with five festive fifty entries in its first five tracks. Does that make it the best Fall album? No, but it's certainly among the best, returning Craig Scanlon to prominence as a songwriter after he'd had little do with the writing on the *Code: Selfish* album and confirming that Fall albums that were heavy on Scanlon's influence have tended to have a pretty good record where festive fifty votes are concerned. The album's two cover versions are Fall masterpieces: 'Lost in Music' complete re-energises the original via Scanlon's lovely mock-disco lick, while 'I'm Going to Spain' takes a piece of largely unknown amateur songwriting and rescues it brilliantly from oblivion, of course making it sound entirely like a song the band might have written themselves in the process.

It offered further comfirmation, if any were needed, of Smith's rare ability to discover something conceptually interesting in the most unlikely places.

4. The Wedding Present
Seamonsters (RCA, 1991)
1218 pts

Dalliance/Dare/Suck/Blonde/**Rotterdam/**Lovenest**/Corduroy*/**Carolyn/**Heather**/Octopussy**

*Featured as a single in 1990
**Featured as a session track in 1990

Producer: Steve Albini

Performers:
David Gedge – guitar/vocals
Peter Solowka – guitar
Keith Gregory – bass
Simon Smith - drums

A change of direction for The Wedding Present and festive fifty evidence, among other things, suggested it didn't lost them a lot of admirers. Indeed, critical reaction, especially in the United States, suggests it won them quite a few more. The recruitment of Steve Albini as producer helped augment a sound already being clearly nurtured in their 1990 session and the result is arguably the band's most adventurous album. Gedge's voice sometimes sounds stranded, stripped raw when bereft of its by then conventional accompaniment of a wall of guitars. The affect is stunning at times, however. The guitars lose their jangle but retain their harshness, providing a startlingly vivid constrast to the emotional lyrics of tracks like 'Corduroy' and 'Heather'. Viewed in the context of The Wedding Present's career, it isn't their best work, at least among those of us who reserve a special fondness for their earlier work. However, it's certainly an important album, allowing the band to unleash elements of their sound many hadn't known existed, while its high points more than bear comparison with what had gone before. It also moved them on stylistically at exactly the right point, a vital album in securing the band's longevity while at the same time opening musical avenues that Gedge would go on to secure long into the future, both with this band and with Cinerama.

3. Pulp
Different Class (Island, 1995)
1350 pts

Mis-Shapes/Pencil Skirt/**Common People**/**I Spy**/**Disco 2000**/Live Bed Show/Something Changed/**Sorted For E's & Wizz**/F.E.E.L.I.N.G. C.A.L.L.E.D. L.O.V.E./ **Underwear**/Monday Morning/Bar Italia

Producer: Chris Thomas

Performers:
Jarvis Cocker – guitar/vocals
Mark Webber – guitar
Steve Mackey – bass
Russell Senior – violin/guitar
Candida Doyle – keyboards
Nick Banks – drums/percussion

Peel's comment that this album would have stood out had it been released in any year was spot-on. On *His & Hers*, Pulp took what they'd honed to a state of near perfection: here, perfection was attained, confirming Jarvis Cocker as unquestionably the most astute lyricist of the nineties and his band similarly the best of its time. The narratives are multi-faceted and yet consistent: Cocker manages to hold together a unified persona throughout the album while combining in its character social inadequacy, adversarial mockery and cruel vengeance, all of which combines to see it through disappointing romances, fake friendships, dead marriages and horrifying sexual altercations to survive and tell the tales with admirable and sometimes amazing frankness. Whether the individual is Cocker himself, which it plainly often is, or a kind of everyman narrator becomes an absolute irrelevance. *Different Class* is, of course, a multiple metaphor: if the concept itself seems to flirt dangerously with triteness, it pulls of the most glorious of all its survival stories to stand as a brilliant exposition of all of its figurative associations, simultaneously exploring the truth and the artifice of its and any time.

2. The Smiths
The Queen is Dead (Rough Trade, 1986)
1422 pts

The Queen is Dead/Frankly Mr Shankly/**I Know It's Over**/Never Had No One Ever/Cemetry Gates/Bigmouth Strikes Again/**The Boy with the Thorn in His Side***/Vicar in a Tuto/**There is a Light That Never Goes Out**/Some Girls Are Bigger Than Others

Featured as a single in 1985

Producers: Morrissey and Johnny Marr

Performers:
Morrissey – vocals
Johnny Marr – guitar
Andy Rourke – bass
Mike Joyce – drums

Their greatest album and, for many people, the greatest by any band in any period. The Smiths had of course been thrilling us for more than three years before this collection saw the light of day, but the band's vision had never seemed so fully realised or unified before its release, which at last saw The Smiths realising their full and considerable potential over a single album. Despite its inevitable comparisons, The Queen is Dead is not a pure descendent of the Pistols' 'God Save the Queen': it's conceptually much closer to Nietzsche's 'God is Dead' metaphor. The old values are dead and, unless we replace them and face up to our responsibility for killing them, we've had it – both personally and politically. Though the album is diverse in terms of content and style, this theme permeates it throughout, whether in the form of disaffected employees, failed romantics, literary retreatists or whatever. It's an honest album that reflects on the difficulties of attaining satisfaction in any of these spheres, rather than simplistically embracing the postures and idealism that sometimes raised their head on Meat is Murder. Such existential honesty was always present in their work but here it stands revealed as that previously elusive quality that raised them well above their contemporaries.

1. The Smiths
Strangeways Here We Come (Rough Trade, 1987)

A Rush and a Push and the Land is Ours/**I Started Something I Couldn't Finish**/Death of a Disco Dancer/Girlfriend in a Coma/Stop Me if You Think

You've Heard This One Before/Last Night I Dreamt Than Somebody Loved Me/Unhappy Birthday/**Paint a Vulgar Picture**/Death at One's Elbow/**I Won't Share You**

Producers: Morrissey, Johnny Marr and Stephen Street

Performers:
Morrissey – vocals/piano on 'Death of a Disco Dancer'
Johnny Marr – guitar/autoharp on 'I Won't Share You'
Andy Rourke – bass
Mike Joyce - drums

Not, it must be said, the best album of all time, nor even the best by The Smiths. While the two previous albums in this list rank among the greatest ever released, this one is merely very very good. The fact that it contributed seven tracks to the 1987 festive fifty appears to be the combined result of differing opinions regarding what the best tracks really were and the recent demise of The Smiths that had exerted an even greater influence over their ever loyal fan base. It is, however, an album that deserves to be regarded as the best among Smiths albums with the exception of its exalted predecessor. Though it lacks the sweeping vision of *The Queen is Dead*, Morrissey's self-mockery attains some unquestionable peaks, while the dark undertones of 'Death of a Disco Dancer' and the direct record industry critique of 'Paint a Vulgar Picture' hinted that the recent split had come at a time when, sadly, they still had much to say and new directions to pursue. *Strangeways Here We Come*, then, can be regarded as a well-crafted album that left their hugely dedicated audience confirmed in their view that this was a premature time to call it a day. Considered together, their last two albums certainly form a stunning body of material.

JOHN PEEL SESSIONS & THE FESTIVE FIFTY

Tracks from Peel sessions had, in theory, been eligible for votes in the festive fifty since the beginning, but those available purely in session version were slow to make an impact, with Peel commenting during the 1981 broadcast that Altered Images' 'Song Sung Blue' (a track to which he contributed some whistling) had come close to becoming the first to make the chart. Although Peel presumably had the option of broadcasting session versions of tracks that made the chart (some of which have appeared in every festive fifty, he chose not to until 1983. The first session track to be played by Peel in the chart rundown ('Television/Satellite' by Sophie & Peter Johnson in that year)then kickstarted a twenty-two year period in which only one chart countdown would pass without Peel playing at least one track from a session.

That isn't necessarily to say that session tracks were voted for in particularly great numbers. Very often the session version would simply be played in preference to the official release of the same track, sometimes because a number of voters had specified it but often simply because Peel wished to play it. This is something that any festive fifty statistician needs to take on board before we make the mistake of assuming a session version broadcast inevitably meant a session version voted for. I've heard it reported, for instance, that The Fall's 'Australians in Europe' became the highest placed session track in a festive fifty when it made number two in 1987, yet so far as I'm aware no evidence exists that, merely because Peel chosen to play the session version of this track, it was the version specified by voters. The song in question also appeared on the 12" release of *Hit the North*.

That isn't to say its broadcast in a session won't have had some influence on the voting. Indeed, there is substantial evidence that a session broadcast increases the chances of a tune making the festive fifty at the end of the year.

Excluding recorded live performances, there were 320 tracks recorded for Peel sessions that entered the festive fifty in the year in which they were eligible, an average of 14.5 entries per chart from 1983 onwards, which of course is almost a third of the chart. The vast majority of these are different versions of songs released elsewhere. In most cases, Peel did not play the session version in the countdown, but there is every reason to believe, session tracks forming such a part of the diet of the regular Peel audience, that their appearance in this form went some way towards pushing the track concerned into the festive fifty in most, if not all, cases.

Having said that, there is every reason to give special consideration to those session tracks that made it into the festive fifty without any alternative version of the track being available. It's necessary, therefore, to approach this section from three different angles:

1. Tracks that made the festive fifty, a version of which had appeared in the festive fifty
2. Session tracks broadcast by Peel in the festive fifty
3. Tracks that made the festive fifty that were only available as a session recording at the time

I must give credit, as you would expect, to Ken Garner's fabulous 'Peel Sessions' book for its enormous assistance in researching parts of this section.

Tracks recorded for sessions that made the festive fifty

Top ten bands/artists

Predictably, The Fall are absolutely streets ahead of everyone else. Perhaps the most interesting achievement is that of The Delgados, whose thirteen festive fifty tracks contain eight that appeared in sessions (two of which, 'Pull the Wires from the Wall' and 'My Blue Sky' made the chart when available only in their session versions)

1. The Fall	35
2. The Wedding Present	13
3. The Delgados	8
4. The Smiths	7
=5. Half Man Half Biscuit	6
=5. PJ Harvey (inc w/John Parish)	6
=5. Siouxsie & The Banshees	6
=8. Babes in Toyland	5
=8. Ballboy	5
=8. Billy Bragg	5
=8. Cinerama	5
=8. Cocteau Twins	5

Number one tracks that had appeared in session

These are surprisingly rare. Although Pulp's 'Common People' and The Delgados' 'Pull the Wire from the Wall' and Jesus & Mary Chain's 'Never Understand' all made number one, they did so in the year after they appeared in session. Instances of session tracks becoming number one in the same year as they were broadcast, even if they also appeared as an official release are restricted to:

1984: How Soon is Now – The Smiths
1988: Destroy the Heart – House of Love
1996: Come Out 2 Nite (Session title: Come Out Tonite) – Kenickie
2001: Chinese Whispers – Melys

Sessions that produced four festive fifty entries

It's one of the most rare festive fifty occurrences of all for all tracks from a single session to make it into the chart.

I'm excluding here 'Hung Over as the Oven at Maida Vale' by Godspeed You Black Emperor!, because that track formed the whole session, as did 'Loving You' by The Orb, which I'm not even sure should have been eligible for the festive fifty anyway. I'm counting only recorded sessions (not live ones) that featured what became the standard four tracks. Also excluded is anything recorded at Phoenix, Groningen or anywhere which was then subsequently given an airing in the show. Once this is all taken into consideration, there is only one instance of four tracks recorded for a single session making the Festive Fifty:

The Fall (3 June 1985)
Cruiser's Creek/Couldn't Get Ahead/Spoilt Victorian Child/Gut of the Quanitifier

Sessions that produced three festive fifty entries

Because of the singular nature of the achievement above, it doesn't seem right for any self-respecting festive fifty researcher to leave it at that, so here is a chronological list of those sessions that yielded three entries. It may be noted that it's often the third track of the four that misses out. I'm not sure what conclusions to draw from that. Incidentally, it's not always the case that the tracks listed reached the chart in the same year of the session. Successful tracks are in bold.

Siouxsie & The Banshees (23 February 1978)
Hong Kong Garden/Overground/Carcass/ **Helster Skelter**

Stiff Little Fingers (13 April 1978)
Alternative Ulster/Wasted Life/Johnny Was/State of Emergency

The Smiths (31 May 1983)
What Difference Does It Make?/Miserable Lie/**Reel Around the Fountain**/**Handsome Devil**

The Smiths (9 August 1984)
William, It Was Really Nothing/**Nowhere Fast**/Rusholme Ruffians/**How Soon is Now?**

Cocteau Twins (5 September 1984)
Pepper Tree/Beatrix (Session title: Whisht)/**Ivo** (Session title: Peep Bo)/Otterley

The Fall (7 October 1985)
L.A./**The Man Whose Head Expanded**/What You Need/**Dktr Faustus** (Session title: Faust Banana)

The Fall (19 May 1987)
Athlete Cured/**Australians in Europe**/Twister/**Guest Informant**

The Fall (31 October 1988)
Dead Beat Descendant/**Cab It Up!**/Squid Lord/**Kurious Oranj**

Babes In Toyland (29 September 1990)
Catatonic/**Ripe**/**Primus**/Spit to See the Shine

The Fall (23 March 1991)
The War Against Intelligence/**A Lot of Wind**/Idiot Joy Showland/**The Mixer**

The Fall (5 February 1994)
M5/**Behind the Counter**/Reckoning/**Hey! Student** (Session title: Student)

Cinerama (24 May 2001)
Careless/Get Smart/**Quick, Before it Melts**/**Health & Efficiency**

The Strokes (27 June 2001)
The Modern Age/**Hard to Explain**/Barely Legal/**Someday**

Most Involved Producers/Engineers

The following are the producers or engineers who have been involved with the most tracks that featured in a Peel session and went on to make on a festive fifty appearance.

1.	Dale Griffin	71
2.	Mike Engles	68
3.	Mike Robinson	64
4.	Nick Gomm	26
5.	Miti Adhikari	22
=6.	Dave Dade	21
=6.	James Birtwistle	21
8.	Tony Wilson	20
9.	Simon Askew	18
10.	George Thomas	16

The Great Session Runs

Unsurprisingly, only the real festive fifty heavyweights have managed to record a run of four sessions or more producing at least one festive fifty entry. Information in brackets shows the date of the session's first broadcast, followed by the tracks that featured in the chart.

The Fall   14   1983-95
(23.8.83: Eat Y'self Fitter; 12.12.83: Pat Trip Dispenser/C.R.E.E.P.; 3.6.85: Cruiser's Creek/Couldn't Get Ahead/Spoilt Victorian Child/Gut of the Quantifier; 29.9.85: L.A./The Man Whose Head Expanded/Faust Banana*; 9.7.86: Realm of Dusk/U.S. 80s-90s; 19.5.87: Athlete Cured/Australians in Europe/Guest Informant; 31.10.88: Dead Beat Descendant/Cab It Up/Kurious Oranj; 1.1.90: Chicago Now!; 23.3.91: The War Against Intelligence/A Lot of Wind/The Mixer; 15.2.92: Free Range/Kimble; 13.3.93: Ladybird (Green Grass)/Service; 5.2.94: M5/Behind The Counter/Student**; 17.12.94: Glam Racket***/Numb at the Lodge+; 22.12.95: Chisillers)

The Wedding Present++   6   1987-95
(3.3.87: A Million Miles/Getting Nowhere Fast; 24.5.88: Take Me I'm Yours/Why Are You Being So Reasonable Now?; 14.10.90: Dalliance/Heather; 17.3.92: Come Play With Me/Flying Saucer; 16.4.94: So Long Baby/Spangle; 3.12.95: Go Man Go)

The Smiths   4   1983-86
(31.5.83: What Difference Does It Make?/Reel Around the Fountain/Handsome Devil; 21.9.83: This Charming Man; 9.8.84: William, It Was Really Nothing/Nowhere Fast/How Soon Is Now?; 17.12.96: Sweet & Tender Hooligan/Half A Person)

*Later released as 'Dktr Faustus'

**Later released as 'Hey! Student'
***This song has already featured in the previous year's festive fifty and was, by Fall standards, already an old song when it appeared in session.
+Later released as 'Feeling Numb'
++This list does not include the band's Ukrainian sessions, which appeared between 1987 and 1990 which, although released under the band's name, I'm regarding as a side-project. The Ukrainian sessions did not yield any festive fifty entries.

Session tracks broadcast in Festive Fifty countdowns

In 1983, Peel played two tracks that were only available in session form plus another, 'Eat Y'self Fitter' by The Fall, whose session version had, pretty much by common consent, captured the song's magic in a way that the version on the *Perverted By Language* album hadn't quite managed. From that point, Peel continued to include some session tracks in all festive fifty broadcasts with the exception of two of his later charts.

Although the practice became rarer in those later festive fifties, along with tracks only available in session form, Peel tended to include session versions apparently either because they appealed to him or because, as he occasionally stated, voters had tended to request that version. This reached a peak in the celebrated festive fifty of 1995 in which eight session versions were featured, including two that had actually appeared in session the previous year and one that was actually four years old.

Full List of Session Tracks Broadcast

What follows is a full list of tracks broadcast during the festive fifty countdown:

1983
Television/Satellite – Sophie & Peter Johnston
Eat Y'self Fitter – The Fall
Reel Around The Fountain – The Smiths

1984
Blue Canary – Frank Chickens
Reel Around The Fountain – The Smiths*
Emma – Sisters of Mercy
Nowhere Fast – The Smiths
Between The Wars – Billy Bragg

1985
A Hundred Words – The Beloved
All That Ever Mattered – Shop Assistants

Cruiser's Creek – The Fall

1986
Felicity – The Wedding Present
I Wish I Could Sprechen Sie Deutsch - Freiwillige Selbst-Kontrolle
Realm of Dusk – The Fall

1987
Athlete Cured – The Fall
Sweet & Tender Hooligan – The Smiths**
You Sexy Thing – Cud
Australians in Europe – The Fall
1988
Samora Machel – Shalawambe
Take Me I'm Yours – The Wedding Present

1989
She Comes in the Fall – Inspiral Carpets
Directing Traffic – Inspiral Carpets
So This Is How It Feels – Inspiral Carpets

1990
Beast Inside – Inspiral Carpets
Dalliance – The Wedding Present
Heather – The Wedding Present
Loving You – The Orb

1992
Circa 1762 – Pavement
Kimble – The Fall
Popeth – Datblygu+

1993
Sirius B – Transglobal Underground
Naked Cousin – PJ Harvey
Ladybird (Green Grass) – The Fall
Olympia – Hole
Glam Racket – The Fall++
Wang Dang Doodle – PJ Harvey+++

1994
M5 – The Fall
Spangle – The Wedding Present
Common People – Pulp

1995
Northern Industrial Town – Billy Bragg
Underwear – Pulp
Kiss Tomorrow Goodbye – Flaming Blue Stars
Violet – Hole $
Nitro – Dick Dale
Alright – Supergrass
Maximum – Dreadzone
Feeling Numb – The Fall (session title: Numb at the Lodge)

1996
Paintball's Coming Home – Half Man Half Biscuit $$

1997
Pull The Wires From The Wall – The Delgados

1998
Shake-Off – The Fall
If I Were a Carpenter – Quickspace
One Louder Solex – Solex

1999
Hung Over as the Oven at Maida Vale – Godspeed You Black Emperor!

2000
Wonderwall – Cat Power
I Hate Scotland – Ballboy

2002
You Got Nothing – Antihero
99.9 – Wire
Mr Blue Sky – The Delgados
You Don't Send Me – Belle & Sebastian

2004
Electricity – The Magic Band
Joy Adamson – Decoration
Big Eyed Beans From Venus – The Magic Band
Joy Division Oven Gloves – Half Man Half Biscuit

*The same version as that which charted in 1983, but now officially released on the album *Hatful of Hollow*
**Originally recorded for a Peel Session, but officially released on the B-Side of the 7" single *Sheila Take A Bow*
***At the time of broadcast, already released on the 12" EP *The Peel Sessions*
+Session track broadcast in 1991, but released on *BBC Peel Sessions* LP in 1992
++Mark Goodier session recording
+++Originally recorded for a Peel session, but officially released on the B-side of the Man-Size single
$ Released on the *Ask For It* album, but originally recorded for a Peel Session in 1991
$$ Mark Radcliffe session recording

Dandelion Radio Sessions

It's worth adding that Dandelion Radio's festive fifties have also included some broadcasts of session recordings, specifically:

2008
Glasshouse – Decoration (Andy Morrison)

2009
Black Hand – Atomizer (Andy Morrison)

2010
Love Love – Ghost Society (Andy Morrison)

Waiting There (Noise) – 93MillionMilesFromTheSun (Mark Whitby)

2011
Salt – Spidersleg (Andy Morrison)

2013
Josephine – Flies On You (Mark Whitby)

2014
Goodbye Cagoule World – (Mark Whitby)
Secret Life – Ill (Jeff Grainger)

3. Tracks only available as a session recording that made the festive fifty

Tracks that made the chart when only available in session form are, inevitably, a much rarer phenomenon. Incidentally, the year in which this happened most was 2004, the year of John Peel's death. Rob Da Bank announced five tracks that had appeared in their session form and with no official release, though one was broadcast in the countdown in its demo version (see footnotes beneath the table below).

In the list below I have excluded even those session tracks (such as PJ Harvey's 'Wang Dang Doodle' or Cud's 'You Sexy Thing') that reached the chart in the year of the session and charted in their session form, purely because the session version gained an official release in the same year.

Applying this very strict criteria, the following top twenty emerges:

	No reached	Year
1. Take Me I'm Yours – The Wedding Present	4	1988
2. Reel Around The Fountain – The Smiths*	6	1983
3. Joy Division Oven Gloves – Half Man Half Biscuit	8	2004
4. Between The Wars – Billy Bragg	13	1984
5. Nowhere Fast – The Smiths*	14	1984
6. Emma – Sisters of Mercy	15	1984
7. Handsome & Gretel – Babes in Toyland	18	1991
=8. You Sexy Thing – Cud	20	1987
Heather – The Wedding Present	20	1990
You Don't Send Me – Belle & Sebastian	20	2002
=11. Hung Over as the Oven at Maida Vale – Godspeed You Black Emperor!	21	1999
Common People – Pulp	21	1994
13. I Tried It, I Liked It, I Loved it – Decoration**	24	2004
14. Athlete Cured – The Fall	26	1987
15. Pull the Wires from the Wall – The Delgados	27	1997

16. Mr Blue Sky – The Delgados	29	2002
17. 24 Hour Garage People – Half Man Half Biscuit	30	1999
18. Naked Cousin – PJ Harvey***	32	1993
=19. I Wish I Could Sprechen Sie Deutsch – Freiwillige Selbstokontrolle	33	1986
Wonderwall – Cat Power	33	2000

*Both Smiths entries were publicised as their next singles shortly after their appearance in session. 'Reel Around The Fountain' was abandoned in favour of 'This Charming Man' due to those professional perverts in the British press alleging that the lyrics advocated child molestation. 'Nowhere Fast' was ditched following the festive fifty success and general critical acclaim directed at 'How Soon Is Now?', which led to its selection as the next single in 1985.

**This track was available in demo form, and indeed this was the version played by Rob Da Bank in the festive fifty countdown. However, it was not commercial available and did appear in the band's Peel Session that year, which qualifies it for inclusion here.

***This track appeared in the same session as 'Wang Dang Doodle' and also gained an official release, but this was not until January 1988 which means that at the time of voting nobody, expect perhaps Peel himself and a few others, could possibly have owned a copy.

THE FESTIVE FIFTY

RECORDS & STATISTICS

Bands/artists with most festive fifty entries, chart by chart

Year	Band/Artist
1976	Bob Dylan (4)
1977	The Motors (3)
1978	Siouxsie & The Banshees (7)
1979	Siouxsie & The Banshees (7)
1980	Joy Division (7)
1981	Joy Division (8)
1982	The Clash (4)
1982T	Joy Division (10)
1983	New Order (5)
1984	Cocteau Twins/The Smiths (7)
1985	The Fall/New Order/The Smiths (5)
1986	The Fall/The Smiths (7)
1987	The Smiths (11)
1988	The Fall (6)
1989	Inspiral Carpets/Pixies/Stone Roses/The Wedding Present (5)
1990	The Wedding Present (6)
1991	The Fall (6)
1992	The Wedding Present (7)
1993	The Fall (10)
1994	The Wedding Present (4)
1995	Dreadzone/Pulp (6)
1996	The Fall/Stereolab (3)
1997	Stereolab (3)
1998	The Delgados (3)
1999	Hefner (5)
1999AT	Joy Division (5)
2000	The Delgados/PJ Harvey/Hefner (4)
2001	The Strokes (5)
2002	Cinerama /Low/Miss Black America (3)
2003	Ballboy (3)
2004	Ballboy/Bloc Party (3)
2005	The Fall (3)
2006	Beatnik Filmstars/Decoration/Lost Penguin/Mogwai/The Nightingales (2)
2007	Beatnik Filmstars/The Fall/The Nightingales (3)
2008	The Fall (4)
2009	Camera Obscura/Fuck Buttons/The Joy Formidable/Los Campesinos!/The Pains of Being Pure at Heart/Sky Larkin (2)
2010	Allo Darlin' (2)
2011	PJ Harvey/The Lovely Eggs (2)
2012	Allo Darlin'/The Chasms/Godspeed You! Black Emperor (2)
2013	The Fall/Fuck Buttons/JD Meatyard/Mogwai/Public Service Broadcasting/The Wolfhounds (2)
2014	Allo Darlin'/Goat/Half Man Half Biscuit/Ste McCabe/Mogwai/Benjamin Shaw/Shellac (2)

Labels with most festive fifty entries (chart by chart)

Totals include entries for labels with releases in a particular chart, even when they this was not the version broadcast (eg in the case of session versions)

Year	Label
1976	Harvest/Reprise (4)
1977	Virgin (5)
1978	Polydor (10)
1979	Polydor (10)
1980	Factory/Rough Trade (7)
1981	Factory (9)
1982	CBS (5)
1982AT	Factory (13)
1983	4AD (9)
1984	4AD (9)
1985	Rough Trade (8)
1986	Rough Trade (8)

Year	Label		Year	Label
1987	Rough Trade (12)		2001	Rough Trade (5)
1988	Beggars Banquet (6)		2002	Integrity (5)
1989	4AD (7)		2003	SL/Too Pure (3)
1990	Creation (6)		2004	Chemikal Underground/SL (4)
1991	Cog-Sinister/Creation (6)		2005	Chemikal Underground/Sanctuary (3)
1992	Big Cat/RCA (6)		2006	Cargo/Cherryade/Rock Action/Rough Trade (2)
1993	Cog-Sinister (8)		2007	Caroline True/Slogan (3)
1994	Island (6)		2008	Sanctuary (4)
1995	Island (9)		2009	Wichita (4)
1996	Chemikal Underground/Stereolab (3)		2010	Fortuna Pop! (4)
1997	Duophonic (3)		2011	Bella Union/Cherryade/Fortuna Pop!/Island/Probe Plus (2)
1998	Chemikal Underground/Pickled Egg/Warp (4)		2012	Fortuna Pop! (3)
1999	Domino (5)		2013	Odd Box (5)
1999AT	Factory (9)		2014	Audio Antihero (3)
2000	Chemikal Underground/Island/Too Pure (4)			

Appearance Records

Top band/artist on most occasions (including joint)

1.	The Fall	10
=2.	The Delgados/Joy Division/The Smiths/The Wedding Present	4

Top band/artist on most occasions (outright)

=1.	The Fall; Joy Division	4
2.	The Wedding Present	3

Most appearances in festive fiftes

Includes every appearance, regardless of how many times the same track or versions of it appeared.

1.	The Fall	103
2.	The Wedding Present	57
3.	The Smiths	37
=4.	New Order/Siouxsie & The Banshees	31
6.	Joy Division	30
7.	The Clash	26
8.	PJ Harvey (incl. w/John Parish)	24
9.	Sex Pistols	23
10.	Half Man Half Biscuit	21
=11.	Cocteau Twins/Pixies	17
13.	Stiff Little Fingers	16
=14.	The Delgados/The Jam/Mogwai/Pulp	15
=17.	Pavement/The Undertones	14
=19.	Cinerama/Stereolab	13

Most tracks to appear in festive fifties

The number of different tracks (regardless of different versions) placed in festive fifties, regardless of multiple appearances.

1.	The Fall	98
2.	The Wedding Present	54
3.	The Smiths	31
4.	New Order	24
5.	PJ Harvey (incl. w/John Parish)	23
6.	Half Man Half Biscuit	19
7.	Cocteau Twins	17
=8.	Mogwai/Pixies	15
10.	Siouxsie & The Banshees	14
=11.	Cinerama/The Delgados/Pulp	13
=14.	Belle & Sebastian/Billy Bragg/Jesus	

	and Mary Chain/ Pavement/ Stereolab	12
=19.	Ballboy/Hefner/Sonic Youth	11

Most entries in a single chart

11	The Smiths	1983
10	Joy Division	1982AT
	The Fall	1993
8	Joy Division	1981
7	Siouxsie & The Banshees	1978
	Siouxsie & The Banshees	1979
	Joy Division	1980
	Cocteau Twins	1984
	The Smiths	1984
	The Fall	1986
	The Smiths	1986
	The Wedding Present	1992
6	The Fall	1988
	The Wedding Present	1990
	The Fall	1991
	Pavement	1992
	Dreadzone	1995
	Pulp	1995

Most appearances in festive fifties: individual performers

1.	Mark E. Smith	109
2.	Stephen Hanley	77
3.	Craig Scanlon	71
4.	David Gedge	70
5.	Bernard Sumner	62
=6.	Peter Hook; Stephen Morris	61
8.	Simon Wolstencroft	54
9.	Morrissey	46
=10.	Johnny Marr; Andy Rourke	40
12.	Keith Gregory	39
13.	Mike Joyce	38
14.	Simon Smith	36
=15.	John Lydon/Pete Salowka/Brix Smith	31
=18.	Steve Severin/Siouxsie Sioux	30

20.	Gillian Gilbert	28

Most tracks in festive fifties: individual performers

1.	Mark E. Smith	104
2.	Stephen Hanley	72
3.	Craig Scanlon	67
4.	David Gedge	66
5.	Simon Wolstencroft	54
6.	Morrissey	40
7.	Keith Gregory	37
=8.	Johnny Marr/Andy Rourke	36
=10.	Simon Smith/Bernard Sumner	35

Top record label on most occasions (including joint)

1.	Rough Trade	6
2.	Chemikal Underground	5
3.	Factory	4
=4.	4AD; Island	3

Top record label on most occasions (outright)

1.	Rough Trade	4
=2.	Factory; 4AD	3

Most appearances in the top ten

1.	The Fall	27
2.	The Wedding Present	14
3.	Joy Division	13
4.	The Smiths	12
5.	New Order	10
6.	The Clash	9
7.	Sex Pistols	8
8.	Mogwai/Undertones	7
=10.	The Delgados/PJ Harvey	6

Runs and Gaps

Longest uninterrupted runs

Bands or artists who have appeared in five or more consecutive festive fifties without a break. The 1982 and 1999 all-time charts are not included.

	Years	From/ To
The Fall	23	1983-2005
Half Man Half Biscuit	8	1998-2005
The Wedding Present	8	1985-1992
Cinerama	7	1998-2004
The Clash	6	1977-1982
The Jam	6	1977-1982
Siouxsie & The Banshees	6	1978-1983
Ballboy	5	2000-2004
Cocteau Twins	5	1982-1986
The Cure	5	1979-1983
Echo & The Bunnymen	5	1981-1985
Jesus and Mary Chain	5	1984-1988
New Order	5	1981-1985
Sex Pistols	5	1977-1981
The Smiths	5	1983-1988
Stereolab	5	1993-1997

Longest uninterrupted runs (individual performers)

	Years	From/ To
Mark E. Smith	23	1983-2005
Stephen Hanley	15	1983-1997
Craig Scanlon	13	1983-1995
Simon Wolstencroft	12	1986-1997
Nigel Blackwell	8	1998-2005
Neil Crossley	8	1998-2005
David Gedge	8	1985-1992
	8	1998-2005
Keith Gregory	8	1985-1992
Keith Hancock	8	1998-2005
Carl Henry	8	1998-2005
Morrissey	8	1983-1990

Longest gaps between appearances

It's rare for a festive fifty career to be suspended over a long period of years, though there have been several instances of it, particularly in recent years, so many in fact the the artist at the top of this list in the previous edition of this book is now down in sixth. The following bands and artists all returned after lengthy absences, though many of them cheated by breaking up for the period in between or, more rarely, not even doing it by their own efforts but via a remix from someone else, although the two artists at the top of the chart provide a genuine case of individuals who carried on making records until one was eventually recognised again by the festive fifty voters. Again, the 1982 and 1999 all-time charts are discounted here, which is why the numbers for Dead Kennedys and Laurie Anderson might vary from those cited elsewhere in the book.

	Years	From/To
David Bowie	34	1979-2013
Neil Young & Crazy Horse	34	1978-2012
Dead Kennedys	31	1981-2012
Public Image Ltd	29	1983-2012
The Membranes	28	1984-2012
Laurie Anderson	23	1981-2004
My Bloody Valentine	22	1991-2013
The Undertones	22	1981-2003
Teenage Fanclub	19	1991-2010
Billy Bragg	16	1998-2014
Daft Punk	16	1997-2013
Morrissey	16	1990-2006
Helen Love	15	1998-2013
Godspeed You! Black Emperor	14	1998-2012
Portishead	14	1994-2008
Shellac	14	2000-2014
Half Man Half Biscuit	10	1986-1996
Cuban Boys	9	2005-2014
Calvin Party	8	1996-2004
Chumbawamba	8	1985-1993
The Wedding Present	8	1996-2004

Longest gaps (individual performers)

	Years	From/To
David Bowie	34	1979-2013
Frank Sampedro/Billy Talbot/ Frank Molina/Neil Young	34	1978-2012
Jello Biafra/East Bay Ray/Klaus		

Flouride/ Bruce Slesinger	31	1981-2012
John Lydon	29	1983-2012
John Robb	28	1984-2012
Drumbo	28	1976-2004
Marco Pirroni	28	1980-2008

Longest periods of waiting for a festive fifty debut

If you're going to make the festive fifty, chances are you'll do it in the earlier years of your existence as a performer. What follows is a top ten of those who've waited an unusually long time for their debut appearance, taking their first official release as the start of the waiting period. Inevitably, the 1999 all-time chart provides a number of entries. I noted in the first edition that the achievement of Dick Dale ought to be credited with a special significance but since then the achievements of Gil Scott-Heron and Pere Ubu have outstripped even Dick.

		Years
Gil Scott-Heron	1970-2011	41
Pere Ubu	1975-2014	39
Beach Boys	1962-1999AT	37
Dick Dale	1961-1996	35
Tim Buckley	1967-1999AT	32
The Velvet Underground	1967-1999AT	32
Nick Drake	1969-1999AT	30
Kate Bush	1977-2005	28
Close Lobsters	1986-2014	28
The Wolfhounds	1986-2013	27

The Great Singles Runs

Only the most powerful of festive fifty contenders need apply here and some, most notably New Order, still don't get a look-in. These are bands or artists who have put together an uninterrupted run of consecutive entries for single releases (A-sides only, though EPs do qualify if at least one track featured) of notable length. One single failing to make it breaks the chain. With a festive fifty 'life' of only five years, it is yet another considerable achievement of The Smiths that they managed to put two such runs together, including a whopper that was only equalled by that far more durable band from Leeds, who took a lot longer to do it. Indeed, during their entire existence, The Smiths only had one single that failed to chart ('Shakespeare's Sister', which itself only just missed out on a festive fifty entry), otherwise they would have continued their mammoth run right up to their split.

	Singles	From-To
The Smiths	11	1985-1987

(That Joke Isn't Funny Anymore/The Boy with the Thorn in his Side/Bigmouth Strikes Again/Panic/Ask/ Shoplifters of the World Unite/Sheila Take a Bow/Girlfriend in a Coma/Stop Me if You Think You've Heard This One Before/Last Night I Dreamt that Somebody Loved Me)

The Wedding Present	11	1983-1991

(Go Out & Get 'Em Boy/Once More/This Boy Can Wait/My Favourite Dress/Anyone Can Make a Mistake/Nobody's Twisting Your Arm/Why Are You Being So Reasonable Now?/Kennedy/Brassneck/ Corduroy*/Dalliance)

The Fall	8	1990-1996

White Lightning/High Tension Line/Free Range/Ed's Babe/Why Are People Grudgeful?/Behind the Counter**/Hey! Student/The Chisilers

Cinerama	7	2000-2004

Your Charms/Superman/Health & Efficiency/Quick, Before It Melts/Careless/Don't Touch That Dial/It's Not You, It's Me

Pulp +	7	1993-1995

Razzamatazz/Lipgloss/Do You Remember the First Time?/Babies/Common People/Mis-Shapes/Disco 2000

Ash	6	1994-1996

Jack Names the Planets/Petrol/Uncle Pat/Kung Fu/Girl From Mars/Angel Interceptor

The Fall	6	1984-1986

C.R.E.E.P./No Bulbs++/Couldn't Get Ahead/Cruiser's Creek/Living Too Late/Mr Pharmacist

Jesus and Mary Chain	6	1984-1987

Upside Down/Never Understand/You Trip Me Up/Just Like Honey/Some Candy Talking/April Skies

Morrissey+++	6	1988-1990

Suedehead/Everyday is Like Sunday/The Last of the Famous International Playboys/Interesting Drug/Ouija Board, Ouija Board/November Spawned a Monster

Pixies   6   1988-1990
Gigantic/Monkey Gone to Heaven/Here Comes Your Man/Velouria/Dig For Fire/Planet of Sound

The Smiths   6   1983-1985
Hand in Glove/This Charming Man/What Difference Does It Make?/Heaven Knows I'm Miserable Now/William, It Was Really Nothing/How Soon Is Now?

The Fall   5   1979-1981
Rowche Rumble/Fiery Jack/How I Wrote 'Elastic Man'/Totally Wired/Lie Dream of a Casino Soul

Hole   5   1991-1995
Teenage Whore/Beautiful Son/Miss World/Doll Parts/Violet

*Featured on the 3 Songs EP.
**Another EP track.
***And another.
+'Babies' was a re-issued track that featured on the *Sisters* EP. Had I discounted this from qualification, it would still have augmented the chain as, in its original release, it immediately preceded 'Razzamatazz'.
++From the Call For Escape Route EP.
+++As The Smiths ended their existence on an unbeaten run of eleven singles, and Morrissey began his solo career with a run of six, he actually managed an astonishing run of seventeen consecutive festive fifty entries.

The great album runs

This concerns those bands and artists who have achieved the not inconsiderable feat of placing tracks from five consecutive albums or more in the festive fifty. Just one track from the album keeps the run going. Compilations and live albums are not included.

The Fall   17   1983-2000
Perverted By Language/The Wonderful and Frightening World of The Fall/This Nation's Saving Grace/Bend Sinister/The Frenz Experiment/I Am Kurious Oranj/Seminal Live*/Extricate/Shift-Work/Code:Selfish/The Infotainment Scan/Middle Class Revolt/Cerebral Caustic/The Light User Syndrome/Levitate/The Marshall Suite/The Unutterable

Half Man Half Biscuit   8   1997-2014
Voyage to the Bottom of the Road/Four Lads Who Shook the Wirral/Trouble Over Bridgwater/Cammell Laird Social Club/Achtung Bono/CSI: Ambleside/90 Bisodol (Crimond)/Urge for Offal

The Fall   7   2003-2013
The Real New Fall LP/Fall Heads Roll/Reformation Post-TLC/Imperial Wax Solvent/Your Future Our Clutter/Ersatz GB/Re-Mit

PJ Harvey   7   1992-2004
Dry/Rid of Me/To Bring You My Love/Dance Hall at Louse Point+/Is This Desire?/Stories of the City, Stories of the Sea/Uh Huh Her

Billy Bragg**   6   1984-1998
Brewing Up With Billy Bragg/Talking with the Taxman About Poetry/Worker's Playtime/Don't Try This At Home/William Bloke/Mermaid Avenue***

Stereolab   6   1993-2001
Transient Random Noise Bursts with Announcements/Mars Audiac Quintet/Emperor Tomato Ketchup/Dots & Loops/Cobra & Phases Group Play Voltage in the Milky Night/Sound Dust

Nick Cave & the Bad Seeds   5   1984-1990
From Her to Eternity/The First Born is Dead/Kicking Against the Pricks/Tender Prey/The Good Son

The Wedding Present   5   1987-1996
George Best/Bizarro/Seamonsters/Watusi/Saturnalia

*Despite its title, this album, essentially put together so that The Fall could get out of their contract with Beggars Banquet, contained a full side of new material recorded live in the studio.
**The breakthrough Life's a Riot with Spy vs Spy was, of course, a mini-album and, despite its immense significance, doesn't fulfil the criteria for inclusion here.
***Billy Bragg & Wilco
+John Parish & Polly Jean Harvey

Miscellaneous Records & Statistics

Earliest releases to register an entry

For a chart that didn't begin until 1976, there ought to be some recognition for releases that made the festive fifty despite being released many years before its inception. Inevitably, most of this top ten comes from that first chart, though some waited until the very last of the all-time charts to register an entry. The Beach Boys' achievement in placing two tracks in the 1999 festive fifty says much about the renaissance they enjoyed during the nineties, emphasised by how often *Pet Sounds* began to top 'best album' lists. Contrast this with its status in similar polls conducted in the late seventies and early eighties. Release dates here are those for the UK, although the majority of bands are from the US, with The Beatles and The Who the only representatives from this side of the pond. Significantly, Dylan grabs the top two places, with two tracks from Highway 61 Revisited, an album that changed the direction of both his music and pretty much everybody else's.

1. Like a Rolling Stone – Bob Dylan   August 1965
2. Desolation Row – Bob Dylan   Sept 1965
3. My Generation – The Who   Oct 1965
4. God Only Knows – Beach Boys   May 1966
5. Visions of Johanna – Bob Dylan   August 1966
6. Good Vibrations – Beach Boys   Oct 1966
7. I Can Take You to the Sun – The Misunderstood   Dec 1966
8. Strawberry Fields Forever – The Beatles   Feb 1967
9. Light My Fire – The Doors   March 1967
10. A Day in the Life – The Beatles   June 1967

Individual performers: appearances with most different bands

Some of the greatest of all Peel performers never managed a single festive fifty entry (David Henderson, Ivor Cutler, Viv Stanshall, among others) and even the great Captain Beefheart only registered in the chart on two occasions, each time with the same song. Others don't seem to be able to stop making the fifty, even when they change bands or latch onto someone else's for a brief spell. While there is a long list of artists who've done it with two different bands, the following is an elite group of those who've made the festive fifty with three or more. In 2012, Amelia Fletcher's entry with Tender Trap, after eleven years with the band, finally brought her level with Mark E. Smith at the top.

6   Amelia Fletcher (Talulah Gosh/The Wedding Present/Heavenly/ Marine Research/Hefner/Tender Trap)
    Mark E. Smith (The Fall/Inspiral Carpets/Long Fin Killie/D.O.S.E./Elastica/Von Sudenfed)

5   Rob Pursey (Talulah Gosh/Heavenly/Marine Research/Sportique/Tender Trap)

4   Elizabeth Fraser (Cocteau Twins/This Mortal Coil/Felt/Massive Attack)
    Johnny Marr (The Smiths/Billy Bragg/Electronic/Modest Mouse)
    John McEntire (Bastro/Stereolab/Smog/Tortoise)
    Tim Rippington (The Flatmates/Beatnik Filmstars/Forest Giants/Short Stories)
    Robert Wyatt (Matching Mole/Robert Wyatt/Scritti Politti/Working Week)

3   Damon Albarn (Elastica/Blur/Gil Scott-Heron)
    David Bowie (Iggy Pop/David Bowie/Arcade Fire)
    Tim Gane (McCarthy/Stereolab/Tortoise)
    Mick Harvey (The Birthday Party/Nick Cave/PJ Harvey)
    Darren Hayman (Hefner/The French/Darren Hayman)
    Lisa Horton (Bearsuit/Hyper Kinako/Mega Emotion)
    Kirsty Maccoll (The Smiths/Billy Bragg/Morrissey)
    Malcolm Middleton (Arab Strap/Malcolm Middleton/Human Don't Be Angry)
    Peter Momtchiloff (Talulah Gosh/Heavenly/Marine Research)
    David Pajo (Slint/Tortoise/Palace Brothers)
    Dave Ruffy (The Ruts/Aztec Camera/Zion Train)

Bernard Sumner (Joy Division/New Order/Electronic)
Tim/Kim Tortoise (Red Cosmos/Cyclic Freeload Unit/Bourbon Somersault the 3rd)
Jah Wobble (Public Image Ltd/Primal Scream/The Orb)
Thom Yorke (Radiohead/PJ Harvey/Atoms For Peace)

Most successful cover versions

Festive fifty voters have never been ones to turn their backs on a good cover version, and this list is predictably full of quality with The Fall, as in so many other cases, especially prominent. A cover version is deemed, somewhat conventionally, to be a song previously recorded by another artist. 'Shipbuilding', although written by Costello and Langer and performed by Robert Wyatt, is not considered to be a cover version because its original and definitive recording was by Wyatt, prior to Costello himself releasing the song.

Some tracks in this list are covers of tracks by bands or artists who made the festive fifty themselves on another occasion, either with the song concerned or, more often, with a different one. This list currently includes Bob Dylan, The Smiths, The Cure, Bob Marley, David Bowie, Prince, Tim Buckley and, at this stage, no others.

I've not included for consideration the many heavily sampled tracks to have made the festive fifty, such as Evolution Control Committee's cover of Public Enemy's 'Rebel Without a Pause', Ollo's remix of The Dodgems or Cuban Boys' desecration of Kenny's 'The Bump' as it seems to be those tracks were recorded in an entirely different spirit. Similarly, Mogwai's 'My Father, My King', inspired by a Jewish hymn, offers a pretty radical translation of the original and is, therefore, also not included. Camera Obscura's 'I Love My Jean', a setting of a poem to music rather than a cover of a song, is also refused entry. Interestingly, although there have been many cover versions in the festive fifty since Dandelion Radio assumed responsibility for the chart, only one has qualified for inclusion here.

The number reached gives the highest placing achieved by the track in the case of those that have appeared more than once.

Top Twenty Cover Versions

1.	Kiss – Age of Chance	2
=2.	The Green Fields of France (No Man's Land) – The Men They Couldn't Hang	3
	Mr Pharmacist – The Fall	3
4.	Song to the Siren – This Mortal Coil	4
=5.	All Along the Watchtower – Jimi Hendrix Experience	5
	Legend of Xanadu – The Fall	5
=7.	F-Oldin' Money – The Fall	7
	Make Me Smile (Come Up & See Me) – The Wedding Present	7
=9.	Step On – Happy Mondays*	8
	The Light 3000** – Schneider TM KPT. michi.gan	8
11.	Why Are People Grudgeful? – The Fall	11
12.	Just Like Heaven – Dinosaur Jr	12
13.	Different Drum – The Lemonheads	13
=14.	Johnny Was – Stiff Little Fingers	15
	Ziggy Stardust – Bauhaus	15
	Emma – Sisters of Mercy	15
	White Lightning – The Fall	15
	Shout Bama Lama – Detroit Cobras	15
=19.	I'm a Mummy – The Fall	17
	What Are They Doing in Heaven Today – Mogwai	17

*Originally released by John Kongas as 'He's Gonna Step On You Again'
**Originally released by The Smiths as 'There is a Light That Never Goes Out'

Top Double-Sided Records

Of course, before CDs, they were all – with occasional exceptions – double-sided and, whilst a CD generally contains more than one track, a track from the 'wrong' side of a 7" single making the festive fifty seemed to carry a greater impact, somehow. I line up happily alongside Steve Albini, Neil Young and Peel himself in lamenting the decline of vinyl, and in celebrating that trend's partial reverse in recent years. As years have gone by, this list has acquired more and more CD releases and rendered the title of the section somewhat anachronistic. Still, in the interests of equity, releases from the CD age like 'Mis-Shapes/Sorted for E's & Wizz' have had to be recognised.

Otherwise, I've been pretty strict on entry requirements. Extra tracks on 12" singles do not count, so The Smiths' 'How Soon Is Now?' has not been allowed to bump up the points total for 'William, It Was Really Nothing'/'Please Please Please...' This achievement will have its moment in the next section.

Points are awarded based on David Gedge's format (CGP means 'Combined Gedge Points'), to give an overall score of the two sides combined. As in the section on cover versions, points are drawn from the year in which a particular track gained its highest entry.. In the event of a tie, the highest position goes to the record with the highest placed side. Joy Division remain top of the tree, as they have been since 1981, with a record they didn't even intend as an official release, though there have been many close challengers since.

		Pos	CGP
1.	Joy Division – Atmosphere/	1	
	Dead Souls	11	90
2.	Chumbawamba & Credit to the Nation – Enough is Enough/	1	
	Hear No Bullshit	12	89
3.	Pulp – Mis-Shapes/	12	
	Sorted For E's & Wizz*	2	88
4.	Decoration – Candidate/	11	
	Job in London	4	87
5.	Nirvana – Smells Like Teen Spirit/	1	
	Drain You**	16	85
6.	The Wedding Present – Nobody's Twisting Your Arm/	2	
	I'm Not Always So Stupid	15	85
7.	New Order – Temptation/	1	
	Hurt	17	84
8.	New Order – Thieves Like Us/	7	
	Lonesome Tonight	12	83
9.	Stiff Little Fingers – Suspect Device/	4	
	Wasted Life	18	80
10.	The Strokes – The Modern Age/	18	
	Last Nite	5	78
11.	The Fall – Why Are People Grudgeful?/	11	
	Glam-Racket	20	71
12.	Cinerama – Pacific/	13	
	Kings Cross	18	71
13.	Pulp – Common People/	1	
	Underwear	31	70
14.	The Clash – Should I Stay or Should I Go?/	26	
	Straight to Hell	6	70
15.	The Strokes – Hard To Explain/	7	
	New York City Cops	28	67
16.	Morrissey – Every Day is Like Sunday/	12	
	Disappointed	23	67
17.	The Wedding Present – Brassneck/	19	
	Don't Talk, Just Kiss***	18	65
18.	The Fall – Mr Pharmacist/	3	
	Lucifer Over Lancashire	37	62
19.	Antihero – Rolling Stones T-Shirt/	5	
	You Got Nothing	37	60
20.	The Smiths – Hand in Glove	9	
	Handsome Devil	33	60

*In the festive fifty countdown of 1995, Peel actually broadcast a version of 'Sorted...' recorded live at the Glastonbury Festival and included as an extra track on this CD single, though the studio version of the track was the actual 'B-side' (if such a term has any currency in these situations).

**The original, US release of 'Teen Spirit' (October 1991) had 'Even in His Youth' as its 'B-side' (though released only in CD and cassette formats), a track that was only included on some versions of the UK release (November 1991), the 7" single of which had 'Drain You' on the reverse.

***'Brassneck' made the festive fifty in 1989 as a track from the Bizarro album. Its flipside made it the following year, after the two had been paired on a single early in 1990.

Triple-sided records

A logistical impossibility, presumably, but shorthand for single/EP releases containing three tracks, all of which made the festive fifty. There are only three instances of this, two of which occurred in the same year, 1983. Both of these were instances of 12" singles where a third track was recognised in addition to the conventional A and B sides. The Wedding Present went on to emulate these achievements with a three track EP in 1990.

The Smiths – William, It Was Really Nothing/Please Please Please, Let Me Get What I Want/How Soon Is Now?

Cocteau Twins – Pearly Dewdrops' Drops/Pepper Tree/The Spangle Maker

The Wedding Present – (The 3 Songs EP) Corduroy/Make Me Smile (Come Up & See Me)/Crawl.

A straight adding up of 'Gedge pts' reveals The Wedding Present's EP to be the most successful of the three.

Three tracks out of four placed

There have been three instances of a four-track EP placing three of those tracks in a festive fifty. The three, with the successful tracks in bold, are:

Cocteau Twins – Sunburst & Snowblind (1983)
Sugar Hiccup/From the Flagstones/Because of Whirl-Jack/Hitherto

The Wedding Present – Nobody's Twisting Your Arm (1988)
Nobody's Twisting Your Arm/I'm Not Always So Stupid/Nothing Comes Easy/Don't Laugh

The Fall – Why Are People Grudgeful? (1993)
Why Are People Grudgeful?/Glam-Racket/The Re-Mixer/Lost in Music

Using the same calculation as that employed in the previous section, the greatest achievement is that of The Fall, in that most golden of all Fall festive fifty years.

Highest placed B-sides, extra/bonus tracks, etc

Eligible for this list is anything that was released on a single, but was not deemed to be the main track. It includes anything from traditional B sides to extra tracks on 12" singles or CD single releases. Excluded from the list are tracks that featured on recognised EP releases where there is no recognised title track (for example, 'From the Flagstones' by Cocteau Twins) and B sides that also featured on an album in the same year (ruling out the likes of 'Sorted For E's & Wizz' by Pulp or 'Cemetry Gates' by The Smiths), but see notes below in relation to this.

Top Twenty B-sides, bonus tracks, etc

		No. Reached
1.	How Soon is Now? – The Smiths*	1
2.	Australians In Europe – The Fall	2
=3.	The Spangle Maker – Cocteau Twins	4
	Job in London – Decoration	4
	Velocity Girl – Primal Scream**	4
6.	Burn Black – Hole	7
7.	Dead Souls – Joy Division***	11
=8.	Hear No Bullshit – Credit to the Nation & Chumbawamba	12
	Lonesome Tonight – New Order	12
10.	Fleshworld – The Wedding Present	14
11.	I'm Not Always So Stupid – The Wedding Present	15
12.	Hurt – New Order	17
=13.	Kings Cross – Cinerama	18
	Wang Dang Doodle – PJ Harvey	18
	Don't Talk, Just Kiss – The Wedding Present	18
	I Lost You, But I Found Country Music – Laura Cantrell & Ballboy	18
17.	Worm Song – The Yobs	19
18.	Love in a Void – Siouxsie & The Banshees	21
=19.	Disappointed – Morrissey	23
	Sweet & Tender Hooligan – The Smiths	23

*Eventually released as an A side but only in the following year. It should be noted, however, that this track was also available on the Hatful of Hollow LP. As this was a compilation rather than a planned album release, the track is allowed to qualify.
**Deserves recognition as the best performing B-side from a single that didn't register its main track ('Crystal Crescent') in the chart.
***As with the Smiths' track, above, this was available on a compilation album (Still) and is allowed to qualify for the same reason. There is a body of opinion that claims 'Dead Souls' to be the A-side of the single with 'Atmosphere'. If this were the case, 'Atmosphere' could not qualify anyway as it was released as an A-side on the Factory release later in 1980. I'm going with 'Dead Souls' as the B-side anyway.

Highest placed tracks by European bands (outside Britain and Ireland)

I commented in the first edition on the rarity of such releases making the festive fifty, but the small upsurge that I also noted has been continued and strengthened in the Dandelion Radio years. Goat join Sugarcubes as the only band to fature twice in this top twenty, thanks to their two entries in the 2014 chart.

		Country	No
1.	Birthday – The Sugarcubes	Iceland	1
2.	Young Folks – Peter, Bjorn & John	Sweden	5
3.	Hearts – LSG	Germany	6
4.	Rollin' & Scratchin' – Daft Punk	France	7
5.	The Light 3000 – Schneider TM	Germany	8
6.	Talk to God – Goat	Sweden	9
7.	Putin Has Pissed Himself (Putin Zassal) – Pussy Riot	Russia	12
8.	Incubus Succubus – Xmal Deutschland	Germany	13
9.	Heaven's On Fire – Radio Dept	Sweden	14
10.	Noir Desir – Vive La Fete	Belgium	15
=11.	Crystalline (Omar Souleyman Version) – Bjork	Sweden	16
	Do You Even Know Who You Are? – Sonic Subjunkies	Germany	16
13.	All Lickety Split – Solex	Holland	19
=14.	Deus – The Sugarcubes	Iceland	20
	We're From Barcelona – I'm From Barcelona	Sweden	20
=16.	One Louder Solex – Solex	Holland	23
	Hide from the Sun – Goat	Sweden	23
18.	Giorgio By Moroder – Daft Punk	France	24
=19.	California Uber Alles (12" Plastic Toys Remix) – Dead Kennedys*	Italy	26
	Ma Simba Bele – Unknown Cases	Germany	26

*Although this is of course a Dead Kennedys song, the release entered the fifty courtesy of a remix by Italians.

Highest placed tracks by bands/artists from outside Europe and North America

The definition of North America is taken from www.worldatlas.com, which includes nations commonly considered to be within Central America (in other worlds, it comprises all nations in football's CONCACAF region). Because of this, Jamaican entries are not included.

1.	Unworldly – Pop Off Tuesday	Japan	4
2.	Lord Lucan is Still Missing – Ollo	Australia	8
3.	The Mercy Seat – Nick Cave	Australia	10
=4.	St Huck – Nick Cave	Australia	11
	We Crossed the Atlantic – Hydroplane	Australia	11
6.	Shield For Your Eyes... – Melt Banana	Japan	12
=7.	Hana – Asa Chang & Junray	Japan	18
	Mother Earth & Father Man-Made – The Venopian Solitude	Malaysia	18
9.	Release the Bats – The Birthday Party	Australia	19
10.	The Ship Song – Nick Cave	Australia	20
11.	In Love – The Datsuns	N.Zealand	21
12.	Chnam Oun Dop Pram Mouy – Cambodian Space Project	Cambodia	22
13.	The Last Goodbye – Postal Blue	Brazil	26
14.	Tetris Wonderland – DJ Scotch Egg	Japan	28
15.	The Owls Go – Architecture in Helsinki	Australia	29
16.	My Foolish Heart – Bhundu Boys	Zimbabwe	30
=17.	Matadjem Yinmixan – Tinariwen	Mali	32
	Open Field – Maher Shalal Hash Baz	Japan	32
=19.	(I'm) Stranded – The Saints	Australia	35
	Tupelo – Nick Cave	Australia	35

UK number one singles that made the festive fifty

Given that only a small minority of festive fifty entries ever got into the national singles charts, it's a significant event when a number one hit single in the UK makes it in. As the following list shows, there have been several instances of this, although they became considerably rarer after 1982. The greatest achievement here, I think, is that of The Prodigy, a number one single that seemed a strange and welcome quirk at the time and seems even odder in retrospect. It occurred eleven years after the last previous instance and, aside from the 1999 all-time festive fifty, there would be no further instances of a single that had already been number one making the chart in Peel's lifetime, although there have been some since. Only the official singles chart (in more recent times that overseen by the Official Charts Company) has been considered and performances in other charts such as those specifically for downloads, streaming or whatever have been disregarded.

	No.	Year
Hey Jude – The Beatles	14	1976
Voodoo Chile – Jimi Hendrix Experience	16	1976
Maggie May – Rod Stewart	34	1976
Jumping Jack Flash – Rolling Stones	39	1976
Are 'Friends' Electric? – Tubeway Army	39	1979
Going Underground – The Jam	13	1980
	23	1981
	17	1982AT
	35	1999AT
Town Called Malice – The Jam	11	1982
Come On Eileen – Dexy's Midnight Runners	19	1982
Pass the Dutchie – Musical Youth	36	1982
Two Tribes – Frankie Goes to Hollywood	25	1984
Pump Up the Volume – M/A/R/R/S	46	1987
Firestarter – The Prodigy	37	1996
Good Vibrations – Beach Boys	46	1999AT
I Bet You Look Good on the Dancefloor – Arctic Monkeys	3	2005
Crazy – Gnarls Barkley	36	2006
Bonkers – Dizzee Rascal	11	2009

The following performances might also be considered worthy of note:

I Am The Walrus – The Beatles   45   1999AT
 (Originally released as the B-side of the number one single 'Hello Goodbye' in 1967)
Crystalline (Omar Souleyman Version) – Bjork   16   2011
 (The single was a number one, but the Souleyman version was clearly that selected by festive fifty voters and this was one of several 'additional tracks' on the release)

The following all made number one in the UK singles chart, but only after they'd appeared in the festive fifty:

Uptown Top Ranking – Althea & Donna   2   1977
 (Reached number one early in 1978)
Too Much Too Young – The Specials   36   1979
 (A live recording of the track that appeared in 1979 reached number one in 1980)
Should I Stay or Should I Go? – The Clash   26   1982
 (Reached number one in 1991, when reissued following its use in a commercial)
Your Woman – White Town   31   1996
 (Made number one early in 1997)
Brimful of Asha – Cornershop   1   1997
 (The only festive fifty number one also to reach the top of the singles charts, albeit via a remix that achieved the feat in 1998)

Most successful performances in festive fifties and UK singles charts

Here I have considered for inclusion all festive fifty tracks that also made the UK singles charts, whether prior to their FF performance or not. The 'score' for both the festive fifty entry and the UK chart entry is based on a common formula (the usual one) and added together to give an overall success rating. The highest possible rating would be 100, for a single that made number one in both charts, and of course there is only one track that has achieved that feat. In the event of a tie, the highest position in either chart determines the higher placing. If two tracks are still tied, it is the higher festive fifty entry placing that counts, simply because that's the order of things as I see it. We end up with a rare festive fifty chart in the sense that there are no entries at all from The Fall (although Mark E. Smith still sneaks in there).

		FF	UKSCSucc.	
1.	Brimful of Asha – Cornershiop	1	1*	100
2.	Common People – Pulp	1	2	99
3.	Uptown Top Ranking – Althea & Donna	2	1	99
4.	Blue Monday – New Order	1	3*	98
5.	I Bet You Look Good on the Dancefloor – Arctic Monkeys	3	1	98
6.	Sorted for E's & Wizz – Pulp	2	2	98
7.	Cognoscenti vs Intelligentsia – Cuban Boys	1	4	97
8.	God Save the Queen – Sex Pistols	3	2	97
9.	Born Slippy – Underworld	5	2	95
10.	Mad World – Tears For Fears	4	3	95
11.	Smells Like Teen Spirit – Nirvana	1	7	94
12.	Alright Now – Free	6	2	94
13.	Layla – Dereke & the Dominoes	2	7	93
14.	This Charming Man – The Smiths	2	8*	92
15.	Sit Down – James	8	2*	92
16.	All Along the Watchtower – Jimi Hendrix Experience	5	5	92
17.	The Message – Grandmaster Flash & the Furious Five	3	8	91
18.	The Story of the Blues – Wah!	8	3	91
19.	True Faith – New Order	7	4	91
=20.	Town Called Malice – The Jam	11	1	90
	Bonkers – Dizzee Rascal	11	1	90
22.	Pretty Vacant – Sex Pistols	6	6	90
23.	Song 2 – Blur	11	2	89
24.	Step On – Happy Mondays	8	5	89
25.	Gangsters – The Special AKA	7	6	89
26.	Where Are We Now? – David Bowie	8	6	88
27.	Going Underground – The Jam	13	1	88
=28.	Mis-Shapes – Pulp	12	2	88
	Only You – Yazoo	12	2	88
30.	Come Play With Me – The Wedding Present	4	10	88
31.	Like a Rolling Stone – Bob Dylan	10	4	88
32.	Hey Jude – The Beatles	14	1	87
33.	Brown Sugar – Rolling Stones	13	2	87
34.	Girl From Mars – Ash	4	11	87
35.	Alright – Supergrass	13	2	87
36.	Love Will Tear Us Apart – Joy Division	3	13	86
37.	Panic – The Smiths	5	11	86
38.	How Soon is Now? – The Smiths	1	16*	85
39.	Voodoo Chile – Jimi Hendrix Experience	16	1	85
40.	Regret – New Order	13	4	85
41.	Seven Nation Army – White Stripes	10	7	85
42.	Crystal – New Order	9	8	85
43.	Young Folks – Peter, Bjorn & John	5	13	84
44.	Suedehead – Morrissey	13	5	84
45.	Public Image – Public Image Ltd	9	9	84
46.	I Want You – Inspiral Carpets ft Mark E. Smith	1	18	83
47.	Strawberry Fields Forever – The Beatles	17	2	83
48.	Down in the Tube Station at Midnight – The Jam	4	15	83
49.	Last Nite – The Strokes	5	14	83
50.	Come On Eileen – Dexy's Midnight Runners	19	1	82

*Indicates those singles that achieved this positon on reissue, after their festive fifty entry.

Record labels: most appearances

This list includes every appearance for a record label, no matter how many times the same track charted. It does not include session tracks that appeared prior to their official release. The first label of release is the one that is counted, regardless of which version was played in the festive fifty countdown: the only exception is where the track only made the chart following its reissue on a different label. This means, for example, that appearances for 'Teenage Kicks' are credited to the Good Vibrations label, not Sire. Similarly, 'Anarchy in the UK', though later released by Virgin on the *Never Mind the Bollocks* album, is considered to be an EMI release. Split releases are credited to both labels involved.

Subsidiaries of major labels are counted independently so, for example, entries for Epic do not count towards the CBS total, while the Beggars Banquet umbrella – which has at various times emcompassed labels like Situation Two and 4AD - is separated into its various parts, so that only Beggars Banquet releases are credited to it. The result is a mixture of the more successful post-punk indie labels with a smattering of majors, mostly gathering points early in the chart's history through being quickest onto the punk gravy train. Fortuna Pop! is the most successful label in the

Dandelion Radio years, with sixteen entries. Seven further appearances for Rough Trade since the first edition of this book have seen them become the first label to reach and exceed 100 appearances.

		Appearances
1.	Rough Trade	101
=2.	Factory	58
	4AD	58
=4.	Polydor	53
	Virgin	53
6.	Island	45
7.	CBS	43
8.	Creation	35
9.	Beggars Banquet	32
10.	RCA	27
11.	Chemikal Underground	26
12.	Probe Plus	23
13.	Too Pure	22
=14.	Domino	19
	Geffen	19
16.	Warp	18
17.	Permanent	17
=18.	Stiff	16
	Fortuna Pop!	16
20.	Duophonic	15

Record labels – Most tracks

This time tracks that appeared more than once, whether in different versions or the same one, are only counted once. This means a significant reduction in the totals for those labels that benefited heavily from multiple appearances in the early all-time charts.

		Tracks
1.	Rough Trade	81
2.	4AD	55
3.	Island	42
4.	Factory	34
5.	Creation	33
6.	Beggars Banquet	32
7.	Polydor	30
8.	Virgin	29
9.	Chemikal Underground	25
10.	RCA	24
11.	Probe Plus	22
12.	Too Pure	21
=13.	CBS	19
	Domino	19
=15.	Geffen	18
	Warp	18
=16.	Permanent	18
18.	Fortuna Pop!	16
=19.	Cog-Sinister	14
	Duophonic	14

Longest tracks

It remains the case that many of the longest tracks in festive fifties featured in that very first one of 1976, though the revival of longer entries that gathered pace in the nineties, and which gave us a number one that will probably be there for ever, has continued in recent times, with a number of tunes gaining entry to this list in the Dandelion Radio years. Two Godspeed You! Black Emperor tracks are the longest to appear in these years, and the re-discovery of the 1977 chart makes Pink Floyd the only other band to match their achievement of three entries here. Mogwai, once held as relatively undisputed kings of the long festive fifty entry, have now dropped out of the top twenty completely. The Dandelion years have also seen The Fall appear in one of a small number of lists they didn't find a place in in the first edition of this book, and indeed they have the only number one track here.

Inevitably, many of the longer tracks here, including the number one, had shorter versions played during the countdown. It's been necessary here to make a judgement call on which versions voters chiefly intended to vote for. In the case of the number one, it seems clear it was the full-length version that would have been the object of their approval, but in other cases this is not so clear-cut. For instance, Peel opted to play the Industry Standard Mix of Orbital's 'Are We Here?' in the chart and it's not clear whether this version was specifically preferred by voters: had the album version of the track been selected, its duration of 15.33 would have warranted inclusion here. I've tended towards including the track used in the broadcast, except where it would seem likely that another version was preferred by voters and have commented on these instances in the footnotes below. Since the first edition, I've removed 'Voodoo Chile' from this list on the grounds that there really wasn't anything solid on which to base my early judgement that voters would have preferred the full-length version to the 7" single version that Peel played.

		Time
1.	Blue Room – The Orb*	39.58
2.	Shine On You Crazy Diamond – Pink Floyd**	26.11
3.	Echoes – Pink Floyd	23.31
4.	Dark Star – Grateful Dead***	23.18
5.	Supper's Ready – Genesis	22.58
6.	Djed – Tortoise	20.53
7.	My Father My King – Mogwai	20.12
8.	Loving You – The Orb+	20.10
9.	We Drift Like Worried Fire – Godspeed You! Black Emperor	20.07
10.	Mladic – Godspeed You! Black Emperor	20.00
11.	Hung Over as the Oven at Maida Vale – Godspeed You Black Emperor!++	18.00
12.	Only Skin – Joanna Newsom	16.53
13.	Walk Like a Giant – Neil Young & Crazy Horse	16.31
14.	Lucy Over Lancashire – Paul Rooney	16.00
15.	Full Fathom Five – Vert:x	15.56
16.	Pipes – Katie Gately	14.00
17.	Genetic – Emeralds	12.08
18.	50 Year Old Man – The Fall	11.33
19.	Pigs – Pink Floyd	11.25
20.	Desolation Row – Bob Dylan	11.18

*The full version was not broadcast in the countdown for obvious reasons, although Peel commented that he would have liked to do so. Instead, he played the 18.45 Part 1 version from Side A of the 12" release.
**The time given is the combined length of parts 1-5, which open the Wish You Were Here album, and parts 6-9, which close it. Parts 1-5 are 13.40 and parts 6-9 a slightly less impressive 12.31. It was Parts 1-5 that Peel played in the countdown.
***The version from Live/Dead, which was also the version played in the countdown.
+There were several versions of this track, but this is the Peel Session version, which was played in the countdown.
++The session actually comprised three tracks, 'Monheim', 'Chart #3' and 'Steve Reich', the first two of which would be released separately on the following year's *Lift Your Skinny Fists Like Antennas to Heaven*

album, but the three 'movements' were brought together as a single continuous track in session and given this name. Peel actually gave the title as 'Hung Over as the Queen at Maida Vale' in the original session broadcast, but this appears simply to be an error.

Shortest Tracks

Post-1977 it became almost a matter of artistic pride to make your records as brief as possible, even though bands like Stiff Little Fingers, The Clash and Siouxsie & The Banshees all made the festive fifty with tracks of five minutes or longer.

Despite that, only the track from The Yobs from the 1977 chart is from the punk era: although there were a number of short tracks in that chart, this is the only one with the level of brevity needed to secure a place in this list Throughout the late seventies and early eighties, a Wild Man Fischer tune from the very first chart still hung on to the top spot in this list, something I managed, embarrassingly, to overlook in the first edition of this book.

The mid-eighties saw a re-birth of the Buzzcocks guitar riff (perhaps exemplified best in this list by the Soup Dragons' 'Whole Wide World') and Primal Scream's 'Velocity Girl' established the post-Fischer benchmark for short tunes, though it now only stands in joint eight position in this list, and of course now that the content of the 1977 chart is fully known, it was always longer than that Yobs track. Pixies, despite holding the last note on 'Allison' for a full seven seconds, managed to take five seconds off the Primal Scream track only four years later before, eleven years after that, Half Man Half Biscuit got into the festive fifty with a tune that was only half the length of that previously unassailable Wild Man Fischer effort.

It will take something truly remarkable, I assume, to take the top position off HMHB. The Dandelion years, however, have seen a number of sub-two minute efforts, the most impressive achievement being that of Big Joan, who now occupy joint fifth place here. Worth noting, in passing, that the only sub-two minute track to make number one in the festive fifty remains 'Come Out 2 Nite' by Kenickie, though it isn't anywhere near short enough to qualify for this top twenty.

		Time
1.	Vatican Broadside – Half Man Half Biscuit	0.28
2.	Go to Rhino Records – Wild Man Fischer	0.56

3.	Dr Dre Buys a Pint of Milk – Grandmaster Gareth	1.00
4.	The Worm Song – The Yobs	1.10
5.	Allison – Pixies	1.15
=6.	Beautiful Idea – Big Joan	1.18
	Open Field – Maher Shalal Hash Baz	1.18
=8.	I Believe I Can Fly – Lost Penguin	1.20
	Velocity Girl – Primal Scream	1.20
=10.	L Dopa – Big Black	1.26
	I Lost You, But I Found Country Music – Laura Cantrell & Ballboy*	1.26
12.	Hot Dog Man – Will & Rick	1.30
13.	All-Nighter – Elastica	1.31
14.	Go Polski Boy – Ste McCabe	1.34
15.	Bob Wilson Anchorman – Half Man Half Biscuit	1.35
=16.	Candy – Dadfag	1.36
	Mentioning No Names – Council Tax Band	1.36
18.	Putin Has Pissed Himself (Putin Zassal) – Pussy Riot	1.40
19.	Kill Twee Pop! – Sarandon	1.40
20.	Whole Wide World – Soup Dragons	1.43

*On the recording and included in the released version is some chatting from Gordon McIntyre at the beginning. I've not included this in the time above, which simply gives the length of the song itself.

Longest titles

Ballboy remain the kings of the long-title, with three entries here, while The Wedding Present now have two.

		Letters
1.	I Don't Have Time to Stand Here With You Fighting About the Sizeof My Dick – Ballboy	59
2.	If You Enter the Arena, You've Got to Be Prepared to Deal With the Lions – The Membranes	56
3.	The Light at the End of the Tunnel (Is the Light of an Oncoming Train – Half Man Half Biscuit	54
4.	There's No Bizznizz Like Propa' Rungleclotted Mashup Bizznizz – Shitmat	51
5.	Where Do the Nights of Sleep Go When They Do Not Come to Me? – Ballboy	45
6.	Shield For Your Eyes a Beast in the Well on Your Hand – Melt Banana	42
=7.	They'll Hang Flags From Cranes Upon My Wedding Day – Ballboy	41
	You Should Always Keep in Touch with Your Friends – The Wedding Present	41
9..	The Thing I Like Best About Him is His Girlfriend – The Wedding Present	40
=10.	Inside the Mind of Sam (Breakfast Serial Killer) – Beatnik Filmstars	39
	Stop Me If You Think You're Heard This One Before – The Smiths	39
	The Last of the Famous International Playboys – Morrissey	39
	When Father Died, Ferrets Licked Away the Tears – Bobby McGee's	39

Shortest Titles

Only one track with a one letter title has appeared in the festive fifty, which is still:

B – Digital Mystiks

There have been four tracks in festive fifties with titles of only two letters (or one letter and a number). Of all the achievements of The Fall in the festive fifty, surely it's the most curious that they've provided three of the four. The four are:

L.A. – The Fall
M5 – The Fall
V2 – That Petrol Emotion
W.B. – The Fall

The 'unofficial' festive fifty number ones

The following tracks were not number ones in the year given. What we have here are, for the years 1967-81, speculative number ones based on an extrapolation of information contained in the all-time festive fifties of 1976 to 1981. In the absence of any other data, this is an attempt to make some kind of informed guess which traks may have been number one in the years from 1967.

The 1976-81 number ones are the tracks that finished highest in that year's festive fifty, the only exception being 1977 which I've left out of this list now that the festive fifty of that year has been awarded official status.

1967	A Day in the Life – The Beatles
1968	All Along the Watchtower – Jimi Hendrix Experience
1969	Whole Lotta Love – Led Zeppelin
1970	Layla – Derek & The Dominoes
1971	Stairway to Heaven – Led Zeppelin
1972	Big Eyed Beans from Venus – Captain Beefheart & The Magic Band
1973	Rocky Mountain Way – Joe Walsh
1974	Freebird – Lynyrd Skynyrd
1975	Shine On You Crazy Diamond – Pink Floyd
1976	They Shoot Horses Don't They? – Racing Cars
1978	Suspect Device – Stiff Little Fingers
1979	Gangsters – Special AKA
1980	Atmosphere – Joy Division
1981	Ceremony – New Order

Most appearances in festive fifties – individual tracks

Now taking the top fifty of the 1977 chart into consideration, one track has now appeared in seven separate festive fifties, while a further six have appeared in six and another eight in five.

As you might expect, these are all from the early period of the all-time festive fifties. They are:

7   Complete Control – The Clash

6   Anarchy in the UK – Sex Pistols
Another Girl, Another Planet – The Only Ones
Holidays in the Sun – Sex Pistols
New Rose – The Damned
Teenage Kicks – Undertones
(White Man in) Hammersmith Palais – The Clash

5   Alternative Ulster – Stiff Little Fingers
Down in the Tube Station at Midnight – The Jam
God Save the Queen – Sex Pistols*
Jigsaw Feeling – Siouxsie & The Banshees
Pretty Vacant – Sex Pistols*

Public Image – Public Image Ltd
Suspect Device – Stiff Little Fingers
Switch – Siouxsie & The Banshees

Since the 1976-82 years, the best any track has achieved is appearances in three festive fifties. Two tracks have done this: 'Common People' by Pulp and 'Pulls the Wires from the Wall' by The Delgados, both of which appeared first when broadcast in a session, then as an official release and finally in the 1999 all-time chart.

*Both of these tracks appeared in the 1977 chart, but not in the top fifty

Appearances for songs recorded by two different artists

There have now been a number of instances of this and two instances of it happening in the same chart, the most recent in the festive fifty of 2014. In the first edition of this book, I recorded the chart's only appearance for Evolution Control Committee as 'Copyright Violation for the Nation', which was the title erroneously given to the release by Peel. It is, and always was, a cover of Public Enemy's 'Rebel Without a Pause' (if one with the unlikely, and brilliant, musical backdrop of a Herb Alpert trumpet-led tune) so its appearance is now recognised here.

Shipbuilding – Robert Wyatt/Elvis Costello
Rebel Without a Pause – Public Enemy/Evolution Control Committee
Heroes – David Bowie/Six By Seven*
Song to the Siren – This Mortal Coil/Tim Buckley
There is a Light that Never Goes Out – The Smiths/Schneider.TM**
Groove is in the Heart – Deee-Lite/Crocodiles
You & Me – Benjamin Shaw/Cloud

*Six By Seven's entry was a German language version, entitled 'Helden'.
**Schneider TM's version was entitled 'The Light 3000'

In addition, there have been remixes of original entries (such as those of Laurie Anderson's 'O Superman' and Dead Kennedys' 'Holiday in Cambodia)

The 'other' festive fifty entries

In the years 1980-1982 and again in 1985, John Peel provided information on what was 'bubbling under' the festive fifty. I haven't included these entries elsewhere in this book because, as far as I'm concerned, they didn't make the festive fifty. However, their existence is worth recognising, as indeed are the achievements of those tracks outside the top fifty listed in the 1977 chart. Peel once revealed, during the dark days of the late eighties, that he'd actually thought about broadcasting the numbers 51-100 instead, because he thought it would make for far more interesting listening. Needless to say, he never went through with it.

What we do have, though, is information on numbers 51-65 from 1980, 51-60 from 1981 and 1982 and 51-70 from 1985, as well as those additional numbers in 1977. I've listed the bands/artists who appeared in those positions alphabetically here but only given information on the personnel involved where this differs from what is already available elsewhere in the book.

Adam & The Ants

| Dog Eat Dog | 53 | 1980 |

Anti-Pasti
(Martin Roper – vocals; Dugi Bell – guitar; Will Hoon – bass; Kevin Nixon – drums)

| No Government | 55 | 1981 |

The Associates
(Added Martha Ladley – keyboards)

| Club Country | 55 | 1982 |

Bauhaus

| Bela Lugosi's Dead | 52 | 1981 |

Big Flame
(Alan Brown – bass/vocals; Greg O'Keefe – guitar; David Green, aka Dil – drums)

| All the Irish Must Go to Heaven | 58 | 1985 |
| Man of Few Syllables | 62 | 1985 |

Bogshed
(Phil Hartley – vocals; Mark McQuaid – guitar; Mike Bryson – bass; Tristan King – drums. Bryson also appeared in the festive fifty as Forkeyes)

| Hand Me Down Father | 65 | 1985 |

Billy Bragg

| Days Like These | 56 | 1985 |

Buzzcocks

| Whatever Happened To | 59 | 1977 |

Cabaret Voltaire
(Now down to central duo of Kirk and Mallender)

| I Want You | 60 | 1985 |

Captain Sensible
(Captain Sensible, aka Ray Burns – guitar/vocals; Paul Gray – bass; Malcolm Dixon – keyboards; Gary Dreadful – drums. Sensible also appeared in the festive fifty with The Damned. For Gray, see also Eddie & The Hot Rods in this list)

| Happy Talk | 59 | 1982 |

The Clash

| Capital Radio | 54 | 1977 |

Cocteau Twins

| Quisquose | 63 | 1985 |

Conflict
(Colin Jerwood – vocals; Steve Ignorant – vocals; John Clifford – bass; Paco – drums)

| Mighty & Superior | 53 | 1985 |

Elvis Costello & The Attractions

| Watching The Detectives | 55 | 1977 |

The Cure

| Close to Me | 67 | 1985 |

Del Amitri
(Justin Currie – bass/vocals; Iain Harvie – guitar; Bryan Tolland – guitar; Paul Tyagi – drums)

| Hammering Heart | 52 | 1985 |

Devo
(Mark Mothersbaugh – keyboards/vocals; Gerald V. Casale – bass/vocals; Bob Mothersbaugh – guitar; Bob Casale – guitar/keyboards; Alan Myers – drums)

| Jocko Homo | 58 | 1977 |

Eddie & The Hot Rods
(Barrie Masters – vocals; Graeme Douglas – guitar; Dave Higgs – guitar; Paul Gray – bass; Steve Nicol – drums. For Gray, see also Captain Sensible in this list)

| Beginning of the End | 57 | 1977 |

Everything But The Girl
(Tracy Thorn – vocals; Ben Watt – guitar)

| Night & Day | 54 | 1982 |

The Fall

Totally Wired	56	1981
Look/Know	58	1982
Rollin' Dany	55	1985

Fire Engines
(Davie Henderson – guitar/vocals; Murray Slade – guitar; Graham Main – bass; Russell Burn – drums)

| Candy Skin | 58 | 1981 |

Gregory Isaacs
(Gregory Isaacs – vocals; Eric Lamont – guitar; Dwight Pinkney – guitar; Flabba Holt – bass; Wycliffe Johnson – keyboards; Wally Badarou – keyboards; Style Scott – drums)

| Night Nurse | 53 | 1982 |

The Jam

| The Eton Rifles | 59 | 1980 |

James

| If Things Were Perfect | 51 | 1985 |

Josef K
(Paul Haig – guitar/vocals; Malcolm Ross – guitar; David Weddell – bass; Ronnie Torrance – drums)

| The Missionary | 52 | 1982 |

Joy Division

| Dead Souls | 64 | 1980 |
| She's Lost Control | 51 | 1981 |

Killing Joke

| Wardance | 52 | 1980 |

Led Zeppelin

| Stairway To Heaven | 63 | 1980 |

Little Feat

| Rocket in My Pocket | 60 | 1977 |

Magazine

| Shot By Both Sides | 61 | 1980 |
| Shot By Both Sides | 53 | 1981 |

The Mo-dettes
(Ramona Carlier – vocals; Kate Korus – guitar; Jane Crockford – bass; Jane Miles-Kingston – drums)

| White Mice | 56 | 1980 |

Motors

| Bringing in the Morning Light | 56 | 1977 |

New Model Army

| No Rest | 66 | 1985 |

New Order

In a Lonely Place	54	1981

Oldham Tinkers
(Larry Kearns – vocals; John Howarth – vocals; Gerry Kearns – guitar/vocals)

John Willie's Ferret	52	1977

Pink Floyd

Shine On You Crazy Diamond	60	1980

The Pogues

And the Band Played Waltzing Matilda	64	1985

Public Image Ltd

Death Disco	62	1980

The Ruts

West One (Shine On Me)	54	1980

Sex Pistols

Pretty Vacant	51	1977
God Save the Queen	61	1977
Pretty Vacant	59	1981

Siouxsie & The Banshees

Love in a Void	51	1980
Hong Kong Garden	60	1981
Cities in Dust	54	1985

The Smiths

Barbarism Beings at Home	57	1985
Shakespeare's Sister	61	1985

Special AKA

Gangsters	57	1981

Stiff Little Fingers

Tin Soldiers	57	1980

The Stranglers

No More Heroes	58	1980
Strange Little Girl	51	1982
Golden Brown	56	1982

10,000 Maniacs

C an't Ignore the Train	59	1985
Just as the Tide Was a-Flowing	69	1985

That Petrol Emotion

Keen	70	1985

Theatre of Hate

The Hop	57	1982

Peter Tosh
(Peter Tosh – guitar/vocals; Al Anderson – guitar; Karl Pitterson – guitar; Abdul Wali – guitar; Robbie Shakespeare – bass; Tyrone Downie – keyboards; Earl 'Wire' Lindo – keyboards; Dirty Harry, aka Richard Hall – saxophone; Harold Butler – clavinet; Sly Dunbar – drums; Skully, aka Noel Sims - percussion)

Stepping Razor	53	1977

The Triffids
(David McComb – vocals; Robert McComb – guitar; Martyn Casey – bass; Jill Birt – keyboards; Alsy MacDonald – drums)

Field of Glass	68	1985

Wah! Heat
(Pete Wylie – guitar/vocals; Pete Younger – bass; Rob Jones – drums. See Wah! for festive fifty entries and later line-ups)

Better Scream	65	1980

The Who

My Generation	55	1980

Yazoo

Don't Go	60	1982

Printed in Great Britain
by Amazon